FOREIGNERS AT ROME

FOREIGNERS AT ROME

CITIZENS AND STRANGERS

David Noy

The Classical Press of Wales

First published in hardback in 2000
This paperback edition 2022

The Classical Press of Wales
15 Rosehill Terrace, Swansea SA1 6JN
classicalpressofwales@gmail.com
www.classicalpressofwales.co.uk

Distributor in North America. E-book distributor world-wide
ISD,
70 Enterprise Drive, Suite 2,
Bristol, CT 06010, USA
Tel: +1 (860) 584-6546
Fax: +1 (860) 516-4873
www.isdistribution.com

ISBN paperback 978-1-914535-28-4; hardback 0-9543845-1-2;
ebook 978-1-914535-07-9

A catalogue record for this book is available from the British Library.

Typeset by Ernest Buckley, Clunton, Shropshire and by Louise Jones, and printed
and bound in the UK by CPI Anthony Rowe, Chippenham and Eastbourne.

––––––––––––––––––

The Classical Press of Wales, an independent venture, was founded in 1993, initially to
support the work of classicists and ancient historians in Wales and their collaborators from
further afield. It now publishes work initiated by scholars internationally, and welcomes
contributions from all parts of the world.

The symbol of the Press is the Red Kite. This bird, once widespread in Britain, was reduced
by 1905 to some five individuals confined to a small area known as 'The Desert of Wales' –
the upper Tywi valley. Geneticists report that the stock was saved from terminal inbreeding
by the arrival of one stray female bird from Germany. After much careful protection, the
Red Kite now thrives – in Wales and beyond

To the memory of
Jean Norris Midgley
1914–1996

CONTENTS

INTRODUCTION

Leaving behind Nicaea in Bithynia while I was still a youth,
I went to the glorious city and the land of the Ausonians.
In hallowed Rome I taught accounts and measures.
I, Basileus, obtained the tomb, the work of my mind.

IGUR 1176

In the second year of the dictatorship of C. Caesar,
with M. Antonius as *magister equitum* [47 BCE],
the site of the tomb was bought from Q. Modius L.f. Qui.
    24 feet wide, 24 feet deep.
C. Numitorius C.l. Nicanor, by birth a Theban, eye doctor.
Numitoria C.l. Philumina, by birth a Phrygian.
C. Numitorius C.l. Stabilio, by birth a native slave.
P. Opitreius C.l. Butas, by birth a Smyrnan.
They built the foundation. In their tomb is buried:
Numitoria C.l. Erotis, by birth a Carthaginian.
Q. Numitorius C.l. Isio is buried there.

AE (1972) 14

Papiria Rhome made this (monument) for herself while alive, and for
Papiria Cladilla aged 19, and for P. Papirius Proculus aged 13(?), her
children. Here the wretched(?) mother held two funerals, and she buried
their bones with rites which are not just. For at Rome a falling roof-tile
carried off Proculus. The deceased Cladilla lay on her funeral pyre at
Sipontum. Your parental wishes did you harm. The cruel gods gave more
good things so they could take more away. Also for P. Papirius Cladus her
husband and for P. Papirius Celerio and Papiria Hispanilla her ex-slaves.

CIL iii 2083 (Salona)

Flavia Valeria placed this inscription for her well-deserving daughter
Flavia Viventia, who lived 18 years. She had her burial on 31st July. This
girl came from the province of Pannonia. She (lived) with her husband
one year 8 months. In peace.

ICUR 13155

Be of good cheer Serenus, child, untimely dead, aged 4 years 8 months
19 days. Fuscinus the emperor's *provocator* his father and Taon his
mother, Egyptians, made this (tomb), being left behind.

IGUR 939 = ICUR 4032

Sacred to the *Di Manes*. Aurelia Marcia, by birth a Thracian from the Promesian city, who lived 36 years 5 months 8 days. Aurelia Zenodora her sister and Aurelius Herodes her husband, *beneficiarius* of the 10th praetorian cohort, made this tomb for the well-deserving woman.

CIL vi 2734

The people commemorated in these epitaphs are a few examples of the countless number of foreigners who made their way to the city of Rome. Male and female, slave and free, soldier and civilian, following their families or bringing their own marketable skills – thousands of newcomers arrived in Rome each year. Some became so well integrated into the city that they left no trace of their origins. Some stayed at Rome for the rest of their lives but, like the people above, left epitaphs recording where they had come from. Some did not die at Rome but returned home first. The purpose of this book is to explore the reality behind the epitaphs: how and why foreigners came to Rome, how they were treated when they were there, how they adapted to life in the city, how far they were able to or wished to retain a distinct 'foreign' identity.

Roman social historians agree that a high proportion of the population of Rome consisted of immigrants and their descendants. Most immigration happened involuntarily through the slave trade, but a substantial part was of a voluntary nature, primarily for economic reasons. The fact that Rome must have depended on immigrants for its population growth and the maintenance of its huge size has been widely acknowledged (see, e.g., Pleket 1993, Morley 1996). However, many important studies of life in the city pay very little attention to the role played by foreigners, e.g. three pages in Stambaugh (1988, 93–5); no specific discussion at all in Robinson (1992). The only existing lengthy work on the subject is a long but now somewhat outdated article: La Piana (1927); this was not intended to be a comprehensive survey, since it was aimed specifically at explaining the spread of Christianity, and much of it has now been superseded by recent epigraphic discoveries. Cecilia Ricci has surveyed the epigraphic evidence for immigration from some of the provinces very thoroughly in a series of articles on Gaul (1992a), Spain (1992b), Egypt (1993a), the Balkans (1993b), Germany (1993c), and Africa (1994b). My debt to these in what follows will be obvious. The epigraphic evidence for Christian immigration is summarized by Avraméa (1995).

My interest in the topic arose from studying the Jews of Rome, primarily through their inscriptions, and beginning to wonder how far their experiences and self-identity were comparable to those of other people who were in some sense 'foreign', as visitors or immigrants themselves, or as the descendants of immigrants who retained some link to their ancestral traditions. I gradually realized that there was a vast amount of evidence available, frustrating in what it does not say but still potentially rewarding in what it can reveal. The bulk of the material is epigraphic:

• inscriptions (mainly epitaphs) where someone's place of origin is explicitly stated, or an 'ethnic' label is used; these may provide information about both foreigners themselves and their descendants.

• inscriptions in Greek (and other non-Latin languages); not necessarily connected to foreigners, but likely to be so.

• inscriptions which use formulae or names characteristic of places other than Rome.

• epitaphs from burial areas used by immigrants and their descendants, e.g. the Jewish catacombs.

• epitaphs from the provinces recording that someone died at Rome.

• inscriptions recording the cults or other institutions of foreigners at Rome.

There is also much literary evidence, from pagan, Christian and Jewish writers:

• complaints about the prevalence of immigration and 'un-Roman-ness' in the city; these are largely of a rhetorical nature and have limited historical value, but may contain some useful information, particularly on motivation.

• references to the periodic expulsions of foreigners.

• neutral or positive references to the presence of foreigners at Rome.

• anecdotes about individual foreigners.

• the words of writers who were themselves immigrants to the city, such as Martial, Galen and Augustine.

Where appropriate, I have also made use of comparative material, drawing on studies of European cities in the medieval and early modern period, and of Rio de Janeiro in the nineteenth century, the only city whose slave population is likely to be commensurate with Rome's. This is particularly helpful in the interpretation of epigraphic evidence, and in attempting to estimate the numbers involved at Rome.

The definition of a 'foreigner' for the purposes of this work is primarily: someone who was born outside Italy and moved to Rome, but continued to have a 'home' (in their own thinking or in other people's) elsewhere. Most foreigners were immigrants, but since some were at Rome for temporary reasons rather than with the intention of settling permanently (see p. 3), it is their status as 'foreign' rather than as 'immigrant' which determines their inclusion here, given the impracticability of separating temporary visitors from permanent migrants in most of the evidence.

People who were born at Rome could still be considered 'foreign', by themselves and others, if their attachment to another place (the birthplace of their ancestors, or the centre of their religion) seemed greater than their attachment to the city of Rome. These people will be discussed in Section 3, where the existence of foreign communities at Rome is investigated, but they are not included in Section 2, which focuses on those who actually moved to Rome during their own lifetimes.

The definition which I am using does not take into account someone's ancestry. A person defined as Spanish here could equally well be descended from, say, native Spaniards or from Roman colonists who had come to Spain two or three generations earlier. Except in a very few cases, it is impossible to make this distinction on the basis of the available evidence: apart from 'foreign' emperors (and not always even for them) there is simply no reliable information about the ultimate ancestry of any individual. This is unfortunate, because people who were (or believed themselves to be) descended exclusively from Roman colonists would probably have had a very different concept of 'home' from people descended from Spanish tribes.

The work concentrates on the presence at Rome of foreigners who were free, civilian, and below equestrian rank. Reference will, however, be made to foreign slaves, soldiers and the aristocracy where appropriate. Italians are excluded from the definition of foreigner used here. This is primarily a decision based on practicalities, since the evidence for provincial and overseas migration is very substantial by itself, and I hope to look at immigrants from within Italy in the imperial period separately; displaced Italian peasants in the late Republic have already been well studied. The difference between a teacher of rhetoric from Tarentum and one from Dyrrachium may have been minimal, but on the whole it seems likely that the situation of non-Italians at Rome would have differed substantially from that of Italians. Apart from the questions of language and proximity, people from Numidia or Pannonia *may* have been more likely to feel solidarity with each other, or at least a specific identity through shared geographical origins, than people from Italy were (even if some 'ethnic' labels were originally imposed by the Romans, as suggested by Matthews 1999, 16). Life at Rome would have been different for someone whose home was twenty days' sea voyage away, as compared to someone who could walk to their birthplace in a day, and the boundary of Italy seems the most practicable cut-off point to separate short-range and long-range migrants. The use of *provincialis* as opposed to Italian shows that the Romans themselves sometimes made the distinction.

For the purposes of this work, 'Rome' includes Ostia and Portus, since residence in the ports was often a preliminary to moving to (or leaving) Rome, and since a number of individuals known from inscriptions, such as M. Antonius Gaionas (see p. 240), were active both at Rome and at the ports.

The book is divided into three sections. Section 1 looks at the background: the nature of the evidence, the demography of the city of Rome, and the attitudes to foreigners taken by writers and by the state. Section 2 deals with the individuals who came to Rome, using the vast number of fragmentary case-histories from inscriptions and literature to try to build up a picture of what sort of people came to Rome, why they came and how they dealt with the practicalities of migrating to the city. Section 3 examines foreigners living at Rome: the ways in which they used (or did not use) tools such as language, religion and names to preserve a separate identity. The second part of this section consists of a region-by-region survey of foreigners at Rome, summarizing the nature of migration from each region and the different ways in which different groups reacted to being at Rome. The Appendix has a complete list of all the epigraphic foreigners (according to the definition given at p. 6) used in the study: while it will no doubt be possible to point out omissions, and there may be disagreement about some inclusions, the total number of individuals (1,284) is large enough for these to be unlikely to affect the conclusions which I have drawn (mainly in ch. 4) from this body of evidence.

Parts of the book have been used as seminar papers, at Lampeter and at the conference on *Race, Religion and Culture in Late Antiquity* at Swansea. I am grateful to the participants for their numerous comments, and to colleagues at Lampeter for providing frequent advice and help. The last stage of the work was almost completed during a term's study leave in early 1999. I am also very much indebted to the people who have read through part or all of the draft work and made many suggestions for its improvement: Danielle de Laborie, Stuart de Laborie, Andrew Erskine, Val Hope, Greg Horsley, Stephen Mitchell, Neville Morley, Margaret Williams, and two anonymous readers of an early version; also to Anton Powell for taking on the book for the Classical Press of Wales and for giving much helpful advice. Additional thanks to Susan Sorek for suggesting the title ('citizens and strangers' comes from a Jewish epitaph from Egypt, JIGRE 36), and to the members of the Ipswich Town Mailing List for providing frequent interruptions.

Chapter 1

THE EVIDENCE AND THE PROBLEMS

This chapter attempts to define the foreigners who are the subject of the book, and to consider how far the Romans themselves had a separate category of 'foreigners'. It investigates the nature of the evidence and the problems which it presents, the socio-legal status of foreigners in the city, and the near invisibility of those who wanted to integrate fully into Roman society – issues which are essential to understanding the material presented later in the book.

i. Latin terminology

The people who are studied here were never neatly categorized by the Romans. Latin does not have a term to match the full range of the English 'foreigner'. *Peregrinus*, defined by Lewis & Short as 'a foreigner, stranger' was primarily a legal term for someone who was free but not a Roman citizen.[1] It was sometimes used in conjunction with *advena*, a more general term meaning 'newcomer' or 'stranger'.[2] A *peregrinus/peregrina* might even come from a family which had lived in Rome for generations, speak only Latin, and have no known kin outside Rome, but the lack of Roman citizenship was the crucial feature of his or her status. Conversely, a *civis Romanus/Romana* might know no Latin, never visit Rome and have no dealings with anyone who did, but was defined by a status which was inherited (or bought, or acquired by manumission). However, when Roman citizenship became almost universal among the free population after 212, the meaning of *peregrinus* changed, and in the fourth century it was the label used for the 'foreigners' who were periodically expelled from Rome. Christianity gave it the additional sense of 'pilgrim', so it again acquired connotations which were different from those of the English word.

Provincialis could be used for the inhabitant of a province as opposed to an inhabitant of Italy, as when Tacitus was asked whether he was an Italian or a provincial,[3] but it did not apply to foreigners from outside the boundaries of the Empire. *Transmarinus* ('overseas') was mainly applied to inanimate things and geographical terms, especially in the phrase 'overseas provinces'; it is only very occasionally used for people, although a character in Plautus introduces himself: 'I am a visitor from overseas'.[4]

Alienigenus/alienigena is a more inclusive term for someone 'born elsewhere', but was used frequently by only a few writers. Cicero and Livy regularly gave it negative connotations, associating it with *externus* and *barbarus*, and opposing it to positive descriptions such as *domesticus* (someone connected with home) and *noster* ('our'); only Valerius Maximus seems to have used it in a neutral sense.[5] Alexander Severus is described as *hominem Syrum et alienigenam* ('a Syrian man and born elsewhere') in an expression of surprise that someone of such a background should make a good emperor.[6] The Vulgate, which uses *alienigenus* frequently, often associates it with *empticius* ('saleable') in the context of slaves. Tacitus refers to *ex Italia aut provinciis alienigenae* ('those born elsewhere from Italy or the provinces'), showing that it could apply to anyone born outside a specific place.[7] Thus it does not exactly match the range of 'foreign'; its semantic force was perhaps closer to 'alien'.

Externus has the basic meaning of 'foreign' or 'external'. It is applied to things (particularly wars) more often than people. When applied to people, it most often goes with 'enemy'[8] or 'kings'.[9] It is sometimes associated with *alienigena*, *advena* or *barbarus*.[10] Very occasionally it can be used as the equivalent of *peregrinus* or the exact opposite of *civis*.[11] According to Cicero, it is one of the good things about Rome that *homines externos* receive hospitality in the houses of great men.[12] The Elder Pliny complains about the *turba externa* of foreign slaves which fills the houses of his day, with accompanying social problems.[13]

According to Dauge (1981, 396–402), these terms were among the many for 'other' which, although often pejorative, could in some contexts be neutral or even favourable; only *barbarus* always had negative connotations. Yet all the words tend to have derogatory implications more often than not; only *peregrinus*, *provincialis* and *transmarinus* seem normally to have been value-free.

A foreigner implicitly had a 'home' somewhere other than at Rome: a place of birth, or of religious or cultural loyalty. There is insufficient evidence to discuss what 'home' actually meant to foreigners at Rome, but individual cases such as Martial and Augustine show that it could retain great importance. Rapport and Dawson (1998, 6–12) discuss some of the ways in which modern migrants conceptualize home. They suggest (p. 9) that 'there is also the paradox that it is perhaps only by way of transience and displacement that one achieves an ultimate sense of belonging.' Home's greatest significance can be for people who do not live there.

ii. Temporary and permanent residence at Rome

Latin is even further removed from having a word for 'immigrant' than it is for having a word for 'foreigner'. [14] In fact, the fullest discussion by any Roman writer of the reasons for people moving to Rome, by Seneca (see p. 90), indiscriminately mixes reasons for temporary visits and permanent migration, suggesting that the Romans themselves did not conceptualize the difference. Some people came to Rome for a specific, time-limited purpose (e.g. legal proceedings, education, military service, embassies). Some came with the expectation of staying there for the rest of their lives, whether this was by their own choice (free migrants coming to find work) or not (slaves sold to residents of Rome).

In the surviving evidence, it is rarely possible to differentiate between temporary and permanent residents. Literary anecdotes show that someone lived at Rome at a particular stage of his/her life, but do not usually indicate whether this was intended to be permanent. Epitaphs record foreigners who died at Rome, but rarely show whether the deceased had intended to die there. Ambassadors were normally there only for a limited period, during which a significant number seem to have died. Soldiers usually returned home on discharge, but some stayed in Rome; the epitaphs of those who died while serving at Rome do not indicate their ultimate intentions. Teachers, craftspeople and shopkeepers *may* have intended to live out their lives at Rome, but some may have wished to earn enough money to be able to afford to return home in their old age.

Some people moved from one category to the other: e.g. a student who decided to remain at Rome as a teacher, or a sculptor who failed to find work and returned home. This possibility is illustrated by some literary sources. Crates of Mallos, sent to Rome as an ambassador by King Attalus in *c.* 169 BC, broke his leg by falling into the opening of a sewer on the Palatine, and while convalescing, gave instruction in grammar;[15] he thus created for himself the economic possibility of becoming a permanent immigrant. Martial in the early second century and Augustine in the late fourth both, for very different reasons, returned home after a period of living and working at Rome (in Augustine's case, part of a more complex migration process), but if they had died at Rome, their epitaphs would not have indicated that they were not permanent immigrants.

3

It therefore seems unrealistic to try to differentiate between tempo-rary and permanent residents (visitors and immigrants) for most of this study.[16] The two groups can be treated separately in the discussion of their motivation, and differences are also likely to emerge in other aspects of their behaviour, but in the epigraphic evidence, and in much of the literary material, they are largely indistinguishable.

iii. Status

Foreigners at Rome can be divided into three broad socio-legal categories:

a) Slaves. These were nearly all resident at Rome through no choice of their own. Some were eventually manumitted, after which they prob-ably tended to remain at Rome; there is little evidence of ex-slaves returning to their original homes.

b) Soldiers. The Praetorian Guard and the various other military units formed a substantial proportion of Rome's population, and from the time of Septimius Severus they were virtually all recruited outside Italy. Most returned home after discharge in their late 30s or 40s, but some remained at Rome.[17] Soldiers could be accompanied by, or joined by, civilian relatives.

c) Civilians. Civilians of all classes came to Rome, from senators to the unskilled poor. Legally, before the extension of citizenship in AD 212, they were either Roman citizens or *peregrini*, and their status could have considerable relevance to how they fared at Rome. *Peregrini* might still be citizens of their original cities, something which could be commemorated on their epitaphs but was probably of little practical value while they were at Rome.

These three categories are clearly separate in theory, but in practice there were permeable boundaries between them. Slaves on manu-mission and soldiers on discharge could make a conscious decision to stay at Rome and effectively join the numbers of the civilian foreigners. There are also indications that people sometimes changed status in ways which the law did not, in principle, allow, primarily by using slavery as a route to acquire Roman citizenship through manumission. Some cases where this may have happened will be discussed below (p. 25).

iv. The limitations of the evidence

Along with the numerous general comments on immigrants in Roman literature, there are many literary references to individuals who came to live at Rome. These are usually in the context of brief biographical information, or as the background to anecdotes. Occasionally, they go beyond the basic fact of moving to Rome to say why someone did it, or to show that their migration history was more complex than simply moving from their birthplace to Rome. One such case is provided by Prisc(ill)a and Aquila, mentioned in Acts and Paul's letters, who moved from Pontus to Rome to Corinth to Ephesus and back to Rome (see p. 259). Their business as tent-makers may explain why they came to Rome, but this is nowhere made explicit. It is typical of the literary evidence for one aspect of someone's life to be mentioned while most of the relevant details are completely omitted.

Most of Rome's leading writers were not natives of the city, but they have left few direct discussions of their position and experiences. Fronto, who came from Africa and achieved great eminence at Rome in the second century AD, was apparently reflecting on his own experiences when he wrote:[18]

> ...for there is nothing of which my whole life through I have seen less at Rome than a man unfeignedly affectionate (φιλόστοργος). The reason why there is not even a word for this virtue in our language must, I imagine, be that in reality no one at Rome has any warm affection.

But he gives no other information about coming to Rome. The most detailed description of the process is by Augustine, who came to Rome from Africa in spring (or later) 383.[19] He provides some information about deciding to move, making the journey, being received at Rome by a Manichaean contact, being followed there two years later by his mother, and eventually choosing to leave for Milan. The information he gives is invaluable, but he was not interested in leaving a full account, and there are many missing details; most notably, whether his concubine came with him.

Quantitatively, it is the evidence of inscriptions which is most important for the study of foreigners at Rome. Among the inscriptions, epitaphs vastly outnumber other relevant material, such as dedications to gods, honorific inscriptions for important people and records of victories at the Capitoline Games. Recognizing that an inscription mentions a foreigner depends primarily on foreigners being clearly identified as such by themselves or their commemorators. This is usually done with a formula such as *natus/natione*[20]/*ex/domo* followed by the name of the birthplace, or simply by the birthplace itself given in the ablative case, or by the use of an 'ethnic' such as *Pannonicus* or *Graeca*. The exact meaning of such designations to the people who used them is not always clear (see further discussion in ch. 8): someone whose birthplace was New Carthage might be descended from Italian settlers, Punic settlers, Spaniards, or any combination of the three.

The description of someone as *Africanus* might mean only that he came from the province of Africa, not that he felt more 'African' than 'Roman'. People's perception of their own ethnicity cannot be discussed properly, at least at this stage of understanding of the inscriptions, although it is occasionally made clear, as in the epitaph of a woman which reads 'Greek by race (Ἕλλην μὲν τὸ γένος), my homeland was Apamea'.[21] Their own designation of the province or area from which they came would not necessarily coincide with the official Roman designation: for example, Ricci (1993b, 143) shows that *Dardanus* might be used for someone who considered himself to be 'Dardanian' (or was so considered by his family), even if he did not come from the area which the Romans officially labelled Dardania.

In this book, people with a single name (e.g. Syrus) or a cognomen (e.g. Publilius Syrus) which could also be an ethnic have not been classed as foreigners unless there is additional evidence.[22] The habit of giving slaves an ethnic name seems to have been fairly common, but some such names acquired wider popularity, e.g. Gallus was the cognomen of many people who certainly had no connection with Gaul. Names imposed by owners might in addition not represent the definition which the bearers of the name might give to themselves, e.g. the daughter of a Syrian slave might still be called Syra although she was not herself an immigrant and did not regard herself as Syrian. People with names with a clear local origin, such as Achiba from Syria–Palestine or Sarapion from Egypt, have also not been counted as foreigners without additional evidence, since it may be the case (to be considered in ch. 7.vi) that the descendants of immigrants, not just immigrants themselves, retained the use of names from their original homelands.[23] The same consideration applies to the use of forms of expression which are usually associated with a particular area; e.g. if the date of death is given according to the Egyptian calendar, the deceased clearly had connections with Egypt, but was not necessarily an immigrant. This will be discussed in ch. 8.v.

For the purposes of identifying immigrants in inscriptions from Rome, I have largely followed the criteria used by Ricci (1993b, 143) to identify people from the Balkans. These are:

• an explicit ethnic or birthplace.[24]
• being the (ex-)slave of a local dynasty.
• connection to someone of explicitly foreign origin by an expression like *corregionarius* (only found in military inscriptions).

She also includes the epitaphs of people who were commemorated at home but had done something which required being at Rome, such as serving in the Praetorian Guard. I have not used inscriptions of this sort in my totals and calculations, as my focus is primarily on civilians and they would distort the evidence even more heavily towards the military.[25] Military epitaphs from Rome potentially provide some information about the soldiers' domestic circumstances while living at Rome, while epitaphs from their places of origin do not, nor do discharge inscriptions or dedications by soldiers while at Rome. I have, however, included people who:

• are siblings, cousins or parents (but not spouses or children) of explicit immigrants, if they appear to have been at Rome with them.

• use a language other than Latin or Greek. The possible association with immigration of the use of Greek, or of particular spellings or terminology, will be considered later (p. 171).

The habit of stating the birthplace in an epitaph was much commoner in some groups than others. It was very common for soldiers based at Rome, but not for civilians. In fact, the likelihood of having an epitaph at all would be affected by someone's origin: soldiers seem to have acquired the 'epigraphic habit', but civilian immigrants from a relatively unromanized area might have much less interest in erecting an inscription, especially if they were illiterate and/ or their first language was not Greek or Latin.[26] Ricci suggests that the presence of immigrants from the Balkans, especially Thracians, increased significantly between the mid-first century and the first half of the second century, and then declined – she found only twelve in inscriptions datable after the end of the third century.[27] Impressions like this may, however, be misleading. Some immigrant groups may have been slow to get the 'epigraphic habit' and therefore fail to turn up in the evidence, and the number of inscriptions recording place of origin appears to undergo a general decline in the fourth century (directly linked to the trend towards simpler epitaphs in the catacombs). If the Jews of Rome were only known from their inscriptions, it would appear that they did not arrive in any numbers until the second century AD, whereas literary evidence shows that there was already a big Jewish community in the late Republic. Social status could also affect the chances of having an epitaph: ex-slaves are much better attested in inscriptions from Rome than are the freeborn poor.

Among civilians, the likelihood of being commemorated as an immigrant, rather than just as an ordinary inhabitant of Rome, might be closely correlated with how recent the immigration was. People who had arrived very recently or who did not intend to stay permanently were probably more likely to have their origins mentioned than those who had been in Rome for forty years. Presumably, commemorators who were also immigrants themselves were more likely to mention the fact than those born in Rome who were commemorating their immigrant parents (discussed further below).

A particular problem of the epigraphic evidence is that, like the literary material, it does not usually indicate if the deceased was in Rome temporarily or permanently. Votive inscriptions (e.g. IGUR 94–214) could be put up by people only in Rome very briefly, [28] and I have therefore not included them unless there is reason to link them to a lengthy stay. Some epitaphs must belong to people who died on a short visit to Rome (e.g. IGUR 815), but it seems safe to assume that most people commemorated at Rome had actually settled there, [29] even if they did not all intend to remain there permanently.

I have also included the small number of epitaphs of people who are said to have died at Rome but were commemorated in their home-lands. Returning the remains for burial never seems to have been a common practice, or at least not a regularly documented one (see p. 191). Occasionally, relatives may have come to Rome from the provinces specially to arrange the burial of someone who died there, or they may even never have come at all but arranged it all from long-distance; this appears to be very unusual, however.[30] Relatives (siblings, parents, cousins) recorded as commemorators at Rome are counted here as foreign residents themselves, on the assumption that usually both commemorators and commemorated were living at Rome. The fact that commemoration by parents is very common for soldiers buried at home and very rare for soldiers buried at Rome is another argument that commemorators were actually at Rome with the people they commemorated.

The nature of the evidence, both literary and epigraphic, means that some types of people are particularly likely to get into it and some are particularly likely to be excluded from it. Among those over-represented in the literature are poets, philosophers and orators, the sort of people who most often receive individual biographies or at least biographical details. In inscriptions, people who went to Rome on embassies are over-represented, since they were members of the local elite with the support of their own community and their fellow-ambassadors, and therefore particularly likely to be given an epitaph if they happened to die at Rome.[31] More significant is the over-representation of serving soldiers.[32] The lack of epitaphs for veterans and *evocati* in comparison suggests that soldiers usually went home after discharge,[33] but if they died at Rome before being discharged, they were more likely than anyone else to be commemorated with an epitaph, often under the terms of their own wills. The institutional nature of military life and the occupational hazard of death on active service clearly encouraged serving soldiers to make arrangements for their own commemoration and to commemorate their friends; recording the place of origin became a common feature of their epitaphs (see p. 60).

The poor and illiterate are certain to be under-represented in the evidence, although it has been observed in studies of modern migration that 'the poorest people are normally under-represented among migrants' anyway.[34] Women migrating alone might be particularly likely to be poor too, and so doubly liable to under-representation. There is also a distinct lack of epigraphic evidence for foreign slaves, even though it is clear that vast numbers of slaves at Rome must have been immigrants rather than home-born *vernae*. The possibility of identifying a foreigner in an inscription according to the criteria used here depends on a conscious decision by that person or (more probably) the commemorator to leave an appropriate 'clue'. The obvious corollary of this is that the clue could be omitted in order to indicate a high degree of assimilation. It seems particularly likely that where a child born at Rome commemorated a parent who had migrated, there would be a tendency not to mention the fact. It is also likely that there would be a substantial number of men who worked away from Rome (e.g. in military or civil service) and who married women in the provinces but later returned to Rome with their families; such women should be visible in the evidence, but very rarely are, presumably because of the desire to show assimilation in this case too.

It should thus be clear that the epigraphic (and literary) population of foreigners is far from being an accurate sample of the real population of foreigners. However, since it is now generally acknowledged that the epigraphic population of Rome as a whole does not accurately reflect the real population, that is not an insuperable barrier to using inscriptions as the principal form of evidence in most of this study. There is some comparability with another area of Rome's social history which has recently been studied using similar evidence. The total number of foreigners recorded epigraphically at Rome (listed in full in the Appendix) is quite close to the number of people with recorded occupations collected by Joshel (1992, 16): 1,262 men and 208 women (Christian inscriptions excluded).[35] She encounters a similar problem about how far her epigraphic population reflects the real population (p. 48):

> The large percentage of slaves and freedmen among those with occupational titles does not mean that freedmen and slaves dominated commerce

9

and artisanry; they simply dominated the use of occupational titles among those who received named burial.[36]

In the same way, some of the features of the inscriptions which are discussed in ch. 4 may not accurately reflect the whole immigrant population. However, I believe that when there are patterns in the foreigners' epitaphs which are substantially different from patterns in Roman epitaphs as a whole, those differences are likely to reflect real underlying differences between the structure or behaviour of the immigrant population and of the urban population as a whole (or at least between the epigraphically active parts of those populations) and therefore to require investigation and explanation.

v. Integration and separation

Foreigners at Rome were faced with various possible courses of action. At one extreme, they could spend as much time as possible in the company of other people from the same place, continue to speak their native language and worship their native gods, and make few concessions to their Roman environment. At the other extreme, they could associate with people of all backgrounds, learn Latin, take part in the cults of the city, and emphasize their status as Roman citizens if they had it. These two extremes are exemplified in stone: on the one hand, carvings of Syrian gods with dedications in Semitic languages; on the other, tombstones depicting a man in a toga making the *dextrarum iunctio* with his wife, with a Latin epitaph setting out their full Roman names underneath. However, the ways in which people were represented in epigraphy do not necessarily show the ways in which they would have seen themselves in all circumstances during their lifetimes: modern studies of immigrants and their children show that people can have different 'situational identities' according to whether they are in the context of their own group or that of the indigenous culture,[37] and burial, given the general absence of special burial areas for national or religious groups (see p. 187), would usually have been seen as a context where the indigenous culture predominated – to the extent that people who were not themselves indigenous could be the most enthusiastic promoters of its practices.

People who pursued the strategy of integration are thus very difficult to identify in the surviving evidence, especially the inscriptions, and they are certain to be grossly underrepresented in this study, as already noted. If they wanted to appear Roman in their epitaphs, or their commemorators wanted them to appear so, then there was no need to mention their place of origin. The most difficult thing for them to change was their names: someone with a Roman praenomen and nomen might still have a very un-Roman-sounding cognomen. People certainly did change their names unofficially from 'native' to romanized ones, particularly when they enlisted in the army (see p. 181), but this was probably not normal practice in the world of slaves and ex-slaves. There are many cases where people's foreign origins are suggested by a non-Roman name in an epitaph of otherwise completely Roman appearance; some of these will be discussed in Section 3.

Manumission could normally, at least in the eyes of most Roman writers, be expected for a slave with talent or ability. For slaves born abroad, whether or not they were eventually manumitted, their lives could be governed more by who owned them than by where they came from, since the choice between integration and separation would largely be taken away from them. An inevitable consequence of the fact that large households in Rome got their slaves through the market as well as through breeding was that people of very different geographical origins came to live and work under the same roof. Relationships must have formed across boundaries in ways which were unlikely to occur among free immigrants. Hence the number of inscriptions commemorating a group of slaves or ex-slaves of which the members are clearly stated to have come from different places.[38]

One consequence of the high rate of manumission and of the ethnic mixing encouraged by the urban slave system is that a large proportion of the population of Rome must have had immigrant slaves among their ancestors. Kolb (1995, 461) cites Frank's view that 90% of the plebs were descended from slaves from the 'Greek Orient' and Huttunen's that 60% of the inhabitants of Rome were freeborn, and shows that the two are not necessarily contradictory, since most freeborn citizens could still have slave ancestors. This too must have been a force for assimilation. The descendants of free immigrants (including soldiers) are much more likely to have maintained some sort of separate communal identity than are the descendants of immigrant slaves.

Urban slavery was therefore likely to be an integrating force, and this is probably the reason for the small number of identifiable foreign slaves in the inscriptions (see p. 78). However, where slaves and ex-slaves do have their place of origin recorded, a surprising number have their home city, rather than just their home area, mentioned. Although some may have been born free and subsequently been enslaved, most were presumably born or reared as slaves in those cities but felt as attached to their homes as free citizens would have done. The route of slavery did not lead everyone on a path of full identification with the city of Rome. However, urban slaves, through their enforced contacts with people of other backgrounds and through the greater accessibility of Roman citizenship to them via manumission, were generally more likely to move towards integration than free non-citizen foreigners were. The extent to which a person's specific background, e.g. from Gaul or Syria, affected the likelihood of integration will be discussed in ch. 8.

The various limitations of the evidence discussed above should be kept in mind throughout the book. Status, background and nationality, as well as individual circumstances and wishes, are all linked to the likelihood of a particular foreigner being identifiable in the literature or inscriptions, in ways which are now unquantifiable. Nevertheless, as will be seen, the evidence is plentiful even if it is not fully representative.

Notes

[1] André and Baslez (1993, 85) note the use of various words based on the adverb *peregre* to signify both 'Romain expatrié et étranger immigré' ('Roman expatriate and foreign immigrant'). *Peregre* itself seems usually to be used as the opposite of *domi* or *domum*.

[2] Cicero, *de Lege Ag.* 2.94; *de Or.* 1.250; Plautus, *Poen.* 1031; Tacitus, *Dial.* 7.4. *Advena* is a term usually applied to people rather than things, and it can be the opposite of 'native' (e.g. Tacitus, *Hist.* 2.2; Plautus, *Aul.* 406) or of 'neighbouring' (Livy 22.14.5). When used in the context of the city of Rome, it often means a recent arrival, e.g. Apuleius, *Met.* 1.1; Suetonius, *D.J.* 39.

[3] Pliny, *Ep.*9.23.2.

[4] Plautus, *Most.* 497; cf. Livy 26.24.4 ('overseas peoples'), 39.46.6 and 40.2.6 ('overseas embassies'). Information from the PHI Latin CD-ROM.

[5] Information from the PHI Latin CD-ROM. Urso (1994) discusses Livy's use of the term, in contrast to *terra Italia*, in the context of the events of 205 BC.

[6] SHA, *Alex.Sev.* 65.1.

[7] Tacitus, *Hist.* 4.65.

[8] e.g. Cicero, *Cat.* 2.29; Hirtius, *B.G.* 8.37.1; Livy 34.60.4.

[9] Pliny, *H.N.* 36.91; Seneca, *Q.N.* 3.pr.5.

[10] Curtius Rufus 5.8.11, 5.11.6; Aulus Gellius 12.1.17; Pliny, *H.N.* 28.6; Livy 30.12.15.

[11] Livy 28.25.12; Pliny, *H.N.* 33.37; Quintilian 8.1.2; Seneca, *Ben.* 4.35; Cicero, *Off.* 3.28.

[12] Cicero, *Off.* 2.64.

[13] Pliny, *H.N.* 33.27.

[14] Doblhofer (1987, 53) suggests that *exilium voluntarium* may be an equivalent to the term 'emigration', which Latin does not have. However, when not given a specific legal sense, the term seems to be restricted almost entirely to the voluntary exile of particularly important people, e.g. Aulus Gellius 1.17.21 (Solon), Velleius 1.2.100 (Scribonia the mother of the elder Julia).

[15] Suetonius, *Gramm.* 2.

[16] Purcell (1994, 649–50) notes the impossibility of separating lifelong residents of Rome from temporary visitors.

[17] Ricci (1994a, 23) notes a third possibility: that they might leave Rome to go to the home areas of their wives.

[18] Fronto, *ad Verum Imp.* 2.7.6 = Loeb vol. 2, pp. 154–5 (tr. C.R. Haines).

[19] Discussed by Perler 1969, 134–6.

[20] *Natio*, the noun derived from the verb 'to be born', sometimes corresponds to its English derivatives 'nation' or 'nationality', but in inscriptions it more often has the significance of 'birthplace' or just 'birth'. I have translated it differently according to context.

[21] IGUR 1287. For discussion of the factors contributing to the formation of ethnicity in the ancient world, see Hall (1997, passim); Laurence (1998, 95–100).

[22] Cf. Solin 1977b, 210–11.

[23] However, there is discussion of the usage of some specific foreign names in ch. 8.

[24] This excludes the various terms meaning 'Jew', since they were religious indicators rather than statements about where someone was born; see p. 255.

[25] Admittedly, however, the praetorians who died at Rome while enlisted (and therefore are included here) were not qualitatively different from those who lived until their discharge and then returned home, just unluckier.

[26] Cf. Kaimio 1979, 23.

[27] Ricci 1993b, 161–2.

[28] Kajanto 1980, 88.

[29] Kajanto 1980, 88.

[30] Ambassadors who died at Rome are, when commemorated, invariably commemorated at Rome by their fellow-ambassadors or at home by their relatives; the relatives did not come to Rome to arrange their funerals. In CIL vi 3456, a soldier whose name is lost, probably an *eques singularis*, was commemorated by his brother and heir, and by a veteran who is described as *corporis curator*; this may mean that the brother was unable to make arrangements for the body and the other man held the funeral.

[31] Cf. Moretti 1989, 13.

[32] Panciera (1993, 263) has a total of 1,328 inscriptions relevant to soldiers serving at Rome, although these do not all give place of origin. They are mainly funerary. 586 refer to the Praetorian Guard; the *equites singulares* are particularly well represented and the *vigiles* particularly badly.

[33] Ricci 1993b, 205; Moretti 1990, 208.

[34] Malmberg 1997, 38.

[35] Only 17.5% of her sample recorded an age at death (p. 18), a much smaller proportion than among the foreigners (see p. 63).

[36] Huttunen (1974, 48), studying the occupations of the deceased in inscriptions, notes that only 9.5% of deceased and 4.4% of dedicators have their occupations stated. Some people no doubt made a living by more than one occupation, but many of the people recorded must have had recognizable occupations which were simply not recorded. Thus, if geographical origin was

omitted as regularly as occupation, the people taken as immigrants in this study might be less than 10% of the real number of immigrants in the inscriptions.

[37] Kelly 1989, 85.

[38] For example AE (1972) 14 (see p. i), which includes ex-slaves described as Theban, Phrygian, Smyrnan and Carthaginian, as well as a *verna*; CIL vi 9675: a Paphlagonian and a Cilician freedman.

Chapter 2

THE DEMOGRAPHIC AND
LEGAL BACKGROUND

This chapter aims to show that the city of Rome, like all big pre-industrial cities, depended on a substantial rate of net immigration to maintain its population level, and that foreigners were a demographically essential element of the population. It considers the importance of civilian and military immigration, and makes some very tentative attempts to estimate the numbers of people involved. The extent to which foreigners held Roman citizenship, and the significance of being a citizen, will also be discussed.

i. The size of Rome's whole population

There are considerable difficulties in estimating how many people lived at Rome at any particular time. The evidence includes totals for recipients of the corn dole and other distributions by rulers (mainly from the time of Julius Caesar and Augustus), statements about the amount of food imported into Rome, totals of the number of residential buildings in the fourth century AD, and the extent of the built-up area within the Aurelianic Walls. Such debatable factors as the proportion of women, children and slaves in the population, the food requirements of an average resident of Rome, and the population density limit the value of all these sources.

There is no doubt that the city expanded rapidly in the Republic. Morley (1996, 38) thinks that the population rose from about 200,000 in the early second century BC to 500,000 in 130 BC. Estimates for the late Republic and early Empire vary between 440,000 and 1,000,000, with most people going nearer to the higher figure although the most recent study prefers the lower one.[1] Morley estimates a total of 870–970,000 for the time of Augustus: 750,000 free *plebs urbana*, 100–200,000 slaves, and 20,000 soldiers, senators and equites.[2] Kolb (1995, 451–3) supposes 600,000 citizens, at least 100,000 slaves, and 100,000 *peregrini*.[3] Lo Cascio (1997, 24) arrives at a similar figure for the citizen population in the time of Caesar, noting that adult males would have been substantially over-represented in it; he does not estimate the size of the other parts, and he suggests (p. 30) a decrease to about 600,000 in the *plebs urbana* by the time of Augustus, due to the colonization projects and the capping of the number who could receive the corn dole.[4] The extremely high population density which a total of up to 1,000,000 would suggest can be made more plausible if it is assumed that the city's population was not entirely within the area subsequently marked by the Aurelianic Walls, but also spread out into the surrounding 'countryside', especially along the main roads.[5] For the purposes of what follows, I shall accept 1,000,000 as a convenient and plausible total, but since the estimates below largely concern proportion rather than specific numbers, the general arguments would not be affected if the actual figure was somewhat lower.

The size of the population was probably roughly stable from the time of Augustus until the second century, but there appears to have been a decline by the Severan period, probably attributable to the outbreaks of plague, to something in the range of 650,000–800,000.[6] The size of the population then seems at least to have maintained its level until undergoing a substantial fall at the time of the Sack of Rome in 410, perhaps to 300,000 or below.[7] There may have been something of a recovery after that, as the number of pigs required for the pork dole increased by nearly 20% between 419 and 452, and the emperors regularly resided at Rome in the period *c.* 440–476.[8]

While there is some ancient evidence for the number of adult male citizens and for the total population, there is virtually none for the number of slaves or the proportion of the population which they formed. MacMullen (1990, 327 n. 3) suggests that in a population of 500,000, 4% would own 175,000 slaves, while the rest would be free; i.e. slaves would form 35% of the population. Morley, as shown above, has a considerably lower estimate, 10–20%, and Kolb's is lower still. The fact that such widely divergent opinions can arise suggests the impossibility of assessing the number of slaves at Rome. It is likely that the proportion would have been highest in the first centuries BC and AD, at the time when wars were still bringing slaves into Rome in large numbers, and that it would have declined after that.

The difficulty of assessing the proportion of foreigners in Rome's population is as great as, or even greater than, that of assessing the proportion of slaves. Some people would of course come into both categories, as the large majority of slaves would not have been born at Rome. Epigraphic evidence for immigrant slaves is extremely limited,[9] but this is probably attributable to the self-image of the slaves who left epitaphs (see p. 9). Beloch estimated that there were 60–70,000 resident *peregrini*,[10] and Friedländer suggested 60,000,[11] but Kajanto thinks the evidence implies that foreigners in Rome were not very numerous.[12] Kolb's suggestion of 100,000 *peregrini* (see above) seems fairly arbitrary. An attempt to estimate a minimum percentage based on some more specific criteria is made at the end of this chapter.

One possible approach is to look at other cities with better records, which may at least indicate the sorts of figures for immigrant populations which are plausible. In rapidly expanding early-modern London, life expectancy would have been comparable to ancient Rome, although female age at marriage was probably later (affecting reproductivity) and there was no equivalent to slavery. In Finley's survey of various social groups at London, those who were born outside England (perhaps roughly comparable to people at Rome coming from outside Italy) varied from 2.5–9.4%.[13] The total 'alien' population of London was counted as 5.3% in 1573, but only 1.0% in 1635. [14]

A rather closer parallel is provided by nineteenth-century Rio de Janeiro, the one modern city with a slave population which may be comparable to Rome's and with immigrants coming almost entirely from overseas. There are still some substantial differences, notably the official abolition of the slave trade in 1830 and its effective abolition in 1850.[15] The city's population was expanding rapidly, and depended on both slave and free immigration to maintain the growth. Slaves seem on the whole to have formed something approaching 40% of the population.[16] Nearly 80,000 slaves were recorded in the 1849 census (38% of the population), a total which was never reached again although the city grew larger.[17] Of those slaves, 72% of the males and 57% of the females were born overseas. In the same census, free overseas-born residents amounted to 24% of the male population and 9% of the female (18% of the total); this almost certainly exceeds the overseas-born population of Rome, since immigration from the rest of Italy to Rome would have been substantially more significant than immigration from the rest of Brazil to Rio.

Comparison with London and Rio thus suggests that it is generally plausible to envisage free overseas immigrants as forming something in the range of 5% or more of the population of Rome during the period when the city was still growing (cf. p. 19). At Rio in 1849, only 20% of those born overseas were female, and there may have been a similar gender imbalance in the foreign population of Rome (see p. 60).

ii. Natural demographic decrease

It is generally agreed that mortality was probably higher in Rome than elsewhere in the Roman world, because of insanitary living conditions and the risk of contagious diseases; diseases such as tuberculosis may have been endemic.[18] Newcomers to London were more susceptible to plague than natives were,[19] and the same point has been made about the greater susceptibility of Rome's immigrants to *plasmodium falciparum* malaria.[20] Tuberculosis might be particularly dangerous to the young adults who probably formed most of the immigrant population. Ammianus commented that 'the inhabitants are peculiarly subject to severe epidemics of a kind which the whole medical profession is powerless to cure'.[21] The bad effect of the climate (*intemperies caeli*) of Rome on the health of soldiers newly arrived there in AD 69 is mentioned by Tacitus,[22] and it is even possible that the high number of young ages at death recorded for the German bodyguards of the Julio-Claudian emperors is connected with newcomers' lack of resistance to disease at Rome.[23] Slaves are likely to have suffered from higher mortality than the free population, and immigrant slaves would have been particularly vulnerable to diseases which were not prevalent in their homelands.[24]

It is also likely that the birth rate would have been lower at Rome than elsewhere. Many migrants coming to the city would already have spent some of their fertile years elsewhere, and the slave part of the population would have been less fertile than the rest.[25] Free male citizen immigrants may have postponed marriage until they had access to the corn dole, which from the time of Augustus was only available to a restricted number of recipients.[26] In London, for similar reasons, the natives were closer to reproducing themselves than migrants were,[27] and the same would almost certainly have been true for Rome.

Statistics for London in the seventeenth–eighteenth centuries reveal some trends in the population of a large pre-industrial city. In the seventeenth century, a population of 250,000 required an annual net immigration rate of 2,500 just to remain stable, and in fact the actual immigration rate must have been considerably more, since the population was growing.[28] London's pull on the rest of England was so great that in the period 1650–1750 the survivors of one-sixth of all English births became Londoners. In the eighteenth century, a greater population (still less than that of ancient Rome) needed a migration rate of at least 6,000 p.a.[29] Marital fertility was probably higher in London than elsewhere in Britain, but people married later and so were fertile for a shorter period.[30] Even if natives and permanent settlers were able to reproduce themselves, they formed too small a proportion of the inhabitants to maintain the city's level of population without additional immigration.[31]

Morley (1996, 39) estimates a net annual growth in Rome's population of 4,000 a year in the second and first centuries BC, probably disguising periods of accelerated and decelerated growth as at London. He suggests that this would require an immigration rate of 7,000 a year among the free population, in addition to the immigration of slaves.[32] A city of 1,000,000 people would need 10,000 immigrants a year to maintain its numbers (p. 44). These are figures for *net* migration; since some people left Rome (sometimes in large numbers, when new colonies were founded), the actual number of people moving in would have to be greater. He believes (p. 46) that most of the free immigrants would have come from Italy, at least in the second–first centuries BC, causing a decline in the free population of Italy (p. 50).[33] The survivors of one-tenth of births in Italy would move to Rome (p. 53).

Morley's figures do not allow for immigrants coming from outside Italy. In the late Republic, while Rome was still growing and the Italian countryside was changing, there can be no doubt that the vast majority of immigrants to Rome came from Italy. However, in the first–third centuries AD, when Rome's population was probably roughly stable, the same 'push' factors no longer applied in Italy, as the process of creating great estates and displacing peasants had largely stopped, and in some cases perhaps even reversed. The large spasmodic influxes of slaves through wars of conquest also ceased after the time of Trajan. Since the rate of immigration must have remained roughly constant while the population remained at the same level, it seems intrinsically likely that free immigrants from the provinces formed a more substantial part of the total number of immigrants in the Empire than they had done in the Republic. This point is noted briefly by Pleket (1993, 16):

> In republican times Rome owed its demographic growth to a politically induced exodus of peasants; in the imperial period it continued to depend on immigration, from the provinces and to a lesser extent from the Italian countryside.

If 10,000 people a year were still coming to Rome in the second century AD, the majority of them would have been free provincials.

iii. The military population
While the size of the slave and free foreign population cannot be

estimated with any precision at all, the military population of Rome, and the foreign element within it, can be treated much more accurately. Le Bohec (1994, 34) calculates the total military presence at Rome in AD 23 as 10,000. Panciera (1993, 262) states that it varied between 11,000 and 27–30,000 in the first–third centuries AD. The general trend was upwards, and there was a sharp increase in the time of Septimius Severus. As there was little military recruitment in Rome itself, these men would largely have been immigrants, and many of them came from outside Italy. According to La Piana:[34]

> The Castra Praetoria between Porta Nomentana and Porta Vimenalis, the Castra Equitum Singularium in the Campus Coelemontanus, the Castra Misenatium in Regio III, the Castra Ravennatium in the Trastevere, and the Castra Peregrina on the Coelian, were most of the time centres of foreign infiltration in Roman life.

Living in barracks and sometimes performing repressive functions[35] cannot have made for good relations between the troops and the rest of the population, and most of them appear to have left Rome when they were discharged. Panciera, *contra* La Piana, believes that the city transformed the soldiers rather than vice versa (as happened with provincial garrisons), and that soldiers in Rome lived in considerable (although decreasing over time) isolation from the rest of the population.[36] However, there is evidence, which Panciera tends to minimize, that some brought members of their families to Rome with them (see p. 70).

Although soldiers rarely came from big cities, the places of origin recorded in inscriptions suggest they usually came from smaller cities and romanized areas in the most accessible areas of the country.[37] The possibility should be borne in mind, however, that the named city may have been where the soldier was living when he enlisted rather than his original home, and that many soldiers really came from very rural backgrounds.

The largest military presence in Rome was that of the Praetorian Guard. Nine cohorts were established by Augustus and billeted in a camp on the Esquiline by Tiberius; each cohort nominally numbered 960 in the second century and 1440 in the third.[38] They were increased to twelve cohorts before AD 47, and to sixteen in 69, but Vespasian returned to nine and Domitian to ten. They were dissolved by Constantine after the Battle of the Milvian Bridge in 312. Their normal term of service was 16–17 years.[39] In the first–second centuries, the vast majority were from Italy, but in the third century, recruitment outside Italy was the norm, due to a change of policy by Septimius Severus.[40] Dobó's study (1975) of their inscriptions indicates that the place of origin of about 63% is unknown. Of the rest, 45.4% came from Italy, 15% Pannonia, 7.7% Thrace, 6% Noricum, 3.8% Moesia, 3.8% Hispania, 3.3% Dacia, 2.7% Macedonia, 2.2% Africa, 1.7% Gallia Narbonensis, 1.7% Germany. Given that large numbers of individuals are involved, this is probably a reasonable reflection of the overall geographical background of the praetorians. However, it obscures a very substantial change over time, as most of the Italians belong to the second century and most of the others to the third. According to Le Bohec (1994, 99), relying on earlier work by Passerini, in the first–second centuries praetorian recruitment was 86.3% Italians, 9.5% westerners (including the Balkans), 4.2% easterners; in the third century it was 60.3% westerners and 39.7% easterners, with no Italians. The change of recruitment policy had a noticeable effect on the city of Rome, according to Dio:[41]

> filling the city with a throng of motley soldiers most savage in appearance, most terrifying in speech, and most boorish in conversation.

German bodyguards are recorded for a number of members of the Julio-Claudian family, and for at least one private citizen too. Augustus used them until the Varus disaster, and they were re-established by Tiberius.[42] By the time of Claudius and Nero, the bodyguards had formed a *collegium Germanorum*. Their legal status was probably usually that of *peregrini*,[43] but they were allowed to have heirs, mentioned in many of their epitaphs. They were abolished by Galba,[44] and replaced as imperial bodyguard under the Flavians or Trajan by the *equites singulares*. These probably totaled 1,000, and needed about 70 new recruits a year.[45] Their camp was first at a site between S. Giovanni in Laterano and the future Aurelianic Walls, but under Severus a new one was built between the present-day Via Torquato Tasso and Via Emanuele Filiberto, still near the Lateran.[46] They had a burial area above what became the SS. Pietro e Marcellino catacomb, and their epitaphs are preserved in large numbers (although they are often very fragmentary through reuse). They were always recruited in the provinces, and if not already citizens they received Latin rights on enrolment and citizenship on discharge.[47] Mateescu suggests that they were originally Thracians, but they soon came to be recruited from much the same places as the praetorians. The origins of about a quarter are recorded: before 193, 56% were from Germany/Britain/Gaul/Raetia/Noricum; after 193, 70% were from Pannonia/Dacia/Moesia/Thrace/Macedonia.[48] Germans dominated before Septimius Severus, and people from the Balkans afterwards. A few of them came from foreign royal families, including a Parthian and (probably) Italicus who became king of the Cherusci.[49] They normally served 27–29 years until AD 138, 25 years afterwards.[50]

The fleets based at Misenum and Ravenna had barracks at Rome, used especially in the winter. The main duty of sailors at Rome was to raise and lower the awning at the Colosseum, although they probably had other functions too.[51] The fleets recruited heavily overseas, especially in areas which did not contribute to the other military presences at Rome, e.g. Egypt. Sailors awaiting allocation to their units apparently waited at Rome,[52] and civilian sailors from the Alexandrian grain fleet also appear to have stayed at Rome while waiting for their ships to make the return journey.[53] Sailors would normally have served a similar length of time to the *equites singulares*, but the Pannonian L. Licinius Capito, a helmsman in the Misenum fleet, died aged 63 after 45 years' service;[54] other examples of over 30 years' service are reasonably common.

The Urban Cohorts formed a regular presence on the streets. They contained a much smaller proportion of overseas soldiers than the other military units in Rome. Of those with a known origin, 85% (235/ 277) are Italian; the biggest provincial group is Macedonians (6%).[55] There were also soldiers from various legions stationed at the Castra Peregrina on the Caelian while on duty in Rome,[56] some of whom would have been non-Italians, but they were probably not very significant numerically.

It is thus possible to form a reasonable estimate of the number of provincial soldiers in Rome at any particular time: at least 15,000 in the third century. With the addition of family members (see p. 70), something over 2% of the city's total population in that period would have been people who had come to Rome from outside Italy for military service. Many died there and left epitaphs. Others are recorded in inscriptions erected when they were discharged, usually just before they returned home. Very few appear to have remained in Rome as veterans and been commemorated as having come from the provinces; if they stayed in Rome, either their military status or their immigrant origin was not recorded when they died.[57]

iv. Fluctuations in immigration

It was suggested above that free immigration from outside Italy is likely to have increased during the first–second centuries AD as slave and Italian immigration declined, and to have been at its highest in the third century in view of the changes in military recruitment then. There would have been fluctuations from year to year caused by events both in the provinces (e.g. bad harvests) and at Rome (e.g. employment provided by large-scale building projects), but these are now irrecoverable. If the population of Rome remained roughly stable in the fourth century, as proposed above, the net immigration rate must have been maintained then too, as the conditions of natural demographic decrease (see above) would have continued to apply to the 'native' population.

Rome may have lost some of its appeal to immigrants in late antiquity. Economic, cultural and political decline should have reduced the numbers of immigrants across a whole social spectrum from slaves to professors to merchants.[58] The foundation of Constantinople provided an alternative destination which must have been particularly attractive to people whose first language was Greek. According to the biographies of the popes in the Liber Pontificalis, of the first twenty, three were born in Italy outside Rome, and nine were born overseas (six in Greece). Of the next twenty, one was born in Italy outside Rome, and five overseas (including Pope Damasus from Spain, the first from west of Italy/Africa).[59]

A close examination of the epigraphic evidence (see ch. 4) does not altogether bear out the expected picture of declining immigration, and instead suggests that it remained significant at least from certain areas, even when the total population of Rome appears to have been declining.[60] The expulsions of foreigners at the end of the fourth century (see p. 40) show that they were still seen to be numerically significant. People continued to come from Asia Minor and Syria (see ch. 5.iv and v) in the fifth century.

The epitaphs of immigrant soldiers, which date almost entirely from the first-third centuries AD, slightly outnumber those of pagan civilians which must be largely from the same period (568 : 521; see p. 57). Soldiers were, however, much more likely to get an epitaph recording their provincial origin than civilians were, so this does not indicate that immigrant soldiers really outnumbered civilians. If soldiers and their families formed something like 2% of the population in the third century (see above), it is probably reasonable to assume that military and civilian provincial immigrants together made up at least 5% of the population by the third century, which is consistent with the figures from London and Rio de Janeiro quoted above. The reality could of course be very much greater.

v. Citizenship among foreigners at Rome
A Roman citizen had, in theory, the right to settle in Rome and to

enjoy the benefits of citizenship, some of which were only available to men: the vote, eligibility for (not necessarily actual receipt of) the corn dole.[61] Under Roman law, a citizen could only be ejected from the city as part of the punishment for being found guilty of a crime; exclusion from Rome or Italy was a recognized legal penalty.[62] The soldiers who served at Rome had in most cases to be citizens, although there is reason to think that some may have been given citizenship only at the moment of enlistment.[63]

The presence of slaves at Rome was entirely at the discretion of their owners, although the state might also intervene in extreme crises. Slaves had no choice about coming to Rome in the first place, and also no choice about whether they stayed there. According to a rescript of Alexander Severus dated to 225,[64] a slave who was sold away from his city must not stay in Rome either, and one who was sold away from his province must not stay in Italy either. Slaves might, however, achieve manumission and (automatically, if properly manumitted by a Roman citizen) citizenship while living at Rome, and thus acquire security of residence and, in most respects, equal rights with other citizens. For the most fortunate, this could be a 'fast-track' means of acquiring citizenship if they were manumitted while fairly young. Some possible cases of slave status being advantageous in this respect are discussed below.

Peregrini were, in some respects, in a midway position between citizens and slaves. Their coming to Rome would normally be a voluntary decision, but once there they did not have security of residence, and could be expelled individually or *en masse*. It also appears to have been much harder for a *peregrinus* than for a slave to obtain citizenship; the chances of a *peregrinus* making some contribution to society which was felt to deserve citizenship, or of bribing an appropriate official (which was apparently the usual route)[65] were much less than the chances of a slave being manumitted. There seems to have been a recognized problem of *peregrini* illegally pretending to be Roman citizens, since Claudius imposed capital punishment for it.[66] While living at Rome, *peregrini* were not subject to special taxation, as metics in some Greek cities were, but they may have been hindered in business dealings by their lack of legal protection. They came under the legal jurisdiction of the *praetor peregrinus*. They do not seem to have been subject to reprisals when their compatriots were at war with Rome; for example, there is no evidence of Egyptians at Rome suffering during the war with Cleopatra, or Jews during the Jewish Revolts. *Peregrini* living at Rome were not necessarily immigrants themselves, but could be the descendants of immigrants several generations back. They might be citizens of another city; inscriptions suggest that many immigrants from Asia and Alexandria had civic rights there, and a few had even held office at home. The Constitutio Antoniniana of AD 212 gave Roman citizenship to nearly all *peregrini*, and after that only people from outside the Empire would have come into the category. However, the fact that expulsion of 'foreigners' (still labelled *peregrini* in Latin) was still possible in the fourth century AD suggests that, by that date, citizen immigrants had no more legal protection than *peregrini* had had before.

Inscriptions concerning foreigners at Rome highlight several cases where the exact status of the people involved is anomalous and may reflect the reduction of a freeborn person to slavery. For example, a bilingual (Greek and Latin) epitaph commemorates a woman called 'Iulia, also called Nana, Eumeneian', daughter of a Eumeneian named Demades, wife of Alexander, and mother of L. Pompeius Itharus, an imperial freedman.[67] It is difficult to see how a woman from a family with citizenship of an Asian city could be the mother of an imperial freedman whose nomen, Pompeius, is not that of any emperor. Itharus, as a freedman, acquired the Roman citizenship which his parents did not possess.[68] Similarly, an *eques singularis* named M. Ulpius Viator was commemorated at Rome by his brother M. Ulpius Dorus, an imperial freedman.[69] Since Viator, in order to become a soldier, would have been of freeborn status, his brother should not have been a slave, and Speidel assumes that 'brother' is not to be taken literally.[70] However, since 'brother' relationships are taken literally in all other *equites singulares* inscriptions by Speidel, it seems more satisfactory to suppose that Viator and Dorus really were brothers, and that they followed two different paths to Roman citizenship, although it cannot be said whether Dorus' was voluntary or not.

Another problem of status is presented by a man mentioned in a private letter from Oxyrhynchus: 'Know, then, that Herminos went off to Rome and became a freedman of Caesar in order to take appointments.'[71] Herminos may originally have been an imperial slave in Egypt who somehow secured his transfer to Italy and manumission. Alternatively, Weaver (1972, 36) mentions several cases of non-imperial freedmen trying to become imperial freedmen, and Herminos could be one of those.[72] Another possibility, which seems more likely in view of the cases highlighted above to which it may also apply, is that he was a free man who followed some otherwise unknown procedure of enslavement and manumission (perhaps in one transaction, achieved through bribery) in order to get Roman citizenship and access to a civil service post.[73]

In principle, possession of Roman citizenship should have been a factor which encouraged foreigners to come to Rome up to 212. In practice, it may have been the desire to obtain citizenship which motivated some individuals. The legal status of the foreigners represented in the inscriptions will be discussed below (p. 75); it seems to have varied somewhat according to their place of origin. Irrespective of their legal status, free immigrants were demographically necessary for Rome, especially after the mass influxes of slaves ended. The third century AD was probably the period when they formed the most substantial proportion of the population, perhaps, as suggested above, something in the order of 5%.

Notes

[1] Pleket 1993, 14; Storey 1997. Storey's calculation, extrapolating the population density he works out for Ostia, overlooks the likelihood of Rome having much taller and more closely-packed high-rise accommodation than Ostia did (cf. Carcopino 1941, 36–7). He does not directly explain the figure of 150,000+ adult male citizen recipients of the corn dole, which is too great for a total population of 440,000, although he implies (p. 976) that many would have come from the 'hinterland' rather than Rome itself.

[2] He estimates a freeborn male population of about 260,000 from the corn dole figures (assuming recipients were aged 10) with perhaps an equivalent number of females; 200,000 ex-slaves on the basis of the 120,000 freedmen excluded from the corn dole by Augustus; something like 60,000 resident foreigners, as suggested by Friedländer (see below).

[3] He takes the figures for distributions by Augustus of 250,000 and 320,000 as referring respectively to adult male citizens and their sons aged 10 or more, and to male citizens and their younger sons. If there were 70,000 sons aged 0–10, there must be 40–50,000 aged 10–16, therefore 200,000 adult male citizens, i.e. the number to which Augustus limited the corn dole; therefore *c.* 100,000 girls of 0–16, and he adds 150,000 women.

[4] Kolb (1995, 452) thinks that there was an increase of population between the time of Caesar and Augustus, which is one of the reasons for the maximum number of recipients of the corn dole being 150,000 under Julius Caesar and 200,000 under Augustus.

[5] First suggested by Quilici 1974.

[6] Lo Cascio (1997, 45), arguing for 650,000–700,000 against Beloch's estimate of 800,000. However, Kolb (1995, 454) thinks 1,000,000 is still plausible for the time of Septimius Severus; he notes the big increase in the military population then.

[7] Lo Cascio (1997, 65–6) and Cracco Ruggini (1997, 159), *contra*, e.g. Robinson (1992, 9; cf. p. 23), who suggests that the population in the time of

Constantine and Constantius was less than 500,000. Lo Cascio's picture is certainly consistent with the impression from the inscriptions that immigration continued to remain very significant in late antiquity.

[8] Barnish 1987, 160, 162.

[9] Ricci 1993b, 166. This is discussed further at p. 78.

[10] Beloch (1886, 403), apparently on the basis of the proportion of Greek to Latin epitaphs.

[11] Friedländer (1907–13, vol. 4, 18), on the basis that this was twice the foreign population of Paris under Napoleon. Morley (1996, 38) comments that this argument 'is hardly overwhelming, but the evidence does not exist on which to base a better estimate'.

[12] Kajanto 1980, 88.

[13] Freemen 1551–3: 5.1%; Apprentices 1570–1640: 3.8%; Inns of Court members 1590–1639: 9.4%; Apprentices 1674–90: 2.5%; Freemen 1690: 3.0% (figures from Finlay 1981, 64 tab.3.5).

[14] Norwich in 1583, however, had 4,679 aliens out of a population of *c*. 13,000: Finlay 1981, 67–8.

[15] Karasch 1987, xxii.

[16] Karasch 1987, 61–6.

[17] Karasch 1987, xxi.

[18] Scobie 1986; Morley 1996, 41.

[19] Finlay 1981, 129.

[20] Scheidel 1994, 162–3. Cf. Morley 1996, 44–5.

[21] Ammianus 14.6.23.

[22] Tacitus, *Hist.* 2.93–4: he describes the Germans and Gauls as 'susceptible to diseases'.

[23] Scheidel (1996, 129), emphasizing that the sample is too small to be relied on.

[24] Cf. Karasch (1987, 109, 146–7) on slaves at Rio de Janeiro.

[25] Kajanto 1980, 93.

[26] Morley 1996, 44.

[27] Finlay 1981, 10.

[28] Finlay 1981, 9.

[29] McNeill 1978, 6. Wrigley (1967) suggests 8,000 p.a.

[30] Finlay 1981, 5.

[31] Sharlin 1978; cf. the debate by Sharlin and Finlay in *P&P* 92 (1981), 169–80. Whether or not Sharlin's claim that there was no demographic decrease among natives and permanent settlers is true, the requirement for a high rate of net immigration remains.

[32] The slave population would need replacing at a faster rate because mortality among slaves would have been higher than among free migrants; slaves would probably have been more susceptible to disease, and would have come to Rome at more vulnerable ages (young and old) than free migrants. Any estimate of the actual numbers involved in slave immigration depends on assumptions about the proportion of the population formed by slaves.

[33] Hopkins (1978, 7) estimates that 1,500,000 people were displaced in the Italian countryside in the period 80–8 BC, although only a small proportion of these would have ended up at Rome.

34 La Piana 1927, 223.

35 Panciera 1993, 274–5.

36 Panciera 1993, 262, 272–3.

37 Ricci 1993b, 207.

38 Scheidel 1996, 126, *contra* Le Bohec 1994, 21. The *effective* strength of a unit would have been lower: Scheidel estimates 90–95%. Kennedy (1978, 301) suggests that the size may have been increased by Commodus, rather than by Septimius Severus as is usually thought.

39 Le Bohec 1994, 64; Scheidel 1996, 126.

40 Dio 75.2.4; Ricci 1993b, 206; Le Bohec 1994, 99.

41 Dio 75.2.6 (tr. E. Cary).

42 Le Bohec 1994, 23.

43 Ricci 1993c, 220. Some appear to have started as slaves, since Ti. Claudius Aug.lib. Ductus was described as 'decurion of the Germans' in his epitaph (CIL vi 8811). Speidel (1994a, 25) also thinks that the Greek names of some suggest slave status. Under Nero, they acquired citizenship (Speidel 1994a, 29).

44 Speidel (1994a, 30) notes that banishment from Rome was a normal punishment for soldiers discharged in shame (in this case, allegedly betraying Nero).

45 Le Bohec 1994, 23; Speidel 1994a, 22.

46 See the plan in Speidel 1994a, fig. 10.

47 Mateescu 1923, 184; Le Bohec 1994, 100.

48 Speidel 1994a, 83.

49 Speidel 1994a, 27.

50 Le Bohec 1994, 64, 100.

51 SHA, *Comm.* 15.6; La Piana 1927, 221; Ricci 1993b, 205. Those from Misenum were barracked on the Via Labicana according to the Forma Urbis and CIL vi 1091, those from Ravenna probably in Trastevere (Giorgetti 1977). I owe some of these references to Domenico Carro and the Ostia e-mail Discussion Group.

52 P.Mich. viii 491.

53 Loeb *Select Papyri* i 113.

54 CIL xiv 238.

55 Pagnoni 1942, 32.

56 Richardson 1992, 78.

57 Epitaphs in which soldiers who served at Rome were commemorated at home, presumably usually because they had returned there to live, are surveyed by Ricci (1994a). She notes (p. 47) the rarity of epitaphs from anywhere recording people explicitly as veterans from the military units of the city.

58 Kajanto 1980, 97.

59 This might suggest that immigration had declined but could be explained by the growth of Rome's Christian community, meaning simply that there were more Christians born in Rome in the 3rd–4th centuries than there had been previously and therefore less likelihood of a pope (or any other individual Christian) being an immigrant.

60 Cracco Ruggini (1997, 188) suggests that the legislation by Gratian against beggars in Rome reflects the prevalence of immigration of the very

poor into the city in the late 4th century, although she envisages this as being mainly from the surrounding countryside.

[61] However, since one of the conditions of eligibility was residence at Rome, newly arrived immigrants would not qualify; they would have to wait until the records were updated. See the discussion by Lo Cascio (1997, esp. 11, 47).

[62] In practice, there was probably much less security from the whim of an emperor or magistrate than legal theory would suggest.

[63] There are many cases where brothers have a different nomen, or a son's nomen is different from his father's. They could all be explained by second marriages, illegitimacy, etc., but granting of citizenship on enlistment is a more satisfactory general explanation.

[64] Cod.Just. 4.55.5.

[65] In Acts 22.26–8, a soldier who has 'bought' his citizenship is surprised to find that Paul is a citizen by birth. Cf. Balsdon 1979, 89.

[66] Suetonius, *Clau.* 25.

[67] IGUR 902.

[68] In discussing some other cases of imperial freedmen with non-imperial nomina, Weaver (1972, 36–7) suggests that the explanation may be the operation of the S.C. Claudianum, under which the child of an imperial slave father and a free mother would be an imperial slave. It is possible that Alexander was an imperial slave, but that would not explain where the name Pompeius came from, as it was not Iulia Nana's name.

[69] CIL vi 3309 and 32787; Speidel 1994c, 347.

[70] Cf. discussion of the term 'brother' at p. 70.

[71] P.Oxy xlvi 3312 = NDIEC 3.1. The word used is *opikia* = *officia*.

[72] As suggested by Horsley in NDIEC.

[73] A fictional case of someone selling himself into slavery so that he would be manumitted and become a Roman citizen is mentioned in Petronius, *Sat.* 57; cf. Gardner 1993, 38.

Chapter 3

ATTITUDES TO FOREIGNERS

This chapter surveys the attitudes to foreigners at Rome found in literature, varying from the very positive to the very hostile and sometimes influenced by prejudice against slaves. It also considers the numerous attempts over a period of five centuries to expel some or all of the foreigners from the city, and the ways in which the state occasionally encouraged specific target-groups to come to Rome. This completes the survey of the social, legal and demographic background against which the experiences of individual foreigners at Rome were set.

i. Positive statements about the presence of foreigners at Rome

The presence of a large and conspicuous number of foreigners at Rome (slave, freed and freeborn) is something which is taken for granted by many ancient writers who describe the city and its living conditions, but their attitudes towards it vary considerably. No-one acknowledges directly that immigration was a demographic necessity for Rome. However, the concept of Rome as the capital of the world, a city to which people flocked from everywhere, could make the foreign presence into something positive. This view is taken by some ancient writers, but not very many. Such positive statements are not only rare but are all written by people who were neither natives of nor permanent immigrants to Rome.

Perhaps the most enthusiastic is Athenaeus.[1] He describes the city as the 'epitome of the world' (ἐπιτομὴν τῆς οἰκουμένης),[2] in which all other cities have settled, including Alexandria, Antioch, Nicomedia and Athens. The cities within Rome are more numerous than the days of the year, and whole nations are settled there, including Cappadocians, Scythians and Pontians.

The idea of an entire nation or city taking up residence in Rome seems to have been too hyperbolic for other writers, but Martial refers to 'all the nations (*gentes*) which Rome holds'.[3] Aelius Aristides, speaking at Rome in the second century AD and in a context which shows that the image is meant to be very flattering, considers Rome the city (*polis*) to which all the Empire is the hinterland (*chora*), and then says that people flow into Rome like rivers flowing into the sea, the city preserving an unchanging appearance although the population, like the water, is in constant flux.[4] The themes were still being repeated much later. According to Ammianus,[5] when Constantius visited Rome in AD 357 he was amazed by the 'numbers of people of every race' whom he encountered there; perhaps a reference to the impression which Rome made on Ammianus himself rather than on Constantius. Sidonius in the fifth century, praising Rome as the capital of the whole world (*unica totius orbis civitate*), says that only barbarians and slaves are foreigners there.[6]

Another approach taken by some ancient writers is to concentrate on the attraction of Rome for the elite. According to Strabo, it was full of learned Tarsians and Alexandrians.[7] On this view, it was the quality rather than the quantity of foreigners in the city which was significant. Such a view was therefore not *necessarily* inconsistent with the hostility to foreigners in general which is expressed by some of the writers discussed below. It may have been encouraged by the gradual appearance at Rome of senators with provincial origins (from the first century AD) and of overseas-born emperors (from the second century). Provincials from the West appeared in the Senate in small numbers under Julius Caesar, Augustus and the Julio-Claudians; senators from the East only arrived in significant numbers from the time of Vespasian, perhaps simply because of the slower appearance of suitable candidates.[8] From that time on, provincials formed a significant if unquantifiable proportion of the Senate.[9]

However, the sources suggest that emperors' foreign origins usually tended to be emphasized by their enemies, as for example when Alexander Severus was called 'a Syrian *archisynagogus*'[10] and to be glossed over by themselves and their supporters. The first senators from a region also seem invariably to have attracted a hostile reaction from the established aristocracy,[11] although they are likely to have become more acceptable over time, especially as the area which produced senators continued to expand so that those who had originally seemed to come from the frontiers later appeared to be from very romanized areas. When Claudian in 404 rejoiced that the consulship was not going to 'a foreign (*peregrina*) image of pretended rights' but to a true Roman (i.e. the Emperor Honorius), his definition of 'foreign' was very different from what someone three centuries earlier would have meant, but he still used the word pejoratively.[12]

Senators too were likely to play down their provincial origins, as when Statius praises his contemporary Septimius Severus from Lepcis:[13]

> Your speech is not Punic, nor your dress.
> Your mind is not foreign – Italian, Italian.

The obvious implication is that Italian is 'good', Punic 'bad'. Even Fronto, who self-deprecatingly describes himself as Libyan and privately prayed to traditional African gods,[14] would probably not have been pleased if others had used the label for him. Talbert (1984, 37) comments:

> Links with native culture had to be severed. Instead, all senators, whatever their geographical origin, were versed in a single heritage.

ii. Neutral statements

A more common attitude, and one taken by a number of writers who spent most of their lives at Rome (although none who were natives of the city), is to accept the presence of a large number of foreigners without treating it either as particularly good or particularly bad. The earliest work where this perspective is found seems to be the 'Guide to Electioneering' attributed to Q. Cicero, where Rome is described as 'a city made from a gathering of nations' (*civitas ex nationum conventu constituta*).[15] It has been suggested that the reference is to Italian tribes rather than overseas immigrants,[16] but already in the first century BC overseas immigration was substantial and *nationes* would naturally refer to more than Italians. The passage goes on to describe the deceit and vice which fill Rome, but does not specifically attribute them to the city's cosmopolitan character.

The clearest and best-known neutral statement is probably Seneca's, part of an explanation prompted by his own exile of how being separated from your homeland is not necessarily a disaster.[17]

> 'To be deprived of one's country (*patria*) is intolerable', you say. But come now, behold this concourse of men, for whom the houses of huge Rome scarcely suffice; most of this throng are now deprived of their country. From their towns and colonies, from the whole world in fact, they have flocked here. Every class of person has swarmed into the city that offers high prizes for both virtues and vices. Have all of them summoned by name and ask of each: 'Where do you come from?' You will find that there are more than half who have left their homes (*relictis sedibus suis*), and come to this city, which is truly a very great and a very beautiful one, but not their own.

Seneca appears to have in mind voluntary migration rather than (or as well as) the forced migration of slavery, which would not suit his argument so well. It is hardly plausible that over 50% of the population really were immigrants, but this may have been the impression which someone like him genuinely had, just as the amount of immigration is regularly overestimated by most people in the modern West.[18]

Neutral statements continue to occur in the second century. A speaker in Tacitus' *Dialogus* refers to people coming from Spain, Asia and Gaul.[19] In the record of the arrest of Justin Martyr, the 'saints' in Rome are all said to have had different native cities, which they refused to name to the authorities.[20] Many important figures in early Roman Christianity are said in passing to have been immigrants, some of whom later left the city.[21]

iii. Negative statements

Negative comments about the number of foreigners seem to be more numerous in Roman literature, and are certainly better known. The statement put by Juvenal into the mouth of his character Umbricius is the most notorious:[22]

> ...I cannot bear, Romans, the city being Greek. But what proportion of the scum is really Greek? For a long time now the Syrian Orontes has poured into the Tiber... One is from high Sicyon, another has left Amydon, one is from Andros, another from Samos, Tralles or Alabandae. They make for the Esquiline and Viminal, to become the life and soul of great houses, and their masters.

Umbricius complains that the rich do not share his prejudices against Greek immigrants, for whom he uses the patronizing diminutive *Graeculus* ('little Greek'), and Juvenal may in any case be seeking to mock Umbricius rather than to endorse his views. Joshel (1992, 4) notes that 'the little Greek, who may have had some actual counterpart in Roman society, becomes a literary vehicle'. However, other writers show comparable hostility towards foreigners, so Umbricius is probably representative of a real-life school of thought, even if it is not necessarily Juvenal's own.

Lucan, himself an immigrant from Spain, complains in an authorial intervention in the *Pharsalia* both about the fields of Italy being full of chained slaves (a source of lamentation since the late second century BC) and about Rome itself being 'aglut with the scum of humanity'.[23] He, and a number of other writers, use the image of Rome as a sewer into which detritus flows from all over the world. Here he perhaps has slaves in mind, as Tacitus certainly does in a speech he attributes to

C. Cassius Longinus, who complains that there are whole nations in slave-households (*nationes in familiis*), bringing with them alien religious practices.[24] According to Gellius, Favorinus was opposed to wet-nursing because most wet-nurses (presumably at Rome) were slaves or of servile origin and 'of foreign and barbarous birth' (*externae et barbarae nationis*).[25] Lucian, echoing Juvenal, complains about the importance of Syrian, Libyan and Alexandrian slaves, and also imagines dinner-guests lamenting that they are upstaged by Greeks who have just come into the household.[26]

Appian, presumably quoting a republican source, says that the common people of Rome are racially mixed, and deplores the equal rights of freedmen and the difficulty of distinguishing slaves from the free; the context thus makes the first point appear derogatory too.[27] Immigrants could also be described in the political debate of the Republic as 'those to whom Italy is only a stepmother'.[28] According to Sallust, lamenting the supposed moral decline of the city, all criminals who were driven from their homes eventually made their way to Rome.[29]

The common feature of most of these passages is that they are complaining about the influence or numerical significance of slaves and ex-slaves. Thus, xenophobia is combined with class prejudice. Few of them seem to be worried about free immigrants. However, Ammianus shows that in times of crisis xenophobia could easily surface without apparent class antagonism; if this happened in the fourth century AD, it may well have occurred during the first centuries BC and AD too:[30]

> Now to turn to the vulgarity of the stage. The players are hissed off unless the favour of the mob has been purchased by a bribe. If there is no demonstration of this sort, they follow the example of the savages of the Chersonese, and clamour for the expulsion of foreigners from the city, though they have always been dependent on the help of these same foreigners for their livelihood.

Ammianus is very unusual in disapproving of such an attitude, as he also does when it is exhibited by the elite.[31] He had a vested interest, as he would have been counted among the foreigners himself. In fact, government policy in the first century AD and in his own time seems sometimes to have been based on the xenophobic prejudice which he finds objectionable (see below).

Ammianus is the only writer who describes a spontaneous outbreak of mass xenophobia. Otherwise, the evidence only shows hostility to foreigners within the very limited circle of the writers who produced the literature. However, one epigraphic case at least shows that it occurred in a specific real-life context. On the second-century tombstone of an *eques singularis* from Arabia, someone appears to have written in Greek: 'death to the Arabs' (Θ. "Αραποι).[32] The circumstances surrounding this are of course irrecoverable. The use of Greek *may* indicate that the writer was also a foreigner, perhaps bringing to Rome prejudices which originated further east, or pursuing a personal grudge.

The Jews were clearly regarded by outsiders as a separate and distinctive section of Roman society. Writers such as Cicero, Horace and Suetonius refer to collective action by them, evidently making them into a recognized pressure group in politics long before the time of the mass influxes of Jewish slaves.[33] They could be derided for their poverty and their eccentric behaviour.[34] They tend to be treated separately from other minority groups in the sources: the same person might display both judeophobia and xenophobia, but one could (and usually did, in terms of surviving writings) also occur without the other. The position of the Jews at Rome will be discussed in ch. 8.viii; the expulsions of Jews are examined below.

The law, at least until the end of the fourth century AD, did not specifically discriminate against foreigners at Rome, although they clearly suffered numerous disadvantages if they were not Roman citizens (see p. 24). However, one aspect of legal life in Rome which may have penalized foreigners, even if it was not intended to do so, was the use of Latin for all official purposes, including proceedings in the courts and official announcements.[35] Greek was occasionally used in the Senate in the first century AD,[36] and may have been permitted in courts at Rome on a few occasions,[37] but no concessions at all were ever made to other languages. The assumption was that all the city's inhabitants would (or should) be able to use Latin.

In 397, legislation forbade '*usum tzangarum adque* (sic) *bracarum*' within the city of Rome.[38] *Bracae* are defined in Lewis & Short as 'trowsers (sic), breeches; orig. worn only by barbarians'. *Tzangae* are defined by Souter's *Glossary of Later Latin* as 'a kind of Parthian shoe', on the assumption that they are the same as the *zancae* or *sangae* mentioned in a list of exotic clothing in SHA, *Claud.* 17.6: 'three pairs of Parthian *zancae*'. The prohibition of such apparel in the city may have been a reaction to its becoming fashionable among native Romans, but could alternatively be seen as a deliberate restriction on barbarians of civilian or military background.[39] If the latter interpretation is correct, it is the first and only example of the state intervening in this aspect of foreigners' lives.[40] Previously, the law might be concerned with whether foreigners were allowed to live at Rome at all (see below), but not with imposing disabilities on those who did live there.

iv. Foreign slaves

A slave's perceived racial background was sometimes an important consideration for a potential buyer, and there was clearly substantial prejudice for and against slaves from certain places.[41] This is set out most clearly in a legal text:[42]

> Those who sell slaves must announce the nationality (*natio*) of each one at the sale. For often a slave's nationality either encourages or deters a buyer; therefore it is in our interests to know the nationality. For it is presumed that some slaves are good because they are not of a discredited nationality, but some seem bad because they are of a nationality which is more notorious.

In a Martial poem, the speaker wants his slave to be 'a rosy youth of the Mytilenean slave-dealer', i.e., presumably, from Asia Minor, and not a Geta or someone from the Hister (Lower Danube), i.e. a Thracian. [43] Elsewhere, Martial refers to slaves from Egypt, Cappadocia, Syria, Spain, Greece, Arabia and Ethiopia.[44] Attitudes to slaves from various regions are discussed in some of the sections of ch. 8.

A slave's knowledge of Latin was apparently considered less important than where s/he came from.[45] In some circumstances, having Greek as a first language would be seen as an advantage rather than a disadvantage, although slaves with other first languages were presumably expected to learn Latin. Not understanding Latin was no doubt one of the many factors which would increase the alienation of slaves arriving at Rome.[46]

v. Expulsions of foreigners from Rome

No general legal measures ever seem to have been taken to prevent migration to Rome, unlike Justinianic Constantinople, where special officers were appointed to vet immigrants.[47] In extreme circumstances, however, the Roman state might take coercive measures against foreigners who were already in the city, or groups which included foreigners. Usually, there was only one such measure available: expulsion. It seems that mass expulsion was only ever used against groups composed partly or wholly of foreigners. The usual form which it took was the exclusion of whichever members of the target group happened to be in Rome at the time, but not a permanent ban on the group living there. Thus it would usually have been possible for the expelled to return later.

Latins and Italians were expelled on a number of occasions in the period 187–172 BC, but at the request of Latin cities which were being depopulated by the number of their citizens moving to Rome.[48] Later measures were aimed at immigrants from overseas as well as, or instead of, Italians. The wholesale expulsion of all *peregrini* is said by Cicero[49] to have been enacted by 'Pennus', probably in 126 BC when M. Junius Pennus was tribune,[50] and by Papius in 65 BC,[51] much to Cicero's disgust: 'to prohibit *peregrini* from the use of the city is clearly inhuman'. It was the operation of this law from which Cicero tried to defend the poet Archias by proving that he was a citizen. The Lex Papia is also mentioned by Dio:[52]

> Meanwhile all those who were resident (aliens) in Rome, except inhabitants of what is now Italy, were banished on the motion of one C. Papius, a tribune, because they were becoming too numerous and were not thought fit persons to dwell with the citizens.

Cicero mentions a man being exempted from 'the law by which *peregrini* were expelled from Rome', presumably the same one.[53] Balsdon (1979, 100) links the expulsions with attempts to extend the citizenship, and suggests that they were temporary measures to prevent non-citizens from trying to vote at such times. Lintott (1994, 76) likewise believes that Pennus' law was passed:

> either because there was a threat to public order from Italians gathering in the city to support Flaccus at the elections, or because it was suspected that Roman citizenship was being usurped.

Purcell, in the same volume, sees the Lex Papia, which according to Dio did not apply to Italians, rather differently (1994, 652–3):

> The unmistakable xenophobia of the measure puts it in the company of those various expulsions of ideologically suspect groups which long characterized Roman policy and reflect a lasting insecurity about the tenacity of the Roman character; but also, concerned with far more than the maintenance of electoral propriety, the Lex Papia is eloquent evidence for the scale of non-Italian presence at Rome.

However, the motivation described by Dio hardly seems plausible, and is certainly inconsistent with the usual *laissez-faire* approach taken by the state. Only two expulsions of 'ideologically suspect groups' are known before 65 BC,[54] so there was not as much precedent as Purcell suggests. There were perhaps other reasons which are not recorded (such as actual or potential food shortage; see below); there must certainly have been particular circumstances which triggered the legislation, even if the attitudes behind it always existed. Neither of the laws can have been in force for very long. Balsdon (1979, 100) even comments that 'there is no evidence that they resulted in any expulsion at all of aliens from the city of Rome'. However, Cicero refers to the condemnation of a painter, a freedman of the painter Sopolis, under the Lex Papia, by which he presumably means the law of 65 BC.[55]

A form of expulsion was recommended by Dionysius of Halicarnassus, writing in the Augustan period, as a way of preserving the moral qualities of the city's population. He complains about the number of undeserving slaves who achieve manumission, and recommends that the censors should make enquiries about the newly manumitted:[56]

> After which they should enrol in the tribes such of them as they find worthy to be citizens, and allow them to remain in the city, but should expel from the city the foul and corrupt herd under the specious pretence of sending them out as a colony.

His worry about the effects of the ex-slaves on the population is ostensibly more moralistic (the immoral means used to achieve manumission) than racialist, which is hardly surprising as he was himself an immigrant. He evidently thought that a general expulsion of undesirable ex-slaves would be unacceptable, and hence felt the need to justify it by making it into the foundation of a colony. However, this proposal seems to have little in common with any measures which were actually taken.

Food shortages certainly led to the temporary expulsion of 'surplus' groups in the time of Augustus and later, which is the reason for suspecting that they may also have been behind the earlier expulsions. In AD 6, gladiators and slaves for sale were banished to 100 miles from Rome according to Dio; Suetonius says that all foreigners except doctors and teachers were removed.[57] This was part of a string of emergency measures to reduce the pressure on the food supply; Augustus and others dismissed most of their retinues, and senators were encouraged to leave, presumably taking their slaves with them.[58]

The only other recorded general expulsions are over 300 years later. In the intervening period, specific groups were frequently targeted, but foreigners *en masse* were not, as far as the surviving evidence goes. If the huge chronological gap between the general expulsions is not just a consequence of inadequate sources, it may be related to the particularly high proportion of foreigners at Rome in the first–third centuries AD. It was perhaps felt that a mass expulsion of all foreigners was not feasible in that period, and that concentrating on smaller groups was more practicable. This could explain the discrepancy between Dio and Suetonius concerning the events of AD 6 which was noted above; Augustus may originally have wanted a general expulsion but decided to settle for a more limited one, or a general expulsion which was feasible in Augustus' time no longer seemed plausible to Dio. If the proportion of people perceived as 'foreign' had fallen by the mid-fourth century, then the Augustan precedent would have made mass expulsion a viable option again in a crisis.

Ammianus, in a digression within the context of events of AD 354 describes a mass expulsion which was clearly motivated by fear of famine:[59]

> Lastly, the ultimate disgrace, not long ago, when foreigners were banished in headlong haste from the city because a famine was expected, no respite whatever was granted to professors of the liberal arts, though very few in number, while at the same time the hangers-on of actresses and those who posed as such for the occasion, together with 3,000 dancers with their choruses and the same number of dancing instructors, were allowed to remain without even being questioned.

By this time the legal distinction between *peregrini* and citizens no longer applied, so presumably the definition of a foreigner was someone not born in Rome or only living at Rome for a certain length of time.[60] This expulsion could be the one also alluded to by Libanius in a speech delivered in 360: [61]

> (Rome) converts a dearth of provisions into abundance by expelling foreigners whenever such an emergency arises.

After this, the expulsion of foreigners by the Urban Prefect seems to have become a fairly common measure as a response to popular xenophobic feeling at times of food crisis.[62] There is an implication that the Prefect may have kept records enabling 'foreigners' (however defined) to be identified. Aradius Rufinus in 376 avoided such an expulsion by obliging 'the honoured and richer men' to help buy corn on the open market to deal with the immediate crisis.[63] In 382, able-bodied beggars of free status were ordered to be removed from Rome and settled as perpetual *coloni*, but the question of whether they were immigrants does not appear to have arisen.[64] However, there is a reference in the life of Alexander Severus to the possibility of having individual beggars at Rome maintained by individual cities[65] – presumably this implies that a city would maintain beggars who originated from that city, people who are likely to have gone to Rome for other reasons and later ended up as beggars. The agenda behind this may well be a fourth-century one rather than one which genuinely belongs to Alexander's reign, since it fits well with the events mentioned by Ammianus and Ambrose, and it suggests that alternatives to expulsion were being considered. Ammianus clearly thinks that a targeted expulsion of 'non-productive' residents would have been preferable to the mass expulsion which he describes, and his comment on the lack of exemption for professors may show awareness of the Augustan precedent.

In 384, a delay in the arrival of grain imports caused another expulsion.[66] This is lamented by Symmachus in a letter to Nicomachus Flavianus:[67]

> We fear a shortage of corn, despite the expulsion of all those whom Rome had taken to the full breast she offered... With how much hatred from the provinces is our security achieved?... If only our city can recall as soon as possible those whom she unwillingly sent away!

According to the interpretation of Palanque (1931, 350–1), Symmachus was himself responsible for the expulsion, while he was Urban Prefect. Themistius, in a speech made at Constantinople in 384/5, is probably alluding to the same event when he congratulates Constantinople on not having to take similar measures:[68]

> We no longer need to continue to send away foreigners, as recently happened in the capital, a remedy worse than the disease.

Ambrose complains, also probably in the context of this expulsion, that 'those who had already spent a substantial time (*plurimam...aetatem*) there went away with their children weeping', with their personal ties (*necessitudines, affinitates*) torn away.[69] There may of course be an element of rhetorical exaggeration in this, but the underlying picture appears to be real.

vi. Expulsions of specific groups

Problems with the food supply motivated most of the expulsions discussed above. Usually, however, expulsion was restricted to a limited group, defined by religion, nationality or occupation. Such expulsions were motivated by the alleged actual or potential misdeeds of the target group. At least until the second century AD, the target group was of non-citizen status and therefore liable to summary treatment by the authorities.[70]

One of the earliest such cases happened in 139 BC, but the exact details are uncertain because the source, Valerius Maximus, is only preserved in epitomes and with different textual traditions.[71] Those expelled were astrologers, Jews and/or worshippers of the Asian god Sabazius. The action was taken by the *praetor peregrinus*, Cn. Cornelius Hispalus. Valerius Maximus describes the event in the context of various religious suppressions which he regards as justified, perhaps, as Slingerland (1997, 43–4) suggests, with the intention of vindicating similar measures in his own time taken by Tiberius. The motivation is stated clearly to be the introduction of objectionable religious practices, although how they were objectionable is not specified. The source material does not allow a reliable reconstruction of what actually happened, and of whether there were really separate expulsions of Jews and Sabazius-worshippers (as argued by Lane) or just confusion in the source. Jews at this date are likely to have been fairly recent immigrants to Rome and therefore readily identifiable as 'foreign', and Sabazius-worshippers were probably Asian immigrants. A precedent may have been set for similar actions in the future against groups perceived as both foreign and religiously suspect.

The Jews were the target of expulsions on at least two later occasions, mentioned by rather more reliable sources. In AD 19, 4,000 Jews descended from freedmen (and therefore presumably citizens but not themselves immigrants) were conscripted[72] and sent to Sardinia, while others who practised Jewish and Egyptian rites were expelled from Italy unless they gave them up.[73] The cause given by Josephus, the embezzlement of money from an aristocratic proselyte called Fulvia, seems out of all proportion to the severity of the measures, and the real motivation has been the subject of much debate: over-zealous proselytizing, participation in disturbances, and state hostility to the Jewish religion have all been proposed.[74]

Claudius also took action against the Jews of Rome, prohibiting their assemblies and perhaps excluding them from the corn dole in AD 41, and expelling them from the city a few years later (probably in 49).[75] According to Suetonius, the Jews were expelled because they were 'constantly making trouble, with Chrestus as instigator' (*impulsore Chresto assidue tumultuantes*), something which has generally been taken as a slightly garbled reference to the arrival of Christianity at Rome.[76] However, Slingerland (1997, 159–68) has recently argued that Chrestus was the name of the instigator of the expulsion rather than of the trouble-making. This suggestion is unconvincing as a way of understanding the Latin, but his thesis of persistent official Julio–Claudian hostility to the practice of Judaism at Rome is a persuasive one. Botermann (1996, 114, 137), on the other hand, thinks that Claudius gradually became more hostile to the Jews of Rome because of trouble among them which may have resulted from the preaching of Peter. Whether Claudius expelled the Jews because of general hostility or some specific alleged misdemeanour is, however, less relevant here than the fact that expulsion was in itself seen as an appropriate measure to use against them – they were still perceived as 'foreign' at this date although the majority had probably been born at Rome (see p. 257). The expulsion again seems not to have been a very long-lasting one, since the Christians Prisc(ill)a and Aquila who left Rome at the time were back there within a few years (see p. 259).

The Tiberian expulsion had an explicitly religious orientation, since people could avoid it by giving up the practice of Judaism. The same does not seem to have been true for the Claudian expulsion, although it could apply to Claudius' earlier measures. It appears that Jews were, as appropriate, defined as a religious or a national group; Suetonius illustrates the interchangeability of the concepts by saying that Tiberius expelled 'the others of the same race' (*reliquos gentis eiusdem*) if they did not obey him by abandoning their rites.

Another religious group which repeatedly fell foul of the authorities was the 'followers of Egyptian rites'. Measures against them are repeatedly presented in the sources as parallel to measures against the Jews, but there were in fact fundamental differences. Suppression of the cult of Isis and Serapis is mentioned by Valerius Maximus immediately after his description of the anti-Jewish measures of 139 BC, although it appears not to have happened until the 50s BC, with further suppression under Augustus,[77] who at this time revived (or invented) the principle that foreign gods should not be worshipped within the pomerium.[78] Isis-worshippers again fell foul of the authorities in AD 19, due to a scandal involving an aristocratic woman. The presumably immigrant priests were crucified, and their shrine was destroyed, but the only expulsion mentioned is the exile of a Roman aristocrat named Decius Mundus. The event is associated with the expulsion of the Jews in AD 19 by Josephus, Tacitus and Suetonius.[79] Tacitus and Suetonius treat the two measures as parallel, but Josephus tries to show that the Egyptian cult deserved repression while Judaism did not. The different treatment given to Isis-worshippers as opposed to Jews can be attributed to the fact that they were not seen as a particularly 'foreign' group for whom expulsion was considered appropriate, but as established inhabitants of Rome whose religious behaviour rather than their right of residence was the point at issue.[80] Isis-worship was quickly rehabilitated at Rome, to the extent that it received imperial sponsorship from Caligula. The reasons for the previous depth of hostility to it are not certain: Dinand (1980, 105, 115) attributes it to an association with supporters of the *populares* in the political conflict of the late Republic, and to anti-Egyptian propaganda at the start of the principate. Beard, North and Price (1998, vol. 1, 161, 299) suggest that the cult was potentially subversive to Roman family and political values.

The Asian worshippers of Sabazius may have been expelled in 139 BC, and another religious expulsion of an Asian happened in the late Republic: Cicero says that the priest of Magna Mater, a man from Pessinus, was expelled by a tribunician law of Clodius.[81] This was despite the fact that the state had arranged for the priests of Magna Mater to be brought from there in the first place.[82] However, only one individual was involved on this occasion.

The expulsion of specific national groups without religious connections is mentioned only twice, at times of great national insecurity for the Roman state. In 171 BC, when Rome declared war on Macedon, a delegation from King Perseus was ordered to leave the city immediately and Italy within thirty days, and other Macedonian residents of Rome were expelled with them.[83] There is a description by Appian of the Macedonians' reaction – it presumably owes more to imagination or to much later events than to any actual records, but it at least tries to give the perspective of the expelled:[84]

> Consternation mingled with anger followed this action of the Senate, because, on a few hours' notice, so many people were compelled to depart together, who were not even able to find animals in so short a time, nor yet to carry all their goods themselves. Some, in their haste, could not reach a lodging-place, but passed the night in the middle of the roads. Others threw themselves on the ground at the city gates with their wives and children.

In AD 9, after the Varus disaster, Germans and Gauls were removed from Rome, again presumably not for what they had done but for what it was feared they might do. Those serving in the Praetorian Guard (who were by definition citizens) were transferred to various islands, and those living in Rome for other reasons (presumably *peregrini* rather than slaves) were ordered to leave.[85] Such measures seem to have been completely exceptional, and must have been very difficult to enforce: while the authorities had some hope of identifying members of a group which shared religious practices, it would have been much harder for them to identify people purely by nationality.

Apart from religion and nationality, occupation could also be a common feature of people targeted for expulsion. Some professions which tended to be practised by foreigners came under official suspicion. It was probably the association of a particular job with foreigners which made expulsion appear a suitable form of repression. Philosophers, who would normally have been perceived as 'Greek', were repeatedly expelled *en masse*, usually at times when their potential political or moral influence was seen as threatening:[86] in 161 BC (along with rhetors),[87] by Nero,[88] by Vitellius,[89] by Vespasian,[90] and by Domitian probably in AD 89.[91] Epictetus left Rome for Nicopolis as a result of the last expulsion, while Artemidorus evidently did not go far, as the Younger Pliny (who was praetor at the time) could still visit him. There were also individual expulsions, such as that of two Epicureans, Alcaeus and Philiscus, in 173 or 155 BC because of their allegedly corrupting influence.[92] The measures taken against them reflect the fact that philosophers were not usually Roman citizens.

Astrologers were also targeted on several occasions from the second century BC onwards, and were sometimes liable to execution if they did not comply. The fact that they are sometimes referred to in Latin by the pseudo-ethnic term *Chaldaei* shows that they were perceived as foreign.[93] Robinson (1992, 201) comments:

> They might be connected with foreign cults, their beliefs might be of foreign origin, and this was clearly an important argument against them: they were not Roman, they had ideas – and might be expected to spread them.

Their first expulsion is mentioned along with that of the Jews in 139 BC.[94] Further expulsions are recorded by Agrippa in 33 BC,[95] in AD 16 along with magicians,[96] in AD 52,[97] by Vitellius in AD 69,[98] by Vespasian,[99] Domitian (with the philosophers),[100] and again in AD 409 'unless they burn their codices and embrace the catholic faith'.[101] From the second–fourth centuries, they remained liable to punishment as individuals but appear (like foreigners as a whole during the same period) not to have been dealt with *en masse*. The Tiberian legislation threatened those who continued to practise with exile if they were citizens or death if they were not. Nevertheless, Ricci (1993a) lists seven astrologers from Egypt who lived at Rome. Like other expelled groups, they invariably seem to have been able to return very quickly in the absence of legislation being enforced which permanently forbade their practices at Rome.

Other occupational groups could also be targeted. Actors, usually of servile and/or foreign background, are mentioned three times. A late source says that there was an expulsion in 115 BC of 'the theatrical art' (*artem ludicram*), except for Latin flute-players.[102] Tiberius expelled the *histriones* and Nero the *pantomimi* from Italy for the purpose of keeping order, since rioting between their supporters had become a serious problem, as well as protecting public morality.[103] It was probably only the most prominent actors who were affected, and on both occasions they were soon able to return. Alexander Severus allegedly expelled male prostitutes.[104] Greek 'general dealers' (*pantapolae*) were expelled from Rome in the early fifth century, apparently on a charge of exceeding statutory prices, and recalled in 440:[105]

> The Greek dealers whom they call *pantapolae*, among whom it is clear that there is a great number and great diligence in buying and selling goods, we no longer permit to be excluded from residence in the holy city, although dissension and the great hatred of shopkeepers rather than the interests of the venerable city of Rome have removed them from business.

The original expulsion seems to have been a reaction to popular pressure, as other expulsions were in the late fourth century, rather than a deliberate policy. The recall should perhaps be seen in the context of the need to open up the market at Rome after the Vandal conquest of Africa.[106]

In the Christian period, either state or papal authority sometimes ejected individuals or groups who had arrived recently and were suspect on religious grounds. In 419, Honorius and Theodosius expelled Pelagius (who had come from Britain) and Celestius 'as pestilent corruptors of the Catholic truth'.[107] Pope Gelasius (492–6) expelled the Manichaeans (who would have included both immigrants and natives), and burnt their books in front of the doors of Santa Maria Maggiore.[108]

The common feature of all the expulsions is that the targets were perceived as foreign. Other circumstances could vary: the motivation could be actual misdeeds, potential misdeeds or food shortage, and the initiative could come from the top or the bottom. Many of the expelled Jews may well have been born at Rome, but it was their connection with somewhere outside Rome which made expulsion seem an appropriate method to use against them.

The practicalities of the expulsions are never specified in the sources. A day by which everyone must leave was probably announced, which could be the next day (Macedonians) or some way in the future (astrologers under Domitian). When small numbers of prominent individuals such as philosophers were involved, there would be no difficulty in using the Urban Cohorts or Praetorian Guard to pick them up. However, when larger groups such as Jews were involved, and even more when all foreigners were the target, the difficulties would have been much greater. As mentioned above, there are hints that the state kept some records in the fourth century, and there was certainly central registration of students from overseas by then (see p. 93). Jews liable to pay the Jewish Tax must also have been registered, but that was only applicable *after* the recorded expulsions of Jews. Purcell (1994, 654–5) suggests that there was a system of registration which made expulsions possible in the Republic, but there is no other evidence for that, and enforcement was probably much more haphazard. In fact, there is no direct evidence of the state keeping general records of foreigners at Rome before the fourth century, although in the *Acts of Justin and Companions* (see above, n. 20), suspects are all asked for their home cities. This does not necessarily mean that they were not kept, since there were certainly records of people's ethnic backgrounds in some provinces, but on the whole their existence seems unlikely, particularly as there is no reason to think that anyone in authority knew the total population of the city. It seems likely that expulsions would have involved a mixture of deliberate targeting of figures already well-known to the authorities like Justin's companions (which would explain why Prisc(ill)a and Aquila were expelled, if they had been involved in troubles within the Jewish community which led to official intervention[109]) and denunciation of individuals by their neighbours and customers. It is unlikely that they could ever have been very thorough, and there must in any case have been difficulty in deciding exactly who was a 'Macedonian' or 'German'. However, the available evidence is enough to indicate that expulsions were normally more than symbolic gestures.

vii. Encouragement of immigration

On the other hand, two groups of non-citizen foreigners were repeatedly encouraged to come to Rome by the state because they had skills which were not felt to be sufficiently available in the indigenous population: doctors and, to a lesser extent, teachers. According to the Elder Pliny,[110] the first doctor at Rome was Archagathus son of Lysanias from the Peloponnese, who arrived in 219 BC and was given Roman citizenship and a *taberna* at public expense. Nutton (1986, 38) and others have suggested that he was specifically invited by the Senate in the way that the councils of Greek cities sometimes invited doctors to take up residence. Despite Pliny's jibes about Archagathus' loss of popularity, doctors continued to receive rewards. Suetonius says that:[111]

> Caesar also granted the citizenship to all medical practitioners and professors of liberal arts resident in Rome, thus inducing them to remain and tempting others to follow suit.

The encouragement given to the immigration of doctors and teachers was continued by Augustus' exemption of them from a general expulsion of foreigners (see above). This implies that citizenship was no longer being granted to all of them by his time, since citizens would presumably not have been affected by the expulsion. Although doctors and teachers continued to move to Rome in considerable numbers after Augustus' time (see pp. 91, 110), the state seems no longer to have offered specific encouragement.

With these exceptions, the state did not deliberately encourage immigrants, and clearly did not need to, since immigration was demographically adequate without specific encouragement. However, according to hostile sources, the establishment of the free corn dole in the late Republic was an unintentional incentive for citizens to come to live at Rome (as well as for owners to free their male slaves).[112] Once the number of recipients was fixed by Caesar and Augustus, the incentive must largely have disappeared, since a male citizen who arrived in Rome could then presumably do no more than go on a waiting list. Lo Cascio (1997, 25) argues that many immigrants would have left when Caesar first reduced the number of recipients. However, potential immigrants did not necessarily know what the actual arrangements were, as a piece of gross misinformation attributed in the Talmud to a third/fourth-century rabbi may indicate:[113]

> Ulla said...'Everyone who resides in the city, even if he was not born there, receives a regular portion of food from the king's household, and so does everyone who was born there, even if he does not reside there'.

People arriving at Rome with this sort of idea would have had a nasty surprise when they found out that the corn dole was not so readily available as they had been led to believe. The possibility of misinformation encouraging people to move to Rome will be discussed further below (p. 89).

Notes

[1] Athenaeus 1.20b–c.

[2] The same phrase is attributed by Galen (18a.347) to the rhetor Polemo.

[3] Martial 8.61.5.

[4] Aelius Aristides 26.61.

[5] Ammianus 16.10.6.

[6] Sidonius, *Ep.* 1.6.2.

[7] Strabo 14.5.15.

[8] Talbert 1984, 31–2. Many provincial senators, and probably most of the early ones, are likely to have been the descendants of Italian settlers, whatever hostile propaganda said about their barbarian backgrounds.

[9] Talbert 1984, 33.

[10] SHA, *Alex.Sev.* 28. This probably did not take place in Rome.

[11] Balsdon (1979, 25) on senators from Gaul.

[12] Claudian 28.7.

[13] Statius, *Silv.* 4.5.45–6.

[14] Fronto, *ad M.Caes.* 1.10.5 says 'I am a Libyan of the nomadic Libyans' (ἐγὼ δὲ Λίβυς τῶν Λιβύων τῶν νομάδων, in contrast with a Scythian); *Ver.Imp.* 2.1.6 (Hammo Iuppiter).

[15] (Q. Cicero), *Comm.Pet.* 54.

[16] Kajanto 1980, 84.

[17] Seneca, *ad Helviam* 6.2–3. The next part of the passage is discussed at p. 90.

[18] In early 19th-century Rio de Janeiro, where slaves never formed more than half the population, travellers consistently estimated that 2/3 of the people were black (Karasch 1987, 62).

[19] Tacitus, *Dial.* 10.2.

[20] *Acts of Justin & Companions* rec.C. 1 (ed. Musurillo).

[21] e.g. Eusebius, *H.E.* 4.11 gives the following cases from the mid-2nd century: Valentinus (quoting Irenaeus, *Ref.Her.* 3) came to Rome in the time of Hyginus and remained until Anicetus was pope (*c.* 140–160); Cerdo (quoting Irenaeus, *Ref.Her.* 1) came in the time of Hyginus; Hegesippus came in the time of Anicetus, and stayed until Eleutherus' papacy (*c.* 160–180).

[22] Juvenal 3.58–60, 68–71. Pleket (1993, 17) describes this statement as 'a literary formulation of the iron law that the population of large pre-industrial megalopolises was incapable of reproducing itself sufficiently'.

[23] Lucan, *Phars.* 7.400–6 (tr. D. Little); cf. 7.535–43.

[24] Tacitus, *Ann.* 14.44.

[25] Aulus Gellius 12.1.17.

[26] Lucian, *On Salaried Posts (De Mercede)* 10, 17, 27.

[27] Appian, *B.C.* 2.120.

[28] Valerius Maximus 6.2.3, quoting P. Scipio Africanus.

[29] Sallust, *Cat.* 37.

[30] Ammianus 28.4.32 (tr. W. Hamilton).

[31] Ammianus 14.6.22.

[32] Speidel 1994c, 265.

[33] Cicero, *pro Flacco* 66; Horace, *Sat.* 1.4.138–43; Suetonius, *D.J.* 84; Schäfer 1997, 108.

[34] e.g. Seneca, fr. 593; Petronius, fr. 37; Juvenal 3.10–18, 3.290–6, 6.542–7.

[35] Kaimio 1979, 63.

[36] Kaimio 1979, 107–9.

[37] Kaimio 1979, 143–6.

[38] C.Theo. 14.10.2 (repeated in 399: ibid. 14.10.3). I owe this reference to Geoffrey Greatrex. The first version specifies the punishment as perpetual exile; the second one only threatens expulsion from the city. Cf. the discussion by Chauvot (1998, 326–9). There was also legislation which could have been similarly motivated against the wearing of skins (*indumenta pellium*) and long hair (*maiores crines*) in the city in 416 (ibid. 14.10.4).

[39] Chauvot 1998, 326–7.

[40] Speidel (1994a, 130) thinks that 'barbarian' soldiers in units at Rome probably abandoned their native dress and hairstyles for ones more acceptable at Rome.

[41] Roman stereotypes about various nationalities are summarized by Balsdon (1979, ch. 4).

[42] Digest 21.1.31.21 Ulpian. The last sentence is probably an interpolation.

[43] Martial 7.80.

[44] Bradley 1994, 43.

[45] Digest 21.1.65.2 Venuleius.

[46] Bradley 1994, 46–7.

[47] Feissel 1995, 366.

[48] Balsdon 1979, 99–100.

[49] Cicero, *de Off.* 3.11.47; cf. La Piana 1927, 223.

[50] C. Gracchus is said to have written on 'the law of Pennus and *peregrini*' (Festus p. 362 s.v. *respublica*).

[51] Balsdon (1979, 100) also mentions expulsion laws in 122 and 95 BC, but these were more probably aimed against falsely claiming citizenship. The punishment for doing this in the late Republic was apparently only to be forbidden to live at Rome (ibid., 101), although it later became a capital offence.

[52] Dio 37.9 (tr. E. Cary).

[53] Cicero, *de Lege Ag.* 1.13.

[54] Macedonians in 171 and several groups in 139; see below.

[55] Cicero, *Att.* 4.18.4.

[56] Dion.Hal., *Ant.Rom.* 4.24.8 (tr. E. Cary).

[57] Dio 55.26; Suetonius, *Aug.* 42; Garnsey 1988, 220–1; Robinson 1992, 141.

[58] Garnsey 1988, 229.

[59] Ammianus 14.6.19 (tr. W. Hamilton).

[60] Cf. Cracco Ruggini (1997, 165), who says that the crucial distinction was between *cives domo Roma* and others. There is no evidence for how long someone had to live at Rome at this time before being considered to be *domo Roma*.

[61] Libanius, *Or.* 11.174, tr. Pack (1953, 187). The speech contrasts Rome with Antioch, where Libanius claims such a thing would never happen. The dating to 360 is followed by, e.g., PLRE i 506.

[62] Ambrose, *de Off.* 3.46; Ammianus 28.4.32.

[63] Ambrose, *de Off.* 3.46–9; Palanque 1931, 348–9; Cracco Ruggini 1997, 189.

[64] C.Theo. 14.18.1.

[65] Cracco Ruggini 1997, 190; SHA, *Alex.Sev.* 34.

[66] Pack (1953, 188) thinks that this is the expulsion referred to by Ammianus, and that Ammianus was among the expelled.

[67] Symmachus, *Ep.* 2.7.3.

[68] Themistius, *Or.* 18.222A.

[69] Ambrose, *de Off.* 3.49; Palanque 1931, 350–1.

[70] Cf. Rutgers 1998, 98.

[71] Valerius Maximus 1.3.3; Lane 1979; Slingerland 1997, 40–5.

[72] The use of conscription as well as expulsion suggests that, at this date, some respect was paid to the different rights of citizens and non-citizens; Jews who were Roman citizens and of the wrong gender or age to be conscripted were presumably exempt from any aspect of Tiberius' measures, although the

sources do not mention this.

[73] Tacitus, *Ann.* 2.85; Suetonius, *Tib.* 36; Josephus, *Ant.* 18.65–84; Seneca, *Ep.* 108.22; Dio 57.18.5a. Views about the exact dating are summarized by Slingerland (1997, 50). The figure of 4,000 comes from Tacitus, who may imply that Isis-worshippers as well as Jews were conscripted, but Suetonius mentions only Jews as conscripts.

[74] Smallwood 1981, 203–7 (following Dio); Williams 1989 and Rutgers 1998; Slingerland 1997, ch. 2.

[75] Suetonius, *Clau.* 25; Dio 60.6.6–7; Acts 18.2; Schol. in Juv. 4.117; Orosius 7.6.15–16 (claiming to quote Josephus). It is likely although not universally agreed that there were two separate anti-Jewish measures: Botermann 1996, 114; Slingerland 1997, ch. 4. The reference to the corn dole is the interpretation of Philo, *Leg.* 155–8 by Slingerland (1997, 66 n. 3). It should be noted, however, that if this is correct, it would only have affected Roman citizens, while the later expulsion would only have affected non-citizens.

[76] If this is correct, the expulsion may only have been aimed at Jewish followers of Christ, not at all Jews (Botermann 1996, 50; Brändle and Stegemann 1998, 126). However, Acts says that all the Jews were affected. Walters (1998, 178) argues that the expulsion had the effect of driving a wedge between the Christians and the non-Christian Jews.

[77] Valerius Maximus 1.3.4; Dio 53.2.4, 54.6.6; Dunand 1980, 103–5, 114–17; Slingerland 1997, 43. Beard, North and Price (1998, vol. 1, 161) think that Isis shrines were probably destroyed in 59, 58, 53, 50 and 48 BC. It is possible (*contra* Slingerland) that Valerius Maximus refers to different, earlier measures from those mentioned by Dio.

[78] Beard, North and Price 1998, vol. 1, 180.

[79] Josephus, *Ant.* 18.65–80; Tacitus, *Ann.* 2.85; Suetonius, *Tib.* 36; Slingerland 1997, 50–5, 67–70.

[80] Dunand (1980, 77) calculates that 43% of cult members in Italy (as indicated by names in inscriptions) were foreigners, but from a variety of backgrounds: Syrians, Asians, perhaps even Ethiopians, as well as Egyptians. However, the basis of the calculation (the use of Greek names) renders it very suspect (see p. 179).

[81] Cicero, *pro Sest.* 56.

[82] Dion.Hal., *Ant.Rom.* 2.19.3–4.

[83] Balsdon 1979, 99. The ambassadors are in Polybius 27.6 and Livy 42.48.1–4; the expulsion of the other Macedonians is only mentioned by Appian, *Mac.* 11.9.

[84] Appian, *Mac.* 11.9 (tr. H. White).

[85] Dio 56.23; Suetonius, *Aug.* 49. According to Speidel (1994a, 19), 'the guardsmen Augustus banished thus were merely the few left in Rome after much of the unit had gone to the Illyrian war of AD 6–9', but this rather understates the significance of the expulsion as it is presented by Dio. The German bodyguard was re-assembled by Tiberius.

[86] The philosophers who were dependents of aristocratic patrons (Balsdon 1979, 42) could easily evade the expulsions by moving to their patrons' houses outside Rome.

[87] Suetonius, *Gramm.* 25.1; Aulus Gellius 15.11.pr-1.

[88] Philostratus, *Ap.T.* 4.47; Robinson 1992, 202.

[89] Dio 65(64).1.4; Suetonius, *Vit.* 14; Robinson 1992, 202.

[90] Dio 66(65).13; Robinson 1992, 202. Musonius Rufus was given a special exemption (Jones 1978, 13).

[91] Suetonius, *Dom.* 10; Dio 67(66).13; Philostratus, *Ap.T.* 7.4; Aulus Gellius 15.11.1–5; Tacitus, *Ag.* 2 (who calls them *sapientiae professoribus*); Pliny, *Ep.* 3.11; Jerome, *Chron.* s.a. 91 (PL 27.601–2); Suda, s.v. Δομετιανός; Robinson 1992, 202.

[92] Athenaeus 12.547a; Plutarch, *Cato Mai.* 22; Cato's objection was that young men might prefer eloquence to warfare.

[93] André and Baslez 1993, 243: 'Tous les astrologues ne sont pas chaldéens d'origine, mais tous les Chaldéens se distinguent assez mal des thaumaturges orientaux venus chercher fortune.' ('All the astrologers are not originally Chaldaeans, but all the Chaldaeans are not very clearly distinguished from the oriental miracle-workers who came to make their fortune.')

[94] Valerius Maximus 1.3.3; see above.

[95] Dio 49.43.5. Robinson suggests that they were under suspicion at the time because of Antony's Eastern associations.

[96] Suetonius, *Tib.* 36; Tacitus, *Ann.* 2.32; Dio 57.15.8–9; Collatio 15.2 Ulpian.

[97] Tacitus, *Ann.* 12.52; he says the expulsion was ineffective. According to Beard, North and Price (1998, vol. 1, 231), the ban was repeated seven times in the 1st century AD.

[98] Tacitus, *Hist.* 2.62; Suetonius, *Vit.* 14. According to Suetonius, the astrologers correctly predicted that Vitellius would be dead by the date on which they were told to leave.

[99] Dio 66(65).9.2.

[100] Jerome, *Chron.* s.a. 91 (PL 27.601–2); Suda, s.v. Δομετιανός.

[101] Cod.Just. 1.4.10.

[102] Cassiodorus, *Chron.* s.a. 115 BC (MGH, *Auct.Ant.* 11.131–2). McGinn (1998, 41) suggests that it may have been a ban on performance rather than an expulsion.

[103] Suetonius, *Tib.* 37, *Nero* 16; Tacitus, *Ann.* 4.14, 13.25; Dio 57.21.3.

[104] SHA, *Alex.Sev.* 34.4.

[105] Nov.Val.III no. 5; Jones 1964, 865; Ricci 1997a, 190.

[106] Brown 1982, 134.

[107] Augustine, *Ep.* 201.

[108] Lib.Pont., *Gelasius*.

[109] Cf. Botermann 1996, 134.

[110] Pliny, *H.N.* 29.12.

[111] Suet, *D.J.* 42 (tr. R. Graves).

[112] Sallust, *Cat.*37.7; Dion.Hal., *Ant.Rom.* 4.24.5; Appian, *B.C.* 2.120. Appian, presumably quoting an earlier writer, complains that it is the unemployed and beggars who are drawn to Rome from all over Italy; cf. Purcell 1994, 652.

[113] b. Meg. 6b (tr. M. Simon), quoted at greater length at p. 145.

Chapter 4

WHO MOVED TO ROME?

This chapter uses comparative material to highlight some of the important features of modern migration patterns which are relevant to Rome. The evidence of inscriptions is used to address some fundamental questions about migration to Rome which have not previously been approached from this perspective. Although only limited answers to these questions are possible, the use made here of epigraphic material helps to confirm or deny some of the assumptions which have previously depended on more impressionistic sources, and also illustrates aspects of migration which have hitherto gone unnoticed, in terms of the gender, age and family situation of people moving to Rome.

i. Patterns of migration

Studies of migration in recent history offer a theoretical framework which may help to understand some of the evidence for foreigners moving to Rome. Tilly (1978, 51–4) identifies four types of migration:
a) Local, where people move to a geographically contiguous market in labour, land or marriage. This would apply to much of the migration to Rome from Italy.
b) Circular, where people return to their place of origin after a well-defined interval for a specific sort of work (e.g. harvest work, transhumance, domestic service) or after accumulating capital. It tends to be, according to circumstances, nearly all-male or all-female (p. 55). Circular migration may be encouraged by the 'host' community (p. 62), which nevertheless often makes it difficult for migrants to obtain full citizenship rights (see p. 24). The extent to which immigrants to Rome were able to (or wished to) return home is completely unquantifiable, except for soldiers, among whom it appears to have been the norm rather than the exception. Surprisingly high rates of return, between 25% and 60%, have been recorded for European immigrants to the U.S.A in the late nineteenth and early twentieth centuries,[1] so it cannot be assumed that foreigners at Rome were necessarily deterred by an expensive and difficult journey, or by the perceived poverty of their homes compared to Rome. Immigrants who

died at Rome did not necessarily intend to die there; some may have wished to return home first. There is information about people who spent a limited time at Rome for education, and then returned home (see p. 92), but those who worked at Rome for a substantial period and then left will only be visible if they happen to have left an epitaph in their home referring to their stay at Rome, or if they are mentioned in literature. The poet Martial, who returned to Bilbilis in Spain with financial help from his rich friends after living in Rome for 35 years, is a well-documented example of an eventual returnee,[2] but there is no reason to think that returning home was a lifelong intention of his. Return was also possible for people of senatorial rank who had been obliged to live in Rome while holding office, like Galen's consular friend Flavius Boethus who went home to Ptolemais, and Cassius Dio who returned to Bithynia after his second consulship in 229.[3] One factor in the modern world which encourages return, the sending home of remittances by the person who has left,[4] would not have been available to Roman migrants. Migration in the ancient world was not a way for one family member to subsidize directly those who remained at home, since the facilities for transferring funds from one area to another without making a personal visit were only available to the very rich.

c) Chain, where people at the destination provide help and encouragement for new migrants from the same place of origin. This may involve a substantial amount of experimental moves and 'backflow', and its importance is proportional to the distance and cost of the move. It can lead to migrants forming 'urban villages' or monopolizing particular trades. Migration from Denmark to the U.S.A. tended to follow this pattern, primarily from economically stagnant towns full of under-employed people who had previously migrated from the countryside.[5] Italians from certain towns moved to South Wales in the early twentieth century by a similar process. It can also be organized by migrant entrepreneurs who bring employees from their home area, or by other types of official or unofficial 'brokers'.[6] The existence at the destination of a large community of migrants from the same place can in itself be an additional reason for more people to follow the same route.[7] Research on modern migration emphasizes the importance of 'migrant networks' linking place of origin and destination.[8] Chain migration helps the creation of networks within immigrant communities too, assisting individuals to adjust to their new lives.[9] There is no doubt that this sort of migration must have been very significant at Rome. Direct evidence for people being encouraged to migrate to

Rome by compatriots already there is hard to find, but that is not surprising in view of the nature of the source material.[10] It can be assumed in a few cases: La Piana (1927, 230) suggests that the future Pope Victor came to Rome from Africa specifically to minister to the Africans already there. Evidence for the existence of immigrant communities at Rome will be considered in ch. 8. Diaspora groups such as Jews (ancient and modern) may have flows of migration between their various communities, and that will be considered in ch. 8.viii. It may be significant that Paul was able to send greetings to 26 people at Rome before he had visited the city.[11]

d) Career, where people migrate in order to benefit from the job opportunities of the destination. People living in the Roman Empire could take advantage of the political unity and (usually) the *Pax Romana* to move to Rome from considerable distances. Certain types of employment required someone to be at Rome: some aspects of government service; the Praetorian Guard. Other types, such as teaching and medicine, probably offered greater opportunities at Rome than anywhere else (see ch. 5.iv–vi).

Tilly's categories are thus potentially illuminating in helping to interpret the reality behind individual cases from Rome. Studies of contemporary migration also show clearly that many migrants do not just make a single move in a lifetime, but move in several stages, 'stepwise': rural people often move to a small town, then a large town, then a metropolis, rather than directly from countryside to metropolis. Migration is not just a once-in-a-lifetime decision.[12] Such behaviour is virtually invisible in epitaphs, which name only the home province or community. An exception is the bilingual epitaph of an imperial freedman of the early second century, M. Ulpius Chariton, who died at Rome aged 35 and was commemorated (in the Latin part) by his sister and a male relative who was also an imperial freedman (but named P. Aelius); the Greek part gives a mini-biography in verse, showing that he had been born in Sardinia and worked at Tarsus.[13] Zeno of Aphrodisias, a sculptor, describes himself on the tomb he built for himself and his wife and son (probably mid–late second century) as 'passing through many cities, faithful in my crafts'.[14] Many similar stories no doubt lie behind inscriptions which only record the places of birth and death.

Migration 'careers' which ended at Rome are mentioned several times in literature. For example, according to Eusebius, Peter went to Pontus, Galatia, Bithynia, Cappadocia and Asia before reaching Rome.[15] The career of Plotinus is particularly well documented.[16] His birthplace is unknown, but he went to Alexandria to study philosophy at the age of 27 in 232; he joined Gordian's army marching against Persia; then returned to Antioch; then went to Rome in 244/5, where he taught philosophy and lived for 26 years.

There are also references to people who arrived at Rome and then moved on somewhere else. A poem written as an epitaph although preserved as literature[17] commemorates a woman taken captive at Athens, taken to Rome, then buried at Cyzicus. Another example of someone moving on is the grammarian M. Pompilius Andronicus,[18] who moved from Syria to Rome to Cumae. A second-century Christian named Aberkios stayed in Phrygia, Rome, Syria and Nisibis.[19]

Other people returned to Rome several times. The craftsman Flavius Zeuxis who sailed 72 times from the East to Italy is an extreme example.[20] A perhaps more typical case is that of the very successful doctor Galen, a native of Pergamum who studied at Alexandria and elsewhere, and came to Rome for the first time in 162. He came to the attention of some prominent men by demonstrating dissection, and one of them, Claudius Severus, recommended him to Marcus Aurelius. He left Rome at an outbreak of plague, to some extent driven away by the hostility of other doctors, but returned in *c.* 166 at the request of the emperors in order to treat a further outbreak.[21] This pattern is also well documented for Christians, people somewhat less successful in Roman society than Galen, so it was not entirely restricted to the most prosperous.[22]

ii. Socio-economic background of migrants

There is rarely any information about the original background in their home communities of people who moved to Rome. When there is, it is almost invariably biased towards the most prosperous, who had the greatest reason to advertise their origins. It can be assumed that those mentioned below are not typical of the foreign population as a whole. Immigrants who practised occupations such as doctor and charioteer at Rome had presumably been trained before they arrived, whereas others may have taken up new work on reaching Rome.

Marcion, who became leader of a Christian sect, was the son of a bishop, and a wealthy shipowner in Pontus before coming to Rome in the mid-second century.[23] Several prominent people from Asia are recorded in epitaphs at Rome: L. Antonius Hyacinthus, a strategos and asiarch from Laodicea commemorated by his freedman;[24] Aurelia Tatia of Thyateira, high-priestess of Asia, commemorated by her husband;[25] a fragmentary inscription may record a high-priest from Laodicea.[26]

They may not have intended to remain at Rome permanently, although someone who had exhausted the available honours at home could move to Rome to seek even higher ones. There are several dedications by Alexandrian *bouleutai*, who may also have been temporary visitors.[27] A priestess of the imperial cult who died at Rome aged 25 had her remains taken back to Lyon by her two sisters.[28] Other provincial priests are mentioned at Rome, e.g. a *sacerdos augustalis* from Gaul.[29]

Moving to Rome was something which in certain circumstances could be done by the upper echelons of provincial society, including people of senatorial class as well as those mentioned above. It was also done by those considerably further down the social hierarchy, as some of the motives discussed in ch. 5 will suggest, but voluntary migration to Rome (as opposed to the enforced migration of the enslaved) was probably not a viable option for the really destitute.

iii. Where did immigrants come from?

Epigraphic evidence, if used with caution, enables an impression to be formed of the homelands of foreigners who died at Rome.[30] It does not justify any conclusions about absolute numbers of immigrants, but it does show fairly clearly that the parts of the Roman Empire (and beyond) divide into three types as sources of migrants, as illustrated below with the table and map.[31] It also seems to confirm something which has been observed about modern migration, that distance is not the most important consideration.[32] In order to illustrate possible changes over time, I have separated pagan inscriptions from Christian and Jewish ones. The pagan inscriptions are usually first–third century, the Christian and Jewish ones third–fifth century AD, so differences between the two categories *may* reflect changes over time. This is clearly a somewhat crude method of dividing them, but seems the most practical one. I am only aiming to show general trends, not to produce any exact calculations. It should be remembered, however, that the large numbers of Christian immigrants from certain areas may be due to the fact that those areas produced more Christians rather than more immigrants; i.e. a fourth-century immigrant from Asia Minor would probably be a Christian, but one from Gaul would probably be a pagan.

Type A contains the areas from which the migrants appear to have come to Rome mainly as a result of enlistment in the army. This covers a continuous geographical area from Britain via Germany to Thrace. The removal of the military units from the city in the fourth century

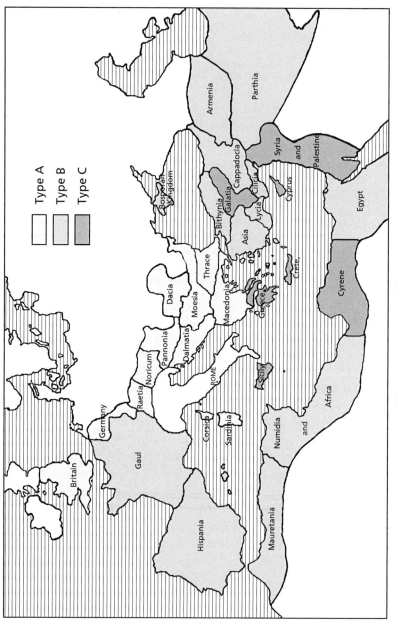

MAP. Home areas of foreigners.

meant that these areas largely ceased to be important sources of immigrants.

Type B contains the areas from which civilian immigrants outnumber soldiers in the inscriptions, and pagan immigrants heavily outnumber Christian and Jewish ones. Asia, Gaul and Hispania provide the bulk of evidence of this type.

In Type C, civilians are still predominant, but Christian and Jewish evidence is a substantial proportion of the total, and in some cases more plentiful than pagan evidence. The geographical area involved here consists of the southern and eastern shores of the Mediterranean, and part of Asia Minor. Overall the Christian and Jewish evidence is scantier than the pagan,[33] but there is enough of it to illustrate that Rome remained an attractive destination even when its political and economic appeal was declining. This is confirmed by the many references in writers like Jerome and Ausonius to highly educated people who migrated to or through Rome. Ammianus' description of how Constantius was struck by the mixed population of the city (see p. 32) certainly appears to reflect the real situation.

TABLE 1. Home areas of foreigners.

Type A: Mainly military

	Pagan mil.	Pagan civ.	Chr./Jewish	Total
Britain	3	0	0	3
Corsica and Sardinia	9	3	0	12
Dacia	30	8	1	39
Dalmatia	11	7	2	20
Germany	112	24	1	137
Macedonia	14	3	2	19
Moesia	15	9	1	25
Noricum	47	9	0	56
Pannonia	109	23	10	142
Raetia	27	2	1	30
Thrace	72	27	3	102

Type B: Mainly pagan civilian

	Pagan mil.	Pagan civ.	Chr./Jewish	Total
Africa and Numidia	11	36	14	61
Armenia, Bosporan Kingdom and Parthia	0	22	4	26
Asia	3	66	11	80
Bithynia	4	24	9	37
Cappadocia	1	11	4	16
Cilicia	3	9	1	13
Egypt	14	23	10	47

(cont.)	Pagan mil.	Pagan civ.	Chr./Jewish	Total
Gaul	22	43	10	75
Hispania	19	60	12	91
Lycia	0	7	2	9
Mauretania	8	10	3	21

Type C: Mainly civilian; substantial (25%+) Christian/Jewish

Crete, Cyrene and Cyprus	2	4	7	13
Galatia	3	12	21	36
Greece	3	18	8	29
Sicily	0	5	9	14
Syria and Palestine	22	48	45	115
Unknown	4	8	4	16
Total	568	521	195	1284

The above figures say nothing about *absolute* numbers of people from any of the areas, but give some impression of *relative* numbers. The places of origin for the soldiers, for whom it was common to give the information, are likely to be an approximate reflection of the actual frequency with which they were recruited in those areas. For the civilians, for whom the information about origin was given much less often, the potential for distortion is much greater (for example, some places of origin may have been more prestigious than others and therefore more likely to be recorded), but the comparison between civilian and military figures, and between pagan and Christian/Jewish, at least suggests some plausible patterns: some places provided few civilian immigrants at any period, some provided substantial numbers in late antiquity.

iv. The gender of immigrants

Modern studies show that migration is usually very gender-selective, but that there is great variability in whether males or females predominate, depending particularly on the type of work available at the destination.[34] At Rome, even if military immigrants are excluded, there is a very heavy bias towards males in the epigraphic evidence. Furthermore, there seem to be almost no cases of a freeborn female immigrant at Rome being said to carry on any sort of work independent of her family or household, e.g. as a midwife, trader or craftswoman in her own right.[35] This, and the generally male orientation of the reasons for moving to Rome discussed in ch. 5, seem to confirm the impression of predominantly male migration found in the inscriptions.

In the pagan inscriptions, the gender can be determined for 509 out of 521 individual immigrants (in the other cases, the broken state of the inscriptions or anonymity makes it impossible to determine gender). The totals are:

TABLE 2. Gender of civilians (pagan).

	Male	Female	Uncertain	Total
Africa and Numidia	29	7		36
Armenia, Bosporan Kingdom and Parthia	20	2		22
Asia	52	14		66
Bithynia	21	3		24
Cappadocia	10	1		11
Cilicia	7	2		9
Corsica and Sardinia	2	1		3
Crete, Cyrene and Cyprus	3	1		4
Dacia	4	3	1	8
Dalmatia	5	2		7
Egypt	17	6		23
Galatia	9	2	1	12
Gaul	33	9	1	43
Germany	22	1	1	24
Greece	11	7		18
Hispania	42	17	1	60
Lycia	6	1		7
Macedonia	3			3
Mauretania	8	2		10
Moesia	8	1		9
Noricum	8	1		9
Pannonia	13	9	1	23
Raetia	2			2
Sicily	4	1		5
Syria and Palestine	34	12	2	48
Thrace	19	5	3	27
Unknown	7		1	8
Total	399	110	12	521
%	76.7	21.0	2.3	

In the Christian and Jewish inscriptions, the gender can be determined for 172 out of 195 individuals. The totals here are:

TABLE 3: Gender of civilians (Christian/Jewish).

	Male	Female	Uncertain	Total
Africa and Numidia	9	1	4	14
Armenia, Bosporan Kingdom and Parthia	3		1	4
Asia	8	2	1	11
Bithynia	6	2	1	9
Cappadocia	3		1	4
Cilicia	1			1
Crete, Cyrene and Cyprus	5	2		7
Dacia	1			1
Dalmatia	1	1		2
Egypt	9	1		10
Galatia	15	2	4	21
Gaul	4	5	1	10
Germany	1			1
Greece	5	1	2	8
Hispania	10	1	1	12
Lycia	1	1		2
Macedonia	1	1		2
Mauretania	2	1		3
Moesia		1		1
Pannonia	5	5		10
Raetia	1			1
Sicily	7	1	1	9
Syria and Palestine	33	7	5	45
Thrace	2	1		3
Unknown	2	1	1	4
Total	135	37	23	195
%	69.2	19.0	11.8	

Some soldiers may have crept into the civilian category. I have counted as 'military' only those explicitly identified as such, and it is likely that some people (especially soldiers' male commemorators) were themselves soldiers although the inscriptions do not say so. However, this is unlikely to create a big distortion, and the preponderance of males is even greater in the Christian and Jewish inscriptions, where soldiers are very rare.

It may also be the case that there was a tendency to mention a woman's birthplace less often than a man's. If so, this would also create a distortion, but there is no obvious reason why it should be true in the civilian world. The gender bias shown here in the immigrant epigraphic population is comparable to that found at Roman military sites. The most likely explanation for the immigrants, as for the military sites, seems to be that it reflects (while perhaps exaggerating) reality: male immigrants really were much more numerous than female ones, at least among those who were likely to get epitaphs. This is consistent with the balance of free foreign immigrants in Rio de Janeiro in the early nineteenth century (85% were male in the 1834 census and 80% in 1849);[36] males formed about 75% of Italian immigrants to the U.S.A. in the early twentieth century.[37]

v. The ages of immigrants

Age at death is given most commonly when the deceased is a soldier. Out of 503[38] deceased military personnel in this sample, ages are recorded for 360 (71.6%). Recording age, birthplace and length of service were all standard features of military epitaphs, clearly encouraged by the nature of the relationship between the deceased and the commemorators, who were usually fellow-soldiers (see below). The demographic profile of the praetorians, *equites singulares* and other military personnel at Rome is fairly clear. Most enlisted at the age of 17–20,[39] served for up to 29 years (see p. 22; praetorians served for much shorter periods), and then retired away from Rome. A few men are specifically said to have served in a legion before coming to Rome, but most give no such indication in their epitaphs. Model life tables suggest that there might be 39–44% mortality between the ages of 20 and 45,[40] with a slightly increasing number of deaths in each ascending age cohort; in other words, if the ages given below reflected the reality of the ages at which soldiers actually died, the number of deaths in each age cohort would increase slightly up to 35–39, the age group in which praetorians would begin to be discharged.

TABLE 4. Ages of soldiers.

Age	Number	%	%
<19	2	0.6	
20–24	27	7.5	[20–29] 23.1
25–29	56	15.6	
30–34	89	24.7	[30–39] 47.5
35–39	82	22.8	

(cont.)	Number	%	%
40–44	48	13.3	[40–49] 22.5
45–49	33	9.2	
50–54	10	2.8	[50–59] 4.5
55–59	6	1.7	
60+	7	1.9	
Total	360		

The pattern shown is fairly consistent with what would be expected, but there is an under-representation of men in their early twenties. This probably indicates that it was commoner to serve in the legions for a few years before coming to Rome than the career patterns recorded in the inscriptions imply.[41] In fact, recruitment among serving legionaries seems to have been the normal way of recruiting praetorians from the time of Septimius Severus.[42] The anomaly in the table could alternatively be explained by the time it would take to establish sufficient links among fellow-soldiers to ensure commemoration, since it was other soldiers rather than relatives who were the usual commemorators.[43] The decline of the numbers from age 35 onwards is the result of retirement from the army, and is not connected to life expectancy.[44] The small number of veterans, i.e. most of those who died aged over 45, confirms the impression that most soldiers serving in Rome left the city on discharge. It is also likely to be the case, however, that the chance of commemoration would decrease substantially once daily contact with the usual potential commemorators (i.e. fellow-soldiers) was lost. Besides, if commemoration was done by relatives, a man's military status might be less sure to be recorded than if other military personnel commemorated him.

Ages at death are recorded much less frequently for civilians; in fact the combination of age and birthplace in an epitaph could be seen as a typically military form of commemoration at Rome, and it may be the case that some of the people included below are in fact military. 370 civilians (71.0%) in the pagan inscriptions are deceased and therefore might have ages recorded. Of those 370, ages are actually recorded for 111 out of 275 males (40.4%) and 43 out of 87 females (49.4%).[45]

TABLE 5. Ages of civilians (pagan).

	Male	Female	%
0–9	3	1	3
10–19	23	11	22
20–29	38	16	35

30–39	23	10	21
40–49	10	3	8
50–59	5	1	4
60–69	4	1	3
70+	5	0	3
Total	111	43	

In the Christian and Jewish civilian epitaphs, ages are rather less commonly given. 173 of the individuals recorded (88.7%) are deceased. Of those, there are ages for 47 males (35%), 17 females (46%) and 7 people of uncertain gender (30%).

TABLE 6. Ages of civilians (Christian/Jewish).

Age	Male	Female	Uncertain	%
0–9	3	2		7
10–19	3	2	1	8
20–29	15	3	4	31
30–39	6	3	1	14
40–49	8	3		15
50–59	2	2	1	7
60–69	4	1		7
70+	6	1		10
Total	47	17	7	

Males who died in their twenties form by far the largest age group among the civilians, both pagan and Christian/Jewish, in contrast to the soldiers where they are outnumbered by those who died in their thirties. The older age groups *may* be under-represented because of the reduced chance of immigration being recorded as someone got older. The proportions of the age groups are much the same for males and for females in the pagan group, but the predominance of females in their twenties has disappeared in the Christian and Jewish group; this may be no more than chance, given the small number of inscriptions involved.

Age at death does not, of course, in itself show anything about the age at which the deceased person came to Rome (except a *terminus post quem non*). The epitaph of a freedwoman named Valeria Lycisca specifically says that she arrived at Rome at the age of 12.[46] Eutactus died aged 14, five years after leaving home.[47] Basileus left Nicaea to come to Rome while 'still a young man'.[48] Literary evidence shows that Martial was in his early twenties when he came to Rome, and that Galen apparently arrived aged 32 or 33, although he actually left his home at Pergamum for Smyrna and other destinations at about 20.[49] Recording this information is extremely unusual, however, either in literature or epigraphy.

Thus, the only way of assessing typical ages of arrival at Rome on a large scale is by trying to extrapolate them from the epigraphic information about age at death. At least 23% of the soldiers whose ages are recorded in the epitaphs had reached Rome by the time they were 30, and at least 72% by the time they were 40, as they had died by those ages. In contrast, at least 60% of the pagan civilians whose ages are recorded had arrived before they were 30, and at least 81% before they were 40.[50] Career records indicate that in reality soldiers were typically arriving in their early-mid twenties. The implication of the epigraphic evidence is therefore that civilians tended to come to Rome at a rather earlier age than that, probably in their late teens and early twenties. Modern migration peaks between the ages of 17–30, which is consistent with the Roman evidence.[51] The epigraphic evidence for Roman civilians thus supports the thesis that males in their late teens and early twenties predominated among new arrivals.

The lack of evidence for children among the foreigners at Rome is a strong contrast to what is normally found in civilian epigraphic populations.[52] One explanation could be that it was less usual to commemorate the birthplace of a child than of an adult. However, this would be very surprising, since the adults who commemorated their children would themselves be fairly recent arrivals in Rome and thus, one would expect, among the most likely to record the fact of immigration. The other explanation is that there simply was a shortage of overseas-born children among the foreign population, suggesting that people tended to come to Rome before they had started to have families. This would be consistent with the typical age of immigration suggested above, and also with some of the commemoration patterns discussed below. It is clearly not a universal rule, since some epitaphs show the presence of young immigrant children, and examples are also known from literature: the future poet Lucan was eight months old when brought to Rome from Spain.[53]

The ages in the epitaphs show that for the immigrants, as for Romans in general, age rounding was a widespread phenomenon. For example, among people from Syria, 8/12 soldiers, 4/10 pagan civilians and 9/10 in Christian/Jewish inscriptions have ages ending in 0 or 5.

For people from Hispania, the figures are 8/11 soldiers, 5/20 pagan civilians, 3/4 in Christian/Jewish inscriptions. For people from Gaul: 8/17 soldiers, 5/11 pagan civilians, 3/5 in Christian/Jewish inscriptions. However, when compared to the calculations of Duncan Jones (1990, 83–5), there is no significant difference between age-rounding for immigrants and for the general slave/freed population of Rome which he studies. The 'rounding index' for the foreigners' inscriptions at Rome is 44.7, very slightly lower than those he calculated:[54] freedmen 47.4, freedwomen 52.9, male civilians and *incerti* 48.4, female civilians and *incertae* 48.9. The numbers involved for the foreigners are rather smaller, but it seems safe to conclude that they fall into the same general range as the slaves and ex-slaves, and do not show the greater age-awareness which Duncan-Jones associates with higher educational standards.

vi. The immigration of individuals and family groups

The immigration of married couples and nuclear families is not well attested in the inscriptions. Only in six cases are a husband and wife both clearly said to be immigrants: an Egyptian couple (the husband is a gladiator) commemorate their son, who died aged 4 and may or may not have been born in Rome;[55] a husband and wife from Gaul erect an honorific inscription for a friend;[56] two hostages from Parthia build a tomb for themselves and their children;[57] a wife who died at 19 is commemorated by her husband, both from Spain;[58] a man commemorates both his brother and his wife, and all seem to be labelled Phrygians;[59] and a couple from Syria were apparently married for 50 years.[60]

On the other hand, there are some instances where a man appears to have come to Rome while his wife remained at home. There are two cases where a man commemorated at Rome is said to have a wife in Spain.[61] In a fragmentary epitaph, a 22-year-old man who died at Rome seems to be commemorated at home in Dalmatia by his wife.[62]

There is also a case where an immigrant's young child is implied to have been born at Rome, although the interpretation is not entirely clear:[63]

> Aged nineteen months I lie in the tomb which my father Proclus made, from Syrian land. My name is Procla. The earth is my fatherland in which I lie (γαῖα...πατρίς...ᾗ παράκειμαι).

The phrase 'from Syrian land' could be understood as applying to daughter or father, but the last sentence seems to be a clear statement that the child was not an immigrant herself. There is no indication of whether Proclus came to Rome with his wife or got married there. An even younger immigrant (although she could have been born at Rome) was the 11-month-old Salome, whose 'still young mother' promised to send her remains back to her ancestors.[64] Where a young child is recorded as an immigrant without details of any family, s/he is presumably still likely to have come in a family group, but this may not always be the case: Kornoution from Sinope, who died aged 10, was commemorated by his *nutritor*, although his parents were apparently still alive – perhaps they had remained in Sinope.[65]

Inscriptions recording whole nuclear families where all members are shown to be immigrants are also rare.[66] There are two for couples with two children,[67] and three showing couples with a son – in one of these cases the mother is free and the father appears to be a slave.[68] There is also a Christian inscription in which the unnamed parents commemorate their son Victor who lived 80 days and 'crossed the seas' (it is not stated from where).[69]

It is commoner to find just one parent and a child identified as immigrants, nearly always where the parent commemorates the child; the other parent is not mentioned in these epitaphs.

Father and son: eight examples, with the son's age, where stated, ranging from 9 to 24.[70] In one case the son is said to be an *eques singularis*; in another he was a Bosporan ambassador to Rome but apparently accompanied by his father.

Father and daughter: one example, a girl aged 12 from Asia.[71]

Mother and son: two examples where there are two sons; in one case the sons are a praetorian and an *urbanicianus* from Gaul,[72] and in the other the mother is free but at least one son is an imperial slave from Africa.[73] There are six examples of mother and one son: in three cases the son is a soldier, and in one a deacon.[74] There is also one case where an *eques singularis* from Dacia seems to be commemorated by his grandmother.[75]

Mother and daughter: three examples, including two Christian families from Pannonia.[76]

Presumably in most cases these represent the surviving members of nuclear families who had all migrated together. However, where the son is a soldier, the procedure must have been different: he would have been accompanied to Rome, or followed later, by his mother, either for his convenience or hers.[77] Presumably this would be most likely if she was a widow. The ban on soldiers' marriage which was in force until the time of Septimius Severus did not apply to soldiers bringing their mothers with them, although they could hardly have lived together if the son was barracked in the Praetorian Camp. One explanation of how the increased number of praetorians were able to fit into the Camp in the third century is that those who married were allowed to live out,[78] and perhaps this applied to others who had relatives at Rome too.

The epitaphs show that foreigners at Rome were commemorated by their siblings surprisingly often, and by their spouses and children surprisingly rarely. This impression may be due to some extent just to the nature of the evidence: a foreigner's brother or sister (or parent) can be assumed to be an immigrant too if apparently present at Rome, whereas the same assumption cannot be made for a spouse or child. The basis of the impression can be tested by looking at who the commemorators of foreigners are, even when the commemorators are not said or implied to be foreigners themselves. Although this does not necessarily give a cross-section of the whole foreign population, it does enable comparisons to be made with the epitaphs of Rome in general; if foreigners' epitaphs show different commemoration patterns from 'ordinary' epitaphs, then there *may* be underlying differences in family structure. The following tables consider the commemoration of soldiers and civilians separately, since the family arrangements of the two groups were clearly likely to be very different.

TABLE 7: Commemorators of soldiers.[79]

	No.	Total	%
Ascendants		7	1.9
Parent	6		
Grandparent	1		
Nuclear family		42	11.5
Wife	28		
Wife and children	4		
Children	10		
Extended family		58	15.9
Brother(s)	48		
Sister	5		
Nephew	1		
Cousin/relative	4		
Non-kin		237	65.1
Municeps	14		
Heir/amicus/soldier	211		
Freedman	10[80]		
Freedwoman	2		
Self /by will	20	20	5.5
Total		364	

The totals in the table can be compared to Ricci's study of commemorations outside Rome of soldiers who served at Rome, where 33% were commemorated by parents, 27% by soldiers, friends or heirs, and 16% by brothers.[81] In comparison, in the present sample, the lack of commemoration by ascendants, the predominance of commemorations by non-kin, and the equal importance of brothers are all significant.

The lack of commemoration by ascendants is readily explained by the fact that the soldiers died away from home.[82] The predominance of commemoration by fellow-soldiers is normal for a military population where most people were far removed from their families.[83] Many more 'fellow soldiers' were probably from the same home community as the deceased than are specifically indicated by terms like *municeps*. Men described as friends and heirs are often not members of the same unit as the deceased. In that case, the friendship seems likely to have been formed before arrival at Rome, either immediately on enlistment, through service together in the same unit initially, or before enlistment, through coming from the same place.[84] Scheidel notes that the possibility of being commemorated by someone other than a fellow-soldier was much greater for a praetorian who died in the second ten years of service than for one who died in the first ten years; the difference is due to the greater number of commemorations by wives for the former group.[85] Relatively new recruits would have few contacts in Rome outside their military unit, unless they were contacts which had been formed before coming to Rome, and that would affect who commemorated them as well as whether they were commemorated at all.

Brothers form an important group of soldiers' commemorators. The term appears to be used to indicate a real relationship,[86] rather than just as a term of endearment (in which case it should be much commoner). Most brothers share a nomen, but a few do not. In those cases they must either have been half-brothers, full brothers of whom one was legitimate and the other was not, or people who were only granted citizenship when they enlisted.[87] Members of the last category are particularly likely to be the illegitimate children of other soldiers by non-citizen women. Although most brother-commemorators were also soldiers themselves, some are not said to be so, and occasionally they are explicitly civilian: for example, one of the commemorators of the Pannonian *eques singularis* T. Aelius Rufus was his brother and heir Titius Marcellus, who is described as *paganus*, apparently 'civilian'.[88]

The occurrence of five sisters as soldiers' commemorators is also noteworthy. A few soldiers apparently brought their sisters to Rome with them, as others brought their mothers (one praetorian may have joined with his father to erect a dedication in Greek to his sister).[89] However, the presence of a sister in Rome might be due not to her accompanying her brother but to her being married to another soldier stationed there. This is never made explicit in the inscriptions but seems plausible, as soldiers' families would probably have tended to be of similar status to each other at home and therefore liable to inter-marry.[90] One man who was commemorated by both his wife and sister presumably did not have them both in Rome to act as housekeepers for him.[91]

A substantial number of immigrant soldiers were commemorated by their wives. Most of these are likely to be from after Septimius Severus' legalization of soldiers' marriages, but some could be earlier, using the language of marriage for a relationship which was not legally recog-nized as such. There is virtually no direct information on whether soldiers' wives met and married the soldiers at Rome, accompanied the soldiers from home when they first came to Rome, or came from home to join them when they were established at Rome. As soldiers normally enlisted before the usual age for male marriage in the Roman Empire, the second possibility is the least likely. It is excluded altogether in the cases of Iulia Carnuntila from Pannonia and Aurelia Gorsila from Aquincum, who died at 19 and 24 respectively, and were buried by their husbands, both already veterans who must therefore have been in Rome for a minimum of 16 years (if they were praetorians), and possibly much longer.[92] It was the practice in mili-tary epitaphs only to give the place of origin of the deceased, not of the commemorator, so there are no cases where the homes of both hus-band and wife are known. However, it may be significant that the homes of the wives, where they are the ones commemorated and their place of origin is stated, are always areas where soldiers were re-cruited, and that several soldiers from the Balkans have wives with distinctively Thracian names.[93] In one case where the backgrounds seem to be different, a German woman named Paterna was commemo-rated by her husband M. Aurelius Diascentus, who may have been a Thracian. [94]

Panciera (1993, 270–1) notes the frequency with which Greek cognomina occur among the wives of praetorians (about one-third of the cases in his sample), and suggests from this that praetorians' wives were often freedwomen or of servile ancestry; he does not consider the possibility that some of the women had Greek names because they were immigrants. Given that soldiers appear often to have taken

71

latinized (or graecized) names to replace original 'barbarian' ones (see p. 181), it may be the case that their wives tended to do so as well. It may also be relevant that wives commemorating their soldier-husbands sometimes give the name of the husband's home village (see p. 219), something which would be consistent with their coming from the same place, since the name of the village can have meant little to outsiders. Although it cannot be proved that the soldiers who married at Rome (evidently only a small proportion of the total of serving soldiers) usually married women from their home areas, the epigraphic evidence is at least consistent with such a proposition.

The fact that some soldiers had family members with them is relevant to a change in migration patterns over time. Since most praetorians from outside Italy were recruited in the third century, there may, if substantial numbers of soldiers brought civilian relatives with them, be a corresponding increase in civilian immigration from the same areas at the same time. Unfortunately, since few of the pagan epitaphs can be dated precisely enough to distinguish second-century ones from third-century with any great reliability, this cannot be tested in the inscriptions. However, it will be suggested below that, at least in the case of Pannonia, civilian immigration increased in the third century.

TABLE 8. Commemorators of civilians (pagan).

	Male dec.	Fem. dec.	Total	%
Ascendants			30	15.2
Parent(s)	23	2		
Foster/step-parent	5			
Nuclear family			68	34.5
Spouse	15	24		
Spouse and children	1	5		
Children	10	10		
Foster-child	2			
Grandchildren	1			
Extended family			38	19.3
Brother(s)[95]	28	1		
Sister	3	3		
Nephew	1			
Cousin/relative	2			
Non-kin			44	22.3
Municeps/colleague/ sodales/conservus	8			
Amicus/heir	7			
Patron	3			

Master	7		
Client	1		
Freedman	12		
Freedwoman	1		
Slaves/workmen	3		
Pupils	2		
Self/by will	14	3	17	8.6
Total	147	50	197	

There are some notable differences from the military pattern. The greater importance of parents as commemorators among the civilians is to be expected, since some civilians would have arrived as part of nuclear families whereas soldiers would very rarely have done so. Commemoration by spouses and children is more important for civilians, but only for civilian women – for men, the proportion is comparable to that for soldiers. Non-kin are, naturally, much less significant for civilians, but still form a substantial proportion of commemorators for males. These points are again consistent with the proposition that males in their late teens and early twenties predominated among new civilian immigrants.

There is one perhaps surprising similarity between the military and civilian samples: the proportion of extended family as commemorators. This is largely brothers commemorating brothers, and is far more significant here than among any of the civilian samples studied by Saller and Shaw.[96] It includes pairs where one appears to be a soldier and the other a civilian, as well as pairs (or trios) where both are civilians. The presence of two brothers together would not necessarily mean that they arrived at the same time, although that is possible. Another explanation would be that one arrived first, perhaps as a soldier or in the imperial service, and the other brother joined him later, coming to Rome for some other sort of work and making use of the first brother's presence there. In the case of a Phrygian family, Aelius Papias (perhaps an imperial freedman) commemorated his *peregrinus* brother Apollonius son of Isonomus.[97] Eutactus, who died aged 14, had 'lived abroad with' his brother for 5 years, and the wording may suggest that he had come to Rome to join a brother who was already there.[98] Family reunion remains an important reason for modern migration even when the economic attractiveness of the destination has reduced since the first family member moved there.[99] At Rome, the presence of a brother who was financially secure must have been a strong 'pull' factor (see p. 86) for another brother who had originally been left at home.

There are some striking differences between the commemoration patterns for male and female civilian deceased. Males are often commemorated by parents; females virtually never. Women are commemorated by spouses much more often than men are. This may be connected with the lack of young ages noted above. It suggests that, by the time they reached the age at which they were likely to be commemorated, women were married and men were not. Artemo from Laconia was already married when she died at 14.[100] The implication may be that, while nuclear families with young children were unlikely to come to Rome, families who arrived with rather older children were more common.[101] Another possibility is that females were coming to Rome specifically in order to marry migrants from their home communities who had preceded them there, as suggested above in the case of soldiers. Septimius Severus' first wife Paccia Marciana was probably a native of Lepcis, but unless he married remarkably young, it is unlikely that they were married before he went to Rome at the age of 17.[102] There could also be a suggestion of this in the unusual wording of the following Christian epitaph:[103]

> Flavia Valeria placed this epitaph for her well-deserving daughter Flavia Vi<vent>ia, who lived 18 years. She had her burial on 31st July. This girl came from the province of Pannonia. She lived with her husband for 1 year 8 months. In peace.

But it is not explicitly said that the husband was an immigrant or that Viventia only came to Rome to get married. It is very unusual for an immigrant to be married to another immigrant from somewhere different unless they were or had been fellow-slaves.[104]

It is also noteworthy that, while males are frequently commemorated by non-kin, females almost never are. This would be consistent with a large number of male immigrants lacking family commemorators because they had come to Rome alone, or at least without relatives. Some examples show that male immigrants might have left their relatives at home. A man who died at Ostia aged 50 was commemorated at home in Gaul by his sons.[105] A 17–year-old *notarius* named Praetorianus who died at Rome in AD 225 was commemorated at home at Sitifis in Mauretania, together with his sister who died there the next year aged 8, by their father; Praetorianus had clearly not gone to Rome as part of a family group.[106] In these cases, the ties they retained with their homes were strong enough to ensure their commemoration there. Most people in a similar situation would either have been commemorated at Rome by non-kin or not commemorated at all. The practice among immigrants from some areas of naming the home village (to be discussed in ch. 8) may also reflect a desire to show ties among compatriots at Rome even when they were not kin.

In the Christian and Jewish inscriptions, the practice of naming the commemorator at all was unusual. The numbers below are therefore very small:

TABLE 9. Commemorators of civilians (Christian/Jewish).

	Male dec.	Fem. dec.	Gender unc.	Total	%
Ascendants				9	26
Parent(s)	5	1	2		
Foster-parent	1				
Nuclear family				11	31
Spouse	5	4			
Spouse and children	1	1			
Extended family				8	22
Brother(s)	5	2			
Relative	1				
Non-kin				2	6
Friend	1	1			
Self	5			5	14
Total	24	9	2	35	

These show some of the same patterns as the pagan inscriptions: the greater importance of commemoration by parents for males than for females; the significance of brothers. The lack of commemoration by children is again noticeable. It is likely that children commemorating their parents, at whatever date, would be less likely to record that they were immigrants, especially if the children themselves were born at Rome.

vii. Legal status of immigrants

Soldiers serving at Rome were Roman citizens, but civilians could be of any legal status (see p. 24). The status of the pagan civilian immigrants in the inscriptions is set out below, as indicated by their names. Status is shown too rarely in the Christian and Jewish civilian inscriptions for the same treatment to be worthwhile for them.[107] The categories are as follows:

1. Slave. Someone clearly shown to be a slave, either by the use of

servus or a similar word, or by an owner's name in the genitive.

2. Ex-slave. Someone clearly shown to be a *libertus/liberta*, either by use of the word, by a designation such as C.l. or P.lib. in the name (i.e. the abbreviated form of the patron's praenomen, followed by an abbreviation for *libertus/-a*), or by calling someone else their patron.

3. Freeborn. A citizen with a nomen and cognomen (sometimes a praenomen too, if male), shown to be freeborn either by a filiation in the name (e.g. C.f.), being the sibling of someone else freeborn, or holding a rank for which free birth was a qualification, such as city councillor.

4. *Peregrinus/peregrina*. Someone who was free but not a Roman citizen, indicated by a single name followed by father's name in the genitive, or a single name with indication of citizenship of a city other than Rome.[108]

5. Single name. Someone recorded with a single name is most likely to be a slave, but could be a *peregrinus/-a*, or occasionally a citizen whose nomen was omitted (e.g. in a metrical or Greek epitaph). M. Antonius Gaionas, a man active in various Syrian cults in the late second century AD (see p. 240), is referred to in most inscriptions only as Gaionas, simply because the context did not require his full name.

6. Duo/tria nomina. Someone whose name shows that s/he was a citizen by using a nomen and cognomen, but not whether s/he was freeborn or freed, e.g. Ti. Claudius Severus, Flavia Eutyche.[109]

7. Unknown. Those who cannot be placed in any of the above categories, through damage to the stone (usually) or anonymity in the inscription.

TABLE 10. Legal status of foreigners in pagan civilian inscriptions.

	Slave	Ex-slave	Free-born	Pereg-rinus/a	Single name	2/3 nomina	Un-known	Total
Africa and Numidia	13	1	9		3	10		36
Armenia, Bosporan Kingdom and Parthia	3	1	3	9		5	1	22
Asia	1	6	6	18	19	12	4	66
Bithynia	1	2	1	5	6	8	1	24
Cappadocia	2	2			3	4		11
Cilicia	1	1	1	3	2	1		9
Corsica and Sardinia		2					1	3
Crete, Cyrene and Cyprus				3	1			4

Dacia		1		2		4	1	8
Dalmatia					1	5	1	7
Egypt		1	2	1	8	9	2	23
Galatia	3			3	3	1	2	12
Gaul	2	4	14	4	2	17		43
Germany	13		2		2	5	2	24
Greece	4	1	1	2	5	5		18
Hispania	4	1	13		12	26	4	60
Lycia	1			1	1	4		7
Macedonia			1		1	1		3
Mauretania	2	1	3		2	2		10
Moesia					2	6	1	9
Noricum	1	1	2		1	4		9
Pannonia			1			19	3	23
Raetia	1					1		2
Sicily				1	3	1		5
Syria and Palestine	5	8	1	5	11	12	6	48
Thrace	2	2		3	2	13	5	27
Unknown					4		4	8
Total	59	35	60	60	94	175	38	521
%	11.3	6.7	11.6	11.6	18.0	33.6	7.2	

Two changes over time are likely to distort these figures. The practice of indicating filiation or libertine status was normal in the first century AD but seems to have declined fairly rapidly afterwards.[110] The category of *peregrinus/peregrina* virtually disappeared after AD 212, when the Constitutio Antoniniana gave Roman citizenship to nearly all free inhabitants of the Empire.

This may partly explain the big variations between regions. For Asia, 18/66 individuals were *peregrini*. This probably reflects the relative slowness of citizenship in spreading in the eastern provinces, and also an attachment to the Greek cities on the part of people who came from them. It also suggests that Asia was an important source of immigrants before 212; those classified as *peregrini* from Asia must have come to Rome before then. Gaul and Hispania show similar patterns to each other (cf. p. 59 above): for Gaul, 14 were freeborn and 17 had duo/tria nomina out of a total of 43; for Hispania, 13 were freeborn and 26 had duo/tria nomina out of a total of 60. For Pannonia, 19/23 had duo/tria nomina. This form of giving the name was normal in the third century, when Pannonia was the main recruitment area for the

Praetorian Guard, so this probably shows that civilian immigration was boosted at the same time, as suggested above.

The highest proportion of certain ex-slaves is for Syria (8/48), although many of those in the duo/tria nomina category may also be ex-slaves. The number of immigrants who had clearly come to Rome as slaves is remarkably small. Despite the comments in the literary sources on the prevalence of Egyptian slaves, there are no Egyptian slaves in the inscriptions, and only two definite ex-slaves. It is possible that some places of origin were felt to carry greater stigma than others and were therefore less likely to be recorded. It may be significant that nearly all the Egyptians recorded in the pagan civilian epitaphs are connected to Alexandria, not to Egypt (see p. 247).

In the study of epitaphs for people with occupational designations by Joshel (1992), over 60% were slaves or ex-slaves (pp. 23, 184). 42% used a formal status indication (corresponding to the ex-slave and freeborn categories above) (pp. 38–9); 27.6% had a single name (she calls them 'uncertain slaves'), and 30.4% had a nomen without status indication ('uncertain freeborn'; the same as duo/tria nomina above). She argues that work was one form of identity readily available to slaves (p. 24), and that therefore slaves and ex-slaves were more likely to have their occupations commemorated than the freeborn were. In contrast, it appears that place of origin was on the whole *less* important in slaves' self-identity than occupation was. Only 15 people in her study used a *natio* ('place of birth') designation, which she explains as follows (p. 41):

> Because of the equation of outsider with slave, foreign origin was closely associated with a servile past. Neither freeborn citizens nor freedmen who wished to hide their ethnicity would have used *natio* on their tombstones if it indicated a non-Italian place.

While the second sentence is clearly true, the first is certainly not, in epigraphic terms. It was soldiers, not slaves, who were most likely to record their 'ethnicity' in inscriptions, as shown above. However, there does seem to be evidence in TABLE 10 for slaves and ex-slaves being less likely than free immigrants (whom they must have outnumbered very substantially, at least until the early second century AD) to have their place of origin recorded, something which may be related to the well-known enthusiasm for romanization of the ex-slaves who put up funerary monuments: people who were depicted wearing togas and with severe and deliberately Roman expressions were unlikely to record that they had been born in Paphlagonia.[111]

Notes

[1] Faist 1997, 205; cf. Boyle, Halfacree and Robinson 1998, 9.

[2] Pliny, *Ep.* 3.20; Martial 12.18, 12.31, 12.68. Galen, another returnee whose movements are recorded in his own writings, left Rome more because of hostility from other doctors and fear of the plague there than from anxiety to return to Pergamum (Nutton 1973; Jackson 1988, 61; PIR² G24), and was later obliged by Marcus Aurelius to return to Rome. Another example, whose return was not necessarily caused by the same feelings, is Ti. Claudius Tyrannus, an imperial freedman and doctor, who returned to Magnesia on the Maeander, where he set up a series of *ergasteria* (probably manufacturing workshops) in a nearby village (Nutton 1986, 35; I.K. Magnesia 113).

[3] Galen 2.215 – but according to PIR² F229, he left Rome to become legate of Palestine; Balsdon 1979, 211. Cf. Symmachus, *Ep.* 6.38 (written before 401): 'our friend Severus, freed from the pressure of public business, will return to the leisure of his homeland'.

[4] Boyle, Halfacree and Robinson 1998, 77, 88–9.

[5] Tilly 1978, 59.

[6] Boyle, Halfacree and Robinson 1998, 97; Faist 1997, 206.

[7] Malmberg 1997, 33–4.

[8] Faist 1997, 193, 209.

[9] McCormack 1984, 358.

[10] Feissel (1995, 368) suggests a similar phenomenon in Constantinople.

[11] Boyle, Halfacree and Robinson 1998, 156; Lampe 1991, 219.

[12] Malmberg 1997, 23; Tilly 1978, 56; Boyle, Halfacree and Robinson 1998, 115.

[13] CIL vi 29152.

[14] IGUR 1222.

[15] Eusebius, *H.E.* 3.1.

[16] Porphyry, *V.Plot.* 1–11.

[17] Gk. Anth. 7.368 (Erucius, *c.* 50–25 BC).

[18] Suetonius, *Gramm.*8.

[19] Lampe 1991, 220.

[20] CIG 3920; Lampe 1991, 219; Pleket 1993, 30.

[21] See above (n. 2).

[22] Justin Martyr, originally from Flavia Neapolis (the former Samaria) came to Rome twice (*Acts of Justin & Companions* 3). Irenaeus, from Smyrna, was in Rome both in 155 and *c.* 177, and may have had other periods there as well: in 155 according to the appendix to the Moscow ms of *Letter to the Smyrnaeans*, cited by Lightfoot, (1889–90, vol. 2, 422). He writes: 'there is no reason for supposing that these two occasions exhausted his residence at Rome'. Irenaeus was there in *c.* 177 according to Eusebius *H.E.* 5.4.

[23] Blackman 1948, 1–3.

[24] IGUR 352.

[25] IGUR 433.

[26] IGUR 1063.

[27] I.Porto 16, 21, 23. They perhaps put up dedications at Portus when about to sail home.

[28] CIL xiii 2181.

[29] BCAR (1949/50), 31 no. 1 = AE (1953) 56.

[30] See the discussion at p. 8 of the nature of the epigraphic evidence.

[31] The regions into which I have divided the empire for the purposes of the following tables and map are basically the provinces of the 1st–2nd centuries AD. Adjacent provinces which produced few immigrants have sometimes been combined, and the areas outside the empire which produced immigrants (Armenia, Parthia and the Bosporan Kingdom) have also been combined. There is an element of uncertainty built into the attribution of individuals to specific regions: if someone's home city is stated, the region is clear, but if s/he is described simply as 'Thracian' or 'Greek', s/he did not *necessarily* come from the province of that name, since some ethnic labels undoubtedly transcended provincial boundaries – a 'Thracian' may have lived in the province of Moesia, or a 'Greek' in the province of Asia. However, the distortion created is unlikely to be very significant.

[32] Malmberg 1997, 33: 'The development of international networks, communication links and interpersonal contacts has been of greater importance to international migration than physical distance.'

[33] This is partly attributable to the tendency of Christian epitaphs to be simpler than pagan ones, conveying less information of any kind.

[34] Boyle, Halfacree and Robinson 1998, 22–3.

[35] One exception is a woman who sold oil from Baetica (AE (1973) 71). Otherwise, female immigrants with jobs mentioned in epitaphs all seem to be slaves or ex-slaves.

[36] Karasch 1987, 61, 66. In the Brazilian-born free population, females slightly outnumbered males in 1849.

[37] Namias 1978, 31.

[38] This is the number of deceased immigrant soldiers, not the total number of immigrant soldiers (which includes commemorators too); hence the difference from the total in TABLE 1.

[39] Scheidel 1996, 111–16.

[40] Model West level 4 males table quoted in Bagnall and Frier (1994, 100); Frier's life table quoted in Parkin (1992, Table 6). Of 1000 people alive at 20, the former gives 606 alive at 45 and the latter 561. This assumes that there would only be 'natural' mortality; it is unlikely that many soldiers serving at Rome died violently, except during civil wars, and their epitaphs never indicate that they died in action.

[41] Scheidel (1996, 126) comes to the same conclusion by a different route: 'Tentatively adding 4 years to a mean recruitment age of 20 of the average legionary selected for transfer, this soldier [i.e. a typical praetorian] will have begun to serve in the capital at the age of 24.'

[42] Dio 75.2.4–5; Kennedy 1978, 289.

[43] Scheidel 1996, 129: 'Irrespective of the actual development of mortality, we should probably anticipate a gradual increase of the frequency of commemoration as soldiers grew older, simply because of their increasing chance of receiving a tombstone inscription.' The anomaly could also be explained simply by soldiers being fitter than the rest of the population due to being

medically tested on enlistment, and therefore less likely to die soon after they enlisted than a normal population of the same age (I owe this suggestion to Howard Toney).

[44] Scheidel (1996, 129) detects an over-representation in his sample of praetorians who died after 6–9 years of service, and suggests that the length of service may be given more accurately than the age of death. For the purpose of this study I have accepted the ages at death given in the epitaphs at face value, despite the doubt which he casts on them; small discrepancies would not seriously affect the picture.

[45] The remaining eight are people of uncertain gender, for whom no ages survive.

[46] CIL vi 28228. Atimetus from Rhegium also came to Rome at 12 to study or perhaps to compete in the Capitoline Games: IGUR 1165.

[47] IGUR 367.

[48] IGUR 1176: ἔτι κοῦρος.

[49] Nutton 1973, 160–2.

[50] If the pagan and Christian/Jewish samples are combined, the proportions become 56% and 75% respectively.

[51] Boyle, Halfacree and Robinson 1998, 111; Clark 1979, 71. There is also a lesser peak in early childhood.

[52] Saller and Shaw 1984, 130. Huttunen (1974, 28), commenting on the prevalence of children's epitaphs at Rome, writes that 'the City had the custom of dedicating an epitaph to children and indicating their age much more often than in other cases'.

[53] PIR² A611. Cf. the two-year-old Cantabrian boy commemorated by his parents in CIL vi 27441. Barnes (1967, 87), thinks that Septimius Severus the friend of Statius was brought to Rome while extremely young by his father, who had bought an estate at Veii.

[54] The method is: for each of the four age cohorts 23–32, 33–42, 43–52, 53–62, the percentage of ages divisible by 5 is calculated; 20 is deducted; each figure is multiplied by 1.25; the mean of the four figures is calculated. This avoids distortion caused by greater rounding of higher ages.

[55] IGUR 939 = ICUR 4032.

[56] CIL vi 1625a.

[57] AE (1979) 78. Although hostages would normally come into the category of temporary residents, these people presumably expected to die at Rome.

[58] CIL vi 21569.

[59] CIL vi 34466; it is possible that the abbreviated ethnic was not meant to apply to the wife.

[60] ICUR 4004.

[61] ICUR 18762, 18995.

[62] CIL iii 9713.

[63] IGUR 1317.

[64] IGUR 1323. The name implies that they were from Syria-Palestine, but the inscription does not specify their home.

[65] IGUR 1255.

[66] I have assumed that, where parents commemorate a child in Rome and

the child is said to be an immigrant, the parents are also immigrants even if not explicitly labelled as such. Nuclear families in which one of the parents is an immigrant but nothing is said about the birthplace of the children are much commoner, and in those cases no assumptions can be made about where the children were born.

[67] ICUR 19659 from Africa, AE (1992) 154 from Spain.

[68] AE (1992) 155, CIL vi 24162, CIL vi 27441 (all from Spain).

[69] ICUR 13226.

[70] CIL vi 3303 (Thrace), CIL vi 20012 (Dalmatia), CIL vi 20121/2 (Gaul), CIL vi 29694 (Bosporus), CIL vi 36324 (Germany), IGUR 508 (Crete), IGUR 326 (Asia), BCAR 43 (1915) p. 305 (Germany).

[71] IGUR 843.

[72] CIL vi 2714.

[73] CIL vi 13328.

[74] CIL vi 2954 (Thrace; the son's wife also has a Thracian name), CIL vi 3171 (Africa), ICUR 5337 (Mauretania; the son is a deacon), ICUR 5568 (Gaul), IGUR 610 (Egypt), AE (1983) 50 (Bithynia).

[75] CIL vi 3236.

[76] ICUR 13155, 13355; IGUR 1323 probably from Syria.

[77] In the 4th century, taking their widowed mothers to Rome with them was an issue for Augustine and Nebridius; see p. 124.

[78] Kennedy 1978, 287.

[79] If more than one *different* relationship occurs, they are all counted, e.g. if someone was commemorated by both his wife and his brother, it is counted in both sections, but if he was commemorated by his two sons, it is only counted once. 'Heirs' are not counted if other relationships are present (e.g. if someone is commemorated by his wife and his heir). Named commemorators with no stated relationship are excluded. The 'by will' category includes only epitaphs where the formula *t(estamento) p(oni) i(ussit)* or *ex testamento* is used and another commemorator is not named.

[80] Includes one case where the gender of the ex-slave is unclear.

[81] Ricci 1994a, 29. She states that the soldiers commemorated by heirs were always buried away from their place of origin.

[82] Panciera 1993, 266–7 counts 44 inscriptions where the parents of soldiers who served at Rome are mentioned (most of the soldiers are not said to be immigrants, and are therefore not included in my sample). Few of the parents are explicitly freeborn. One is a *peregrinus* (CIL vi 2422, Hierax Apolloni f.). Most of the parents in 1st–2nd century inscriptions have Greek cognomina and are likely to be ex-slaves or their close descendants. In contrast, only two out of 86 brothers and sisters of praetorians and *urbaniciani* have Greek cognomina.

[83] Saller and Shaw 1984, 133.

[84] Panciera (1993, 265) takes previous service in the same unit as the usual explanation for the relationship.

[85] Scheidel 1996, 131. Since most praetorians only served 16–17 years, the 'second 10 years' must include discharged soldiers.

[86] The same view is taken by Ricci (1994a, 30). Some doubt is expressed by

Panciera (1993, 266). He notes that 11 out of 63 brothers of praetorians did not share the same nomen, but the explanations proposed below seem more likely to cover these cases than the non-literal use of the term 'brother'.

[87] *Frater* can also be used in Latin to signify 'cousin', as pointed out to me by Tony Brothers.

[88] CIL vi 3183; Vulpe 1925, 190. Despite the different nomina here, the use of the term 'brother' obviously cannot be an expression of affection between fellow-soldiers.

[89] IGUR 134; the name of the deceased is lost, however, and the relationship with the commemorators is not certain.

[90] On the tendency of soldiers to marry the daughters of other soldiers in North Africa, rather than to intermarry with the indigenous population, cf. Cherry (1998, 133). Wells (1997, 574) makes a similar suggestion for all frontier regions.

[91] CIL vi 2482.

[92] CIL vi 37271, 3454.

[93] CIL vi 2760, 2954, 3202. In EE ix 658 from the Ager Albanus, a soldier of Legio II Parthica Severa named M. Aurelius Diza is commemorated by his wife Brais, both Thracian names (Mateescu 1923, 200).

[94] CIL vi 3452; Speidel 1994b, 157. Speidel suggests that they met while Diascentus was serving in Germany and that Paterna then accompanied him to Rome, but it is also possible that they met at Rome.

[95] Including foster-relationships.

[96] Saller and Shaw 1984, 136.

[97] CIL vi 34466. See p. 25 on the anomaly of the different statuses of the two brothers.

[98] IGUR 367; see discussion at p. 195 of where they came from.

[99] Boyle, Halfacree and Robinson 1998, 28, 36.

[100] IGUR 1161.

[101] Among British emigrants to Canada, families with children old enough to be wage-earners were particularly encouraged (McCormack 1984, 359).

[102] SHA, *Sev.* 1.

[103] ICUR 13155.

[104] The only civilian example where they were not certainly fellow-slaves before manumission is IGUR 1293, where a man from Ceraunus in Caria is married to a woman from Athens; it is possible that even in this case they had been slaves together, as part of the inscription is lost.

[105] CIL xii 2211.

[106] CIL viii 8501.

[107] Cf. Kajanto 1963a.

[108] This category may have been slightly inflated by the tendency in some Greek inscriptions for Roman citizens not to give their full names; cf. Kajanto (1963b, 4). He concludes, however, that the much greater frequency of single names in Greek than in Latin epitaphs (64% against 15–16%) shows that 'a considerable part of the persons bearing only a single name must have been immigrants'.

[109] Junian Latins would have the same forms of names, but are unlikely to

have been of any numerical significance in this context.

[110] Kajanto 1963a, 5–9.

[111] Cf. Walker 1985, 45–6. The rarity of ethnics for slaves is also noted by Solin (1977b, 208).

Chapter 5

WHY DID PEOPLE MOVE TO ROME?

This chapter is based largely on literary evidence for the very extensive range of reasons why people moved to Rome, sometimes reinforced from inscriptions, and with comparative material helping to put the numerous anecdotes into context. Special attention is paid to Seneca, the one ancient writer who specifically addresses the question. The motives have been divided into some broad categories in order to illustrate the main recurrent themes: Rome's attractions as an educational and political centre and as the largest market for goods and services.

i. Evidence

While inscriptions enable some suggestions to be made about the ages and family situations of people coming to Rome, they are largely uninformative about why they came.[1] For the two groups which were probably the most numerous, soldiers and slaves, the motivation is obvious. Soldiers came when it was part of their job, although it is not clear whether it was entirely personal choice which assigned a recruit to the Praetorian Guard rather than to a legion, or which moved him from a legion to Rome. Slaves came to Rome through the slave-trading system, usually with no element of choice. For others, there may be circumstantial evidence, but even if people are recorded as having done a particular type of work at Rome, they did not necessarily come to Rome *intending* to do that type of work (unless it was something they had already been specifically trained for). An extreme example is Timagenes from Alexandria, who came to Rome as a slave in 55 BC and worked as a cook and litter-bearer, but after his manumission became a teacher of rhetoric.[2]

Two other possible sources of insight into immigrants' motivation are ancient literature and comparative material on migration in later history. The literature consists mainly of anecdotal information about individuals, and therefore tends to be much more informative about some sorts (particularly the well-educated and ultimately influential) than others, but there is a lengthy discussion by Seneca of why people came to Rome (see p. 90 below).

Rabbinic literature gives a little insight into some of the thought processes of individual Jewish migrants, even if they are usually presented for particular tendentious reasons (mainly to emphasize the disadvantages of leaving the land of Israel). Being forced into emigration by food being too dear or scarce is considered (and discouraged):[3]

> A person should not go abroad unless wheat sells at the price of two *seahs* for a *sela*. R. Simon said: Under what circumstances? Only in a case when he cannot find any to buy (even at that price). But if he finds some to buy, even if one *seah* sells for a *sela* – he may not go abroad. For thus would R. Simon teach: Elimelech was one of the great men of his generation and a leader of the community, and because he went abroad (Ruth 1.1) he died there with his sons in famine, while all of Israel survived in their land, as it is written: '[And when they came to Bethlehem] all the city was stirred because of them' (Ruth 1.19); this teaches that all of the town had survived, but he and his sons died in the famine.

Also considered is the possibility that the success of one emigrant would encourage others:[4]

> It once happened that a disciple of R. Simon b. Yohai went abroad and returned wealthy; and all the disciples saw him and wished also to go abroad; R. Simon was aware and removed them to the valley near his town of Miron. There he prayed before God: 'O valley, fill up with golden dinars!' and it filled up with golden dinars. He told them: Whoever wishes to take – let him come and take, but know you that whoever takes now makes a withdrawal against his reward in the next world.

Despite the obviously imaginative nature of these texts, they illustrate some of the push and pull factors at work in migration decisions, whether the destination was Rome or elsewhere.

ii. Push and pull factors

The actual process of making the decision to move to Rome is extremely badly documented. The fact that it was natural for a provincial to consider the possibility of the move is suggested by Artemidorus' reference to a young man of Bithynia who dreamed of moving to Rome and then died; Artemidorus' interest is in the significance of the dream, but it must come from an environment where moving to Rome was a real possibility.[5] The only case in which the process is described in ancient literature is that of Augustine, for whom it was very much an individual decision, influenced by the advice of friends but also prompted by his dissatisfaction with his life at home as well as the attractions of working at Rome.[6] Augustine was prosperous enough at the time of his move to be able to afford it without undue difficulty;

other people must have had to assess the financial arguments much more carefully. Family circumstances would also have influenced most potential migrants more than they did Augustine. If, as argued in ch. 4.iv–vi, most migrants were young males, their decision to move to Rome is likely to have been influenced by the whole family rather than taken entirely individually.

A decision to migrate will be influenced by push and pull factors, both of which were at work in the case of Augustine, and no doubt for most others who decided, rightly or not, that Rome was a better option than staying at home.[7] Push factors encourage people to leave their homes. They include: economic decline of the home area, poor employment opportunities at home, cultural alienation, and natural or humanly-created catastrophe (war, famine, etc.). Some are personal, some could apply to whole sections of a community. Pull factors encourage people to choose a particular destination, in preference to their home area or to other possible destinations. They include: greater or more lucrative employment opportunities, opportunities for specialized training or education, and the perceived attraction of the new environment – in particular, the appeal of city life to rural people. Rome could certainly be seen as attractive for more than economic reasons: the idea of the city as the centre of *libertas* was still current in late antiquity,[8] and Martial shows some of the ways in which life there could be thought preferable to living in a small town.[9] Pull factors can also arise from family circumstances: some people may be pulled into 'movement as a result of dependency on someone else who has moved, such as a spouse'.[10] In some contexts, the spread of the idea of emigration as cure for all ills has been noted,[11] which may also be relevant to some of the people coming to Rome but is now completely untraceable.

The combination of push and pull factors will have different effects in different individual cases, according to personality, family circumstances, the behaviour of others, etc.[12] The attractions of Rome are well documented in the ancient literature, as is the fact that they ceased to be perceived as attractions by some people who were living there.[13] Push factors influencing the decision to leave home are much harder to detect. Long-distance migration to Rome may have been the answer which some people found to problems in their home communities. This is certainly attested by the sources for Italians moving to Rome, particularly those who had lost their land in the second–first centuries BC; frequent attempts were made to force them to return home.[14] It is, however, very difficult to make a specific link between socio-economic problems in any area outside Italy and migration to Rome. Avraméa (1995, 17) notes the prominence of people from Northern Syria among immigrants to Rome in late antiquity. She links this with demographic expansion in the North Syrian countryside in the fourth–sixth centuries, when previously uncultivated land was brought under cultivation, and asks:

> Peut-on supposer que ces agriculteurs enrichis ont investi leurs revenus agricoles en d'autres métiers, devenant des citadins loin de la patrie?[15]

Surely a much more likely link is that people were forced to leave Syria at this period because of lack of land and work, and eventually found their way to Rome, directly or indirectly.[16] However, clear evidence of a direct link would require precise dating both of individual migrations and of events at home which may have caused them, and that is very rarely possible, although some considerations applicable to people from a particular region will be suggested in ch. 8. Push factors which encouraged people to leave home would not necessarily encourage them to move to Rome rather than to somewhere else; the reasons why Rome was felt to be a preferable destination to any of the alternatives are now very hard to detect except in the case of individuals pursuing a career which could best be advanced at Rome, but some will emerge below.

It must be remembered that in one important way Rome was much less attractive as a destination for free migrants than big cities in the medieval and modern worlds. The presence in Rome of substantial numbers of slaves meant that employment opportunities for the free, especially the unskilled and capital-less free, were fewer than in cities dependent on free labour.[17] The corn dole (as well as the competition from slave labour) may have contributed to keeping down wages for free workers.[18] There certainly was work available for the unskilled or relatively unskilled, for example on building sites[19] and at the quays,[20] but some areas of employment which have absorbed large numbers of immigrants elsewhere (particularly domestic service) were, at Rome, mainly the province of slaves. Large-scale manufacturing seems to have been very limited, although there was some production of lamps, bricks and tiles for export.[21] The compensations such as the corn dole and free entertainment would not be enough to maintain a family without paid work, although an individual male might manage, at least if he was a Roman citizen. There may have been a similar effect to that noted by Karasch (1987, 70) for immigrants to Rio de Janeiro:

> Because of the monopoly of low status occupations by slaves and free

people of color, the Portuguese had to use their common ancestry and regional ties in Portugal to help each other enter middle-status occupations and work as clerks, commercial agents, shopkeepers, retailers, tavern owners, slave traders and merchants.

The importance in present-day migration patterns of 'skilled transients' who are willing to change countries regularly[22] may echo what happened in the Roman Empire, where people such as teachers and sculptors could clearly be very mobile, for whom Rome might be a particularly rewarding destination (see pp. 94, 113 below). The rich who required 'luxuries', in terms of goods and services, could well afford them, whether it involved hiring free labour or buying slaves. Highly skilled labour and luxury imported goods were readily available. The market for luxury goods would certainly have created employment, but, in areas where capital was required, it is likely that it would have been provided by the rich and used by their ex-slaves,[23] again reducing the openings for free immigrants. The 'trickle-down' effect of the spending of the very wealthy would therefore have had less effect on employment than in later cities where all labour was free.[24]

Migrants do not, of course, necessarily have all the relevant information when they set out. Even if they do, their behaviour does not always appear to an outsider to be totally rational.[25] For someone in Gaul or Egypt, the streets of Rome might be imagined to be paved with gold, even if the reality turned out to be very different.[26] A passage from the Talmud suggests that Rome may also have had this image in Palestine:[27]

Ten ḳabs of wisdom descended to the world: nine were taken by Palestine and one by the rest of the world. Ten ḳabs of beauty descended to the world: nine were taken by Jerusalem and one by the rest of the world. Ten ḳabs of wealth descended to the world: nine were taken by the early Romans and one by the rest of the world.

Martial's poem about a man from Spain who turns back at the Milvian Bridge when he finds out that cash handouts from the rich to their clients have been replaced by food parcels is clearly meant as a joke, but is one of the few pieces of literature to acknowledge that immigrants might change their minds.[28] It was certainly possible for some people to return home if they found they had made a mistake, but presumably not for the very poor who would have used all their available resources to make the one-way journey. A modern example of migration based on misinformation which may have ancient parallels, is that of middle-class young men from Senegal to Italy; having found that the job opportunities they expected were not available, they tended to remain in Italy rather than return home, making a living as best they could, and not to inform other people at home of what had happened, because of the loss of face it would entail.[29] People who moved to Rome may have been similarly motivated to stay there by feelings of pride. In the Senegalese case, the reluctance of the first migrants to correct the original misinformation contributed to a form of chain migration; people who spread ideas like those in the talmudic passages may have done the same for Rome.

iii. Types of motivation suggested by Seneca, *ad Helviam* 6.2–3

As an immigrant himself, who came to Rome while young as part of a family migration, Seneca was probably more interested in the process than most Roman writers.[30] He is certainly the only one who gives a lengthy list of the reasons why people come to Rome. The list is not comprehensive, and it also shows that he (and probably Romans in general) did not differentiate between coming for a visit and coming to settle. He wants to explain why so many people in the crowds are not natives of Rome, and so it is not really relevant for him to separate those who have come temporarily from those who are there permanently.

> From their *municipia* and *coloniae*, from the whole world they have congregated here. Ambition has brought some; the requirement of public office (*necessitas officii publici*) has brought others. For some, it was an embassy imposed on them; for others, it was luxury, seeking a convenient and wealthy setting for its vices. Eagerness for liberal studies (*liberalium studiorum cupiditas*) brought some; the shows (*spectacula*) brought others. Some were led by friendship, others by industry taking the ample opportunity for showing virtue. Some have brought beauty for sale, some have brought eloquence for sale. Every race of humans has flowed together into the city which offers great rewards for both virtues and vices.

The passage contains a mixture of moralizing and reporting. As suggested at p. 33, Seneca's attitude to immigration is on the whole fairly neutral. He regards it as neither intrinsically good nor bad, although the context of the passage makes him emphasize that people who have left their homes are not necessarily unhappy. He is aware that people come to Rome for a wide variety of reasons, of which he approves of some and not others. The list is heavily weighted towards the wealthy, and makes no mention at all of the most numerous groups of immigrants: soldiers and slaves. The latter would hardly fit the argument that people do not mind leaving home. There is no reference to push factors, which also would not suit the argument; for Seneca, pull factors are entirely responsible for people coming to Rome. The reference to friendship perhaps shows awareness of the possibility of chain migration, although he probably has in mind wealthy people from Spain rather than Syrians living in tenements in Trastevere.[31]

Most of Seneca's categories fit well with motivation known from other sources, and will be discussed below. The comment on luxury, a variation on the *topos* of Rome as the world centre of debauchery, seems rather out of place in the list. It is not clear exactly whom Seneca has in mind: the profligate rich? People who make a living from the profligate rich (such as sellers of luxury goods)? His description could be applied to anyone who preferred the city to country life. The phrase about 'industry' is also rather enigmatic. Since Seneca nowhere else mentions the traders and craftspeople whose sometimes immigrant origins he must have been aware of, it seems most likely that the 'industry' he has in mind is that shown by small-scale artisans whose products did not offend against his dislike of luxury.

Seneca's somewhat disorganized and incomplete list does not provide a very satisfactory basis for an analysis of the great variety of reasons attested in other sources for people to come to Rome. In what follows, I have divided the motivation into four very broad categories: education, including providers and recipients; government and politics; the provision of goods and services; family and religion. Coming to Rome as a career move, or in order to make money, could fall into any of those categories, according to what sort of career or what form of money-making was in view. In some cases push factors (e.g. expulsion from home) could be most important, but it is largely pull factors which predominate in the evidence. In some fields, such as education and medicine, the provision of effective services at Rome virtually depended on a continuous stream of qualified immigrants – hence the encouragement offered by the state (see p. 47). In some, presence at Rome was essential to perform a political or governmental function. But most people who came to Rome came for reasons which could equally well have taken them to a smaller city. It was Rome's other attractions, and the greater scope offered for economic or career success, which brought them there rather than to any of the alternatives.

iv. Education

'Eagerness for liberal studies' is one of the motives given by Seneca, applicable to students, teachers and others; the Latin adjective *liberalis* can be taken to include all aspects of education for people of free status. Rome is naturally well documented as a centre for education, attractive to teachers and students from all over the empire, speakers of Greek as well as of Latin.[32] Prominent Romans in the Republic often brought educated Greeks back to Rome with them, either as family tutors or as personal advisers; these would normally be men of *peregrinus* or slave/freed status.[33] Students would normally come to Rome temporarily, unless they were being trained for a career which required them to remain in the city. Teachers probably gravitated to Rome in the expectation of staying there, although there are signs of a tendency for Rome to be just one stop in a career which took the most successful around a series of major cities. Philostratus' *Lives of the Sophists* give details of many such careers, and later writers such as Ausonius attest more.

Literature records many males (mainly teenagers or in their very early twenties) coming to Rome to study. The possibility of a *filiusfamilias* having gone to Rome 'for the sake of his studies' is mentioned in a number of legal texts:[34] complications which might arise include paying him an allowance and getting him to deliver a letter to the emperor. Students might come from very privileged provincial or foreign backgrounds: Herod the Great's sons Aristobulus and Alexander studied in Rome for about five years from *c.* 22 BC, living with Asinius Pollio.[35] Septimius Severus, the future emperor, came to Rome aged 17 from Lepcis 'to pursue his studies', and to obtain the *latus clavus* with the help of a consular relative.[36] Information is scarcer about less advantaged students, unless they happened to be Christians (Justin Martyr's pupils included Tatian from Nisibis and Irenaeus from Smyrna[37]) or were recorded in epitaphs. One of the latter is Alexander from Dacia, who died while in Rome to study, aged 20, in the third or fourth century.[38] In the same period Principius died while 'enjoying his studies at Rome', apparently aged nearly 22, and was commemorated at home (Scardona in Dalmatia) by his father.[39] In an epitaph from Lyon, A. Vitellius Valerius was commemorated by his parents;[40] he appears to have died while studying at Rome aged 10 (*annorum X*), but perhaps the text means that he was studying there for 10 years.

When the subject of study is specified, it is most likely to be literature or oratory, as taught by *grammatici* and *rhetores*. In the fourth century, Jerome went to Rome from Dalmatia at 12 to study under the top *grammatici*; he moved on to Trèves when he was 20. Bonosus, who grew up with him, studied with him at Rome.[41] Sidonius refers to his friend Burgundio being in Rome to make a reputation for oratory and to meet the 'senatorial youth'.[42] The possibility of making important contacts through fellow-students might be as important in a family's decision to send their son to study there as the standard of the education was. It was always sons; there is no evidence for daughters being sent to Rome to be educated.

In late antiquity, someone who left home to study was liable to come under suspicion of trying to avoid the financial burdens to which he was liable at home, since most students must have come from local office-holding families. In 360, the state intervened in the whole procedure. The emperors wrote to the Urban Prefect in a way which illustrates some of the realities of student life as well as the limitations which were to be placed on it:[43]

> Those who come to the city out of eagerness to learn should, in the first instance, take to the *Magister Census*[44] letters from provincial judges, by whom the opportunity to come is given, stating their towns, birth and merits. This is also so that on their first entry they should state immediately what studies in particular they propose to devote themselves to. And, thirdly, so that the *Officium Censualium* should know precisely their lodgings. Thereby they can make arrangements for the thing which they claim they were seeking. The *Censuales* should threaten the same thing, so that they each behave themselves in gatherings as they should. They should wish to avoid shameful and base reputation and company, which we think is next to criminality. They should not attend the games too frequently, or seek out unseasonable public parties. Furthermore, we confer power so that, if any of them do not behave themselves in the city in the way which the dignity of liberal studies demands, they can be publicly beaten, and immediately put on a ship, thrown out of the city and sent home. Those who work diligently at their studies are permitted to remain at Rome up to their twentieth year. After that time, someone who failed to return spontaneously would return to his homeland all the more shamefully for having worried the Prefect's Office. So that these things are not enforced only perfunctorily, Your Excellency should warn the *Officium Censuale* that each month notes should be taken of who these people are, where they come from and in what length of time they are to return to Africa or other provinces. Those people are exempted who are subject to the burdens of *corporatores*. Similar notes should be sent to the *scrinia mansuetudinis nostrae* each year, by which we may judge through the merits of individuals and by their educational activities being found out (*institutionibus conpertis*) whether and when they are useful to us.

It was not the quality of education which the emperors were interested in at this time, but the behaviour of the students, and in particular the possibility that they would stay away from home longer than necessary.

Rome was also a centre for legal training. Philostratus refers to a boy from Messene in Arcadia who was sent to Rome by his father to study legal science; after resisting Domitian's advances, he returned home.[45] There is an epitaph for a Cappadocian youth who was probably studying law when he died at Rome.[46] Augustine's friend Alypius, a member of the curial class at Thagaste in Africa, went to Rome to study law after having studied at Thagaste and Carthage; he moved on to Milan, but eventually returned to his home town as bishop (394–419).[47] The existence of recognized law schools, rather than just classes gathered around an individual teacher, is suggested by Aulus Gellius' references to places which he calls *stationes* where law was taught at Rome.[48]

Many male immigrants are attested as working in 'liberal studies' at Rome, usually making a living as a teacher although their reputation might be more as a writer or philosopher; a few achieved enough financial patronage not to need to earn an income. The Younger Pliny comments on Rome as a 'centre for liberal studies' in the context of the philosopher Euphrates, whom he had met while doing military service in Syria 15–20 years earlier; he now knew him as a teacher and moralist at Rome.[49] For teachers of rhetoric, the chairs of Greek or Latin rhetoric at Rome with a salary of HS 100,000 p.a. were the pinnacle of their career from the time of their foundation by Vespasian.[50] The Greek chair at Rome was regarded as a promotion over the chair at Athens, since several holders of the post at Athens moved on to Rome: e.g. Philagrus of Cilicia,[51] Hadrian of Tyre who died at Rome aged about 80 in *c*. AD 190,[52] and Pausanias of Caesarea in Cappadocia.[53] The duties were not restricted to teaching, since Euodianus of Smyrna, when he held the chair, was also expected 'to supervise the artisans around Dionysus' (i.e. actors).[54] The Latin chair was held first by Quintilian, an immigrant from Spain although he was already living at Rome.[55]

Well-known teachers at Rome in the late Republic and early Empire, before the creation of the state-sponsored chairs, also appear nearly all to have been immigrants from outside Italy. Most of those known came from Greece or the province of Asia; people from Gaul and Syria are also mentioned. Such immigrants were not always wholly welcome: two Epicureans were expelled in 173 or 155 BC (see p. 45); the teaching of rhetoric was suppressed by the censors in 92 BC; and Demetrius the Cynic who came to Rome from Corinth was removed by Tigellinus.[56] Some teachers were of relatively high social status before they came to Rome, although often not Roman citizens unless they took advantage of Julius Caesar's offer of citizenship (see p. 47). Freedmen and slaves are also mentioned, such as M. Antonius Gnipho, born free in Gaul but brought up as a slave, who taught Cicero and Julius Caesar;[57] P. Valerius Cato, a successful teacher in the time of Sulla, who claimed to be freeborn but was said by some to be a freedman from Gaul;[58] L. Ateius Philologus and Cn. Pompeius Lenaeus, from the same period, who were freedmen from Athens.[59] Eros, the teacher of Brutus and Cassius, came on a slave-ship from Antioch.[60] Some teachers achieved substantial wealth: Epaphroditus of Chaeronea, a *grammaticus Graecus* in the first century AD, owned two city houses and an extensive library; a portrait statue survives with a Latin inscription by his freedman.[61] However, successful teachers could still die poor, and the success of a well-documented few is probably not representative of the mass of people who came to Rome to teach.[62]

Some teachers arrived at Rome as the result of a specific invitation. Aristodemus of Nysa had schools at Nysa (where Strabo studied) and Rhodes; he came to Rome to teach the children of Pompey.[63] Apollonius of Chalcis came to Rome at Antoninus Pius' request to become tutor of Marcus Aurelius.[64] Others came of their own accord after building up experience and reputation elsewhere. Another of Strabo's teachers, Xenarchus of Seleuceia, a Peripatetic, taught at Alexandria and Athens before coming to Rome, where he became a friend of Augustus. [65] Isaeus, a sophist from Assyria, came to Rome *c.* AD 97 at the age of 60, preceded by his reputation according to Pliny; he evidently made his living as a teacher but gave public performances of his own rhetoric.[66] There are a number of epitaphs commemorating immigrants from this sort of background, people who probably made their living from teaching although their epitaphs give them other designations, e.g. Papirius Heraclitus, a sophist of Laranda in Lycaonia;[67] Alexander, a philosopher from Tarsus.[68]

Teachers at Rome were normally self-employed. Most newcomers presumably arrived with the intention of setting up a school but without any guarantee of its success; the ones who are mentioned in the sources are invariably those who succeeded. Basileus of Nicaea is described in his epitaph as coming to Rome while still a young man and teaching mathematics and geometry there,[69] but most teaching careers probably began at home. The early acquisition of influential pupils or patrons at Rome would help a new arrival to become established. Cornutus, a philosopher from Lepcis, taught Persius and Lucan;[70] he used Latin for writing about grammar, Greek for philosophy. Sextus, a Boeotian philosopher, had Marcus Aurelius in his audience at Rome.[71] Julius Pollux of Naucratis taught rhetoric to Commodus, to whom he dedicated his *Onomasticon*, and was rewarded with the chair at Athens.[72]

There is very little evidence that teachers and sophists tended to bring family or friends to Rome with them, although it is unlikely that the wealthier ones would have travelled without a retinue of slaves.

P. Aelius Samius Isocrates, a sophist who was a citizen of Nicomedia and Ephesus, was commemorated as 'patron and foster-father' by someone called Aratus, a *mousikos* (presumably in this context a scholar), who perhaps combined the functions of servant and student.[73]

The motivation for moving to Rome for someone who was already an established teacher at home seems to be discussed specifically only by Augustine. He was encouraged by his friends to go to Rome for 'greater earnings and higher dignity', presumably the usual attractions, but actually went (he says) because he expected the students to be better disciplined.[74] Another attraction might be the facilities which Rome offered for research. Strabo says that the grammarian Tyrannion acquired Apellicon's library which Sulla had brought back to Rome from Athens,[75] and the other library facilities provided by various emperors would have been important to scholars; Strabo also mentions Alexandrian scholars at Rome.[76] Diodorus Siculus made use of the research materials available at Rome to write his *Universal History*, although he does not actually say that was why he went there in the first place.[77]

The tendency of 'professional men' to migrate over greater distances than anyone else has been noted in early modern England.[78] The geographical mobility of Roman teachers, philosophers and sophists is illustrated by the teacher and philosopher Favorinus. He was born at Arles, went via Rome to Asia Minor, was successful at Athens, then died at Rome in the reign of Antoninus Pius.[79] Epictetus the Stoic came from Hierapolis in Phrygia; he was a slave of Nero's freedman Epaphroditus, but was presumably free by the time Domitian expelled the philosophers from Rome (see p. 45), when he moved to Nicopolis.[80] There was still great mobility in late antiquity: Ausonius knew many people who taught in various places, for example Ti. Victor Minervius, a rhetor from Bordeaux who taught at Bordeaux, Constantinople and Rome. Ausonius claims somewhat hyperbolically that a thousand of his pupils went into the courts and two thousand into the Senate.[81]

The same person might come to Rome first as a student and then again as a teacher. Quintilian, from Calagurri in Spain, must have come to Rome as a student since he studied under Remmius Palaemon, and came back again as an adult in AD 68 in the retinue of Galba, going on to establish himself as the first holder of the Latin chair.[82] Tatian, from Assyria, seems both to have studied under Justin Martyr and to have taught at Rome before returning to the East after an ecclesiastical dispute in 150 or 172.[83] Porphyry, born in 233, was brought up at Tyre, studied at Athens, and came to Rome to become a disciple of Plotinus in 263 (i.e. when he was substantially older than most students). He spent six years at Rome before moving to Sicily, but returned to Rome after Plotinus' death. He married his friend's widow Marcella and became head of the Neo-Platonic school there. According to Eunapius:[84]

> After Porphyry's early education had thus been carried on and he was looked up to by all, he longed to see Rome, the mistress of the world (τὴν μεγίστην Ῥώμην), so that he might enchain the city by his wisdom.

It was occasionally possible for immigrants whose reputation was based on oratory or teaching to acquire political influence as well. Fronto, originally from Africa is one such example; through his association with the Antonine emperors he achieved high office and considerable powers of patronage. A less well known one is Eutychius Proculus, a *grammaticus Latinus* from Sicca Veneria in Africa who was promoted to the proconsulate by Marcus Aurelius.[85] Alexander, a sophist of Seleucia in Cilicia sent to Rome by his father, became secretary *ab epistulis graecis* to Marcus Aurelius.[86] Palladius, a native of Athens, taught rhetoric at Rome and became famous as a Latin rhetor; he was summoned to court in 379 and served as *Magister Officiis* in the East in 382–4.[87]

Some people are attested only as philosophers or litterateurs, with no indication that they did anything to earn a living. In such cases, it is usually impossible to say whether they were able to live off their own resources, were supported by wealthy patrons, or did actually make money by teaching. Statius' friend Septimius Severus (from the same family as the later emperor, and presumably an ascendant of the ex-consul who helped him) came from Lepcis and joined a literary circle at Rome.[88] Some people were commemorated just as philosophers, such as Cn. Artorius Apollo, 'Stoic philosopher from Perge', whether or not they made their living by other means.[89] Aelius Aristides could apparently afford to come to Rome to show off his eloquence without needing financial recompense;[90] most sophists came from very well-off backgrounds.[91] Another way to eke out a living is suggested for Serapio of Alexandria, a member of Plotinus' circle:[92]

> who began as a rhetorician and afterwards took to the study of philosophy as well, but was unable to free himself from the degradation of finance and money-lending.

v. Government and politics
Public office
When Seneca put ambition at the beginning of his list of reasons for

coming to Rome, he probably had in mind desire for success in public life through standing for office or seeking favour with the emperor or those around him.[93] The pattern of members of provincial elites coming to take up residence at Rome in order to pursue power was well established. The tendency is derided by Plutarch:[94]

> Yet there are others, Chians, Galatians or Bithynians, who are not content with whatever share of reputation or power among their own countrymen has fallen to them, but rather weep because they do not wear the shoes of a patrician; yet if they do wear them, they weep because they are not yet Roman praetors; if they are praetors, because they are not yet consuls; and if consuls, because they were proclaimed not first but later.

If they wished to hold office at more than local level, they had no choice about moving to Rome, although they could still maintain strong ties with their homelands (see p. 166), and sometimes returned to them later (see p. 54). Some of the most successful, such as Hadrian and Septimius Severus, were descended from Italian colonists, but people without predominantly Italian ancestry were increasingly able to achieve senatorial rank. Some of the leading figures of second-century politics, such as Herodes Atticus from Greece and the Servilii Pudentes from Africa built suburban palaces rather than taking up residence in central Rome.[95] Trajan encouraged them to transfer their main residences to Italy. [96]

This reason for going to Rome still applied as the city's political importance declined, although Constantinople became an alternative destination. In the fourth century Anatolius, surnamed Azutrion, from Berytus, studied law at home.[97]

> Then he sailed to Rome where, since his wisdom and eloquence were elevated and weighty, he made his way to court. There he soon obtained the highest rank, and after holding every high office and winning a great reputation in many official positions...he finally attained the rank of Praetorian Prefect...

In his case, it is not clear if it was ambition for public office which brought him to Rome in the first place, but if he did have such ambitions, he had to go to Rome to fulfil them. The importance of Rome as the place to which you must go for public success was still being trumpeted by Sidonius Apollinaris to his friend Eutropius in the fifth century.[98]

'The requirement of public office' comes second on Seneca's list. If this is a different category from 'ambition', it must imply the duties of those who already held office, rather than the desire to obtain office. This would not be restricted to people of high standing. For example, soldiers were frequently sent to Rome to guard prisoners: there are examples of this in the soldiers who guarded Paul on his voyage from Caesarea in Palestine to Rome,[99] and the ten 'leopards' who travelled with Ignatius from Smyrna.[100]

Soldiers would presumably discharge their duties and then leave, but imperial slaves might be sent to Rome permanently. According to La Piana (1927, 296), slaves from the imperial estates in Phrygia and Asia were sent to work at Rome, and were probably influential in getting the privileges of the Magna Mater cult extended by Claudius. One specific example from an epitaph is 'Trophimus, imperial freedman, a boy, once a Phrygian shepherd', apparently sent to Rome at an early age.[101] This suggests an unusual amount of both geographical and social mobility. The influence of a few imperial freedmen was notorious in the Julio-Claudian period, but the presence of considerable numbers was always essential to the running of the administration, and some of these must have been immigrants.

In late antiquity, emperors who were seldom or never at Rome themselves sent their ministers there instead. Constans, while ruling Gaul, sent Proaeresius to Rome 'because he was ambitious to show them there what great men he ruled over'.[102] Proaeresius also sent to Rome one of his own pupils:[103]

> Eusebius, who was a native of Alexandria. He seemed to be peculiarly suited to Rome, because he knew how to flatter and fawn on the great; while in Athens he was regarded as a seditious person.

Maximinus, appointed *vicarius urbis* by Valentinian I, was the son of a clerk of Carpian [104] stock from the governor's office in Sopianae in Valeria; he had a superficial education and undistinguished career at the bar; then became governor of Corsica, Sardinia, Tuscany; then he was put in charge of the corn supply of Rome before being promoted again.[105] He was assisted in his purge of senators by another Pannonian who had worked his way up the civil service: [106]

> Leo was then a notary and later master of the offices, a grave-robbing brigand from Pannonia, slavering like a wild beast in search of prey and as thirsty for human blood as Maximinus.

The law

The law brought litigants and the accused to Rome whenever civil or criminal cases arose which could not be dealt with at provincial level. As long as Rome was the centre of the legal process, someone who wanted to make a living from speaking in court (as opposed to using it just to supplement a private income) would be likely to move there.

The ones who are mentioned in the sources are the most successful, such as Cn. Domitius Afer who came to Rome from Nîmes.[107] Quintilian, when he came to Rome in the retinue of Galba, at first made a living by pleading cases as well as teaching rhetoric.[108] There is an interesting poem by Martial[109] in which the speaker asks a man called Sextus why he has come to Rome. 'You say: "I shall plead cases more eloquently than Cicero himself"'. The speaker replies: 'Atestinus pleaded cases, and Civis – you know them both – but for neither was it their whole livelihood.' The alternatives which Sextus considers are writing poetry or 'cultivating great houses'.[110] The implication seems to be that it was very difficult to make a living just by speaking in court. It could, however, lead to greater things, as the verse epitaph of Eventius of Vienne, dated 407, suggests:[111]

> Here is buried a man who once, with a famous name, pleaded cases and deserved to be considered a senator. At no great age he spoke the law at Vienne. From there, (he made) the journey to Italy, to accumulate much honour, if Eventius had not died, leaving the sad city in grief, departing from life to associate deservedly with the saints.

Appian of Alexandria, the second-century historian, having held office in his own city, came to Rome as an *advocatus fisci*.[112] This was one way of beginning a career as an advocate at Rome, established under Hadrian.

Apart from those who spoke in court, several important jurists from the second-third centuries are known to have been immigrants. Cervidius Scaevola was a Greek; Papinian was probably related to Julia Domna and therefore a Syrian; Paul originated somewhere in the East.[113] Ulpian, from Tyre, is first recorded working at Rome as a praetor's *assessor*.[114] This was an alternative way of using the law to make a living, but again must have been available only to a very few.

Embassies

The people discussed above came to Rome as a career move, but the city's role as centre of government brought others there for more transient reasons. 'An embassy imposed (on them)' occurs in Seneca's list. This is one of the best-attested reasons in literature for people to come to Rome,[115] and is also mentioned in many inscriptions. Some ambassadors died there while performing their duties; they might be recorded at Rome by fellow-ambassadors[116] or at home by their families.[117] The most important ambassadors from friendly states could be entitled to a public funeral at Rome,[118] but there is no epigraphic record of this. Others received honorific inscriptions at home recording the success of their missions. In theory, an embassy should have required only a short stay in Rome, but difficulties in performing it, or personal complications, sometimes led to an extended visit. There are hints of some of the difficulties which might be encountered in an inscription honouring two citizens of Abdera who had pleaded at Rome on behalf of the city of Teos in a territorial dispute with King Cotys of Thrace in the 160s BC:[119]

> As ambassadors on behalf of the people they endured both mental and [physical] suffering. They met the [leaders] of the Romans and won them over by daily [perseverance]. They also persuaded the patrons of the [city] to come to the assistance of our people. By explaining the state of affairs and by means of the daily round of calls at the *atria* they made friends of [some of] those who looked after and championed our opponent.

In less fraught circumstances, however, taking part in an embassy might be a perk rather than an imposition. Ambassadors were legally obliged to complete the business of their embassy before acting on personal matters,[120] presumably to prevent people coming to Rome at their city's expense in order to carry out private business. Embassies seem to have been so common that in the late Republic the Lex Gabinia could require the Senate to sit daily in February just to deal with them.[121] There is no record of this in the principate, perhaps because autocracy enabled embassies to be dealt with more swiftly, but there must still have been tens or even hundreds of ambassadors in Rome at any one time when the emperor was in residence or the Senate was sitting. Accommodation was provided at state expense in the Villa Publica,[122] but presumably only for a limited number of important ambassadors. Several legal texts deal with the complications which could result from going to Rome on an embassy, and it clearly became a serious issue for provincial elites.[123]

In the third and second centuries BC, embassies usually came from independent or client states seeking alliance or peace.[124] Book 7 of Pausanias, for example, contains many references: e.g. the Spartans were allowed to send an embassy to Rome against the Achaean League, contrary to what had been agreed, so the Achaeans sent one too.[125] The numerous embassies sent to Rome by cities, leagues and kings in the aftermath of the defeat of Perseus of Macedon are recorded by Polybius and in inscriptions.[126] Augustus allegedly received embassies from many different nations (not necessarily always when he was at Rome): Indians, Scythians, Parthians, Sarmatians, Garamantes, Bactrians, Albanians, Iberians, Medes.[127] Tacfarinas sent envoys from North Africa to Tiberius demanding land.[128] Parthian, Armenian and

German envoys attended the theatre at Rome during Claudius' reign,[129] and he also received envoys from Sri Lanka.[130] Mithridates of the Bosporan Kingdom sent his brother Cotys with a message of friendship to Claudius in AD 46, but Claudius gave Cotys the kingship instead.[131] Such ambassadors might well bring their own staff with them; as members of their home elites, they are unlikely to have travelled alone. For example, an ambassador from Bosporan Phanagoria is commemorated together with a Bosporan translator of Sarmatian who must have accompanied him to Rome.[132] Embassies could disguise other things: Damocles, who came to Rome with a Macedonian delegation in 205 BC, is said by Polybius (13.5.7) to have been a spy.

A king might even come himself. The most spectacular example of this was when Tiridates of Armenia came to Rome in AD 63 to receive his crown from Nero. He brought a huge entourage with him: his own sons, other members of the royal family of Parthia and Armenia, 3,000 Parthian cavalry and a large number of Romans.[133] A less edifying spectacle was Archelaus, son of Herod the Great, who went to Rome in 4 BC to plead for his father's throne, accompanied by a family party including his mother, aunt and cousins (who worked against his interests); his mother Malthace died at Rome.[134]

An individual ambassador could become a regular visitor to Rome. The poet Crinagoras of Mytilene, born *c.* 70 BC, went on embassies to Julius Caesar at Rome in 48/7 and 45, and to Augustus in Spain in 26/5. He apparently spent enough time in Italy to become familiar with Roman high society.[135] The sophist Scopelian performed many embassies to the emperor for Smyrna, and one to Domitian for all Asia about the vine edict; he eventually retired as an ambassador on the grounds of old age.[136]

In the Empire, provincial cities (and eventually provincial councils too, and some semi-official bodies within cities) sent numerous embassies to Rome offering congratulations or condolences to the emperor or to other prominent individuals. An inscription from Messene refers to sending an embassy to Tiberius in AD 14 'to lament that the god [Augustus] is no longer manifest among us', to congratulate the new 'world ruler', but also to ask him about some local difficulties 'and to implore him that we may receive some consolation'.[137] A Trojan delegation later offered Tiberius belated condolences on the death of Drusus.[138] The real motivation of such embassies could be to ask for immediate imperial intervention, as the Messenians did, or to build up goodwill against a future need for it. In some cases, it was necessary to decide whether the embassy should approach the emperor or the

Senate; Mytilene came up with an ingenious solution, that the ambassadors should thank Augustus in front of the Senate and the Senate in front of Augustus.[139]

Provincials honoured their non-imperial patrons and their ex-governors at Rome too. CIL vi 1508 is a partly Latin but mainly Greek inscription honouring a proconsul of Bithynia, naming the ambassadors of various cities who had come as a joint provincial delegation. In AD 153, five Dacians went to Rome for the inauguration of the consulship of M. Sedatius Severianus, former legate of Dacia.[140] In 158, four envoys from Uselis in Sardinia came to invest M. Aristius Balbinus Atianus as their patron.[141] The Lycian *koinon* sent a number of embassies to Rome concerning the honours which they wished to give Opramoas in the mid-second century.[142] The practice continued in late antiquity. The cities of Sicily honoured, in Greek, Vetitius Perpetuus *signo* Arzygius, corrector of Sicily 312–324.[143] A series of Latin inscriptions was erected by cities of Africa in AD 321–2,[144] honouring Q. Aradius Rufinus Valerius Proculus, *praeses* of Byzacena in 321.[145]

Provincials or client states also sent embassies to Rome to complain, or to ask for better treatment, special rights or the settlement of local disputes. In 155 BC, Athens sent the philosophers Carneades of the Academy, Diogenes the Stoic and Critolaus the Peripatetic to plead to the Senate against a fine imposed for the sack of Oropus; the senator C. Acilius acted as interpreter, as they could not speak Latin.[146] A Julio-Claudian inscription from Mantinea honours a man who went on two embassies to Rome 'taking not accusations against proconsuls but praise', implying that accusations were common.[147] According to the Elder Pliny, every emperor was approached by provincial delegations complaining about monopolies.[148] Pleas for help after natural disasters such as earthquakes were also made frequently.[149]

Much later, M. Servilius Draco Albucianus of Gigthis secured the right of *Latium maius* for his city on his second attempt in Rome;[150] although only successful embassies are recorded in inscriptions, this man's experience shows that not all embassies actually were successful. Literature, on the other hand, frequently records unsuccessful or rival embassies. The range of business which could be brought is shown by the following selection from the many embassies received by Tiberius and/or the consuls and Senate during his reign: a delegation from Hispania Ulterior asking permission to build a shrine to Tiberius and Livia in AD 25; a dispute between Sparta and Messene; a request from Segesta to rebuild the temple of Venus on Mount Eryx; a request by

Marseille for confirmation of a bequest to the city; a request by eleven cities of Asia to build a temple to Tiberius.[151]

Embassies by Jews living in Judaea and Egypt are particularly well documented thanks to Philo and Josephus, although they were probably no more numerous than those of any other provincial group; presumably similar circumstances arose with similar frequency in most parts of the empire. Jews and Greeks from Alexandria sent rival delegations to Caligula to complain against each other; their stay was prolonged by the difficulty of getting access to him.[152] The Jews of Jerusalem sent an embassy to Claudius over the issue of the High Priest's vestments during the procuratorship of Cuspius Fadus (AD 44–46), and received support from Agrippa II, who was in Rome at the time.[153] They sent another delegation in AD 61 after a dispute with the procurator Festus and Agrippa II concerning a new wall blocking Agrippa's view of the Inner Court of the Temple.[154] Festus allowed them to send a delegation of twelve, of whom two, Ishmael b. Phiabi the High Priest and Helchias the treasurer, were kept at Rome by Poppaea. Josephus went to Rome in AD 64 as part of an embassy to secure the release of some arrested priests; he was probably there for about a year.[155]

Ambassadors were usually, at least in the East, highly educated men from their cities' elites, often with reputations in philosophy or rhetoric. Bowersock (1969, 46), writes:

> The sophists were in a unique position to gain the ear and sympathy of the emperor, and it was in their power thereby to enhance the prestige, beauty, and affluence of their chosen cities.

Although ambassadors tended to be wealthy men in their own right, some found employment while in Rome, sometimes leading to their staying there. There might be a long delay before they could put their case or receive an answer, as with the Alexandrian Jews. Ambassadors from Plarasa and Aphrodisias were officially and permanently promised the right of audience in the Senate and a reply within ten days, which was presumably unusually swift.[156] Crates of Mallos, sent by King Attalus of Pergamum in *c.* 169 BC, fell down a manhole and broke his leg, as previously mentioned (p. 3); while recovering, he gave lectures.[157] The philosopher Carneades came as part of the delegation from Athens in 155 BC and lectured to 'large and admiring audiences' while he was in Rome.[158] Chaeremon, a Stoic philosopher from Alexandria, came to Rome as part of the Alexandrian delegation in AD 41, and presumably used contacts he made then to become one of Nero's teachers.[159] Apollonius of Athens, who held the Greek chair there, went on an embassy to Severus in 196/7, and while in Rome took part in a declamation competition against the sophist Heracleides.[160] The philosopher Julius Africanus, originally from Aelia Capitolina (Jerusalem), was sent to Rome by the inhabitants of Emmaus, and Alexander Severus put him in charge of organizing the Pantheon library.[161] It was thus not unusual for an ambassador to change from being a temporary visitor to Rome to being a permanent resident there.

An ambassador could be handsomely rewarded at home if he achieved something for his city. Artemidorus of Ephesus got some decisions at Rome in favour of the city and the Temple of Artemis, 'and in return for this the city erected in the temple a golden image of him'.[162] There could also be rewards available from the emperor or his family. Josephus received 'many presents' from Poppaea before he left. In several cases, ambassadors are said to have received Roman citizenship from the emperor:[163] for example, two Frisians who impressed Nero by their behaviour when they visited the theatre.[164] A decree of the Senate promised seats among the senators at the games for ambassadors from Plarasa and Aphrodisias.[165]

Some emperors apparently wished to discourage excessive numbers of embassies, or at least excessive expenditure. They must have been aware of the gravy-train possibilities for civic leaders, who regularly seem to have shown great enthusiasm for being sent to Rome. There was a precedent in the late Republic: a law which limited the amount a city could spend on embassies bringing votes of thanks to retiring governors.[166] In AD 63, provincial councils were forbidden to send embassies to deliver votes of thanks to retiring governors;[167] this presumably post-dates the Bithynian delegation mentioned above. Vespasian limited embassies to three men.[168] The Younger Pliny discovered that Byzantium sent a delegate to Rome annually with an allowance of HS 12,000 to offer a loyal address to the emperor; he stopped the practice, and Trajan approved.[169] Antoninus Pius also seems to have restricted the sending of embassies, at least those on 'routine' business.[170] Some imperial replies to embassies say that the ambassadors should be paid their expenses (unless they had undertaken to go at their own expense); the omission of this statement probably implies that the emperor thought the embassy had been an unnecessary one.[171] The fact that someone undertook an embassy at his own expense is often acknowledged in honorific inscriptions, such as:[172]

> For Q. Caecilius Gal. Rufinus of Saguntum, son of Q. Caecilius Valerianus, for an embassy which he performed at no charge (*gratuita*) to the great emperor Hadrian Augustus at Rome. The province of Hispania Citerior.

In some cases, it was a summons from Rome, either from the emperor or Senate, which led to a delegation being sent.[173] Ambassadors from Heraclea appeared before the praetor Q. Metellus over the case of Archias' citizenship.[174] Tiberius summoned the magistrates of Rhodes to Rome because they 'sent him a public report without adding the usual complimentary formula'; he then sent them home again.[175] Delegates from the cities of Asia were called to the Senate to discuss their rights of asylum in AD 22.[176] In AD 43, a delegation was summoned from Lycia during an investigation by Claudius and the Senate into Lycian misconduct, and one ambassador was deprived of Roman citizenship for not knowing Latin.[177] Larger contingents must also have arrived, at least some on a more permanent basis, on the various occasions from Magna Mater in the late third century BC to Elagabal in the early third century AD when a foreign god was officially 'summoned' to Rome.

In theory, embassies were motivated by local circumstances and caused only short-term movement of people. In practice, they may often have provided a convenient way for members of provincial elites to visit Rome for their own reasons; they sometimes led to extended stays at Rome and even to permanent migration there. They were so numerous that they created a substantial (probably amounting to hundreds) although constantly changing foreign presence in the city.

Hostages and prisoners of war

Other temporary foreign residents of Rome were there for political reasons but not by their own choice. There was a long tradition of taking hostages from enemy states to live at Rome. This gradually developed into members of the ruling families of client states being brought up at Rome and eventually sent back home as (it was hoped) pro-Roman rulers. The official reason for the sons and grandsons of King Phraates of Parthia being sent to Augustus was that Phraates was 'seeking our friendship through the pledging of his children'.[178] Maroboduus, who was brought up at Rome in the time of Augustus, became a very pro-Roman ruler of the Marcomanni.[179] Italicus, son of Flavus of the Cherusci (Arminius' brother), and grandson of Actumerus of the Chatti, was born and brought up at Rome, and was sent by Claudius to rule the Cherusci in AD 47.[180] In 49, a Parthian delegation came to ask for a man who had been a hostage at Rome as their new king.[181] This 'civilizing' policy was still followed much later: Aurelian took the sons of the Vandal leaders back to Italy in 270s.[182] There seem to be no recorded instances of reprisals ever being visited on hostages by the state, although Aristobulus II, former ruler of Judaea, was murdered during the civil war of Pompey and Caesar.[183] Antiochus II of Commagene was summoned to Rome and executed in 29 BC for having murdered an ambassador,[184] but that was a rather different case. Most hostages seem to have been kept in the manner to which they were accustomed: the first Parthian hostages seen at Rome sat two rows behind Augustus at the games,[185] and Demetrius I (see below) went on regular wild-boar hunts with Polybius.[186]

Hostages might come in large numbers. 100 Carthaginian hostages (males aged between 14 and 30) were taken in 202 BC.[187] 1,000 Achaeans were taken to Rome in 166 BC and distributed to Italian towns; the Achaean exiles in Sparta were persuaded to go to Rome to work for their return. 300 survivors including the historian Polybius were released in 151.[188] Domitius Corbulo sent the children of kings of central Asia Minor as hostages after his campaigns in the time of Nero.[189] Female Dacian hostages being sent to Rome are depicted on Trajan's Column.[190] There were also many important individual hostages. The future Seleucid king Antiochus IV Epiphanes was a hostage at Rome from 189 BC, when still very young, to 175 when he returned home to take the throne.[191] He was replaced as hostage by his 10–year-old nephew, the future Demetrius I Soter, who later escaped after failing to get his status as hostage altered.[192] Agrippa I, the grandson of Herod, was theoretically a hostage when he lived at Rome from his childhood until he was in his thirties, but became a great friend of members of the imperial family including Caligula and Claudius; he was given the status of a client king with a growing kingdom, but continued to visit Rome. The last recorded hostage likely to have been kept at Rome is Huneric son of Geiseric in 442.[193]

There are many examples of such people in literature, but a number also left inscriptions. These were usually erected when one of the hostages happened to die at Rome, and say nothing about whether they expected to return home eventually, but in at least one case hostages built their own tomb at Rome while still alive, so presumably expected not to leave. Two Thracian hostages, brother and sister, were commemorated in the time of Augustus.[194] There is a Latin epitaph for two sons of an Arsacid King Phraates,[195] and another where a woman named Ulpia Axse, described as 'Parthian hostage', and (presumably) her husband whose name is lost, commemorate their daughter and grandchildren.[196] A dedication to Jupiter by 'King Ariobarzanes' and his wife and sons probably refers to Pompey's client-king of Cappadocia.[197] The fact that the inscriptions of nearly all the eastern hostages are in

Latin suggests that romanization was quite effective even when the people involved were not in Rome voluntarily. However, the epitaph of a man named Dicaenetus who probably came from the same milieu (he was 'reared at the hands of kings' and 'had noble blood'), is in Greek.[198]

Some foreign leaders were brought to Rome as prisoners of war rather than hostages, although the distinction seems sometimes to have become rather blurred. They might be displayed in triumphs and executed afterwards, but the fate of most is unrecorded.[199] Perseus of Macedon was displayed with two sons, a daughter and 250 officers in 167 BC; Perseus was kept in custody afterwards, but what happened to the others is not mentioned.[200] The Attalid rebel leader Aristonicus was captured by M. Perperna and sent to Rome, where he died in prison in 128 BC.[201] Caratacus, handed over to the Romans by Cartimandua in AD 51, was taken to Rome, but Claudius released him with his wife and brothers; he remained in Italy with his family.[202] Simon bar Gioras, one of the leaders of the Jewish Revolt displayed in the triumph of Vespasian and Titus, was immediately executed; 700 other prisoners were also sent for the triumph.[203] Zenobia was captured by Aurelian and taken back to Rome for his triumph in 272, but was then allowed to live in retirement at Tivoli. Women were not necessarily treated more mercifully than men, however: in AD 79 both Julius Sabinus, rebel leader of the Lingones, and his wife Epponina were executed.[204]

Most royal hostages would not have come to Rome alone, however destitute they may sound in the literary sources. Polybius' description of the escape of Demetrius I from Rome shows that he was surrounded by a large entourage.[205] Inscriptions provide occasional reminders of the presence of relatives and slaves; Matthews (1989, 39) even suggests that they could have formed small foreign enclaves in the city. There is an epitaph for a freedman of King Sampsiceramus of Emesa, from the time of Julius Caesar or the Julio-Claudian period.[206] Zia, Dacian wife of King Pieporus of the Costobocesians, was commemorated at Rome by her grandchildren *c.* AD 175–85, implying that the whole family had gone there after defeat by Marcus Aurelius *c.* 170.[207] The family of Abgar IX (or X) of Osrhoene, who was summoned to Rome and deposed by Caracalla, evidently came to Rome with him, since one of his sons commemorated another, aged 26, there.[208] Abgar X (or XI) Phraates, who was restored by Gordian *c.* 242–4, commemorated his wife at Rome, presumably while in exile.[209]

Hostages and prisoners must have been less numerous than

ambassadors, but individuals stayed at Rome for much longer. The two groups are likely to have moved in similar social circles while at Rome, and between them would have formed a foreign presence which was quite significant numerically and even more significant in terms of its contacts and public profile.

Political refugees

A study of modern political refugees divides them into three categories: activists (who oppose the ruling regime), targets (who belong to special groups singled out for violence) and victims (caught up randomly in violence).[210] Rome was normally a place where people were exiled *from* rather than one which exiles went *to*. There are, however, records of a number of exiles coming to Rome from outside the boundaries of the Empire. They belong to the 'targets' category, although the best-known ones were displaced rulers rather than the victims of existing regimes. They are all from the same background as the hostages discussed above. Ptolemy VI Philometor of Egypt came to Rome in 164/3 BC after being driven out by his brother.[211] Ptolemy XII Auletes spent some time at Rome in the 50s BC after being ejected by his subjects. When the Alexandrians sent a delegation of one hundred to Rome to complain against him, he had most of them murdered en route or in the city, and bribed or terrified the rest.[212] His exile proved to be a fairly short-lived one, as he was restored by Gabinius in 55 BC. Augustus lists 'the kings who fled to me as suppliants' from Parthia, Media, Britain and Germany.[213] One non-ruler in the same category is Apelles, who was accused of plotting against his former friend Philip V of Macedon, fled to Italy in 179 BC, but was persuaded to return home by Perseus and murdered there.[214]

Some exiled royals never returned home. A man named C. Iulius Artabasdes, son of Artabasdes and grandson of King Ariobarzanes, who died at Rome aged 39 and was commemorated in Greek and Latin, was probably the son of the king of Armenia and Media who was expelled in AD 3[215] – apparently the family went into exile at Rome and stayed there. In an inscription on a sarcophagus, Aurelius Pacorus, 'King of Great Armenia', commemorated his brother Aurelius Merithas, who had lived with him for 56 years. This seems to be another case of an Armenian ruler being expelled from his kingdom (probably by Verus) and taking refuge at Rome with his family.[216] Amazaspus, commemo-rated as 'the famous son of a king, the relative of King Mithridates', belonged to the royal family of Iberia and was commemorated at Rome after being killed fighting against the Parthians near Nisibis;[217]

he was presumably an exile from his homeland. Refugees of this sort of background would no doubt have moved in the same social circles as hostages and ambassadors.

Most of the refugees who came to Rome from another part of the Empire also appear to have fallen into the 'targets' category. Heraclius of Syracuse and Epicrates of Bidis came to Rome after having been (Cicero says) ejected from their property by Verres. They stayed there for two years before leaving with L. Metellus for his province.[218] It is not clear whether they had previous connections with the Metelli, but that seems likely. Josephus was in effect a refugee at Rome, unable to return to Judaea after the end of the Judaean revolt despite being a landowner there. In his case it was the patronage of the Flavians which made Rome a suitable place of exile for him. In late antiquity, people who found the borders of the Empire unsafe (i.e. the 'victims' category) might go to Rome, although this was likely to be an unwise move in the fifth century. People from Savaria in Pannonia fled to Rome when the barbarian incursions began, bringing with them the remains of St Quirinus.[219] Fabiola left Jerusalem for Rome when the Huns were thought to be approaching.[220]

vi. Provision of goods and services
Medicine

For those with the necessary skills, Rome provided a vast market for goods and services of all kinds. In some fields, the city depended on the foreign presence to provide what it required. Medicine, at least until the second century AD, seems to have been one, where the role of foreigners was much more important than that of indigenous practitioners. Ways in which the state encouraged doctors to come to Rome and stay there were noted at p. 47. The city evidently acquired something of a reputation as a centre for medical treatment, visited by people like a speaker in one of Lucian's dialogues who went there to see an oculist.[221] Galen comments on how it is possible for very specialized doctors to proliferate at Rome;[222] the scope for specialization would be attractive to doctors as well as patients. Doctors in the East often travelled from city to city anyway, so moving to Rome might seem only an extension of existing practice.[223] The growth of Rome's population meant the appearance of new diseases, and hence a growing demand for doctors.[224] Medical training was available at Rome, as well as in the traditional centres in the East such as Cos and Alexandria.[225] There were alternatives to orthodox medicine there too: miraculous cures were also available, at least to Christians, and

Sidonius claimed to be cured of malaria by going straight to the Tomb of the Apostles.[226]

Most of the doctors at Rome for whom any biographical details are known were Greek-speaking immigrants from the East (mainly Greece and Asia), and prejudice against doctors in the sources thus overlaps with prejudice against Greeks.[227] Some were slaves and freedmen, so class prejudice can also be involved. The following are some of those recorded in literary sources with specific places of origin; the list is not intended to be exhaustive, but to show the range of backgrounds. This type of evidence inevitably concentrates on the doctors who had the most prominent patients. Archagathus son of Lysanias from the Peloponnese became Rome's first state-recognized doctor in 219 BC,[228] but there would probably have been slave doctors brought back as prisoners of war before then. In the late Republic, Asclepiades of Bithynia was active,[229] but the lack of known individuals from this period may reflect a real lack of doctors which Caesar and Augustus tried to counteract (see p. 47). Athenaeus of Attalia worked there in the time of Claudius.[230] Nero's chief doctor was Andromachus of Crete, who was succeeded by his homonymous son.[231] Charmis of Marseille was working successfully at Rome in the time of the Elder Pliny.[232] Thessalus of Tralles was also there in the Flavian period.[233] Archigenes of Apamea was in Rome in the early second century; Rufus of Ephesus worked in Rome and Egypt slightly later.[234] Soranus of Ephesus flourished c. 98–138.[235] Galen, coming to Rome from Pergamum for the first time in 162, had a particular 'push' factor behind him: the envy and malice of the other doctors at home.[236] He mentions a doctor from Sicily, and also his own fellow-countryman Quintus.[237] Philostratus says that the doctors who attended Philiscus of Melos were Seleucus of Cyzicus and Stratocles of Sidon, accompanied by over thirty students[238] – successful doctors could earn money from teaching as well as treatment, and presumably some of the students tended to be immigrants too, although there were alternative centres in the East for medical training. A doctor named Zethus, an Arabian, was a friend of Plotinus, and married the daughter of Theodosius, a friend of Ammonius the Egyptian philosopher (a possible example of intermarriage between immigrants of different backgrounds); he was successful enough to acquire a country property near Minturnae.[239]

Egypt was also an important source of doctors for Rome.[240] The Elder Pliny, a notorious hater of doctors, comments on their coming from Egypt to make a profit by treating a new skin disease called *mentagra* which had spread from Asia,[241] and mentions a doctor from

Egypt called to treat Nero's friend Cossinus.[242] The Younger Pliny was treated for a serious medical condition, presumably at Rome, by an Egyptian *iatralipta* (translated by Lewis & Short as 'ointment-doctor' and OLD as 'masseur') named Arpocras, for whom he successfully asked Trajan for Roman citizenship.[243] This man was the freedman of a *peregrina* named Thermuthis wife of Theon, evidently an Egyptian herself. Plotinus was treated until his death in 270 by an Alexandrian doctor, Eustochius.[244]

There is also epigraphic evidence for many doctors who are clearly shown to be immigrants, for example C. Iulius Themison from Tralles;[245] Claudius Zosimus from Ephesus;[246] L. Fonteius Fortis Asclepiades from Ephesus, aged 40;[247] Nicomedes from Smyrna;[248] Q. Aelius Archelaus from Nicomedia, who died at 22;[249] the freedman C. Numitorius Nicanor from Thebes, an eye-doctor who joined in building a tomb in 47 BC;[250] T. Flavius Coelius Severus of Side.[251] The doctor Patron who had a very elaborate tomb on the Via Appia may have been an immigrant from Lycia, but Moretti thinks he was probably born at Rome (or came there very young).[252] Immigrant doctors are much less evident in late antiquity, but Rapetiga from Spain, who died at 25 in AD 388, shows that they were still arriving; as he was commemorated by his father (not specifically said to be a doctor), they may have practised together.[253] The availability of citizenship to doctors is shown by the names of nearly all the doctors in the inscriptions.

Doctors, like teachers, were self-employed and would have depended on reputation to establish a viable business. Some may have brought a big reputation with them (and even been specifically invited to Rome, like Archagathus), perhaps with testimonials from cities where they had worked;[254] others would have had to create it. Having a famous patient or achieving a spectacular success would help. The best-documented case is Galen, who made his name by curing some important people and giving anatomical demonstrations to select audiences. No doubt many doctors and teachers failed to establish themselves in Rome and either returned home or died very poor. According to Galen (14.620–3), numerous doctors came to Rome from Asia because they had been found to be incompetent at home. They may have been able to leave their pasts behind them, but when so many doctors were moving to Rome, it is quite likely that an individual's reputation would eventually have caught up with him.

One immigrant who may have worked on the fringes of the medical profession is the notorious poisoner Lucusta, allegedly patronized by Agrippina and Nero. She is said to have come to Rome from Gaul.[255]

Her 'official' profession was perhaps as some sort of wise-woman providing herbal or magical remedies. Otherwise, although women were clearly active in medicine at Rome, especially as midwives, there seem to be no records of foreign women working in this area. Soranus does not comment on the preferable background of midwives, although he says that wet-nurses (whom he probably expects to be slaves) should be Greek.[256]

Craftspeople and building workers

Sculptors and other highly skilled craftspeople are mentioned as immigrants to Rome several times in literature. According to the Elder Pliny, a Helvetian named Helico, working at Rome as a sculptor (*fabrilem ob artem*), took home with him dried figs and grapes which encouraged the Gauls to invade Italy.[257] After the date of this no doubt spurious and anachronistic story, sculptors seem to have come from the East. Some of the most prominent in the time of Julius Caesar and Augustus were Athenians.[258] Zenodorus, who had made a colossal statue of Mercury for the Arvernes, was brought to Rome by Nero to make his Colossus;[259] his name suggests he was originally of eastern origin (although he might be a Massilian). The sculptor Diodorus came from Egypt in the late first century AD.[260] In the mid–late second century, Zeno of Aphrodisias, who had 'passed through many cities', made 'a tomb and stele and statue I myself sculpted' for his deceased son, his wife and himself now aged 70.[261] Eutyches the Bithynian was the sculptor of a work associated with athletics.[262] There is also an epitaph for a painter (ζωγράφος) from Laodicea.[263]

Craftspeople producing luxury goods with precious metals or stones were often ex-slaves, but occasionally free immigrants. One example from an inscription is the goldsmith Euboulus from Corinth.[264] Kolb (1995, 467) shows that Rome was a production centre for gold and silver, and 138 of 187 gold and silver workers known from inscriptions are from Rome; 80 of them were independent, rather than slaves or ex-slaves working for their owners/patrons. There was a high degree of specialization, and it is likely that the size of the market at Rome allowed people to specialize in making, for example, finger-rings or arm-rings, whereas elsewhere they would have had to act as general gold- and silversmiths (cf. the specialization of doctors discussed above). Augustine comments on the number of specialists in 'Silver-smiths' Street' (*vicus Argentarius*) in Rome who are required to produce a single object which could more easily have been produced by one craftsman.[265]

People described as *marmorarii*[266] were involved in the marble trade, which must have been a very important source of employment, or worked with marble. Apart from the use of marble in building, the fashion for marble sarcophagi at Rome from the early second century AD also provided work. Some of the marble for building and for sarcophagi was imported from Greece (Mount Pentelicus), Egypt, Numidia and Asia (Docimaeum,[267] Ephesus, and especially Proconnesus),[268] and the occurrence of Asian styles of sarcophagus at Rome suggests the presence of Asian craftsmen there as well as the importation of complete sarcophagi. Most known immigrants connected directly or indirectly with the marble trade come from Asia Minor, particularly from Bithynia. A *leukourgos* (worker in marble or other white stone) from Nicomedia aged 54 is commemorated at Portus.[269] Another Bithynian who had his own *statio* (probably a workshop or warehouse in this context) at the 'Petronian Warehouses' was described on his sarcophagus as 'first of *lithemporoi*' (i.e. stone dealers).[270]

Q. Iulius Miletus, from Tripolis in Asia, left a Greek inscription on a large marble altar recording that he came to Rome to see the games in the time of Severus, and that he erected some sort of building at his own expense while there. Since he also asks, 'Serapis, save the race of *marmaroi*', he is likely to have been a *marmorarius* himself. A cippus with an inscription in Greek and Latin records his workmen and his *alumnus* Q. Iulius Faentius honouring him, so his visit to Rome appears to have been more than a sightseeing trip.[271]

Other building-workers travelled long distances to Rome too.[272] Timotheus, a *structor*, came from Laodicea, although he was well enough acculturated to have a Latin epitaph,[273] unlike most first-generation immigrants from that area. Another Bithynian, Maximus from Nicomedia, a builder-carpenter aged 22, has details of his parents in his epitaph, and may have come as part of a family group.[274] Architects are among the Greek immigrants complained about by Juvenal's Umbricius, and known immigrant architects in the real world include Apollodorus from Damascus who designed Trajan's Forum.[275]

Trade/business

Grain, wine and oil, as well as other foods and luxury goods, were imported to Rome from overseas. The trade in oil and wine seems to have come to be dominated by people from Spain in the second century AD.[276] Most traders would have been at Rome only temporarily,[277] like a Phrygian commemorated at Portus who died on his travels,[278] the Nicomedians who honoured Caracalla there,[279] or a man from Egypt who travelled to Rome via Syria, Asia and Greece, and corresponded with people at home about cotton and purple dye.[280] Two other papyrus letters from the second century AD may also refer to trading voyages to Rome. In one, a correspondent asks: [281]

> Find out whether Dioscorus has come from Rome, and give him hearty greetings in my name. Meet Ptolemaeus, the agent of Dioscorus, and ask what he has done in regard to my letter which you delivered to him; and if he has finished the business which I set upon him, good luck to him! But if Dioscorus is not present, send Ptolemaeus so that from him Dioscorus...and when he comes, may give a personal promise...himself.

Decianus, an opponent of Cicero attacked in the *Pro Flacco*, was in business at Pergamum for 30 years before coming to Rome, presumably not as a permanent settler, to sell Tyrian purple.[282] According to Minucius Felix in the second century AD,[283] his friend Octavius Ianuarius 'had made his way to Rome for the purpose of business and of visiting me.'

Particularly important trading groups established *stationes* (see p. 160), which must have been staffed by people who stayed at Rome or Ostia for long periods if not permanently. They might be financially dependent on prosperous compatriots: the *statio* of Tralles in the Forum Romanum was built by a woman named Galene for her *patris*, *c.* 211–217, and the Tyrian *statio* had close financial links with the home city (see p. 161). Ostia also had its own *corpus inportantium et negotiantium vinariorum* for people in the wine trade; in practice if not in theory, this may have been an organization of people from Spain.[284] At Ostia, some individuals involved in trade appear to have taken up permanent residence, such as L. Caelius Aprilis Valerianus, described as *curator* of the Carthaginian ships (*navium Kartha[g.]*), who built a tomb for himself and his wife there. [285]

Someone who wanted to carry on an import/export business embracing both Rome and the homeland would need an agent based at one end. The most likely procedure seems to have been for the head of the firm to remain at home while installing an agent at Rome. Legal texts consider cases where the merchant uses his slave or his son as agent there.[286] Similar scenarios can be imagined behind some of the traders mentioned in inscriptions, although their exact situation is usually unclear. The freedman L. Numisius Agathemerus from Hispania Citerior was a trader at Ostia and a *sevir Augustalis*.[287] P. Clodius Athenio, a *negotians salsarius* (dealer in garum) from Malaga, was an officer of the Corporation of Traders of Malaga, and is recorded at home although he died at Rome and was commemorated there by his wife.[288] C. Sentius Regulianus, an *eques* and a *sevir* at Lyon but buried at Rome, imported wine from Lyon and oil from Baetica.[289] The Fadii at Ostia may have been agents of Sex. Fadius Secundus Musa of Narbonne, who also traded in Spanish oil.[290] The D. Caecilii involved in the same trade at Ostia as *diffusores* had connections with Astigi in Baetica.[291] Coelia Mascellina, the daughter of a *negotiatrix* involved in the trade from Baetica, seems to have continued in it herself.[292]

Foreign traders did not only deal in food and wine. In a combined epitaph of a Cilician freedman, his freedwoman wife and a Paphlagonian freedman, the Cilician is described as *negotiator sagarius* and the Paphlagonian as *mercator sagarius*.[293] Both dealt in mantles: the first one wholesale (not necessarily just at Rome), and the second one retail. M. Licinius M.l. Laetus was a *vestiarius* from Narbonne,[294] a city where a number of other *vestiarii* are recorded.[295]

People recorded in inscriptions at Rome as selling produce which might be from their homelands may also represent one end of an import/export business. L. Lutatius Paccius, an incense-dealer (*thurarius*), was originally a member of the household of 'King Mithridates', probably the one defeated by Pompey, and had therefore come from somewhere in Asia, a likely source of the produce he sold.[296] L. Faenius Telesphorus was an *unguentarius* from Lyon;[297] L. Iulius M.f. Fuscus was an *olearius* from Aix-en-Provence.[298] The wine-dealer Eusebius came from Syria.[299] Oil from Baetica is specified as the commodity for sale several times,[300] and its dealers had their own corporation in the second century AD.[301] International businesses may also exist where a direct link is not made clear; for example, Ricci suggests a connection between Spain, the main producer of *minium*, and the two *miniarii* known at Rome.[302]

In other cases, there is no apparent link between homeland and the nature of the business carried on at Rome. Aurelius Diza from Moesia is described just as *negotians*; possibly a retired soldier since he was commemorated by a soldier serving in the Urban Cohorts,[303] but, as he died at 40 and there is no indication that he had been in the army himself, more likely a civilian with a military friend or relative. T. Aurelius Primus, a *librarius* (perhaps a bookseller or copyist), came from Noricum;[304] M. Ulpius Castoras is described as *librarius Arabicus*.[305] M. Ulpius Chariton, an imperial freedman who may have been a banker, was from Sardinia.[306] Two bankers who were in partnership in the Roman Forum were respectively a Phrygian and a Syrian from Antioch.[307] A *nummularius* (money-lender or -changer) who worked at the Basilica Iulia was a Bessan.[308] In some cases these people may have come to Rome with the intention of going into a particular business, or they may have been freedmen receiving financial backing from their patrons, but they may also have had more complicated employment histories in which they worked at various jobs before the ones they are commemorated with.

Entertainment

Seneca lists 'the shows' as a reason for coming to Rome, and may have been thinking of spectators rather than performers. The games at Rome were allegedly an attraction for visitors at an early period in Roman history: a late source says that Hiero of Syracuse came to watch them after the Punic War, and made a gift of grain to the Roman people.[309] Large numbers were certainly coming by the imperial period. Ovid says that 'a great world was in the city' for Augustus' Naumachia.[310] Martial, no doubt with some exaggeration, lists the places from which people had come for the opening of the Colosseum:[311]

> What race is so secluded or so barbarous, Caesar,
> That there is not a spectator from it in your city?
> The Thracian farmer has come from Orphic Haemus,
> The Sarmatian has come, fed on what he has drunk from his horse,
> And those who drink the first waters of the discovered Nile,
> And those whom the waves of furthest Tethys strike.
> The Arab hurried, the Sabaeans hurried,
> And the Cilicians were drenched with their clouds here.
> The Sigambrians came, with their hair twisted into a knot,
> And the Ethiopians with their hair twisted in a different way.

The partly preserved work by Florus, *Vergilius Orator an Poeta*, set in the early second century, begins with some men from Baetica who have been to Rome for the games being blown off course on the journey home.[312] Enough people came from Cadiz in the third–fourth centuries to have their own designated seats at the Colosseum.[313] In 403, the monk Telemachus came from the East to try to stop the gladiatorial games at Rome, and was lynched as a result.[314]

Spectators presumably came to Rome for the games and then returned home. However, entertainers at Rome were very often temporary or permanent residents. For some, especially charioteers, Rome was probably their ultimate destination. If they were not successful, they could move on to somewhere smaller, like the actor Theocritus who was given his chance on stage at Rome by Commodus' chamberlain Saoterus of Nicomedia, but was unsuccessful and went to Lyon, 'where he delighted the people, since they were rather countrified'.[315] Other entertainers, particularly actors and musicians, may have belonged to travelling troupes which moved on after performing at Rome. Many of these people were slaves who had no choice. Phoebe, an *emboliaria* (interlude-performer) from Vocontia in Gaul, 'skilled in the art of everything' but dead at 12, was probably a slave.[316] Ecloga, who died at 18, was a mime-actress of King Juba, presumably while he was resident at Rome.[317] Others achieved manumission, and freeborn entertainers are recorded too.

Actors and dancers of various sorts often came to Rome from the East. Antipater of Thessalonica has a poem about the dancer Pylades coming from Thebes to Italy to perform as Bacchus,[318] and Bathyllus, a very popular *pantomimus* in the time of Augustus, came from Alexandria.[319] The *comoedus* is one of the undesirable Greek immigrants listed by Juvenal's character Umbricius,[320] and the fact that actors were temporarily expelled on several occasions also suggests their perceived immigrant status (see p. 45). Verus in particular was thought to have brought a large number of stage-performers to Rome:[321]

> Verus also kept the actor Agrippus, with the cognomen Memfius, a man whom he had also brought out of Syria like a Parthian trophy, and he named him Apolaustus.[322] He had brought with him also both flute-players and pipe-players, actors, jesters, mime-actors and conjurors, and all the sorts of slaves which Syria and Alexandria take pleasure in, to such an extent that he seemed to have finished not a Parthian war but an actors' war.

Foreign actors occur in a number of inscriptions. There is an epitaph by M. Volcius (cognomen lost), an actor in Latin plays from Bithynia, for his one-year-old son.[323] M. Aurelius Pylades, a *pantomimus* who was 'approved' by Valerian and Gallienus and who was a city-councillor of Ascalon and Damascus, received an honorific inscription at Ostia, where he had presumably performed.[324]

Most gladiators came to Rome in anonymous masses of prisoners like the Dacians and Suebians who fought a mass combat in 29 BC.[325] Some, however, are shown by their epitaphs to have established families and to have achieved free status (although that does not necessarily mean that they had come to Rome voluntarily in the first place). Wiedemann (1992, 114) suggests that gladiators were a group particularly keen 'to claim a distinct ethnic background' in their epitaphs. For example, M. Antonius Exochus, an Alexandrian, fought at the Parthian triumph held after Trajan's death.[326] Fuscinus the *provocator* and his wife Taon, both Egyptians, commemorated their 4-year-old son Serenus.[327] Another Alexandrian, Macedo, a *Thraex tiro* who died at 20, was commemorated by his fellow 'Thracians'.[328] Pardus, an Egyptian veteran *hastarius*, fought eight times.[329] The predominance of Egyptians can be linked to an inscription, first recorded at Puteoli, put up by a man whose equestrian career included being in charge of the emperor's gladiatorial troupe at Alexandria;[330] it appears that there was an imperially-controlled system for bringing Egyptian gladiators to Rome. Other individuals are recorded from the West: for example, M. Ulpius Aracinthus, a *retiarius*, came from Spain,[331] and the 'Samnite' Thelyphus was from Thrace.[332]

The games in the amphitheatres also required animals to be brought from all parts of the empire, and from outside it. The exact details of the process by which they reached Rome are little known,[333] but specialist keepers must often have come with them. Strabo records that people from Dendera in Egypt came to Rome with the crocodiles sent from there.[334] Such people would presumably return home after the animals had been killed, but it is likely that some would have made repeated journeys with new batches of animals. Performing elephants appear sometimes to have had handlers with them at Rome who came from the same home areas as the animals, such as Ethiopia.[335]

Charioteers tended to come from the West in the first–second centuries AD. The opportunities available to them at Rome were clearly far greater than those available anywhere else, and the city must have had an attraction like that of Serie A for top-class European footballers now. Those who began their careers as slaves were presumably sent to Rome because of the greater scope for making a profit for their owners or patrons there. C. Appuleius Diocles, whose career began in AD 122 and who made his reputation with the Reds, came from Lusitania;[336] he died at 42. Crescens, a not particularly successful Blue charioteer who died at 22 in AD 124 after a 9-year career, was from Mauretania.[337] The Green charioteer M. Aurelius Liber received a dedication from his son on account of three victories; both are said to be Africans.[338] The Red charioteer Aurelius Polyphemus, said to be 'Caesarean by race', is therefore probably from Caesarea in Mauretania.[339] In 401, Symmachus was still having charioteers and actors sent to Rome from Sicily.[340] There may, however, have been something of a change over time, since later inscriptions attest charioteers from the East: one from Cappadocia[341] and another from somewhere in the Diocese of the Orient.[342] Elagabalus' favourite, the charioteer Hierocles, was a Carian. [343] Charioteers were perhaps less likely to be first-generation immigrants than other entertainers, since there was something of a tendency for the job to run in families.[344]

Caligula held contests at Rome for the best boxers of Africa and Campania, and various other one-off Greek-style games were held at Rome in the late Republic and early Empire.[345] The founding of the Capitoline Games by Domitian made Rome a more attractive place for athletes, as well as high-status musicians and performance poets.[346] A number of anecdotes recorded by the dream-interpreter Artemidorus suggest that the games had considerable importance for people in the East, for example:[347]

> The Syrian wrestler Leonas, when he was about to compete in the contest in Rome, dreamt that he had died and was being buried.

Most would have visited once in four years, when the games were held, probably competing at Naples and, from the second century AD, Puteoli too.[348] If they were professionals, they would have followed the circuit of games around the eastern Mediterranean at other times. However, some of the people mentioned below appear to have settled at Rome, at least temporarily, and some retired athletes probably stayed on at Rome or in Italy.[349] T. Flavius Artemidorus, a pancratiast who was a citizen of Adara and Antioch in Syria, won the first Capitoline contest in 86, and was perhaps rewarded with Roman citizenship;[350] he was also victorious at the Olympian, Pythian, Nemean and Actian Games, among many others, and was presumably a professional in view of the large number of places at which he competed. Other cities rewarded victors with citizenship, so it would fit the ethos of the games if Rome did the same. Caldelli (1993, 90–4), provides the following list of origins for known participants (nearly all victors):

TABLE 11. Origins of competitors at Capitoline Games

Italy	6	Crete	1
Gallia Narbonensis	1	Bithynia et Pontus	6
Greece	1	Galatia	3
Asia		Lycia et Pamphylia	1
Mysia	3	Cilicia	3
Lydia	8	Syria	3
Caria	8	Egypt	
Chios	1	Alexandria	5
Cos	1	Egypt	4
Cyprus	1	Africa	2

Athletes were invariably geographically mobile, and the fact that a successful athlete was honoured at Naples by an Alexandrian athletic association may indicate that the whole group had come to Italy together.[351] The place of the Capitoline Games on the circuit is shown by a number of inscriptions from Naples honouring people who were victorious at Rome, Naples and elsewhere; for example P. Aelius Antigenidas of Nicomedia in the mid-second century AD. He had 'played the *aula* to the Roman people for 20 years' before retiring at the age of 35 (perhaps to return home), and his successes included one at the first Eusebeia at Puteoli, two at Rome, and three at Naples, where he received local citizenship.[352]

Moretti thinks that Aurelius Herodes from Philadelphia in Lydia, commemorated in a Roman epitaph as 'chief-secretary of the association' (ἀρχιγραμματεὺς ξυστοῦ), was chief secretary of the *xystos* (association) of athletes,[353] since Philadelphia was a centre for athletes. The *synodos xystike* (association headquarters) building near the Baths of Trajan was founded by M. Ulpius Domesticus, a successful pancratiast from Ephesus.[354] He probably got the promise of a site from Hadrian and the implementation of the promise from Antoninus Pius.[355] A building described in a late fourth-century inscription as *acletarum* (sic) *curia*, with members called *xystici*, must be the same one, so it was a long-lived institution.[356] It would have accommodated athletes visiting Rome, and may have been the administrative headquarters for athletic clubs too.[357] Athletes could be of high status at home: the wrestler M. Aurelius Sarapion put up a dedication at Portus to his father, an Alexandrian city-councillor.[358]

The Capitoline Games were also an attraction for poets, who must be among the people Seneca describes as coming to Rome with 'eloquence for sale'. The poet P. Annius Florus came from Africa to compete as a boy, but was deprived of the crown by Domitian 'not because he begrudged it to you as a boy, but so that the crown of great Jupiter would not fall to Africa', and left Rome, eventually settling at Tarragona.[359] Martial refers to the poet Diodorus wishing to travel from Alexandria to Rome for the Games in 94.[360]

However, Rome already attracted poets before the time of Domitian. A number of writers in the Greek Anthology mention staying (although not necessarily settling) there.[361] Archias came to Rome from Antioch via Asia, Greece and southern Italy, preceded by his reputation. If Cicero can be believed, he was taken in by the Luculli while still *praetextatus*, i.e. a teenager.[362] This illustrates what a poet would normally have to do to make a living without teaching: find a rich patron. Even Martial was dependent on the Younger Pliny and others to pay for his return to Spain (see p. 54). The Cretan Mesomedes, a lyric poet who was a freedman of Hadrian, owed his success to a panegyric of Antinous.[363] An inscription with the text of a poem dedicated to C. Caeionius Rufius Volusianus, Urban Prefect in 365–6, by Eudemos of Laodicea (in Phrygia) may indicate the same process of patronage at work in late antiquity.[364] Another fragmentary inscription records an oracle given at Rome to Septimius Nestor, a poet from Laranda, probably in the first half of the third century.[365]

Musicians are rarely mentioned in inscriptions (outside the context of the Capitoline Games) or literature, although they are included in the list of people brought to Rome by Verus quoted above. Livy mentions lyre-girls and sambuca-girls (*psaltriae sambucistriaeque*) among the luxuries which arrived in Rome from Asia in the second century BC.[366] There is an epitaph for Alcimas of Smyrna, a trumpet-player (*tubocantius*).[367] A flute-player whose by-name was Euphemus, described as *pythaules*[368] and chorus-accompanist (πυθαύλης καὶ χοραύλης), may have been from Cyprus.[369] Flavius Terpnus from Alexandria was a cithara-player who died aged 20.[370] Most musicians at Rome were probably slaves, like the Alexandrian *tibicen* Eucaerus who was alleged in AD 62 to be Octavia's lover.[371] There are several references to associations of musicians or actors, and their members may have tended to be immigrants,[372] but they were trade associations rather than associations of foreigners.

Individuals who could become peepshow attractions might also come to Rome, like a man from Arabia named Gabbaras, sent in the time of Claudius and, presumably, exhibited as the Tallest Man in the World (9' 9" in Roman measurement according to the Elder Pliny[373]). A Jew named Eleazar with similar qualifications ('seven cubits tall') was sent to Tiberius by Artabanus III of Parthia in the retinue of his son Darius, who went to Rome as a hostage.[374] It is unnecessary to suppose that Gabbaras and Eleazar were really the same man;[375] the anecdotes more probably illustrate that such people would naturally end up at Rome. Claudius was presented with a hermaphrodite from Antioch on the Meander,[376] and Plutarch refers to a market at Rome for people with deformities;[377] they were presumably considered desirable because they were profitable attractions.

Prostitution was another aspect of 'entertainment' by which immigrants could make a living. When Seneca writes 'some have brought beauty for sale', he must mean prostitution, although he may also have in mind people who hoped that their good looks would help them in other ways. Prostitution could certainly be associated with immigrants, but most prostitutes would presumably have been slaves rather than free migrants. At the more glamorous end of the sex trade were people like Cytheris, the lover of (among others) Antony. However, these seem usually to have been ex-slaves, and they too probably came to Rome as slaves rather than after they were freed.

Evans (1992, 140–1) argues that prostitution was a way of earning a living for Italian women who had been displaced from the country-side and moved to Rome, since little other employment was available to them. The same may be true for people from outside Italy. Immigrants who work as prostitutes in large cities are usually either lured there under false pretences, or turn to prostitution when their original plans for earning a living fail or prove too unremunerative; prostitution is likely to be a way of supplementing income more often than the sole source of income.[378] A reference to Alexander Severus having the prostitutes arrested and expelling the males and enslaving the females may indicate that they were no longer normally slaves by the third century.[379]

vii. Family and religion

The reasons for coming to Rome discussed above are all linked to self-improvement of one sort or another. People might also be drawn to the city because of personal loyalties which did not necessarily coincide with advancing their own interests, although both factors might operate at the same time. Seneca mentions 'friendship' as a reason for going to Rome. People could go briefly to visit their friends. A poem by Crinagoras has the speaker saying, 'I am getting ready to sail to Italy, for I am on my way to my friends from whom I have been absent for so long' – sailing there via the Cyclades and Corcyra.[380] The real Crinagoras of Mytilene went on embassies to Julius Caesar (see p. 102); the chance to visit friends at public expense was perhaps an additional reason for people to try to get themselves included in embassies. In the case of Octavius Ianuarius (see p. 115), he combined business with a visit to his old friend Minucius Felix. The presence of friends or relatives at Rome might be a decisive factor in someone's decision to travel there temporarily or permanently, even if other motives were also involved.

People might go to Rome in the footsteps of a relative, especially if a pattern of chain migration was established from a particular area; as immigrant groups in the city grew larger, the city would automatically become a more attractive destination because more people had connections already living there. This is rarely mentioned in literature, although suggested by a number of inscriptions (see p. 67). Septimius

Severus already had a male relative in Rome; when he became emperor, he was followed there by his sister, whom he hurriedly sent back to Lepcis allegedly because of her embarrassing inability to speak Latin.[381] When Augustine decided to go to Rome, his mother Monica wanted him to take her with him; he did not do so at the time (for reasons which he does not explain), but she followed him there later.[382] He was apparently accompanied, or followed later, by his concubine, whom he fails to mention in his description of the departure and arrival; it is unclear whether their son was born at Rome or in Africa.[383] On the other hand, the mother of his friend Nebridius refused to accompany her son.[384]

The possibility of women coming to Rome to marry was suggested at p. 71, on the basis of epigraphic evidence. There are two epitaphs for women who came to Rome 'because of their husbands', but in both cases it was probably because they moved with their husbands rather than because they came to Rome to get married;[385] the wording would, however, be consistent with following the men to Rome in order to marry them. I have only been able to find one piece of literature to support the idea of women coming to Rome to marry: according to a poem by the fourth-century writer Palladas, probably not to be taken seriously, a woman went from Alexandria to Antioch to Italy looking for a husband.[386] However, it is clear that most of the reasons for coming to Rome discussed in this chapter and ch. 4 are specific to men. The migration of women is even more under-represented in the literary evidence than it is in the inscriptions. If something like 20–25% of free migrants were women (see p. 63) as the inscriptions suggest, then it seems very likely that many of them came either with their families, like Monica, or in order to form new families. Many modern immigrant groups have strongly endogamic tendencies which, if combined with virilocal marriage, tend to result in brides being sent from the place of origin to join husbands already established at the destination; this may even result in girls born at the destination being sent back to be brought up in the place of origin, because it is felt to make them more attractive as wives.[387]

A freedman could be required to go to Rome to perform services (*operae*) for his patron. There was a proviso: the patron must 'live at Rome like a good man and a diligent *paterfamilias*'; if he just moved about from place to place, he could not require the freedman to follow him.[388] What the *operae* might be is not specified: the most likely situation would perhaps be if the patron had business interests both at Rome and overseas.

Religion could also draw people to the city. For pagans, Rome had some importance as a religious centre, to which people might come to honour the gods or present vows.[389] Certain cults, such as that of Cybele, seem to have brought at least some of their priests from their native areas.[390] People with less formal religious attachments could also come, such as the Syrian prophetess Martha who advised Marius.[391]

Philosophers established a tradition of travelling to see the 'holy places' of their sects for themselves,[392] although that would probably not have brought them to Rome. Touristic sightseeing at Rome was, however, a possibility for those with available time and money, like Antonius Theodorus, a Phoenician who became an important official in Egypt, and who 'a citizen in sovereign Rome, spent much time there and saw the wonders in that place and the things there'.[393]

It was the advent of Christianity which made Rome into an important centre of pilgrimage, primarily through the presence of the martyrs' relics, and despite the increasing difficulty of travelling around the Mediterranean world.[394] The epitaph of Bishop Abercius of Hieropolis refers to the 'sovereign majesty' of Rome, but Rome as the 'seat of Peter' gradually replaced Rome as a city of architectural marvels in the minds of visitors.[395] Ambrose refers to crowds from the entire world visiting the tombs of Peter and Paul,[396] and the regret which Prudentius in Spain and John Chrysostom in Constantinople express at being unable to make the journey to Rome shows how it was a natural desire for Christians in the late fourth century.[397] The attraction for African Christians is well documented: for example, Augustine corresponded with the brother and sister Paulinus and Therasia, who made an annual visit to Rome.[398] The festivals of Peter and Paul, Hippolytus[399] and Laurence were particularly important pilgrimage days,[400] although presumably those coming from a long distance would make their visit cover a number of festivals. People described as *peregrinus* in Christian epitaphs may be pilgrims who died while at Rome;[401] others recorded their ethnics when they wrote graffiti near the tombs they visited.[402] Pilgrims, like ambassadors, occasionally settled at Rome.[403]

Church conferences became another important reason for visiting Rome, even before the legalization of Christianity. Eusebius records a council at Rome in the time of Pope Victor (*c.* 190–198) to discuss the date of Easter, and another to discuss the Novatianists which was attended by sixty bishops in the time of Pope Cornelius (251–3).[404] In 313, Constantine ordered a church council to be held at Rome to discuss the case of Caecilian and Majorinus, presided over by Pope Melchiades.[405] Paula met Epiphanius of Salamis and Paulinus of

Antioch when they came to Rome for the council of 382.[406]

Rome as the established headquarters of western Christianity gradually came to have similar attractions to those it had as the centre of government, bringing people to it on church business or seeking advancement within the church. Irenaeus was sent from Lyon to Rome while presbyter to discuss 'ecclesiastical questions'.[407] Polycarp went to Rome *c.* 154 to consult Pope Anicetus about the date of Easter, and apparently met Marcion there.[408] Origen visited Rome in the time of Pope Zephyrinus (199–217), 'to see the ancient Roman church', and returned to Alexandria after a short stay. While there, he heard a homily by Hippolytus and went to a meeting of Plotinus' school. [409] During a period of 25 years, Origen also studied at Antioch, Caesarea in Palestine, Athens, Caesarea in Cappadocia, Nicomedia, Bostra and Tyre.[410] Bardy (1949, 228) lists many bishops who came to Rome for reasons of church politics in the late fourth century.

Leaders of new Christian movements tended to move to Rome if things became difficult for them at home.[411] Bardy (1948, 88) lists: Valentinus from Egypt; Cerdon from Syria; Marcion from Pontus; Florinus from Asia; Proclus from Phrygia/Asia; Theodotus from Byzantium; Praxeas from Asia.[412] In Cyprian's time as Bishop of Carthage, a number of people who were expelled from the Carthaginian church immediately sailed to Rome, hoping to be accepted in the church there,[413] and Novatus sailed from Africa to Rome to avoid expulsion from his home congregation.[414] Priscilian came to Rome from Spain to try to see Pope Damasus before his enemies could.[415] Pope Innocent I also had to deal with leaders of the Spanish church coming to Rome to complain about other Spaniards.[416] Inscriptions suggest the presence of a number of Montanists at Rome, although it cannot be determined whether their religious affiliation was the reason for their being there.[417] The arrival at Rome of 'heretics' led to the establishment of a system of letters of introduction for Christian visitors (see p. 148).

Exiled bishops and other prominent church figures sometimes gravitated to Rome, probably in the hope that the pope would use his influence to restore them to their sees. Bishop Basilides from Spain, replaced for having lapsed, went to Rome and tried to persuade Pope Stephen to restore him.[418] Athanasius stayed at Rome (as well as at Trèves and in the desert) while exiled from Alexandria,[419] and in the late fifth century the exiled Alexandrian Bishop John Talaïa went to Rome.[420]

Christian charity may eventually have become a pull factor as well. The ejection of beggars in the late fourth century, and attempts to find other ways of supporting them, were discussed at p. 40. Beggars were often characterized as belonging to foreign groups, such as Juvenal's reference to Jewish beggars.[421] In the absence of any welfare system or, outside Christian and Jewish circles, private charity for the very poor, begging would have been the last recourse for immigrants whose original plans did not work out, and it is therefore likely that beggars really did tend disproportionately often to be foreigners.

The reasons for coming to Rome discussed in this chapter are primarily ones which would have motivated males aiming at self-advancement of one form or another. It is impossible to achieve any real sense of the relative importance of the different reasons, and many foreigners at Rome may in any case have had more than one reason for coming. Broadly, it was Rome's position as the political, cultural and economic centre of the Mediterranean world which drew people to it across vast distances.

Notes

[1] Cf. Stanley (1990) for similar conclusions about migration in Roman Lusitania.

[2] RE vi A1.1063.

[3] t. 'Abod.Zar. 4.4, quoted from Gafni (1997, 67).

[4] Midrash Exod.R. 52.3, quoted from Gafni (1997, 69).

[5] Artemidorus 4.34; André and Baslez 1993, 93–5.

[6] Augustine, *Conf.* 5.8.

[7] Conveniently summarized by Boyle, Halfacree and Robinson (1998, 67).

[8] Servius, *in Bucol.* 1.27; Sidonius, *Ep.* 1.16.

[9] Martial 12.pr.; Millar 1981, 157.

[10] Boyle, Halfacree and Robinson 1998, 67.

[11] As described by Panayi 1994, 35.

[12] Boyle, Halfacree and Robinson 1998, 63; Fischer, Martin and Straubhaar 1997, 73.

[13] Laurence (1996) criticizes modern interpretations of Rome as 'dystopia', but the concept in ancient literature is not restricted to Juvenal 3 as he implies.

[14] See e.g. Livy 39.3.4–6, 41.8.7–12, 42.10.3; Servius, *in Aen.* 1.pr., *in Bucol.* 1.pr. In the case of Virgil, as described by Servius, it was the hope of using influence to regain his family's land which brought him to Rome.

[15] 'Can it be supposed that these farmers who had become rich invested their agricultural revenues in other occupations, becoming city-dwellers far from their homeland?'

[16] Cf. Panayi (1994, 25–6) on the link between population growth at home and emigration.

[17] La Piana 1927, 192.

[18] Hopkins 1978, 39.

[19] Brunt 1980. Pleket 1993, 19–20: in early modern Paris and Rome, 25–33% of the adult male population worked in the building trade. Kolb (1995, 485) estimates that there would have been 100–150,000 building workers in Rome in the 1st and early 2nd centuries AD.

[20] Brunt (1980, 93) suggests that people would go from Rome to work at Ostia during the summer; this work would presumably end with the sailing season. Kolb (1995, 486) estimates that 4,000 men would have been involved in transport between Ostia and Rome, and several thousand more would have worked at the quays and warehouses in Rome.

[21] Pleket 1993, 21; Lampe 1989, 38.

[22] Boyle, Halfacree and Robinson 1998, 85; cf. Fischer, Martin and Straubhaar 1997, 59.

[23] Cf. Pleket 1993, 23–4; Purcell 1994, 663.

[24] Nevertheless, the comment by Hopkins (1978, 13; cf. ibid. 49, 105), that 'large numbers of the displaced citizens migrated to the city of Rome to take advantage of the increased expenditure there' still stands.

[25] Boyle, Halfacree and Robinson 1998, 104.

[26] On the lure of the city in the modern world, cf. Boyle, Halfacree and Robinson 1998, 128–140.

[27] b. Ḳidd. 49b (tr. H. Freedman); cf. p. 48 on R. 'Ulla's misinformation about the corn dole.

[28] Martial 3.14.

[29] Bjerén 1997, 243. Cf. Moretti (1989, 9) on the possibility of a similar situation at Rome.

[30] Cf. Doblhofer 1987, 253–4.

[31] Saller (1982, 179–81) notes the importance for *communicipes* of patronage by Africans who were already established in aristocratic circles at Rome.

[32] Greek-speaking teachers sometimes swapped languages. The rhetor L. Cestius Pius from Smyrna taught in Latin (PIR[2] C694). Hierius, a Syrian orator known to Augustine at Rome, taught first in Greek and then in Latin (Augustine, *Conf.* 4.14.21; PLRE i 431(Hierius 5)).

[33] Balsdon (1979, 54–8) gives a lengthy list.

[34] Digest 5.1.18.1 Ulpian, 12.1.17 Ulpian, 47.10.5.5 Ulpian, 50.1.36 Modestinus.

[35] Josephus, *Ant.* 15.342. The text only refers to him as 'Pollio', and it is not completely certain that Asinius Pollio is meant.

[36] SHA, *Sev.* 1.

[37] Bardy 1948, 89; Barnard 1967, 12–13.

[38] ICUR 23076.

[39] CIL iii 6414.

[40] CIL xiii 2040.

[41] Gorce 1925, 15; Jerome, *Ep.* 3.5.

[42] Sidonius, *Ep.* 9.14.

[43] C.Theo. 14.9.1; cf. Jones 1964, 707.

[44] See Jones 1964, 691.

[45] Philostratus, *Ap.T.* 7.42.

46 IGUR 1186.

47 Augustine, *Conf.* 6.8; PLRE i 8.

48 Aulus Gellius 13.13.1; Robinson 1992, 142.

49 Pliny, *Ep.* 1.10.

50 Hopkins 1978, 79; Bonner 1977, 161.

51 Philostratus, *V.S.* 580.

52 Philostratus, *V.S.* 589–90; the age is an exaggeration according to the Loeb introduction, xxxviii.

53 Philostratus, *V.S.* 594.

54 Philostratus, *V.S.* 596.

55 Bonner 1977, 161.

56 Philostratus, *Ap.T.* 4.42; Bonner 1977, 66.

57 Suetonius, *Gramm.* 7.

58 Suetonius, *Gramm.* 11.

59 Suetonius, *Gramm.* 10, 15. Lenaeus achieved fame by translating Mithridates' medical treatises into Latin.

60 Bonner 1977, 60; see p. 235.

61 Bonner 1977, 154 and fig. 8.

62 Iulius Hyginus (a freedman of Augustus, originally from Alexandria), died poor despite being a well-known teacher, writing a commentary on Virgil, and being in charge of the Palatine Library: Suetonius, *Gramm.* 20.

63 Strabo 14.1.48.

64 SHA, *Ant.* 10.

65 Strabo 14.5.4.

66 Pliny, *Ep.* 2.3.

67 IGUR 872.

68 IGUR 320.

69 IGUR 1176.

70 Bardy 1948, 86.

71 Philostratus, *V.S.* 557.

72 Philostratus, *V.S.* 593; Loeb introduction, xxxviii–xxxix.

73 AE (1947) 162.

74 Augustine, *Conf.* 5.8.

75 Strabo 13.1.54.

76 Strabo 14 p. 675. On the Palatine Library, see Horsfall 1993.

77 Diodorus Siculus 1.4.2.

78 Clark 1979, 68.

79 Chevallier 1988, 296.

80 PIR^2 E74.

81 PLRE i 603–4; in Rome in 358 according to Jerome, *Chron.*, s.a. 358 (PL 27.687–8); Ausonius, *Prof.* 2.3–4.

82 PIR^2 F59.

83 Whittaker 1982, ix.

84 Eunapius, *V.S.* 324 (tr. W.C. Wright).

85 SHA, *Marcus* 2.3; Saller 1982, 184.

86 PIR^2 A503. He was much travelled: he lectured at Antioch, Rome, Tarsus, and in Egypt (Philostratus, *V.S.* 271).

[87] PLRE i 660 (Palladius 12).

[88] Statius, *Silv.* 4.pr and 4.5.

[89] IGUR 371.

[90] PIR² A145.

[91] Bowersock 1969, 21.

[92] Porphyry, *V.Plot.* 7.

[93] This is often the significance of his use of *ambitio* elsewhere, e.g. *de Ira* 1.21.3 'the *ambitio* of a great mind is not content with yearly honours'; *Cons. ad Marc.* 23.2: Marcia's son sought *honores sine ambitione*; *de Brev.Vit.* 6.1: Livius Drusus' youthful interference in judicial affairs showed *inmatura ambitio*; ibid. 15.3: *honores* and *monumenta* are examples of what *ambitio* builds impermanently.

[94] Plutarch, *Mor.* 470C (tr. Talbert 1984, 67).

[95] Patterson 1992a, 204.

[96] Pliny, *Ep.* 6.19.

[97] Eunapius, *V.Ph.* 490 (tr. W.C. Wright).

[98] Sidonius, *Ep.* 1.6.

[99] Acts 27.42.

[100] Ignatius, *Rom.* 5.

[101] CIL vi 27657. It could also be translated 'as a boy once a Phrygian shepherd'.

[102] Eunapius, *V.Ph.* 492; PLRE i 731.

[103] Eunapius, *V.Ph.* 493 (tr. W.C. Wright); PLRE i 303 (Eusebius 12).

[104] A tribe transferred to Pannonia by Diocletian.

[105] Ammianus 28.1.5.

[106] Ammianus 28.1.12 (tr. W. Hamilton).

[107] PIR² D126.

[108] PIR² F59. Cf. Champlin (1980, 18) on successful advocates from Africa.

[109] Martial 3.38.

[110] i.e. the sort of lifestyle satirized by Lucian in *On Salaried Posts* (*De Mercede*).

[111] AE (1953) 200, vv.1–6.

[112] PIR² A943.

[113] La Piana 1927, 278.

[114] PIR² D169.

[115] There have been a number of studies of the topic, and no attempt will be made to give a complete list here; see Chevallier (1988). I was unable to consult Canali de Rossi (1997). Affortunati (1994) gives a full survey of all the evidence for German embassies at Rome.

[116] In a particularly unlucky group, two of the three men from Termessos in Pisidia died of disease at Rome and were commemorated there (IGUR 1204). Nicias of Xanthus in Lycia died on his third embassy (IGUR 815).

[117] e.g. CIL xii 1750 (a decurio of Lyon).

[118] Affortunati 1994, 108.

[119] SIG³ 656 (tr. Erskine 1994, 47–8).

[120] Digest 50.7.13.pr Scaeuola.

[121] Talbert 1984, 208, 412.

[122] André and Baslez 1993, 105; Richardson 1992, 430.

[123] Digest 4.6.35 Paul, 4.8.32.9 Paul; 5.1.39.1 Papinian.

[124] Chevallier 1988, 206. He gives some statistics at p. 236.

[125] Pausanias 7.9.4.

[126] Erskine 1994, 50.

[127] Suetonius, *Aug.* 21, *Tib.* 16; Strabo 15.1.4, 15.1.73; Aurelius Victor, *de Caes.* 1.7; Augustus, *R.G.* 31.

[128] Tacitus, *Ann.* 3.73.

[129] Suetonius, *Clau.*25. Friedländer (1908–13), vol. 3, 12–17, has a lengthy list of ambassadors from outside the empire.

[130] Pliny, *H.N.* 6.84–91.

[131] Dio 60.28.7.

[132] IGUR 567 = CIL vi 5207. The *leg(atus) Bosp(h)or(anorum)* commemorated in CIL vi 29694 seems more likely to be from the Crimean Bosporus than a Thracian as claimed by Ricci (1993b, no. T4).

[133] Suetonius, *Nero* 13; Tacitus, *Ann.* 16.24; Dio 63.1–2; Pliny, *H.N.* 30.16–17.

[134] Josephus, *B.J.* 2.21, 2.39; *Ant.* 17.219, 17.250.

[135] Penguin *Gk.Anth.*, 179.

[136] Philostratus, *V.S.* 520–1; Bowersock 1969, 44–5.

[137] Summarized in *JRS* 87 (1997), 211.

[138] Suetonius, *Tib.* 52.

[139] Talbert 1984, 423.

[140] ILS 3896; Williams 1967, 475.

[141] ILS 6107; Williams 1967, 475.

[142] Williams 1967, passim.

[143] IGUR 60.

[144] CIL vi 1401 (Bisica Lucana), 1684 (Chullu, AD 321, honouring the magistrates who undertook the delegation at no expense to the city), 1685 (Thaenae, AD 321), 1686 (Zama, AD 322, listing the people who apparently came to Rome), 1687 (Hadrumetum, 321), 1688 (the Faustianenses, 321).

[145] PLRE i 749.

[146] Aulus Gellius 6.14.8–10; Pliny, *H.N.* 7.112; Cicero, *Rep.* 3.8–9.

[147] SIG³ 783B; Talbert 1984, 414.

[148] Pliny, *H.N.* 8.135; Talbert 1984, 416.

[149] Talbert 1984, 417.

[150] CIL viii 22737, discussed by Saller 1982, 70.

[151] Tacitus, *Ann.* 4.37, 43, 55.

[152] Philo, *Leg.*, passim.

[153] Josephus, *Ant.* 15.403 ff.

[154] Josephus, *Ant.* 20.193–4.

[155] Josephus, *Vita* 16; Lichtenberger 1996, 2146–8.

[156] Reynolds 1982, nos. 8, 9; Talbert 1984, 394.

[157] Suetonius, *Gramm.* 2.

[158] Plutarch, *Cato Mai.* 22.

[159] PIR² C706.

[160] Philostratus, *V.S.* 600–1.

[161] Bardy 1948, 90, citing P.Oxy 412, but the eds. follow the Suda that he was φιλόσοφος Λίβυς.

[162] Strabo 14.1.26.

[163] Millar 1977, 483.

[164] Tacitus, *Ann.* 13.54; cf. PIR[2] M117.

[165] Reynolds 1982, no. 8 (probably 35 BC), restated in no. 9; there were no doubt similar provisions for others.

[166] Cicero, *Fam.* 3.10.6; Williams 1967, 478.

[167] Tacitus, *Ann.* 15.20–2.

[168] Digest 50.7.5.6 Marcian. Williams (1967, n. 62) shows that one or two members was the norm.

[169] Pliny, *Ep.* 10.43–4.

[170] Williams 1967, passim.

[171] Williams 1967, 472–3.

[172] RIT 331.

[173] Talbert 1984, 418.

[174] Cicero, *pro Archia* 5.

[175] Suetonius, *Tib.* 32.

[176] Tacitus, *Ann.* 3.60–3.

[177] Dio 60.17.4.

[178] Augustus, *R.G.* 32.

[179] PIR[2] M329.

[180] Tacitus, *Ann.* 11.16.

[181] Tacitus, *Ann.* 12.10; cf. Augustus, *R.G.* 33.

[182] Lee 1991, 368.

[183] Josephus, *B.J.* 1.183–4, *Ant.* 14.123–4. He was killed because he was caught up in the Civil War, not as a reprisal.

[184] Dio 52.43.1.

[185] Suet, *Aug.* 43. Matthews (1989b, 40), comments: 'Hostages moved in high social circles, attended schools with leading Romans and members of the official classes, and learned their languages.'

[186] Polybius 31.14.

[187] Polybius 15.18.

[188] Pausanias 7.9.6, 7.10.12.

[189] Pliny, *H.N.* 6.23.

[190] Chevallier 1988, 236.

[191] Athenaeus 10.438d.

[192] Athenaeus 10.440b; Polybius 31.11–15.

[193] Procopius, *Wars* 3.4.13; PLRE ii 573. The place of captivity is not mentioned, but Rome is likely in the context.

[194] CIL vi 26608. The sister, but not the brother, had become a Roman citizen.

[195] CIL vi 1799.

[196] AE (1979) 78; Di Stefano Manzella (1976–7, 332–4 no. 3), who suggests that they may have come to Rome after the peace of 116.

[197] AE (1968) 19.

[198] IGUR 1190. The lettering is 2nd-century according to Moretti. The 'kings' could be the emperors.

[199] Strabo 12.3.35 describes how Adiatorix, a tetrarch from Galatia, was

brought to Rome with his family for Augustus' triumph, after which he and his eldest son were put to death but his wife and younger son were not; the 'younger' son was in reality the elder, but was allowed to return home. The assumption that prisoners would not necessarily be executed is clear.

[200] Diodorus Siculus 31.8–9.

[201] Strabo 14.1.38.

[202] Tacitus, *Ann.* 12.36–7; PIR² C418.

[203] Josephus, *B.J.* 6.424–5, 7.36, 7.137, 7.154; Dio 66(65).7. Simon's rival John of Gischala was sentenced to life imprisonment rather than execution, apparently without being taken to Rome.

[204] PIR² E81.

[205] Polybius 31.12.

[206] CIL vi 35556a.

[207] CIL vi 1801; Ricci 1993b, nos. Da6–8; RE xx.1 col. 1220; Mateescu 1923, 99–100.

[208] PIR² A9 and 10; IGUR 1142; Dio 78.12. The fact that the epitaph is in Greek may suggest that they were relatively new arrivals, since long-standing hostages and exiles normally used Latin.

[209] PIR² A11; CIL vi 1797. As that epitaph is in Latin, he may have been at Rome for some time.

[210] Ahmed 1997, 173.

[211] Diodorus Siculus 31.18; Valerius Maximus 5.1.1 f.

[212] Dio 39.13.

[213] Augustus, *R.G.* 32.

[214] Livy 40.55.6, 42.5.4; Tataki 1998, 229.

[215] IGUR 602 = CIL vi 32264, as interpreted by Pani (1979–80); also PIR² A1044. He has also been linked with the Cappadocian royal family.

[216] IGUR 415; PIR² A1566.

[217] PIR² A555; IGUR 1151; Moretti dates it to 114–117.

[218] Cicero, *Verr.* 2.2.62.

[219] Bertolino 1997, 121.

[220] Jerome, *Ep.* 77.8.

[221] Lucian, *Nigrinus* 2.

[222] Galen, *De part.art.medic.* 2.

[223] André and Baslez 1993, 312–15.

[224] Nutton 1973, 166; 1986, 40.

[225] Moretti 1989, 10.

[226] Sidonius, *Ep.* 1.5.

[227] Balsdon 1979, 36–7.

[228] Pliny, *H.N.* 29.12. Nutton (1986, 38) notes the likelihood that he was not actually the first doctor in Rome.

[229] Scarborough 1969, 150; Jones 1978, 1.

[230] Scarborough 1969, 151.

[231] PIR² A585 and 586.

[232] PIR² C720; Pliny, *H.N.* 29.10.22.

[233] Scarborough 1969, 160.

[234] Scarborough 1969, 150, 158.

235 Scarborough 1969, 159.

236 Galen 14.621–3.

237 Galen 8.361–6, 17b.151.

238 Philostratus, *Ap.T.* 8.14.

239 Porphyry, *V.Plot.* 7.

240 Ricci (1993a) lists the known doctors from Egypt.

241 Pliny, *H.N.* 26.3.

242 Pliny, *H.N.* 29.93.

243 Pliny, *Ep.* 10.5–6.

244 Porphyry, *V.Plot.* 7.

245 IGUR 607.

246 IGUR 682, commemorating his son.

247 IGUR 1355.

248 IGUR 1283+102.

249 IGUR 299; commemorated by his *syntrophos* (foster-brother).

250 AE (1972) 14.

251 CIL vi 9580.

252 IGUR 1303.

253 CIL vi 9597 = ICUR 17495. Nutton (1986, 37), notes that 'Greekness' is less common in the names of doctors in the West in the 3rd century than in the 1st.

254 Nutton 1973, 166.

255 PIR² L414.

256 Soranus, *Gyn.* 1.3–4, 2.19.

257 Pliny, *H.N.* 12.5.

258 Friedländer 1908–13, vol. 2, 322 (he thinks that native Italians were predominant in painting, however); Pliny, *H.N.* 36.38 (he also mentions someone from Tralles); IGUR 370.

259 Pliny *H.N.* 34.46.

260 Martial 9.40.

261 IGUR 1222. According to Ward-Perkins (1992, 102), Aphrodisian sculptors enjoyed particular prestige.

262 IGUR 251.

263 IGUR 1425.

264 CIL vi 18175.

265 Augustine, *Civ.Dei* 7.4; he is comparing the proliferation of workers with the proliferation of pagan gods.

266 e.g. Aurelius Agathias, a Syrian: ICUR 1860.

267 Strabo 12.8.14 describes the export of Docimaean marble to Rome for building purposes.

268 Walker 1985, 18–35; Ward-Perkins 1992, 21–4, 31–7.

269 I.Porto 38.

270 IGUR 413; Rigsby 1997. Ward-Perkins (1992, 69), suggests that he dealt in 'any stocks from the adjoining marble-yards that were surplus to official requirements.' He argues for the great importance of Nicomedia as a centre of the Roman marble trade.

271 CIL vi 10091 = IGUR 1567; Vidman, SIRIS 432 = IG xiv 1093.

272 Avraméa 1995, 4.

273 CIL vi 9907. Another *structor* with a Greek name and a Latin epitaph, Cn. Cornelius Anthus, had a Greek wife but his own origin is not stated: CIL vi 9906.

274 IGUR 1263.

275 Solin 1983, 671; PIR^2 A922.

276 Loane 1938, 20–3.

277 Pleket 1993, 23.

278 SEG xxxv 1039, interpreting I.Porto 45.

279 AE (1983) 111, interpreting I.Porto 1.

280 P.Mich. viii 500–1; see p. 165. Another possible trader is Sohaemus, probably a Syrian, who is described in his epitaph as 'both traversing the land and crossing the waves in ships' (IGUR 1334).

281 P.Fouad i 77 (tr. W.G. Waddell). Cf. P.Mert. ii 81.

282 Cicero, *Pro Flacco* 71.

283 Minucius Felix, *Octavius* 2.1.

284 NS (1953) 240 no. 2.

285 CIL xiv 4626.

286 Digest 5.1.19.3 Labeo; 40.2.22.2 Paul.

287 CIL xiv 397.

288 CIL vi 9677; Ricci 1992b, no. a6 and p. 137.

289 CIL vi 29722, discussed at p. 208.

290 Meiggs (1960, 289), but he thinks the name is too common to be sure.

291 Granino Cecere (1994a, 211), and her new reading of CIL vi 1885; AE (1980) 98.

292 AE (1973) 71; Panciera 1980, 244–5; Taglietti 1994, 162–3, 172–4.

293 CIL vi 9675; Loane 1938, 36.

294 Di Stefano Manzella 1976–7, 277–8 no. 11.

295 Cf. Stanley 1990, 250.

296 CIL vi 5639 = i^2 1334; Solin 1983, 675. For the purposes of the statistics in this book, he has been counted as a Bithynian.

297 CIL vi 9998.

298 CIL vi 9717.

299 ICUR 19790.

300 AE (1973) 71: a female dealer in the 2nd century AD. CIL xv 3782–3: amphorae from the stock of D. Caecilius Onesimus, found at Monte Testaccio. CIL vi 1935: a man who was both *viator tribunicius* and a dealer in oil from Baetica (not shown to be Spanish himself). Cf. p. 208.

301 CIL vi 1625.

302 Ricci 1992b, 129.

303 CIL vi 2933; Ricci, 1993b, no. Mo2.

304 CIL vi 33036; cf. p. 271 n. 105.

305 CIL vi 8883; Solin 1983, 672. His job could also be a military rather than civilian one.

306 CIL vi 29152.

307 Bevilacqua 1978.

308 CIL vi 9709.

[309] Eutropius, *Brev.* 3.1.

[310] Ovid, *A.A.* 1.174.

[311] Martial, *Spect.* 3.

[312] Florus, *Vergilius Orator an Poeta* 1.1.

[313] CIL vi 32098 l, m. They may, of course, have been in Rome for other reasons.

[314] Theodoret, *H.E.* 5.26 (PG 82.1256).

[315] Dio 78(77).21.2 (tr. E. Cary). He achieved great influence under Caracalla.

[316] CIL vi 10127.

[317] CIL vi 10110.

[318] Gk.Anth. 16.290.

[319] PIR² B91.

[320] Juvenal 3.93–5.

[321] SHA, *Verus* 8.10–11.

[322] An honorific inscription for this man by one of his freedmen is preserved on a marble altar: CIL vi 10117. Apolaustus' legal status at the time of the inscription was imperial freedman.

[323] BCAR 51 (1923), 74 no. 16.

[324] CIL xiv 4624, with additions in JIWE i 15 and JIWE ii p. 571.

[325] Dio 51.22.

[326] CIL vi 10194.

[327] IGUR 939 = ICUR 4032.

[328] CIL vi 10197.

[329] AE (1988) 24; Ricci 1993a, no. A19.

[330] CIL x 1685 (place of origin unknown): *procur(ator) ludi famil(iae) glad(iatoriae) Caesaris Alexandreae ad Aegyptum.*

[331] CIL vi 10184.

[332] CIL vi 10187. Wiedemann (1992, 114) describes this as 'perhaps an example of double deracination'.

[333] See Toynbee 1973, 65–6, 82–3; André and Baslez 1993, 338–40.

[334] Strabo 17.1.44.

[335] Toynbee 1973, 48.

[336] CIL vi 10048.

[337] CIL vi 10050.

[338] CIL vi 10058. He was also honoured by the town council at Teanum: AE (1979) 155.

[339] CIL vi 33939 (including 10060), apparently dated 275.

[340] Symmachus, *Ep.* 6.33, 6.42.

[341] ICUR 10549.

[342] ICUR 5688, as interpreted by Feissel (1982a, 353–7).

[343] Dio 80.15.1.

[344] e.g. M. Aurelius Polynices had two sons; all three were charioteers, and all three were born slaves but died free: CIL vi 10049.

[345] Suetonius, *Cal.* 18; Moretti 1989, 15.

[346] The games were still attracting Olympic champions in the early 3rd century, e.g. Aurelius Helix, a Phoenician (PIR² A1520). An inscription from

the reign of Commodus refers to the departure of competitors to Rome from Aphrodisias, presumably for the Capitoline Games: Reynolds 1982, no. 59.

[347] Artemidorus 4.82 (tr. R.J. White). Cf. 4.42, the pancratiast Menippus of Magnesia.

[348] Moretti 1989, 15.

[349] Pleket 1973; IGUR 237.

[350] PIR² F221; I.Napoli 50. His father, referred to simply as Artemidorus, was apparently not a Roman citizen.

[351] I.Napoli 51; André and Baslez 1993, 218–20.

[352] I.Napoli 47. Cf. I.Napoli 51: T. Flavius Archibios, a pancratiast from Alexandria victorious at Rome four times, AD 94–106. IGR iv 1636 records a musician from Philadelphia in Lydia who was crowned at all the sacred games from Rome to Antioch.

[353] ICUR 12841 = IGUR 404.

[354] Caldelli 1992; I.K.Ephesus iv 930, 3581.

[355] Pleket 1973; Palmer 1981, 390–1; Bollmann 1997, 214; IGUR 26, 235–6.

[356] Caldelli 1992; CIL vi 10154.

[357] La Piana 1927, 267.

[358] I.Porto 16.

[359] Florus, *Vergilius Orator an Poeta* 1.3–4; PIR² A650.

[360] Martial 9.40; this is presumably what he means by the 'Tarpeian crowns'.

[361] Antipater of Thessalonica 27, Crinagoras 24, Antiphilus of Byzantium 16, Leonidas of Alexandria 8, Lucillius.

[362] Cicero, *pro Arch.* 3.4–5.

[363] Suda, s.v. Μεσομήδης.

[364] AE (1986) 109.

[365] SEG xv 620; SEG xxvii 678 with a new version by M. Guarducci.

[366] Livy 39.6.8.

[367] CIL vi 10149.

[368] Defined by Liddell & Scott as 'one who plays the *nomos* expressing the battle between Apollo and the Python'.

[369] IGUR 551. The inscription is fragmentary, and *Kyprios* could be a personal name of someone else. This man has not been counted as an immigrant in ch. 4.

[370] IGUR 1034.

[371] Tacitus, *Ann.*14.60–1.

[372] La Piana 1927, 266–7.

[373] Pliny, *H.N.* 7.74.

[374] Josephus, *Ant.* 18.103. The same man is probably meant by Columella, *R.R.* 3.8.2, 'a man of the Jewish race higher than the tallest German'.

[375] As in PIR² E50 and Solin 1983, 601–2.

[376] Phlegon, *Mirab.* 35 (6.4 ed. Hansen); cf. Pliny, *H.N.* 7.34 on hermaphrodites as attractions ('once they were counted among prodigies, now among pleasures').

[377] Plutarch, *Mor.* 520B (*de Curiositate* 10).

[378] Cf. Gilfoyle 1992, 59. In 19th-century New York, immigrant prostitutes were outnumbered by those born in the U.S.A., even at the height of

immigration. However, after 1845, 75% or more of the teenage prostitutes in the House of Refuge had immigrant parents, although the death of a parent (rather than ethnic or class background) was the most important factor in their turning to prostitution (Gilfoyle 1992, 62–6).

[379] Or at least by the 4th century, when the text (SHA, *Alex.Sev.* 34.4) was written.

[380] Gk.Anth. 9.559.

[381] SHA, *Sev.* 15.7; Barnes (1967) shows that it is highly unlikely that Latin was really not her first language.

[382] Augustine, *Conf.* 5.8, 6.1.

[383] Augustine, *Conf.* 6.15.

[384] Augustine, *Conf.* 6.10.

[385] IGUR 1262 (Lyka from Crete); ICUR 4209 (Helpis from Sicily). Cf. CIL vi 17690, where a man commemorates his wife and says 'out of duty you travelled with your husband in (his?) province' (*pietate coiugi* [sic] *in provincia peregrinata es*).

[386] Gk.Anth. 11.306.

[387] Bjerén 1997, 229–31.

[388] Digest 38.1.20.1, quoting Proculus.

[389] Chevallier 1988, 205; André and Baslez 1993, 250.

[390] See IGUR 77 = Vidman, SIRIS 384: an inscription of AD 146 about an Egyptian named Embes, involved in the cult of Serapis. Solin 1983, 683; Turcan 1996, 37.

[391] Plutarch, *Marius* 17.

[392] Matthews 1989b, 43.

[393] IGR i 1211 = SB 1002.

[394] Discussed by Bardy 1948, 90; André and Baslez 1993, 264–7; Di Stefano Manzella 1997b, 338.

[395] Bardy 1948, 90; André and Baslez 1993, 265.

[396] Ambrose, *Hymn.* 12.25–32 (ed. J. Fontaine, 1992).

[397] Bardy 1949, 226–7.

[398] Augustine, *Ep.* 95.6 (408).

[399] Prudentius, *Peristeph.* 11.203–8 describes people coming from all over Italy.

[400] Gorce 1925, 4.

[401] e.g. ICUR 1491, 2274. Cf. *MGR* 18 (1994), 177–285, no. 87: someone (not necessarily male, as in the editor's restoration) who died *in peregre* and was probably buried, if the restoration is correct, *[in terra a]liena*. However, the same Latin terms would be used for 'on pilgrimage' and just 'while abroad'; e.g. someone who put up a dedication to the Genius Castrorum Peregrinorum described himself as *peregre [c]onstitutus* (CIL vi 231).

[402] e.g. ICUR 15978.

[403] Solin 1983, 625.

[404] Eusebius, *H.E.* 5.23, 6.43.

[405] Augustine, *Ep.* 42.4, 53.5, 88.3. There was a subsequent council at Arles on the same matter.

[406] Gorce 1925, 11.

407 Jerome, *Vir.Ill.* 35.

408 Eusebius, *H.E.* 4.14 and 5.24, quoting Irenaeus, *Ref.Her.* 3.

409 Eusebius, *H.E.* 6.14; Jerome, *Vir.Ill.* 61; Porphyry, *V.Plot.* 14.

410 Gorce 1925, 15.

411 La Piana 1925, 211.

412 Tertullian, *adv.Prax.* 1: 'For he first brought this sort of perversity from Asia to Roman soil.'

413 Cyprian, *Ep.* 54.

414 Cyprian, *Ep.* 48.2–3.

415 Priscillian, *Liber ad Damasum* 51–2 (CSEL 18.41).

416 Innocent I, *Ep.*3.1 to bishops at Synod of Toletum (PL 20.486).

417 Tabbernee 1997, nos. 72 (ICUR 4437), 93 (IGCVO 134); nos. 73, 74, 94 are possibly Montanist.

418 Cyprian, *Ep.* 67.5 (ANCL edn).

419 Gorce 1925, 23.

420 Pietri 1987.

421 Juvenal 6.543.

Chapter 6

THE PRACTICALITIES OF MOVING TO ROME

This chapter looks at the mechanics of moving to Rome and settling into life in the city. The process by which people arranged to leave their homes and made their way to Rome is very poorly documented, and the evidence is heavily biased towards the most prosperous migrants. The chapter concentrates on free, civilian immigrants; slaves and soldiers would have had very different experiences.

i. How to get to Rome

Although people still travelled to Rome in times of disturbance, it was the protection of the *Pax Romana* for travellers by land and sea which facilitated the journey, and made long-distance movement possible on a large scale.[1] The nature of the journey would have been dictated by the traveller's starting-point, financial means and other personal circumstances. Divine influence might also help to decide what form of travel to use, since, according to Lucian, whether to make the journey to Italy by land or sea was a plausible question to ask the oracle at Abonouteichos in Paphlagonia.[2] Travel overland was aided by the empire-wide network of roads, but was extremely slow compared to water-borne transport. The *cursus publicus* averaged only 45 km daily, and most travellers would probably have been using asses rather than the best horses, and therefore travelling much more slowly, perhaps at a daily rate of 30 km.[3] A traveller on foot might have managed a similar rate without baggage. There is a description of some of the hazards of the journey by Aelius Aristides, who travelled overland from Pergamum in AD 144 (the sea voyage would not usually be possible in the winter, since there was normally no long-distance sailing between November and March or April):[4]

> I set out for Rome in the middle of winter... After [crossing the Hellespont], there was rain, frost, ice and all the winds. The Hebrus just now had been chopped up, so that it was viable by boat, but if it had not been, it was all solid ice. The fields were swampy as far as the eye could see. There was a dearth of inns, and more rain came in through their roofs than from the sky without. And in all this, there was my haste and

speed contrary to the season and the strength of my body. For not even the military couriers passed us, to say no more, and the majority of my servants traveled leisurely. I myself sought out the guides if there was any need, and this itself was no easy matter. For it was necessary to drag the men, who fled like barbarians, sometimes by persuasion, sometimes even by force... And I lay at Edessa [in Macedonia, on the Via Egnatia] by the cataract, and scarcely on the one hundredth day after I started from home, I arrived at Rome.

Aristides was clearly taking a substantial number of people to Rome with him, as anyone of his standing would; large quantities of baggage would require a number of porters.[5] To make the overland journey in 100 days was evidently regarded as something of an achievement in winter. Presumably most people would try to travel at a more favourable time of year.[6] The description of a typical immigrant in Juvenal 3.83 as 'brought to Rome' (*advectus Romam*) assumes arrival in a vehicle or at least on the back of a beast of burden rather than on foot. When the exiled Ptolemy VI is described by Diodorus as approaching Rome on foot, the intention is probably to emphasize his impoverishment.[7] Overland travel had the advantage over travelling by sea that someone with a marketable skill might be able to use it en route to finance the journey.[8]

Travel by ship was relatively speedy and was therefore usually seen as preferable; something like 30 days for a journey from Rome to Egypt was thought to be good, but travelling from east to west could take twice as long because of the prevailing winds.[9] Sea travel was also potentially very dangerous. Shipwreck and piracy are mentioned as equal dangers in legal texts, although piracy appears in reality to have been considerably less likely, at least while the *Pax Romana* was in force in the Mediterranean.[10] The fear of shipwreck may have been one of the reasons for potential travellers to ask for divine advice on whether or not to go by sea. Paul was shipwrecked three times during his travels around the eastern Mediterranean.[11] He and Josephus are among those recorded as being shipwrecked on their way to Rome, and the elite were equally vulnerable, since Marcus Aurelius was nearly wrecked in a very bad storm while sailing from Greece to Brindisi.[12]

The journey might begin in a very public manner, as people of importance could apparently expect to be seen off from their home port by a large escort. Augustine told his mother that he was going to the harbour to see off a friend when he was actually leaving himself, and (although this is a case of emigration *from* Rome), a large party saw off Paula at Ostia when she sailed for Palestine.[13] However, most travellers would perhaps have been more concerned with finding a suitable ship and negotiating the arrangements for their journey. This might in itself be problematic, especially in late antiquity, when the volume of shipping seems to have fallen substantially.[14] Passengers would normally need to provide not only the fare but also their own food and wine. Only drinking water and materials for preparing food were provided by the shipowner according to the normal *naulum* contract entered into by passenger and owner.[15] Fares were relatively cheap, however, and adult male passengers could sometimes work their passage.[16] The possibility of someone making the journey without basic supplies is illustrated by the story of the Egyptian monk Serapion (who had spent time at Athens and elsewhere): he sailed from Alexandria to Rome without provisions, and was maintained by the others on board.[17] What would happen to someone who did not inspire the charity of fellow-voyagers is stated nowhere, but in times of danger it was probably normal for people to share their provisions.[18] There may be a hint of dangers from others on board in a fragmentary second century AD papyrus letter from a woman to her 'son':[19]

> ...first and to choose either that you should remain or proceed to Rome. So, if you sail there...when are you likely to return? Be on your guard against those with whom you eat and drink.

People who made the larger part of their journey to Rome by sea would still complete it overland from Brindisi, Puteoli, Ostia or Portus (depending on date and starting place). Travellers from Greece normally arrived at Brindisi. Aulus Gellius (19.1) describes making the journey from Cassiopa (on Corcyra) to Brindisi in the company of a famous Stoic philosopher he had met at Athens, and 'a rich Greek man from Asia with, as we saw, much ornament and provision of goods and household'. This was the route followed by Galen in reverse when he left Rome to return to Pergamum; the slave whom he had left at Rome to sell up his house was told to go home via Sicily, however.[20]

Others came to Puteoli up to the first century AD. Josephus, travelling from Judaea with (he says) about six hundred other passengers, was shipwrecked in the Adriatic Sea, rescued by a ship of Cyrene, and landed at Puteoli.[21] Apollonius of Tyana sailed from Asia to Corinth to Sicily to Puteoli, and a favourable wind got him there in four days according to Philostratus, perhaps meaning from Corinth.[22]

Reaching the port was not necessarily the end of the dangers of the journey. The final stage, overland, was presumably when the Syrian sophist Pausanias had an accident in which he fell out of his carriage, injuring his back and left hand.[23] It may also have been the point at which R. Nahum of Gimzo was robbed at an inn of the gift he was bringing for the emperor.[24] Even in such a peaceful time as that of the Younger Pliny, there were two cases of prosperous men disappearing without trace while travelling in Italy,[25] and kidnapping travellers for use as agricultural slaves was said to be rife under Tiberius.[26] In the early third century, the bandit Bulla Felix specialized in robbing and kidnapping travellers:[27]

> For he learned of everybody that was setting out from Rome and everybody that was putting into port at Brindisi, and knew both who and how many there were, and what and how much they had.

Arrivals from Brindisi and Puteoli would reach Rome via the Via Appia. Those coming from Ostia and Portus would use the Via Ostiensis or Via Portuensis. The Historia Augusta claims that when Septimius Severus built the Septizodium (at the corner of the Palatine and the Circus Maximus), 'he had no other thought but that his building might present itself to those approaching from Africa'.[28] As the building would actually face those using the Via Appia, this appears to be an anachronism for Severus' own time.

ii. First impressions of Rome

Seeing the city for the first time must have made a great impression on someone arriving after a long journey.[29] By at least the mid-first century BC, Rome was so much larger than any other city that even an Alexandrian or Antiochene must have been impressed by its size. There are no direct first-hand accounts of what it felt like,[30] but some of the views expressed by characters in literature may reflect the experiences of the authors themselves when they first came to Rome.[31] Thus, the impact made on Virgil's character Tityrus may reflect how Virgil himself felt when first coming to Rome from northern Italy:[32]

> I was a simpleton, Meliboeus. I used to think that the city they call Rome was like our market-town, where we shepherds are accustomed to drive down our new-weaned lambs. Arguing from what I knew, from a dog's likeness to a puppy and a goat's to her kids, I measured big by little things. But I soon saw that Rome stands out above all other cities as the cypress soars above the drooping undergrowth.

Dionysius of Halicarnassus thought that the most impressive features of Rome were the aqueducts, roads and sewers.[33] Nearly 400 years later, it was still equally plausible for a writer who was himself an outsider to describe another outsider being impressed by the scale of the city, in this case Ammianus describing Constantius II's first visit to Rome in 357: [34]

> As soon as he entered Rome, the home of empire and of all perfection, he went to the Rostra and looked with amazement at the Forum, that sublime monument of pristine power; wherever he turned he was dazzled by the concentration of wonderful sights... When he surveyed the different regions of the city and its environs, lying along the slopes and on level ground within the circle of the seven hills, it seemed to him that whatever his eye first lit on took the palm.

Edwards (1996, 97–8) shows that Ammianus is far from giving a realistic description of the city as it existed at the time, since he conspicuously omits any reference to Christian monuments, but the sense of wonder can still be taken as genuine. People might be disappointed with the realities of life at Rome, but they were likely to be impressed, at least at first, by its physical setting.[35]

Most references to the city of Rome in rabbinic literature concern a visit there by a group of rabbis in AD 95: Gamaliel II, Eleazar b. Azariah, Joshua b. Ḥananiah and Aqiba.[36] There is a little anecdotal information about their experiences of the trip, giving more of an outsider's view than any other literary source.[37] They travelled by sea to Puteoli, and suffered from a lack of provisions on board ship: when Gamaliel had consumed all his bread, he had to rely on Joshua's flour.[38] They completed the journey from Puteoli to Rome on foot, and could hear the noise of Rome when they were still at Puteoli;[39] this is, as far as I know, the only reference to the fact that the city's noise must have been one of the most impressive things for a newcomer. They sailed home from Brindisi.[40]

There is disappointingly little information about what the stay at Rome of these or any other rabbis was actually like. One of them noticed that the dogs of Rome knew how to deceive men so that they could rob bakers' shops.[41] R. Aqiba sent out 'a member of his household' to buy some food in the market, which may indicate that they usually travelled with their servants, as would be expected for people of their status.[42] There is also a rather bizarre description of the whole city, apparently set at a somewhat later date:[43]

> Ulla said: Greek Italy is the great city of Rome, which covers an area of three hundred *parasangs* by three hundred. It has three hundred markets corresponding to the number of days of the solar year. The smallest of them is that of the poultry-sellers, which is sixteen *mil* by sixteen. The king dines every day in one of them. Everyone who resides in the city, even if he was not born there, receives a regular portion of food from the king's household, and so does everyone who was born there, even if he does not reside there. There are three thousand baths in it, and five

> hundred windows the smoke from which goes outside the wall. One side
> of it is bounded by the sea, one side by hills and mountains, one side by
> a barrier of iron, and one side by pebbly ground and swamp.

This is probably based on an eye-witness account from after the building of the Aurelianic Walls. It suggests that the size of the city was hard for a newcomer to take in, and that the smoke (as well as the noise) impressed people as they were approaching.

iii. Where to go when you reached Rome

A new arrival in Rome with relatives or friends already there would naturally turn to them first. They might already have been involved in arranging the move if it was part of a process of chain migration. The future emperor Severus apparently went to his consular relative Septimius Severus.[44] When his own sister and nephew arrived (after he had become emperor), they came to him and were rapidly sent home with gifts.[45]

Another possibility would be to go to someone influential; preferably someone with whom the newcomer had already had dealings, or at least someone who could be given a letter of introduction.[46] This might be the emperor himself. Diogenes, a professor of literature from Rhodes, came to Rome and went to pay his respects to Tiberius at the Palace, presumably in the expectation that some arrangements would be made for him.[47] Aelius Herodianus, a *grammaticus* from Alexandria, was received into the friendship of Marcus Aurelius when he came to Rome.[48] When a new emperor came to power, this might in itself encourage people who felt they had claims on him to come to Rome; Dio Chrysostom intended to travel to Rome when 'his old friend Nerva' became emperor, although he did not actually get there before Nerva's death.[49]

Alternatively, the approach could be to an aristocrat who might have reason to be sympathetic, perhaps because he was a patron of the new arrival's profession, or of the home area. When the poet Archias arrived at Rome in 102 BC, he was immediately taken into the house of the Luculli[50] – Cicero does not make clear whether this was just because they were well-known patrons of the arts, or because Archias had some previous connection with them. The complaints of Juvenal's Umbricius about how Greek hangers-on of great houses leave no room for native ones may be motivated by occurrences such as this.[51] In some cases, a tie of *hospitium* might exist between a provincial (presumably only an important one) and a Roman aristocrat, perhaps deriving from the aristocrat's term of office in the province, or from a hereditary link between families. Cicero, in a letter of 46 BC, refers to the *hospitium* relationship he had with a man named Lyso of Patrae, who had stayed at Rome for a year and 'almost lived' with Cicero.[52] Individual provincials who put up honorific inscriptions at Rome for leading Romans may have been immigrants to Rome marking useful ties (which they might have formed at home), or may have been sent to Rome specially to honour someone who had helped their home community. For example, Caerellius Pollittianus, proconsul of Macedonia, was honoured for 'innumerable benefits' by a number of men from Africa with the nomen Bon(i?)cius.[53]

Ammianus gives a cynical description of how the process of making the first contact worked in the fourth century, perhaps based on personal experience:[54]

> But nowadays, if you come as a respectable stranger from the provinces to pay a first call on a man who prides himself on his ample means, you will be received like a long-lost friend. You will be asked so many questions that you are driven to invent the answers, and you will be so surprised to find an important personage who has never seen you before paying earnest attention to your slender claims that you will be sorry that you did not visit Rome ten years earlier to enjoy such exceptional favour.

The favour rapidly declines, however, and a client who attends his patron for three years and is then absent for three days goes back to the bottom of the pecking order. Ammianus does not point out that the reason the new arrival would go to the wealthy man in the first place was (presumably) the hope of being provided with work, accommodation or useful contacts.

Membership of the church gave access to a more regularized system of contacts for newcomers. A Christian, at least one of standing, could expect to receive hospitality from fellow-Christians at Rome. Roman members of the Jesus movement met Paul even before he reached the city;[55] the fact that this was the practice of the first Christians suggests that it may have been borrowed from the Jews. Providing help for visitors was seen as an important use of Christian communal funds in the second century:[56]

> The wealthy and willing each gives what he wants as each sees fit, and what is collected is deposited with the president. He helps orphans and foreigners staying with us; in a word, he takes care of everyone in distress.

Considering the number of 'heretics' who made their way to Rome (see p. 126), the danger of hospitality being abused (in orthodox terms) increased. For example, Marcion was welcomed as a benefactor by the Roman church, who did not know about his doctrinally suspect past in Pontus.[57] This eventually led to the church hierarchy carrying letters of introduction (*litterae communicatoriae/formatae*) to show their orthodoxy.[58] Cyprian wrote to Rome to warn of a case where he had refused to give such letters.[59] In the fourth century, making contact became much easier as the number of Christian institutions proliferated, and the contacts could be of higher social standing as the elite gradually became christianized. The monk Serapion enquired for other monks and nuns when he arrived at Rome.[60] Athanasius, during a three-year stay in the city, lived with the emperor's aunt Eutropium and the senators Abuterius and Sperantius.[61]

Fellow-feeling could benefit members of other religions too. Josephus made the acquaintance of an influential Jewish actor named Aliturus.[62] When Apuleius' character Lucius comes to Rome as a devotee of the cult of Isis, he regularly attends the Isis temple in the Campus Martius and 'is received there not as a stranger'.[63] Augustine was a Manichaean when he arrived at Rome, and stayed at the house of a Manichaean auditor, where he fell seriously ill.[64]

Compatriots could also be expected to help, at least if the immigrant was of the appropriate social standing. Licinius Montanus of Cirta stayed with Fronto whenever he came to Rome, and had rights of *hospitium* with others.[65] Saller comments (1982, 185):

> This last clause suggests that a Roman aristocrat, especially a recent migrant who still had numerous ties with his *patria*, was expected to host provincial visitors as a routine duty, and so renew and strengthen his bonds with them.

The sons of Sardius Saturninus, another African, came to study and live with Fronto at Rome.[66] Apollonius of Tyana was allegedly helped at Rome by a tribune who had been a boy at Ephesus when Apollonius cured the city of the plague.[67] When Galen came to Rome from Pergamum, one of his first important patients was Eudemus, another Pergamene and a friend of his father's who had been at Rome for at least ten years.[68] Much earlier, when Ptolemy VI arrived in Rome as an exile, accompanied by a eunuch and three other slaves, he moved into the lodgings ('garret') of the Alexandrian painter Demetrius, until the Senate provided him with better accommodation.[69] According to Diodorus, he obtained Demetrius' address during the journey, and claimed his hospitality because as king he had often entertained him at Alexandria. Later, shared geographical origin might still be important among Christians. The Pannonian mother and daughter Nunita and Maximilla were commemorated in the S. Sebastiano catacomb by Lucceia, daughter of the Urban Prefect Viventius, who was himself a Pannonian.[70] The hospitality system must have operated on class lines, however: Fronto would presumably not have offered accommodation to an African mule-driver, although he might have pointed him in the direction of other African mule-drivers.

The first port of call for a new arrival might be an inn or wineshop, even if it was only a temporary halt before going on to pursue other contacts. This was allegedly the case for Septimius Severus before he met up with his relative:[71]

> On his arrival at Rome he chanced upon an innkeeper who was reading the Life of the emperor Hadrian at that very time.

Apollonius of Tyana and his companions are described as going to an inn near the gates when they first reached the city,[72] and in a story about the birth of Ablabius, who became Constantine's Praetorian Prefect, Eunapius writes:[73]

> A certain Egyptian of the class devoted to the study called astrology... pushed his way into one of the more expensive wineshops, and called out that he was parched after finishing a long journey...

While all these stories are unlikely to have any factual basis in themselves, they probably illustrate a general assumption about the behaviour of newcomers.

iv. Where to stay

Those who were not able to find accommodation through their contacts had to make use of the various sorts of lodging available at Rome.[74] A number of Latin words are used for rented accommodation, and the exact significance seems to vary between writers. A *caupona* ('inn') might provide rooms on a long-term basis as well as overnight accommodation for travellers.[75] Sidonius stayed in a *deversorium* ('lodging-house') in Trastevere, presumably a higher class one than some *deversoria* mentioned in literature.[76] Jerome lived in a *hospitiolum* ('guest-house') for three years after coming back from the East.[77] Paulinus stayed in a *hospitium* for his annual visit.[78] These types of accommodation must have varied considerably: Paulinus is unlikely to have stayed anywhere too down-market, but they would also have included the cheapest rental accommodation available, probably paid for on a daily basis.[79]

Rather than using ordinary lodging-houses, Jerome may have taken advantage of the *xenodochia* and *hospitia* which the Council of Nicaea decreed should be provided in all cities for poor and ill travellers.[80] His friends Pammachius and Fabiola founded the Xenodochium at Portus, which catered for travellers to and from Rome, not only destitute ones.[81] Melania and Pinianus went one better by opening up their own suburban house 'to the holy bishops and priests and all foreigners arriving'.[82] Some newcomers might have accommodation already arranged for them. Josephus, when he reached Rome, was able to go to the house which Vespasian had previously occupied as a private citizen.[83]

Another possibility for those unable to afford regular accommodation would be the erection of shanties, as seen in many expanding modern cities. These are probably what is meant by *tuguria* ('huts') when the word is used in an urban context, and a derogatory reference to 'the buildings of those who live outside the Porta Flumentana or in the Aemiliana' may have the same sort of thing in mind.[84] Huts erected within the city were liable to demolition as a fire-risk. Penalties for those who tried to build *'casas seu tuguria'* on the Campus Martius were enacted in 397.[85] The occupants of such accommodation would not necessarily be immigrants, since people already in Rome were liable to be made homeless through fire, flood, collapse or eviction, but it would be natural for poor newcomers to gravitate to such areas. The homeless who lived under bridges and in tombs, and begged on the Clivus Aricinus,[86] no doubt also included immigrants.

v. Finding work

For those who came to Rome as a career move, the nature of their profession would determine how they went about finding work. Augustine relied on word of mouth when he began to recruit students,[87] and Galen seems to have recruited patients in the same way, which would be normal for teachers and doctors. As already mentioned (pp. 95, 112), acquiring prominent students or patients might be the quickest way to establish a remunerative clientele.

Juvenal's Umbricius lists the jobs which 'Greeks' will do – teacher of grammar, rhetoric or geometry, painter, wrestling-master, fortune-teller, rope-dancer, doctor, magician – but the person he describes as turning his hand to all this is a 'hungry little Greek' (*Graeculus esuriens*),[88] presumably not someone who is really qualified, but some-one who is willing to pretend to be qualified at anything which will earn him a living. In reality, letters of recommendation would pre-sumably be the only way in which a foreigner's skills could be vouched for before they were put into practice, except in cases where the reputation arrived first.

Unfortunately there is no evidence at all about how unskilled or semi-skilled immigrants set about finding work. Foreigners could join the ranks of the unskilled hoping to be hired for the day, but the details of how the process worked are unknown. There may have been an informal system of agents who put newly arrived workers in touch with potential employers, as is often the case with modern immigrants, and it is likely that contacts within an existing immigrant group were used to find employment, or premises in the case of those intending to become self-employed.[89] A foreigner with capital would probably be at no disadvantage compared to an indigenous freeborn Roman in getting started, but both would have been in a less favourable position than an ex-slave with a patron's backing.

vi. Location of housing

The tendency of immigrant groups to cluster in specific areas of a city is well-known in studies of modern migration.[90] This may be partly a matter of choice by people who want to live among others of a similar background, and partly a matter of necessity if housing is difficult to obtain or landlords are liable to be prejudiced against foreigners. The existence of immigrant residential neighbourhoods can allow the preservation of separate identity at local level, through shared language, businesses and cultural organizations, in ways which would be too difficult if the same people were spread all over the city.[91]

There is no direct evidence of landlord prejudice at Rome, but housing was in short supply for everyone in the city. Trastevere is generally thought to have been the area of Rome where eastern immigrants tended to live, although the evidence is probably not as compelling as it is sometimes made to sound. According to MacMullen, 'The whole of this vast Regio of the city was largely from the eastern Mediterranean.'[92] The evidence is mainly the number of shrines of oriental cults located in the area (see p. 240), the (allegedly) high number of burials of Asian and Syrian ex-slaves on that side of the city (see p. 187), and a few literary references such as Philo's comment that the Jews of Rome mainly lived there.[93] Since both banks of the Tiber for a distance of about 2 km south of the Tiber Island seem to have been dominated by docks and warehouses,[94] Trastevere would have been close to much of the work which was available to immigrants. It was certainly an area where Christianity flourished early, partly among immigrants, and it seems to have been the most densely populated region of Rome.[95] However, detailed information about housing arrangements is completely lacking, so it is unclear whether within Trastevere there were separate streets or blocks of Syrians, Galatians, etc., or whether immigrants were crammed indiscriminately into the available accommodation.

The Aventine with its surroundings was also an important area in which foreigners could settle, at least until its gentrification in the first century AD.[96] Like Trastevere, it was outside the pomerium and therefore available for the use of foreign cults. It was also near the docks and warehouses, and it was another important area for the early Christians of Rome.[97]

There is a possible source of evidence for immigrants' residence in the names of some *vici*. If streets in a particular part of the city tended to derive their names from a certain area overseas, it is possible that immigrants from that area were predominant. It must be admitted, however, that this method would produce some completely erroneous results if applied to modern Rome. The *vicus Capitis Africae*,[98] running near the Colosseum roughly along the line of the modern Via della Navicella, may originally have been an area of African settlement, especially if the *vicus Stabuli Proconsulis*, *vicus Syrtis*, *vicus Byzacenus* and *vicus Capsensis* were all located in the same area.[99] However, Richardson (1992, 70–1), believes that it was named after an allegorical sculpted head of Africa, and therefore has no relation to the people who lived there.

There has been a tendency to assume that people who were buried together also lived together in the same part of Rome. Some catacombs contain clusters of burials which appear to belong to people from a similar background (see p. 188).[100] It *may* be true that these people all lived close to each other and to the catacomb, but it is not necessarily so, as Pietri (1976) has shown clearly that there is no automatic connection between where people lived and where they were buried. Therefore the occasional concentration of, for example, Galatian burials in a particular catacomb does not have to represent a Galatian residential area, although it could do so. In general, there is little firm evidence for any concentration of individual nationalities anywhere in residential Rome, although it is highly likely that such concentrations did exist. For newcomers to Rome, the support and companionship of compatriots or co-religionaries of their own status (as well as the patronage of those of higher status) may well have been crucial factors in adjusting to life in the city.

Notes

[1] André and Baslez 1993, 123–5; Chevallier 1988, 409; Aelius Ar. 26.94–104.

[2] Lucian, *Alex.* 53.

³ André and Baslez 1993, 388–409, 489.

⁴ Aelius Ar. 48.60–62 (tr. C.A. Behr; the descriptions of Aristides' ailments have been omitted); Duncan-Jones 1990, 25. Galen also made an overland journey from Pergamum on his first visit to Rome (and probably his second), travelling through Thrace and Macedonia on the Via Egnatia: Nutton 1973, 168; Galen 12.171. Cf. the description of a much more comfortable journey from Gaul by Sidonius, *Ep.* 1.5, but most people are hardly likely to have had his network of friends and relatives to stay with, or his access to the *cursus publicus*, including its river transport.

⁵ André and Baslez 1993, 473–7.

⁶ André and Baslez 1993, 486. For example, Symmachus (*Ep.* 4.63) refers to travel 'as soon as the spring sailing-season opens the sea'.

⁷ Diod.Sic. 31.18.1.

⁸ André and Baslez 1993, 469.

⁹ Duncan-Jones 1990, 17, 26; André and Baslez 1993, 487: Rutilius Namatianus preferred to travel by sea from Rome to Cisalpine Gaul, but was becalmed at the mouth of the Tiber for fifteen days. Ibid. 489: it was possible to travel from Ostia to Africa in one day, from Ostia to Cadiz in seven, and from Puteoli to Alexandria in nine. However, Duncan-Jones shows that these times were exceptionally fast.

¹⁰ e.g. Digest 4.9.3.1 Labeo.

¹¹ 2 Cor. 11.25.

¹² SHA, *Marcus* 27.2.

¹³ Gorce 1925, 106–7.

¹⁴ Duncan-Jones 1990, 29. In the early 5th century, Synesius (*Ep.* 147) gave as an excuse for the non-payment of tribute that no ships sailed from Cyrene to the capital.

¹⁵ André and Baslez 1993, 424; Digest 20.4.6, 30.1.39.1. Digest 4.9.4.2 Vivianus mentions clothing and a daily food supply as items which might be taken on to a ship in addition to the real cargo.

¹⁶ André and Baslez 1993, 424.

¹⁷ Palladius, *H.L.* 1.66.

¹⁸ Midrash Eccl.R. 11.1.

¹⁹ P.Mert. ii 81 (ed. B.R. Rees, H.I. Bell, J.W.B. Barns).

²⁰ Galen 12.648–9.

²¹ Josephus, *Vita* 15.

²² Philostratus, *Ap.T.* 7.10.

²³ Galen 8.213.

²⁴ JE xii 796; Ginzberg 1925–38, vol. 4, 203.

²⁵ Pliny, *Ep.* 6.25.

²⁶ Suetonius, *Aug.* 32, *Tib.* 8.

²⁷ Dio 77.10.2 (tr. E. Cary).

²⁸ SHA, *Sev.* 24; Richardson 1992, 350.

²⁹ André and Baslez 1993, 153–60; Edwards 1996, 15–16, although, as she notes (p. 111), this perspective is rarely found in literature.

³⁰ Aelius Aristides 26 does perhaps reflect some of his first impressions, particularly in his emphasis on the height of the buildings ('the cities which

are now up in the air'), but with very heavy oratorical embellishments. Balsdon (1979, 208) comments: 'There is nothing in it to suggest that Aristides knew anything at all about Roman history or that he was interested in the city of Rome itself.' Cf. the other writers quoted by Dudley (1967, 219–27) in praise of Rome.

[31] Cf. Dyson and Prior 1995.

[32] Virgil, *Ecl.* 1.19–25 (tr. E.V. Rieu).

[33] Dion.Hal., *Ant.Rom.* 3.67.5; it is unclear whether he is thinking of the city only, or of the empire as a whole.

[34] Ammianus 16.10.12–14 (tr. W. Hamilton).

[35] Cf. Edwards 1996, 129.

[36] References include: b. 'Abod.Zar. 54b; Midrash Gen.R. 13.9, 20.4; Midrash Ex.R. 30.9; Midrash Deut.R. 2.24; Midrash Eccl.R. 10.7. Some or all of these men probably made more than one visit: Solin 1983, 660.

[37] The historicity of any details about this trip or any other 'factual' event in rabbinic literature is of course very questionable, but the impressions of Rome may be real ones experienced by travellers, if not necessarily by the rabbis to whom they are attributed.

[38] b. Hor. 10a.

[39] b. Makk. 24a = Midrash Lam.R. 5.18; b. Yoma 20b. Bacher (1896, 195–6) suggests reading 'Palatine' rather than 'Puteoli', on the incontestable grounds that it would not be possible to hear the noise of Rome from Puteoli, but it seems more likely that the passage is deliberately exaggerating to make its point.

[40] m. Erubim 4.1.

[41] Midrash Gen.R. 22.6, attributed to a R. Tanḥum.

[42] Midrash Ruth 6.1.

[43] b. Meg. 6b (tr. M. Simon). Cf. the discussion by Bacher (1896). Part of the passage was discussed above, p. 48.

[44] SHA, *Sev.* 1.

[45] SHA, *Sev.* 15.

[46] André and Baslez 1993, 452–4.

[47] Suetonius, *Tib.* 32.

[48] PIR i² A189.

[49] Jones 1978, 52; Dio Chrys., *Or.* 45.2.

[50] Cicero, *pro Archia* 4–5.

[51] Juvenal 3.119–122.

[52] Cicero, *ad Fam.* 13.19. The 'almost' seems to show that Lyso frequently visited but did not actually live in Cicero's house.

[53] CIL vi 1366; PIR² C159.

[54] Ammianus 14.6.12 (tr. W. Hamilton).

[55] Acts 28.15.

[56] Justin Martyr, *Apol.* 1.67 (tr. Beard, North and Price 1998, vol. 2, no. 12.7d).

[57] Bardy 1948, 100.

[58] Gorce 1925, 173.

[59] Cyprian, *Ep.* 29.

[60] Palladius, *H.L.* 1.66.

[61] Gorce 1925, 139.

[62] Josephus, *Vita* 16.

[63] Apuleius, *Met.* 11.29; La Piana 1927, 337.

[64] Augustine, *Conf.* 5.9–10.

[65] Fronto, *ad Amicos* 1.3 = Loeb vol. 2, 278–283. As noted above, *hospitium* could exist between Romans and provincials as well as between compatriots.

[66] Fronto, *ad Amicos.* 1.9; Saller 1982, 184; Champlin 1980, 15.

[67] Philostratus, *Ap.T.* 7.21.

[68] Nutton 1973, 159; PIR² E109.

[69] Diod.Sic. 31.18; Valerius Maximus 5.1.

[70] ICUR 13355; Bertolino 1997, 117.

[71] SHA, *Sev.* 2.

[72] Philostratus, *Ap.T.* 4.39.

[73] Eunapius, *V.Ph.* 463 (tr. W.C. Wright).

[74] André and Baslez 1993, 461–5. Cf. Frier 1980 on the types of accommodation.

[75] Digest 4.9.6.3 Paul.

[76] Sidonius, *Ep.* 1.5.9; Gorce 1925, 142.

[77] Gorce 1925, 142; cf. the usage of the word by Jerome, *Comm. in Is.* 58.7 (PL 24.566), *Comm. in Matth.* 8.20 (PL 26.53), where it represents the cheapest form of accommodation available.

[78] Gorce 1925, 142.

[79] Scobie 1986, 402.

[80] Council of Nicaea, *Canon* 75; Gorce 1925, 147.

[81] Jerome, *Ep.* 66.11, 77.10; he calls the building both *hospitium* and *xenodochium*.

[82] *Vita S.Melaniae* 7; Gorce 1925, 150.

[83] Josephus, *Vita* 423.

[84] Varro, *R.R.* 3.2.6. Cf. Scobie 1986, 402.

[85] C.Theo. 14.14.1. The punishment was perpetual exile.

[86] Martial 10.5.

[87] Augustine, *Conf.* 5.12.

[88] Juvenal 3.74–8.

[89] Cf. Marett 1989, 81, 96.

[90] Panayi 1994, 4.

[91] Panayi 1994, 78.

[92] MacMullen 1993, 62–63.

[93] Philo, *Leg.* 155: Augustus knew that 'the great section of Rome cut off across the Tiber was occupied and inhabited by Jews'.

[94] Castagnoli 1980.

[95] Cracco Ruggini 1997, 177–8; Lampe 1989, 38–42.

[96] La Piana 1927, 213–15; Balsdon 1979, 16; Lampe 1989, 46.

[97] Walters 1998, 176; Lampe 1989, 13, 30, 46–8, 52. Lampe's doubts about the presence of Christians there in the 1st–2nd centuries AD rest on the absence of specific evidence for Jews there, which is not in itself very significant and in any case does not exclude Christians of non-Jewish background.

[98] This area contained the Paedagogium of the imperial pages, but it seems unnecessary to imagine that they were of African origin (Bardy, 1948, 96), as the toponym was surely established before then. It was a well-known name: according to the *Appendix Probi* (Keil, *Gramm.Lat.* iv, 198), one should write *vicocapitis Africae* not *vicocaput Africae*. An imperial slave commemorated his son as *Caputafricesi* (CIL vi 8987).

[99] La Piana 1925, 226; 1927, 220–1.

[100] The possibility of a residential area of Armenians in the Via Appia area is suggested by Lega and Ricci 1997, on the basis of two epitaphs found there.

Chapter 7

ASPECTS OF FOREIGNERS' LIVES AT ROME

This chapter looks at some of the institutions and practices which may have been shared by foreigners who had settled at Rome, and which perhaps contributed to feelings of solidarity, or at least of separateness from the indigenous population. It deals with them mainly in general terms; those specifically applicable to only one group will be examined in the relevant part of ch. 8. After discussion of the importance of group identity, it looks first at institutions which facilitated contact with 'home' and then at various ways in which, directly or indirectly, people might preserve some of the culture of their homelands while they lived at Rome.

i. Group identity – and lack of it

The extent to which foreigners felt any sense of identity with others from the same area must have varied considerably. Alexandrians may have felt strong solidarity with each other but little or none with people from the rest of Egypt.[1] Jews from Asia perhaps had more in common with Jews from elsewhere than with other people from Asia. Some newcomers to Rome were undoubtedly anxious to take on a 'Roman' identity, and slaves and ex-slaves may have had more loyalty to their household than to their homeland (see p. 11). Considerations of class may have played a part in this too: for example, Champlin (1980, 16) believes that the African elite who moved to Rome in the second century AD were particularly anxious to play down their non-Latin heritage at a time when the Punic language was associated with ignorance. Thus, while it is possible to see ways in which some foreigners maintained a degree of separateness or communal identity in particular aspects of their lives, it is not possible to assess how widespread this was among foreigners in general. As noted above (p. 9), those who preferred to blend into the Roman background are now largely invisible in the sources. Non-Roman names[2] or incidental biographical details may give away the origin of a few, but such cases must be exceptional.

La Piana was the first to pay serious attention to the question of how far foreigners preserved a separate identity at Rome, approaching it primarily from the perspective of the history of the early Christians there:[3]

> ...first of all, it seems that the various foreign races which had a large representation in Rome formed at times special groups bound together by their common origin from the same province or from the same city, by their common traditions, and yet more by their peculiar religious cults of national deities. Through the process of adaptation and amalgamation those groups would be continually losing individuals and families merged in the racial mixture or fortunate enough to climb to the upper Roman classes, but the loss of these was more than offset by newcomers who filled the gaps and perpetuated the existence of the groups as long as the stream of migration continued to flow. Moreover, the process of absorption of the foreign elements into the general environment was very slow.

He thought that there was a tendency to maintain some aspects of separateness (in terms of language and customs) while immigration continued; the implication is that once immigration ceased, a group would lose its identity and become integrated into the city. I have already argued (p. 59) that immigration never did cease in the period under consideration, but it will be suggested below that the preservation of separateness, or at least exclusiveness, was more the exception than the rule, and that the forms which it took varied very much from one group to another.

The type of separate identity which was felt by foreign groups in Rome invites the use of the modern terminology of ethnicity. Panayi (1994, 5) defines ethnicity as:

> ...the way in which members of a national, racial or religious grouping maintain an identity with people of the same background in a variety of official and unofficial ways.

The ways may include residence, marriage, and religious or social activity. In some cases, the sense of ethnicity can be encouraged from above, when leading members of an immigrant community, or even natives of the host community, develop institutions for religion, education or philanthropy targeted specifically at the immigrant group. Some modern immigrant groups have worried about losing their identity and have consciously formed their own cultural and social organizations to try to preserve it.[4] Hall (1997, ch. 2) adds some other considerations in his discussion of Ancient Greek ethnic identity:[5] the difference between *criteria* which really determine ethnicity and *indicia* which merely denote it; the association with common territory and (real or imagined) common descent; the dependence of one ethnic identity on other opposing ethnic identities to give it its self-definition.

The extent to which an immigrant group can preserve a separate identity may be influenced by the demographic make-up of the group, irrespective of the wishes or intentions of the members. If a substantial majority of the immigrants are young males, as was probably the case at Rome (see p. 66), many are likely to have to marry outside their group, simply through lack of alternative; their children are therefore much less likely to consider themselves members of the group. According to Panayi (1994, 18), black ethnicity developed in London by the end of the eighteenth century, but disappeared in the nineteenth century because black immigration dried up and the lack of women forced men to marry out.

On Panayi's and Hall's definitions, the Jews of Rome would count as an ethnic group, even though they were not necessarily homogenous racially (as there would have been both proselytes and descendants of Jews from the land of Israel) or socially (new immigrants would be mixed with people whose ancestors had been in Rome for many generations), since an exclusive religion with a notional common homeland and common ancestors provided the basis of their shared identity. People from Egypt as a whole would not count as an ethnic group, although Alexandrians would, certainly according to Hall's requirements. Some foreigners at Rome clearly felt that there was more to their identity than their place of origin, like the woman whose epitaph reads: 'My race was Greek, my homeland was Apamea';[6] a sense of Greek ethnicity might override basic geographical criteria. However, apart from such extreme cases, it is now very difficult to assess how people in Rome saw themselves in ethnic, rather than more rudimentarily geographical, terms. Writers such as Juvenal (or at least some of his characters) were happy to use labels like Egyptian, Syrian and Greek, but perhaps in ways which the people so labelled would never have used about themselves.[7] When someone described a deceased relative as *Galla*, it might mean that she was an inhabitant of the province(s) of Gaul rather than another province, a member of the 'race' of Gauls rather than another race, an inhabitant of Gaul as a whole rather than of Lyon or Narbonne, or someone who happened to have been born in Gaul rather than at Rome.[8] Reaction to romanization might in itself encourage the formation of new local identities,[9] and such identities might even be expressed more readily at Rome than they would be at home – identification primarily with a town or village while at home might be replaced by identification with a region or province while at Rome.[10] Most of the discussion which follows will therefore concentrate on shared geographical origin, which is slightly less difficult to determine than shared ethnic identity on the basis of the evidence we have.

It is possible to look for signs that foreigners at Rome tried to preserve their separate identity, but much harder to look for signs that they did not, just as individual foreigners are unlikely to be detectable in the epigraphic evidence unless they or their commemorators deliberately made themselves detectable. If they wished to blend into the background, they would not leave inscriptions recording special practices in, for example, religious cult or naming patterns. It should therefore be remembered that the evidence is heavily biased towards those who left traces of separateness, in epigraphy or literature, and away from those who did not. It was suggested above (p. 78) that slaves were acculturated more quickly than free immigrants, and it is therefore among the free foreigners resident at Rome that traces of separate identity are most likely to survive.

ii. *Stationes*

The institution run by foreigners at Rome and Ostia which has left the most obvious trace is the *statio*. A substantial number of inscriptions have survived in both Greek (at Rome) and Latin (at Ostia) referring to buildings called *stationes*. Their exact function is not specified anywhere, but they were closely associated with traders and shipowners from specific cities or areas. They sometimes contained statues of emperors and gods. Apart from one for Tibur,[11] the known ones from Rome are nearly all for eastern Mediterranean cities, with inscriptions in Greek which were presumably meant to be read by others from the same area rather than by Roman passers-by.[12] Most of the *statio* inscriptions from Rome were found in the Via Sacra in front of the Temples of Romulus and of Antoninus and Faustina, near the Porticus Margaritaria, suggesting that the *stationes* had a prominent and prestigious location in the late second/third century AD, the period to which most of the inscriptions have been assigned.[13] The buildings themselves have not been preserved. Their existence began earlier than the date of the inscriptions: there is a reference from the time of Nero (see below), and, according to the Elder Pliny, Vespasian located the *stationes municipiorum* in Caesar's Forum.[14]

The following *stationes* are known at Rome:
• Anazarbus (Cilicia). IGUR 78: a third-century inscription from the Via Sacra. The identification of the city is based on Moretti's interpretation.[15]
• Ephesus (Asia). IGUR 26 is a building dedication to Antoninus Pius and Marcus Aurelius, and to the shipowners and traders of Ephesus,

probably by M. Ulpius Domesticus (the name is restored). Although not from a *statio* itself, it implies the existence of an Ephesian trading organization.

• Heraclea. Moretti thinks that IGUR 88, a marble base of the late second or third century found in the Basilica Aemilia with a dedication to Heracles 'the god of the homeland', probably denotes a *statio* for one of the numerous cities called Heraclea.

• Mopsuestia (Cilicia). IGUR 24, a marble base with a Greek dedication to Antoninus Pius, dated AD 140, may be from an otherwise unknown *statio* according to Moretti.

• Noricum. CIL vi 250 = 30723, a dedication in Latin to the Genius Noricorum by L. Iulius Bassus, their *stationarius*.[16] This *statio* is the only one at Rome that was organized by a province rather than a city, and the only one from Europe.

• Nysa (Asia). According to Moretti's interpretation of IGUR 162, a second-century cippus with a dedication to Hestia by Iulius Maior Antoninus, it may come from a meeting-place for Nysans at Rome.[17]

• Sardis (Asia). Probably the city in the fragmentary IGUR 85. IGUR 86–7, with dedications to 'the virgin goddess of the Sardians', may come from the same building.

• Tarsus (Cilicia). IGUR 79, a third-century inscription from the Via Sacra. A marble base honouring Gordian III probably comes from the same building.[18]

• Tiberias and Claudiopolis (Syria Palestina). IGUR 82, 83; the latter is the base of a statue of a woman, dated to the late second or third century.

• Tralles (Asia). IGUR 84: the *statio* was built 'from the foundations' by ...lia Galene for her homeland (*patris*), in the time of Caracalla or Elagabalus.

• Tyre (Syria). The existence of a Tyrian *statio*, probably in the Forum, is known indirectly. In AD 179, the members of the Tyrian *statio* at Puteoli wrote to the city-council of Tyre complaining that they were unable to pay their rent, and that the *statio* at Rome had ceased to make an annual contribution of 100,000 denarii to them.[19] The Roman *statio*, unlike the one at Puteoli when the letter was written, received financial contributions from Tyrian shipowners and merchants.

At Ostia, the *stationes* were small rooms arranged in a double colonnade around the so-called Piazzale delle Corporazioni. Not all the rooms were used by overseas traders; some were for local guilds. The rooms had mosaics in front of them which depicted the name of the place represented, sometimes with symbols of its produce. The mosaics overlaid an earlier set, so do not belong to the Augustan date of the colonnade itself, but probably to the late second/early third century AD; i.e. the same period as the *statio* inscriptions from Rome.[20] Occasionally the representatives of different cities apparently co-operated with each other, as there is also a statue set up to a patron by 'the masters of all the African and Sardinian ships'.[21] A pediment with the inscription *naviculari Africani* ('African shipowners') was found on the eastern side of the colonnade, and cannot have belonged to one of the individual rooms.[22]

The following cities are recorded as having *stationes* at Ostia. The number after CIL xiv 4549 indicates the number of the *statio* in the layout of the colonnade.

• Alexandria. CIL xiv 4549.40. *[Ale]xandrin[i]/[orum]* is the probable restoration.[23] A dedication to Commodus by the shipowners (ναύκληροι) of the Alexandrian fleet was found at Portus.[24]

• Carales (Sardinia). CIL xiv 4549.21. The mosaic of the *navi(cularii) et negotiantes Karalitani* depicts a ship and two corn measures, showing the importance of the corn trade from Sardinia.[25]

• Carthage. CIL xiv 4549.18.

• Curubis (Africa). CIL xiv 4549.34. If part of the inscription is correctly interpreted as *s(tatio) n(egotiatorum) f(rumentariorum) c(oloniae) C(urubitanae)*, the traders are specifically said to be corn-merchants.

• Gaza (Syria Palestina). A dedication from Portus (so not found in the Piazzale) has the city of Gaza honouring Gordian according to the order of 'the ancestral god'.[26] This was presumably set up by a Gazan trading organization.

• Gummi (Africa). CIL xiv 4549.17. The mosaic depicts a corn-measure.

• Hippo Diarrhytus (Africa). CIL xiv 4549.12.

• Hippo Regius (Africa). P. Aufidius Fortis, who was a *decurio* both at Ostia and at Hippo Regius, was also *quinquennalis* of the Guild of Corn-Merchants at Ostia.[27] His presence may indicate that Hippo Regius had a *statio* at Ostia.

• Mauretania Caesariensis. CIL xiv 4549.48. This is the probable interpretation of the letters *M.C.* between two jars of wine and two date palms in a mosaic.[28] If so, it is the only Ostian *statio* for a province rather than a city.

• Misya (Africa). CIL xiv 4549.10. The mosaic of the *navicularii* depicts two ships.

• Musluvium (Mauretania). CIL xiv 4549.11. The restoration of the name *Mu[s]lu[vit]a[ni]* is not certain.

• Narbonne. CIL xiv 4549.32. The mosaic depicts a ship and the Claudian lighthouse of Ostia.[29]

- Sabratha (Africa). CIL xiv 4549.14. The mosaic with the inscription *stat(io) Sabratensium* depicts an elephant, probably reflecting the trade in ivory.[30]
- Syllectum (Africa). CIL xiv 4549.23. The mosaic of the shipowners from Syllectum depicts two ships and the Claudian lighthouse of Ostia.[31] There is also an epitaph for a man from Syllectum who died at Ostia.[32] Meiggs (1960, 287) thinks that the trade from there was probably mainly in oil.
- Turris Libisonis (Sardinia). CIL xiv 4549.19.
- Meiggs (1960, 286) also believes that Arles may be symbolized by a mosaic depiction of the confluence of a river, probably the Rhône.

If the Tyrian *stationes* of Rome and Puteoli were typical, they were not entirely autonomous organizations, but were subject, at least in theory, to their home city councils. They also had some involvement in the cult of the gods of the homeland. In the case of cities involved in Rome's corn supply, the *stationes* probably acted as intermediaries between the shipowners and the office of the *Annona*. The Tyrians at Puteoli apparently should have been financially self-supporting, and only had to ask for a subsidy from Tyre because of the difficulties they were experiencing. Although their financial arrangements are unknown, the rarity of the names of individual benefactors probably suggests that contributions from a number of users were more common than dependence on an individual patron.

The nature of the *statio* buildings at Rome is unclear: they may have contained storage and retail facilities,[33] but it seems unlikely that there would have been extensive warehousing at their site away from the docks.[34] They were apparently hired directly from the state, as a would-be private landlord in the time of Nero found himself in trouble:[35]

> Salvidienus Orfitus was accused of hiring out three shops in his house around the Forum to cities for use as a *statio*.

The *stationes* in the Piazzale delle Corporazioni at Ostia were extremely small, and could not have accommodated more than a few people at one time, let alone any retail goods. They probably served as offices for taking orders and making business arrangements.[36] It is not clear whether the *stationes* had only commercial functions or whether they could act as a focus for social activities too. Pleket (1993, 16) takes the latter view, that they 'were centres for traders from those cities or for citizens who lived in Rome for other purposes'. La Piana (1925, 255) sees them as entirely commercial, however:

> Evidently they were merely headquarters of the foreign merchants,

meeting-places for their officers, and reference-bureaus for all purposes concerning their associations.

The small size of the Ostian *stationes* would certainly have prevented any large-scale social activity from taking place inside them, although it could still have been organized and publicized from them.

iii. Contact with the homeland

The *stationes* certainly formed part of a commercial network between Rome or Ostia and the homeland, and may have facilitated communication between the two, perhaps, for example, providing information about ships coming to or returning from Italy. Individual foreigners living at Rome could remain in touch with their family and friends at home by letter, but there must have been considerable difficulty in getting letters delivered over a long distance for people who were not important enough to use the *cursus publicus*, and the *stationes* could have been useful in this respect. Otherwise, it would normally be necessary to know someone who was going to make the journey. The lack of official addresses, and in some cases of a permanent place of residence, could also mean that the person delivering the letter needed to know the recipient personally. One surviving letter has instructions for how it is to be forwarded first to Alexandria and then on to the family in Philadelphia.[37] The chances of such correspondence going astray must have been high.

The speaker Aper in Tacitus' *Dialogus* (20.4) comments on students sending letters home. Martial sent a book home to Bilbilis, and assumed that people there would have up-to-date information about his success at Rome and his praise of Bilbilis, implying the existence of a regular news link between the two places.[38] He suggests that the home cities of well-known writers working at Rome always take pride in the successes of their famous sons, although he is of course hardly a disinterested witness. The fact that less well-connected people could also get letters delivered successfully is shown by the preservation of several papyrus letters which were written at Rome and apparently received safely in Egypt. Since there are very few of these, they may, however, be the exception rather than the rule; the surviving ones are from soldiers, sailors or traders, people with the best access to communication networks. Their content tends not to be very informative, and it was perhaps the sending of a letter at all, showing that the sender was alive and well, which was more important than anything which he or she had to say.

Apollinarius, probably a soldier, wrote to Egypt from Rome, to a friend or relative ('most esteemed brother') Sempronius of Karanis, in the early second century; Sempronius had previously been at Rome himself, but left before Apollinarius arrived there, and Apollinarius sent 'our (man) Eros' back home.[39]

Another Apollinarius wrote two letters to his mother Taesion/Taesis, who lived at Karanis, in the second century.[40] He had joined the Roman fleet and travelled via Cyrene to Portus, where he wrote his first letter. He asks his mother to write to him, revealing how such a letter would be sent: 'If you do not find anybody coming to me, write to Socrates and he forwards it to me.' He sends greetings to various people at home, and passes on greetings from someone called Asclepiades. In the second letter he writes:

> I wish you to know, mother, that I arrived in Rome in good health on the fifth of the month Pachon and was assigned to Misenum. But I have not yet learned my century, for I had not gone to Misenum when I wrote you this letter.

This letter also ends with numerous greetings to people at home. The two letters are completely different from each other in writing, style and spelling, so presumably at least one was not written by Apollinarius personally.

Another second-century letter mentions a journey to Rome via Syria, Asia and Greece; the last preserved line contains the phrase 'from Rome to Alexandria'. There is a reference to purple dye, and it appears to have been a trading trip. The editors think that the writer was yet another Apollinarius, the recipient of a letter sent to him probably at Rome by Rullius, complaining about the lack of a letter from him and asking him:[41]

> Send the white cottons, as I requested of you when I was with you, to Menon. 'If there are soft ones', he said when he was with you, 'let them be sent from Rome.'

Another letter sent by someone who had only gone to Rome briefly went from Irenaeus, a sailor on the grain fleet, to his 'brother' Apollinarius, reporting that the ship had arrived on June 30th, he had gone up to Rome on July 9th, and the fleet was still awaiting its discharge papers when he wrote the letter on August 2nd.[42] Presumably someone sailing on a private ship took the letter. The presence in Rome for at least fifteen days of considerable numbers of Egyptian sailors with money to spend and little to do must have been good for some businesses in the city. It would also have been a good opportunity for the delivery of letters from Egypt, and for Egyptians settled at Rome to send letters home.

This sort of evidence for continued contact between immigrants and their homes is only available for people from Egypt. Another possible source, although in a different and very limited way, is epigraphy. It is occasionally possible to detect the same people in inscriptions at home and at Rome, but the chronological sequence is not always clear. Aurelius Ingenuus, a Dacian praetorian in the early third century who died aged 25 and was commemorated by his brother at Rome, seems previously to have commemorated his mother and sister at Sarmizegethusa while he was still an ordinary legionary.[43] Iulius Modestus, an *urbanicianus*, along with two legionary brothers and a sister, commemorated another brother at Lambaesis.[44] P. Clodius Athenio, a merchant from Malaga who built a family tomb at Rome, is also mentioned in an inscription from Malaga.[45] C. Cornelius Iunianus, who died at Rome aged 18, previously made a dedication to his brother at home at Saetabis in Hispania Citerior.[46] Identifying such cases from inscriptions is largely fortuitous, and it is likely that they represent a more widespread phenomenon of people maintaining strong links with their homes, although some may simply date from shortly before and shortly after those involved moved to Rome.

People who continued to own property in their homeland would have to remain in close contact with whoever looked after it for them.[47] Special legal concessions were made to senators' freedmen who managed their home property.[48] However, the owner's personal intervention might be required at times: the future emperor Septimius Severus went home after being quaestor to settle affairs after his father's death.[49] Provincial property could apparently be bought and sold at Rome, however, so not all business required returning home.[50] Until the second century, property-owners below senatorial rank might also have financial responsibilities to their home cities, if they were rich enough to be liable for civic *munera*.[51] They were therefore theoretically liable to be called back home to hold office there and spend their money on their home cities, although there is no evidence for this actually happening to anyone who had taken up residence at Rome.

People who achieved senatorial status and, effectively and for legal purposes, transferred their main residence to Rome (see p. 98) could still be anxious to emphasize their achievement at home. Talbert (1984, 36) lists a number of inscriptions in which people are recorded as the first from their homeland to become a senator or hold a particular office. This could extend to such a detailed claim as being:[52]

> The fifth man ever to enter the Senate from the whole of Asia, and from Miletus and the rest of Ionia the first and only one.

Those who remained at home could still take pride in being described as the relative of a senator.[53]

Some people from the office-holding class continued to make benefactions at home while living at Rome. Claudius' doctor C. Stertinius Xenophon of Cos used his influence to get the island freed from taxation, and erected new buildings and restored old ones at the sanctuary of Asclepius there, although he also acquired estates of his own in the Naples area.[54] L. Minicius Natalis (cos.106) and his son L. Minicius Natalis Quadronius Verus (cos.139) were from Barcelona, where they continued to own land on which, in the early 120s, they built baths, porticoes and an aqueduct.[55] L. Cuspius Pactumeius Rufinus, cos.142, originally from Pergamum, was staying there again in *c.* 145, and built a temple of Zeus Asclepius, being honoured as 'the benefactor and founder of the fatherland'.[56] Bowersock (1969, 29) suggests that the second century was a time at which people who made an impression at Rome would still be benefactors to their own cities; later, concentrating on their careers at Rome made them neglect their homelands. Senators had exemption from performing *munera* in their home cities, but there are numerous examples of them declining to take advantage of this.[57]

There is evidence for some particular forms of ongoing contact between the Jews of Rome and the land of Israel which will be discussed at p. 266. The basis of this was theological and institutional rather than personal, so it is very different from the sorts of contact discussed above.

iv. Homesickness

The possibility of an immigrant deciding that a mistake had been made and leaving Rome quickly was discussed at p. 89. Such occurrences are, inevitably, unlikely to be mentioned in any type of source. There is, however, rather more evidence about how some people remained very attached to their original homes during a prolonged absence. Martial (10.103) said that, although he left Bilbilis 34 years previously, it still owed him as much as Verona owed Catullus for making it famous. He also becomes lyrical about the virtues of his home in a poem written to celebrate his impending return there, beginning:[58]

> That I should too often talk of far-off peoples, Avitus,
> When I have grown old in the city, should not surprise you,
> And that I should thirst for gold-bearing Tagus and my native Salo,
> And return to the rough countryside of a replete cottage.

167

Lucian has this sort of nostalgia in mind when he describes how migrants in general (he does not particularly mean at Rome) can become increasingly attached to 'home':[59]

> No-one was ever known to be so forgetful of his country as to care nothing for it when he was in another state. No, those who get on badly in foreign parts continually cry out that one's own country is the greatest of all blessings, while those who get on well, however successful they may be in all else, think that they lack one thing at least, a thing of the greatest importance, in that they do not live in their own country but sojourn in a strange land; for thus to sojourn is a reproach! And men who during their years abroad have become illustrious through acquisition of wealth, through renown from office-holding, through testimony to their culture, or through praise of their bravery, can be seen hurrying one and all to their native land, as if they thought they could not anywhere else find better people before whom to display the evidences of their success. The more a man is esteemed elsewhere, the more eager is he to regain his own country.

The concept of homesickness is rarely mentioned directly, although philosophical writers acknowledged its existence by frequently arguing that being far away from your homeland was not in itself a bad thing. People such as Ovid wrote about the feelings caused by their absence *from* Rome.[60] There is no Greek or Latin word with precisely the same meaning as homesickness, but Athenaeus, writing about a man called Larensis, says: [61]

> Again by his invitations to hospitality he made all feel that Rome was their native land. For who can suffer from homesickness (τὰ οἴκοι ποθεῖ; literally 'miss the things at home') when in the company of one who keeps his house wide open to his friends?

A Latin inscription from an altar may also refer to homesickness, although it could be the dangers of the journey which the writer had in mind:[62]

> In a foreign place, you should ask the god that you can return to your people safe and sound.

The cure for homesickness was of course return, which was discussed at p. 53. Someone who appears to have been desperate to return home wrote the following enigmatic curse in Greek on a lead tablet, probably in the third century AD:[63]

> Bind Artemidorus the doctor of the third cohort in the Praetorian Camp. The brother of the late Demetrius is (your?) servant,[64] who wishes now to go away to his own land. So do not allow(?) him,[65] but bind the Italian

land, strike(?) the gates[66] of Rome. But bind Artemidorus, the son of
Artemidorus the doctor. (A list of divine or magical names follows.)

The person for whom the curse was written, presumably Demetrius'
brother, was angry at Artemidorus, Italy and the 'gates of Rome' for
preventing him from returning home. Gager thinks that he was
a slave, but there are many possible reasons why a free immigrant
might be forced to stay at Rome unwillingly. The desperation of this
man was no doubt felt by many other immigrants, but only his words
have survived.

v. Language

Language can be a significant factor in the acculturation of immigrant
groups (if they quickly adopt the language of the host community), or
in the preservation of a separate identity (if they consciously retain
their own language). The Romans themselves were aware of this to
some extent: Laurence (1998, 100) notes that 'for Strabo, a crucial
element in the determination of ethnicity was language'. Evidence
about the languages used at Rome comes from literature and inscriptions. Both these sources are extremely inadequate: literature tends to
note only cases where something unusual happened (in terms of
language use), and inscriptions do not necessarily reflect everyday
spoken language, as will be suggested below. Nevertheless, there is
enough evidence to form some impression of the complexity of language use among foreigners at Rome.

Latin

Immigrants from the West probably spoke Latin already as a first or
second language, before they came to Rome. Soldiers would have
learned it in the army if they did not know it before. Civilians from the
East are much less likely to have known Latin before arriving in Rome.
It is not clear whether previous knowledge of Latin would have had
any effect on the decision to come to Rome in the first place, although
it is almost certainly true that the provincials most likely to move to
Rome were those who were most thoroughly imbued in Graeco–
Roman culture (see pp. 56, 181). According to a study of the use of
English by immigrants in the contemporary U.S.A., the immigrants'
proficiency is determined by: informal selection processes which
encourage those with knowledge of English to come; similar counter-
selection processes which encourage those without knowledge to
leave; and processes for increasing proficiency while living in the
U.S.A. Immigrants who come as children increase their proficiency

more than those who come as adults, but those who already know English are more likely to come in the first place.[67] If knowledge of Latin had a comparable effect on migration to Rome, it is now irrecoverable. However, the story of the emperor Septimius Severus' sister being sent back to Lepcis because of her lack of knowledge of Latin has no relevance to people outside the elite – a non-Latin-speaking relative would not have been an embarrassment lower down the social scale at Rome.

Language proficiency does not seem to have been an important consideration for the purchasers of slaves for use in Rome (see p. 37).[68] Slaves who were intended to do manual work might be expected to pick up some Latin, but their initial lack of knowledge would probably not be important. Presumably, however, slaves with different first languages who worked together would tend to communicate with each other in Latin.[69] Younger slaves were no doubt likely to pick up Latin more quickly, and it is possible that, in some circumstances, owners would discourage slaves from using their native languages, at least publicly.[70] Sometimes, however, depending on the sort of work for which the slave was intended, it was knowledge of Greek rather than of Latin which was required by owners.

Even immigrants whose first language was Latin must still have spoken it with a wide variety of regional accents. This receives very little attention in the sources, although Septimius Severus is said to have retained his African accent into old age;[71] Hadrian was mocked for his Spanish accent when he first came to Rome, but soon lost it.[72] One of the reasons for recommending that wet-nurses (who are expected to be 'Greek' by Soranus) should be chosen very carefully was that the child could pick up bad speech habits from them, but this probably includes grammatical mistakes as well as non-standard pronunciation.[73]

Among the Roman Christians, Greek was originally a *lingua franca* for people from a variety of linguistic backgrounds, but Latin replaced it as the liturgical language during the third century. La Piana attributes this change to the predominance of immigrants from Africa and their descendants in the church.[74] If that is correct, it shows that the adoption of Latin could be part of a more complex process than direct 'romanization'.

As Latin was Rome's official language, and also the language which people would expect to be understood by those outside their own group, it was the natural language to use for epitaphs. The fact that Latin inscriptions (principally epitaphs) outnumber Greek ones in Rome by about 50:1 does not necessarily reflect the proportion of people whose first language was Latin.[75] There are numerous epitaphs in Latin for immigrants whose home areas suggest that they almost certainly spoke Greek (see below).[76] Kajanto (1980, 94) suggests that families of ex-slaves might tend to speak Greek at home but use Latin for official documents and epitaphs; he notes that the proportion of slave/freed in Greek-language inscriptions is much lower than in Latin ones. This matches the relatively small proportion of slave/freed designated as foreigners in their epitaphs (p. 78), and suggests that a Latin epitaph with no reference to non-Roman origin might in itself be a conscious statement of acculturation, whatever the real background of the person commemorated.

People from the following areas have left only Latin inscriptions at Rome: Africa, Britain, Corsica, Dacia, Dalmatia, Germany, Moesia,[77] Noricum, Pannonia, and Raetia. All the military inscriptions except two (one soldier from Palestine, one from Thrace) which have been included in this study are in Latin, so it is clear that for soldiers, Latin was the automatic epigraphic language, whatever an individual's background. This is probably associated with the fact that soldiers were likely to be buried near each other in military burial areas, sometimes on public land.[78] It does not necessarily mean that individual soldiers were all fluent Latin speakers, although they would have needed a basic knowledge of it; the language of the military inscriptions was very stereotyped and can have required little input from the people who commissioned them.

Greek

Greek was familiar as a spoken language in Rome at least by the time of Plautus. It gradually came to be associated with people of Asian and Syrian origin as well as those from Greece itself and from southern Italy.[79] Juvenal's Umbricius complains about the use of Greek by such people, and implies, as someone of such prejudiced views naturally would, that they did not make much effort to learn Latin.[80] It also seems to have been the language of some 'eastern' religions, such as the cults of Isis and Serapis.[81] Kajanto (1963b, 10–11) notes a tendency for *peregrini* to have Greek epitaphs, but there is a danger of overestimating this, since there are several definite examples of someone who had a full Roman two- or three-part name being designated in Greek only by a cognomen, so some of the people who are known only by a Greek single name and therefore appear to be *peregrini* may in fact have been Roman citizens (see p. 76).

An anecdote about the philosopher Favorinus, who presumably spoke Latin as his first language since he came from Arles although he used Greek for 'professional' purposes, illustrates the widespread use of Greek among the educated at Rome:[82]

> When he delivered discourses in Rome, the interest in them was universal, so much so that even those in his audience who did not understand the Greek language shared in the pleasure that he gave; for he fascinated even them by the tones of his voice, by his expressive glance and the rhythm of his speech.

Similarly, Hadrian of Tyre 'inspired even those who did not know the Greek language with an ardent desire to hear him declaim'.[83] This literary *topos* shows the high status of Greek at Rome as a language associated with philosophy and literature; no-one would have been similarly praised for their inspiring declamation in Punic. At the same time, however, Greek was also a low status language associated with immigrants and ex-slaves.

It is not the case that Greek epitaphs at Rome were composed only by first generation immigrants. Kajanto (1980, 91) notes two cases of Greek epitaphs for people who were explicitly born at Rome, and observes that anyone with a Greek epitaph and no ethnic *might* have been born there.[84] About 30% of the pagan Greek epitaphs from Rome are in verse, a much higher proportion than from anywhere else,[85] but this reflects the importance of Greek as a literary language in the city. In the case of the Jews, most of those with Greek epitaphs were probably natives of Rome, but there was an incentive within the group to retain the use of Greek (see p. 264). Kajanto observes (1980, 91) that one-fifth of people in the Greek inscriptions have Latin cognomina, which he takes as further evidence that they were not all immigrants. The extent to which foreigners kept Greek (or any other minority language) as their first language, so that it remained the first language of their Rome-born children, could also depend partly on their residential arrangements; it would be much easier to do so if living among other Greek-speakers, whether immigrants or not, than if surrounded by Latin-speakers.[86]

According to Kajanto (1980, 90), most of the slaves (N=9) and ex-slaves (N=34, including a few imperial freedmen) in Greek inscriptions seem to be of foreign origin; the small numbers of people in these status categories was noted above, and reflects the high level of acculturation of inscription-writers from this sort of background, who would normally prefer to use Latin. He made a detailed survey of the origins of all those commemorated in pagan Greek inscriptions and with a place of origin indicated (1980, Tab. 1).[87] Asia and Bithynia predominate, suggesting that people from those areas may have been particularly ready to use Greek as a sign of their identity. He notes that, where the work of the deceased is given, it shows that people with Greek epitaphs could be among the more affluent part of the population. According to his count,[88] the best attested group is doctors (N=17). He also notes that the Greek used is generally correct, which may say something about the economic and educational background of its users.

Kajanto (1980, 100) further suggests that speakers of Greek probably had a greater chance of a Greek epitaph among Christians than among pagans, since Christian epitaphs tended to have a less 'official' character, and were often done by amateurs rather than by professional stonecutters, factors which would favour the epigraphic use of Greek among those for whom it was their first language. Of the epitaphs he surveyed in ICUR, 1109 out of 9359 (11.8%) were in Greek;[89] the proportion varied from 7.6% to 16.9% in different cemeteries. He observes that Greek is commoner in the earlier parts of the catacombs, and appears to decrease drastically from the mid-fourth century.[90] All the popes from Urban to Gaius (222–296) except Cornelius had Greek epitaphs,[91] but Latin was the usual language for later popes. The areas of provenance for people in the Greek Christian epitaphs remain similar to the Greek pagan epitaphs, but with Syria rather more prominent.[92]

The following table, based on a larger number of inscriptions than was available to Kajanto, shows the area of origin of foreigners commemorated in Greek, and the number of Latin epitaphs for people from the same places. I have divided pagan from Christian/Jewish as in ch. 4. It includes only those areas which have produced *some* foreigners' epitaphs in Greek.

TABLE 12. Places of origin mentioned in Latin and Greek epitaphs.

	Pagan			Christian/Jewish		
	Latin	Greek	Mixed[93]	Latin	Greek	Mixed
Armenia	1	1	2	2	2	
Asia	14	38	3	3	6	1
Bithynia	4	17			9	1
Bosporan	2	2				
Cappadocia	7	4		2	2	
Cilicia	3	7			1	
Crete		2		1		
Cyprus		1			2	
Egypt	9	14		1	9	
Galatia	6	5		2	17	

(cont.)		Pagan		Christian/Jewish		
	Latin	Greek	Mixed[93]	Latin	Greek	Mixed
Gaul	36	2		8		
Greece	6	6	3	2	6	
Hispania	47			7	1	
Lycia	2	3	1		2	
Macedonia	2	1		1	1	
Mauretania	6		1	2		
Numidia	2			3	1	
Palestine				1	6	
Parthia	5	1		1		
Sardinia			1			
Sicily	1	3		3	5	
Syria	20	14	4	4	31	1
Thrace	16			2	2	
Unknown		3	1	3		
Total	189	124	16	48	103	3
%	57.4	37.7	4.9	31.1	66.9	2.0

There are some surprising anomalies, such as why were Cappadocians more likely to produce Latin inscriptions than Galatians, but, as the numbers from individual areas are small, too much cannot be read into them. However, there is a clear trend overall: as Kajanto suggested, Greek is used proportionately much more often in the Christian/Jewish inscriptions than in the pagan ones. This is true for most of the areas analysed: e.g. for Syria, less than half the pagan inscriptions but nearly all the Christian/Jewish ones are in Greek. The reason is probably context rather than any change over time in the language spoken by immigrants. Many of the pagan inscriptions come from columbaria, where Latin was almost universally used, as the common language of large *familiae* and of burial associations.[94] Many of the Christian/Jewish ones come from catacombs. Greek was predominant in the Jewish catacombs throughout their use, and in the Christian catacombs in the third century. Kaimio (1979, 73) places the decision, for someone whose first language was Greek, about whether to write an epitaph in Latin or Greek in the context of in-group and out-group language:

> The explanation seems to lie in the fact that the Jews and Christians buried their dead in catacombs – or it is usually only the catacomb epitaphs that we can identify – while the other epitaphs were exposed along the roads, in cemeteries common to everyone. In other words, when an epitaph was set up in a place where everyone could see it, the

out-group language was commonly chosen for it, and in Rome this was Latin. But as soon as an ethnic or religious group makes use of its own cemeteries, closed to outsiders, the burying process becomes an in-group matter and the epitaphs acquire ethnic and religious symbols, and the in-group language is normally reserved for them.

Hence Syrians who were not Christians or Jews tended to write epitaphs in Latin, because they did not have their own exclusive burial areas. Christian and Jewish Syrians were much more likely to use Greek, even though all Syrians would probably have tended to prefer Greek over Latin as a spoken language. The use of Greek was not normally enough in itself to differentiate one foreign group from others, since it could equally well apply to people from Alexandria, Antioch and Athens. However, it did enable them to differentiate themselves from the indigenous Roman population, possibly to pass on their linguistic practices to their children, and, for the Jews, to differentiate themselves from Christians once Latin had become the main language of commemoration in the Christian catacombs.[95]

Bilinguality

Latin-Greek bilinguality was normal among the elite of Roman society, as Cicero's letters illustrate. It is likely also to have been common among immigrant groups: Kaimio (1979, 319) thinks that 'the Greek-speaking population of slave origin in the West' was generally bilingual, and Polomé (1983, 515) envisages people from the Eastern Mediterranean speaking Greek at home and Latin outside. Writing a bilingual inscription was, however, a rather different matter. It was sometimes done on behalf of Greek-speaking cities at Rome. An inscription in which the people of Laodicea ad Lycum honour the people of Rome as their saviour and benefactor has parallel texts in Latin and Greek, but with a mistake in the Latin.[96] When the cities of Bithynia et Pontus put up an honorific inscription for their governor, each city was named in Latin but gave details of its ambassadors in Greek, and Greek was probably the primary language of composition. The governor is called *patrono* in Latin but πάτρωνι καὶ εὐεργέτηι in Greek, perhaps because the Latin term needed explanation for a Greek audience. [97]

Writing a fully bilingual epitaph, i.e. one with the whole text in both languages (rather than part in one and part in the other) was very unusual. Kaimio (1979, 176) counts only fourteen instances, and associates them with people from the East and with attempts to emphasize their own importance by making the epitaphs both look and read impressively.

Epitaphs which use a mixture of Latin and Greek to say different things in the two languages are rather commoner. Kajanto (1980, 94) thinks that they suggest bilinguality among the composers and the potential readers. He sees a tendency to write the factual part of the epitaph in Latin, but epigrams, reflecting the feelings of the bereaved, in Greek. This is consistent with a situation of diglossia, where people use one language for one form of expression and another language for another form, something which I have argued elsewhere applied to the Roman Jews, who certainly regarded some parts of an epitaph as appropriate to one language or the other.[98] The people commemorated in mixed language epitaphs nearly always have Greek cognomina; two came from Greece, and only one was explicitly a freeborn citizen (a competitor in the Capitoline Games). [99] The table above shows that mixed language epitaphs are relatively unusual for people clearly identified as foreigners. Very occasionally such an epitaph uses different languages for different people: in IGUR 902, Latin is used for the commemorator's wife, Greek for his Phrygian mother, suggesting an attempt to make the languages fit the people they are commemorating.

Kajanto sees the greatest evidence of Latin–Greek symbiosis in the epitaphs which are written in one alphabet and the other language. He counts three Greek epitaphs in Latin letters, and fourteen Latin epitaphs in Greek letters, although there are in fact many more.[100] He associates them with ex-slaves or their descendants, and notes the predominance of Greek cognomina again. He suggests that they were intended to show that the deceased was bilingual, and that Latin might be used because the deceased was a Roman citizen.[101] While I would agree that this type of inscription requires people to be bilingual (or, more precisely, diglossic), it also suggests that their proficiency in the written language was not as great as in the spoken language, and that they could only cope with one alphabet although they could speak two languages.[102]

For most immigrants to Rome, bilinguality was probably a temporary situation in their family history, as with immigrants to the U.S.A. First generation immigrants who spoke Greek much better than Latin would have children who were equally at home in both languages and grandchildren who spoke only Latin.[103] For immigrants who were themselves already bilingual when they arrived, the decline of Greek may have been even more rapid, as with the Welsh language among bilingual immigrants to Pennsylvania.[104] Only among the Jews is there any clear evidence that the use of Greek was retained by people whose immigrant ancestry was several generations back.[105]

Other languages

With foreigners coming to Rome from all parts of the empire and outside, many new arrivals undoubtedly had first languages other than Latin or Greek. There are, however, very few echoes in literature of the possibility of hearing other languages spoken, and the fact that Juvenal's Umbricius does not complain about them may reflect their lack of perceived importance.[106] Suetonius mentions plays being performed in the *vici* of Rome 'by actors of all languages', i.e. not just Latin and Greek – he does not make clear which other languages he means.[107] Other indications of special arrangements being made for minority languages are completely lacking, perhaps not surprisingly as all the literary sources are composed by people who would have had little or no interest in such matters. When the speech made by King Tiridates to Nero, presumably in Armenian, had to be translated into Latin, it was an ex-praetor who did it, not an Armenian living at Rome, and there is no clear evidence for foreigners living in the city ever being called on to act as interpreters.[108] Furthermore, people who spoke minority languages may well have appeared to outsiders to have Latin as their first language. Polomé (1983, 516) seems to go well beyond the evidence when he says that Mercurius, imperial treasurer in AD 355, 'was of Persian origin...but he hardly spoke the language of his native country'. Ammianus (15.3.4) says nothing about Mercurius' first language, but in any case he would not have got very far by speaking Persian at court, even if he would have preferred to do so.

Languages such as Punic, Egyptian and Thracian, and various forms of Semitic, Celtic and Germanic languages, certainly must have been spoken at Rome, but largely as 'private, in-group languages'.[109] For example, Tatian's first language was probably Syriac,[110] but the number of people he would have been able to talk to in Syriac at Rome must have been limited. Even if they had an epigraphic tradition at home, these languages very rarely achieved permanent written form at Rome. The possibility that one Thracian word has found its way into a Latin inscription will be discussed below (p. 219), but there is no evidence for more than an individual word of any immigrant European language being inscribed on stone.

Semitic languages are slightly better documented than European ones. Palmyrene was used jointly with Latin or Greek in three inscriptions from a Palmyrene shrine outside the Porta Portuensis (see p. 242). MacMullen (1993, 48) treats this as evidence that 'some very significant minority of the capital, even after many generations, had not become thoroughly Romanized', but in fact there seems no reason to doubt the more obvious explanation, that the people involved were relatively new arrivals in Rome. Nabataean occurs jointly with Latin twice in epitaphs;[111] its use is anything but 'typical', as Polomé (1983, 517) claims. Hebrew or Aramaic was used very occasionally at the end of a Greek or Latin Jewish epitaph,[112] and there is one epitaph entirely in Aramaic but of very uncertain meaning.[113] There appears to have been some difficulty in finding people who could inscribe alphabets other than Latin or Greek: for both Palmyrene and Hebrew inscriptions, the lettering is generally of a much lower standard than it is for the Greek or Latin parts of the same inscriptions: smaller, irregular, with uneven alignment, and lacking serifs.[114]

Calendars

Another possible echo of linguistic and cultural difference lies in the use of different dating systems. At Rome, the usual epigraphic way of giving the year was by the names of the consuls, and the day and month were given according to the Julian calendar. The dating system *ab urbe condita* was virtually never used in inscriptions. Its one epigraphic use in a context associated with foreigners, by a devotee of some Syrian cults, and written side by side with a consular date, seems like an extra expression of artificial 'Romanness'; the author protests too much in using a Roman dating system which indigenous Romans would not normally have used themselves in such a context.[115] There were, of course, many alternative calendars throughout the Empire, with years given according to local eras (e.g. from the foundation of a city or province), and months having different names and covering different periods. It might be expected that foreigners would bring their own systems of recording time to Rome with them, like Apollinarius in the letter quoted above (p. 165), and that these would emerge in their inscriptions. It should be noted, however, that pagan epitaphs rarely give a date at all; Christian epitaphs quite often give the day of the month, but not the year. Hence most of the relevant inscriptions are Christian.

There are a few traces at Rome of the months used in Greek calendars in the East, all in Greek-language inscriptions. A very fragmentary Christian inscription uses the month Panemos.[116] A man from a village in Phoenicia died in the month Dystros.[117] Someone from a village near Apamea died in the month Daisios, probably in AD 431.[118] The month Gorpaios is used in a Jewish epitaph.[119] There is one example of another dating system in a bilingual Greek–Palmyrene inscription from the Palmyrene shrine (see p. 243).[120] The year is given as 547 in both languages, and the month is Peritios in Greek and Sebat in Palmyrene. There is also a dedication to a form of Ares (Ἄρη θεῷ πατρῴῳ ἐπηκόῳ) for the safety of Hadrian, which gives the year as 445 and the month as Xanthikos;[121] Moretti takes the dedicant as a Palmyrene. The years are according to the Seleucid era, and correspond to AD 236 and 134 respectively.

In fact, the only non-Roman calendar which has left any significant trace at Rome is the Egyptian one, occurrences of which will be discussed at p. 248; Egyptian dates are reasonably common in Greek-language Christian epitaphs. The reluctance to use any other dating form is probably a result of the difficulty which outsiders would have in understanding it. Unless a group had its own private burial area, it would tend to use terminology which meant something to others, so local calendars were avoided in inscriptions for the same reasons as local languages – which does not mean that they were not in everyday use among foreigners. The Egyptian calendar, through the cults of Isis and Serapis, perhaps had wider recognition than any other, but its use was certainly not confined to Isis-worshippers, since most of its occurrences are in Christian inscriptions. The general lack of epigraphic evidence for the use of non-Roman calendars certainly shows a reluctance to inscribe them, but not necessarily an abandonment of them in daily use.

vi. Names

There *may* be some correlation between the extent to which people used the languages of their homelands and the extent to which they used names from their homelands. The correlation is certainly not a direct one, since foreigners who forgot or deliberately abandoned their original language would still retain their original names (unless they were replaced by Latin or Greek ones, which was often not the case among slaves and ex-slaves). Kajanto (1980, 85) counted only 530 slaves/ex-slaves with local (i.e. not Greek or Latin) cognomina,[122] out of a total of 25,000 slave names. He notes that the use of, e.g., a Thracian name does not necessarily prove that someone's mother tongue was Thracian. Names which were not Latin or Greek could be passed down among people who actually spoke Latin or Greek,[123] and conversely, Latin or Greek names could be adopted by people who themselves knew little of those languages. Solin (1983, 634–5) notes that slaves with local names tended to have well-known ones such as Malchio and Martha which could be adapted to the case-endings of Latin or Greek, while more 'exotic' names such as Habibi and Thabibu were restricted to *peregrini*. He also observes that 'oriental' names (i.e.

local names from the eastern provinces) were very rare for slaves at Rome: only 1.9% in a total of 26,300.[124] *Vernae*, i.e. slaves born at Rome, were almost invariably given Latin or Greek names, irrespective of their parentage.[125]

In most Roman contexts, local cognomina were names of low prestige. Elton (1996, 146) notes that many barbarian officers in the late Roman army had Latin names, but no Roman officers had barbarian names. The usual trend seems to have been for Latin, and to a lesser extent Greek, names to replace other types. In a sample of pagan inscriptions from Rome, Kajanto found that the cognomina were about 41.5% Latin, 56% Greek and only 2.5% local; the local (including Semitic) proportion increases to 3.5% in Christian inscriptions, where Latin names outnumber Greek by two to one.[126] For Christians, the positive biblical connotations of some Semitic names outweighed the negative barbarian connotations which the same names had traditionally had.

It is generally thought that Greek names were associated with slavery.[127] Kaimio and Solin note the extent to which slaves born in Italy still received Greek names, and that slave-traders tended to give slaves Greek names which, in the context, were perhaps seen as more desirable than either Latin or local ones.[128] Of the slaves from the East with ethnics, Solin counts 139 with Greek names, 33 with Latin and 4 with local ones. Until the second century AD, he argues, this meant that Greek names tended to be avoided for free people at Rome, but, as people with Greek cognomina began to become senators and hold high office, the servile associations of the names gradually disappeared. On the other hand, Kajanto associates the decline of Greek names which he observes in Christian inscriptions before the fifth century with the decline of slavery. However, he also shows that the tendency for fathers with Greek names to have children with Latin names is greater in the pagan inscriptions than in the Christian ones.

There is thus a possibility that a close study of naming patterns among foreigners and their children might indicate a continued sense of 'foreign' identity (by the continued use of local names) or a trend towards romanization (by the use of Latin names). Unfortunately, there are very few cases in the inscriptions where a foreigner with a local name has a child who was clearly born after the parent's arrival at Rome, to test whether such people would give their children local or Latin/Greek names. In cases where the parent is explicitly an immigrant and the child is not said to be one (and is therefore *likely* to have been born at Rome), the following pattern emerges:

TABLE 13. Types of name used by immigrants and their children.

Parent's name	Child's name	
Latin	Latin	24[129]
Latin	Greek	4
Greek	Greek	7
Greek	Latin	5[130]
local	Latin	2
local	local	1

In over half the cases, both parent and child have a Latin name. Local names are almost as rare for parents as they are for children.[131]

It is commoner to find a parent with a non-Latin name and a child with a Latin name than vice versa, but the numbers are extremely small. The two cases where immigrant parents with (probably) local names gave their child a Latin name are:

IGUR 939 = ICUR 4032: mother Taon, son Serenus.

CIL vi 3454: mother Aurelia Gorsila, son Felicissimus.[132]

However, in both cases the father had a Latin name, so the choice of a Latin name for the son may be nothing to do with the fact of moving to Rome, but might have occurred anyway.

This evidence does not provide much insight into the question of how foreigners at Rome named their children, but it does raise another question: why did so many foreigners have Latin names themselves? The names of soldiers are particularly suspicious: for example, all the 4 Bithynian soldiers at Rome had Latin cognomina, whereas only 7 out of 28 civilians did. It seems fairly certain that soldiers often adopted Latin cognomina on enlistment.[133] This is sometimes recorded explicitly in papyri, e.g. in the case of Apion, an Egyptian who joined the fleet at Misenum in the second century AD and took on the name of Antonius Maximus.[134]

Among civilians, Latin cognomina are also unexpectedly common, and local names are extremely rare: for example, out of the civilian immigrants from Egypt, there are 16 Greek names, 10 Latin, 3 Egyptian and 1 Semitic (a Christian). It seems possible that some immigrants took on a Latin (or Greek) name when they came to Rome, perhaps for the practical reason that local names could be difficult for Romans to say or write. Another possibility, which could be an additional factor in explaining the lack of local names, is that people who already had Latin or Greek names (and therefore came from the more romanized/ hellenized part of their society) were more likely to migrate to Rome

181

than those with local names and, implicitly, a less romanized/hellenized background.[135]

Some people clearly could, for a variety of reasons, have both a local and a 'Roman' name, and would use each in the appropriate contexts. This is by definition very unlikely to appear in inscriptions (except for those people who were recorded as having a double name with the *qui et*/ὁ καί formula[136]), since an inscription would normally be a context for the Roman name. However, there is an exception in the case of a dedicant at the Palmyrene sanctuary in Trastevere: in a Latin and Greek inscription he is called simply Heliodorus, but in a Greek and Palmyrene inscription he is called Aurelius Heliodorus Hadrianus son of Antiochus in Greek, and Iarhai son of Haliphi son of Iarhai son of Lisams son of Soadu in Palmyrene.[137] The unusual context and language-choice of the inscription provides considerable information about the various names by which the same man could be known, and although the information is exceptional, there is no reason to think that the naming practices which it illustrates were.

There are numerous attestations of people at Rome with distinctively local names who are not said in their inscriptions to be immigrants. Since it is impossible within the scope of this book to make a thorough survey,[138] and many names are of uncertain provenance anyway,[139] some particularly distinctive names will be studied in the sections of ch. 8 concerned with the areas from which the names originated. The occurrences of these names show that their bearers seem almost invariably to be from a slave/freed or military milieu, except where Semitic names were 'rehabilitated' by Christianity. While Syrian names were common for slaves, the occurrence of a Syrian name for the child of a slave or ex-slave is very unusual, as Solin observes.[140] One exceptional case where a Syrian name was still used in the second generation is:[141]

> To the *Di Manes*. Mariame, lived 6 years. Iaso, peasant from the Marian estate, for his well-deserving daughter.

One name of originally Syrian origin which seems to have been integrated into Latin onomastics is Gamala: a family at Ostia had members named P. Lucilius Gamala in both the first century BC and second century AD, each with at least three generations of free ancestors.[142] In this case, as the name of a city, it perhaps did not have the same connotations as Syrian personal names.

It seems that some names which would have had high status elsewhere (Pharnaces[143] was a royal name, Malchio[144] comes from the root *mlk* = king, Horus[145] was a divine name) acquired low status at Rome.

Their bearers had Latin epitaphs, and appear not to have passed on their names, or other names of similar linguistic background, to their children. The known bearers of these names seem to have been romanized slaves and ex-slaves, and therefore not necessarily typical of free immigrants although, like free immigrants, few children are attested for them. Solin's suggestion that feelings of national pride and solidarity might encourage free immigrants to pass on Semitic names to their children does not seem to be borne out by the available evidence except from the Christian period.[146] He notes elsewhere that 'oriental names', which were rare anyway, were borne by slaves from the East and were not passed on to the next generation born at Rome.[147]

Typically Thracian names could also be borne by slaves, but are mainly attested for soldiers (see p. 220). There was not necessarily a different attitude to the names themselves, but their occurrence among a different and more prestigious group of immigrants would have lessened their negative connotations. Bithus was a fairly Latin-sounding name which did not need latinizing in the way that some local names did. If the Praetorian Guard had recruited more in Parthia, Syria or Egypt, then more examples of free men called Pharnaces, Malchio and Horus might be known at Rome. Perhaps, however, the first two would still have been discarded on enlistment as sounding too un-Latin. The suspicion remains that free immigrants as well as new soldiers may have adopted new names if their original ones sounded inappropriate, a choice which was probably not available to slaves who were expected to keep their original names or whatever names were assigned to them. Slaves and ex-slaves with local names did not emphasize their origins by stating in inscriptions that they were Egyptians or Syrians. Perhaps they felt that the names were sufficient indication of this, but more probably, especially in the context of the Latin inscriptions which they invariably produced, they did not want to mention their origins at all.

vii. Cults

Many foreigners, particularly those from the East, came from areas with their own distinctive local gods, and the importation of those gods to Rome was potentially a way of maintaining communal identity among foreign groups, and of differentiating themselves from their surroundings. Since many migrants must have lacked kin at Rome, they might be able to use contacts made through worship to create substitute networks for themselves, in the same manner that modern migrants have sometimes used church institutions.[148]

While foreigners often appear to have taken part in the worship of the usual Roman gods in the city, some worshipped their own deities as well (or instead). Dionysius of Halicarnassus refers to 'the influx into Rome of countless foreigners, who are under a firm obligation to worship their ancestral gods according to the customs of their home-land'.[149] These were perfectly compatible with the main gods (either by direct identification or by an expansion of the pantheon), but would not otherwise have been worshipped at Rome. In some cases they gradually achieved popularity which took them outside the control of people from the original area (e.g. Isis, Serapis),[150] but more often the cults seem to have remained small, although not usually exclusive. It was also possible for a cult to be spread by returned soldiers who had been stationed in its original locality;[151] thus the spread of a cult does not guarantee that it was foreigners who brought it. However, military votive inscriptions from Rome almost always show a close link between the place of origin of the soldiers and of the god(s) in question, e.g. Thracian soldiers honouring local Thracian gods. It is therefore probably safe to assume that most local gods were brought to Rome by military or civilian immigrants from the gods' localities, rather than by people who were just passing through.

Cult-centres for local deities had to be located outside the pomerium of the city, but otherwise the state took no interest, except on the few occasions when a cult was associated with criminal or subversive activity and suppressed (see p. 41). With the exception of Judaism (see p. 255), these cults did not need to be exclusive, and perhaps therefore had less significance as a means of denoting (or creating) identity than, for example, Islam among Turkish immigrants in Germany or Pakistani immigrants in Britain.[152] Nevertheless, as La Piana (1927, 225) noted:

> The need of practising in their new residence the religious cults of their land of origin is undoubtedly one of the leading causes which led immigrants to form associations of a religious character.

The cults required buildings and furniture. In some cases, these are likely to have been donated by wealthy members of the group such as merchants:[153]

> To that class also the small associations of humble workers of their nationality turned to secure *patroni* and protectors who would dignify the college with their names and help the *arca communis* by their gifts.

Some inscriptions have survived recording such donations, although they do not usually give the desired information about the donor's background, and La Piana's comment goes beyond what the evidence really shows. The evidence for the worship of some of the imported deities will be discussed in the appropriate sections of ch. 8, with the aim of determining whether the cults really contributed to the preservation of identity by immigrant groups.

Slaves who came to Rio de Janeiro often left their homes before they had been fully initiated into their traditional religions, and therefore brought only an incomplete knowledge to Brazil with them.[154] The same may apply to slaves brought to Rome; thus the cult of a local deity might assume a different form at Rome from that which it took at home, even without being joined and influenced by people from other backgrounds. Slaves at Rio who had few compatriots might be obliged to go outside their own group to practise something like their original religion; some brought with them from Africa a tradition of religious adaptation, with the incorporation of new elements. Considerations such as these could also have impeded the continued exclusive worship of local gods by local groups at Rome. Nevertheless, an attempt to recreate the religious practices of home (whether or not this is done accurately) can be a way of maintaining an emotional link with home.[155]

In most cases, the existence of the cult of a local deity is known only from one or two inscriptions, and it is therefore impossible to say how widespread it was, or how far the participants tended to be immigrants. Only cults which produced inscriptions are likely to be known at all. Calzini Gysens (1996a, 261) notes that most inscriptions attest only individual participation in a cult and do not give much insight into how it was organized.

The evidence discussed in ch. 8 shows that the cults which maintained the strongest local identities, apart from Judaism, are those from Syria, practised mainly by civilians, and the Balkans, whose practitioners seem to have been almost exclusively military. Since the soldiers stationed at Rome were such uniform users of Latin epitaphs and names, their tendency to continue to worship their local gods seems somewhat surprising. However, it is consistent with the emphasis placed by the Thracians in particular on their home villages. They do seem to have made considerable efforts to retain their own identity, and presumably they normally returned home at the end of their period of service.

For the Syrian civilians who worshipped Syrian gods, return home is less likely to have been an issue, and some, such as the prominent cult member M. Antonius Gaionas, appear to have been well integrated into other aspects of city life. It therefore seems likely that, for them, religion provided a sense of community, although the very limited information about the functioning of their cults prevents this from being understood fully.

The habit of recording the home village which is found among the Thracian soldiers (see p. 219) also occurs among some Syrians and Galatians in the Christian inscriptions (see pp. 232, 237). As Christians, these people had no scope for showing the same local religious loyalty as the Thracian soldiers (or the Syrian pagans). They may have been attached to the cults of local saints, but that would not be apparent in the evidence which they have left. However, non-orthodox Christian groups seem sometimes to have been generally associated with particular places of origin. This is made clearest by Augustine in a letter dated to 400:[156]

> But, reversing the natural course of things, the Donatists sent to Rome from Africa an ordained bishop, who, putting himself at the head of a few Africans in the great metropolis, gave some notoriety to the name of 'mountain men', or Cutzupits, by which they were known.

The association of the Donatists with Africa was seen as strong, although of course not all Africans were Donatists, and Donatism did not only appeal to Africans. The existence of a sizeable African contingent already in the church at Rome no doubt helped the Donatist cause there, and they had their own Bishop of Rome for much of the fourth century.[157] It may be that Donatism at Rome, like the worship of Syrian gods, provided a communal focus for a particular group of foreigners in the city even though it was not exclusive to that group.

Montanism began in Phrygia in the second century, but spread rapidly and widely. Tabbernee (1997) alleges that there was a Montanist community from Asia Minor at Rome. This is based on rather flimsy evidence; only one epitaph is clearly both Montanist and belongs to someone explicitly from Asia Minor.[158] The sect *may* have been particularly strong among Asians, but there is no firm evidence for this.

It does seem to have been the case, however, that some 'national' groups within the Roman church retained different practices which they had brought with them to Rome. The Asians observed their own date for Easter, something which Pope Victor failed to stop.[159] This implies that they formed a substantial contingent within the Roman church. The replacement of Greek by Latin as the official and liturgical language of the church in the mid-third century may have been connected with the influence of Africans rather than that of indigenous Romans.[160] It seems that Christianity, instead of creating uniformity among its adherents, still enabled religion and local identity to complement each other in some circumstances, even if these are now hard to identify.

viii. Burial practices

The disposal of the dead is potentially a way in which immigrants can give expression to some form of communal identity, in the rituals used or the site where the remains are placed, and the desire to ensure the 'correct' form of disposal can even lead to the formation of community organizations which acquire other functions as well. The prominence of burial associations (*collegia funeraticia*) is well known as a way by which ordinary residents of Rome (although not the very poor) could ensure a burial in a columbarium by making monthly 'friendly society' contributions. La Piana (1927, 272–3) suggests a link with the cults of foreign deities, claiming that the associations 'were indeed not an importation but a local institution, created to satisfy a special need of the immigrant groups in the capital of the empire'. This is certainly a plausible picture, and there is no doubt that some foreigners belonged to such societies, but evidence for the associations being dominated by foreigners or being directly associated with foreign gods is lacking.[161] The use of columbaria seems to have encouraged the standardization of burial practices rather than the preservation of local peculiarities.

In fact, there is very little evidence that groups with a common geographical origin ever established their own separate burial areas at Rome. Slaves and ex-slaves were more likely to be buried with other members of their *familiae*. Other immigrants used collegial columbaria (and later, catacombs), or, if they were prosperous enough, had their own tombs alongside the main roads. In one epitaph, a Theban, Phrygian and Carthaginian are among those sharing a burial plot.[162] In any of these circumstances, people would not normally be buried alongside their compatriots. The tendency to write epitaphs in Latin in such contexts is discussed at p. 170. It should, however, be acknowledged that if there were exclusive burial areas, they would be very hard to identify now, because there would be no point using ethnic or geographical labels in them: it would make sense to label someone *Syrus* in an area full of people of all backgrounds, but it would be irrelevant if the whole area was known to be occupied by Syrians.[163]

The Jewish catacombs provided a communal and probably exclusive site for one religious group, and the Christian catacombs offered the same for the growing number of Christians in the city.[164] It does not seem to be the case that any catacombs were reserved for particular

187

national groups. Nuzzo (1997, 709) finds that there were foreigners in nearly all the catacombs but that they predominated nowhere. The highest proportion of foreigners was at the catacombs of S. Pancrazio, S. Paolo, SS. Marco e Marcelliano (where they were especially people from Syria and Asia Minor), and Ciriaca. In the Praetextatus catacomb, they were mainly found in the so-called *area greca*, whose name is derived from the predominance of Greek epitaphs noted by the excavators.[165] In no case, however, could a whole catacomb be seen as dominated by foreigners. A concentration of Africans has been suggested at Commodilla[166] or at Callistus,[167] but this is based on the prevalence of supposedly African names and does not seem to be reliable.

The possibility of a Pannonian burial area in the S. Sebastiano catacomb at the 'Platonia' mausoleum, raised by Styger but rejected by Ferrua, has been argued quite convincingly by Bertolino (1997, 116). He suggests that the mausoleum, which formed part of the catacomb, was originally the family tomb of the Urban Prefect from Pannonia, Viventius, in which some of his compatriots were also given burial, as indicated by epitaphs. Pannonians fleeing from the barbarian invasions brought with them to Rome the relics of St Quirinus, Bishop of Siscia, and the mausoleum was adapted to accommodate these. Apart from Viventius, four Pannonian pagans, probably all with military connections, are known to have been buried in the same area, suggesting that it was already attractive to Pannonians. The presence of Quirinus' relics probably increased the attraction for Pannonian Christians.[168] However, they only predominated in a limited area, not in a whole catacomb.

There is another more substantial exception to the general lack of a real concentration of burials of people from the same area. A number of Galatians were buried in the Octavilla catacomb on the Via Aurelia.[169] Five epitaphs which explicitly concern Galatians are recorded as coming from there.[170] Three more which come from the Octavilla catacomb seem most likely to concern Galatians because of the similar terminology used.[171] Another six follow a similar pattern, although their place of origin is not known; all could be from Octavilla.[172] Most are only partially preserved, and the names of the deceased are missing in nearly all. Many use the common expressions ἐνθά(δε) (κατα)κῖτε and ζήσας + age, but most contain some more unusual formulae: Γαλάτης after the name; χωρίου followed by the name of the home village[173] (see p. 232); the father's name; τελευτᾷ and the date of death. Ricci (1997a, 190) suggests that there was a Galatian residential quarter in the area of the Via Aurelia, which is certainly possible, but not provable; there was not necessarily a correlation between where in the city people lived and where they were buried (cf. p. 152).

Epitaphs provide the best evidence for foreign burials, but burial practices and tomb style and contents can also suggest a foreign presence. Cremation was normal at Rome until the early second century AD, when inhumation began to replace it gradually. It is likely that some people from areas where inhumation was normal continued to use inhumation at Rome even during the city's cremation period,[174] and it has been suggested that the influence of immigrants was one of the reasons for the general change to inhumation.[175] There are also traces of other burial practices which may be associated with immigrants. However, since C. Cestius, a man of senatorial family, was buried in a pyramid and Poppaea was embalmed, it was certainly also possible for such practices to be adopted by people born at Rome.[176]

Three mummies have been found at Rome (a mid-second century AD one from the Via Cassia, and two from the Via Appia), but the importation of this practice was clearly exceptional.[177] One of them may actually be a case of embalming in honey rather than full Egyptian-style mummification.[178] There is also a possible reference to embalming in honey in an epitaph for a Laodicean.[179] There must have been embalmers available at Rome: apart from the above examples, Lucretius mentions embalming in honey as a possibility in his time, and Statius says that Priscilla, the wife of Domitian's secretary Abascantus, was embalmed.[180] Bodies which were to be sent home for final burial were embalmed if they could not be cremated (see below). In the fragmentary epitaph put up by a man named Gyges for his son Skymnos, the word κηροχυτῶν is used, which Moretti takes as referring either to making a wax image or to preserving the body in wax, a Persian custom which might be consistent with the 'oriental' names of the people involved (who are not specifically said to be foreigners).[181]

The Jewish catacombs of Rome, while not modelled on any pre-existing type of cemetery in the land of Israel, do show some signs of Palestinian influence, particularly the use of *kokhim* in one part of Vigna Randanini. These are burial places cut into the gallery wall at ground level, so that the body could lie at right-angles to the gallery (whereas in a normal *loculus* it lay parallel), with a ledge to enable two bodies to be placed in one *kokh*. Rutgers (1995, 61–5) notes that the Vigna Randanini *kokhim* are very similar to those of the 'tomb of the Prophets' on the Mount of Olives.

Tomb Z in the Vatican necropolis has been labelled 'the tomb of the

Egyptians' because of the representation of an Egyptian god on each of the three surviving walls: 'no Hellenized deity in western guise, such as Isis, Serapis or Harpocrates, but a fully-fledged native divinity in national costume'.[182] One of these gods is probably Horus. The tomb was built for inhumations only, and Toynbee and Ward-Perkins (1956, 55) explain its unusual form as follows:

> There can be little doubt that Tomb Z was built, in the first instance, for an Egyptian family resident in Rome and practising there some aspects of its native cult. This in itself would be sufficient to account for the absence of cremation-burials, since the Egyptians never burned their dead.

There were no inscriptions associated with the first (second-century) phase of the tomb, although one of the mid-third-century sarcophagi found there has an epitaph. Subsequent reuse may have removed any original inscriptions, but it seems likely that people who were anxious to create an Egyptian-style tomb would have avoided using Greek or Latin in it. It is possible that the users of this tomb were, like C. Cestius, simply attracted to Egyptian funerary architecture, but in the case of a tomb interior which would have made no visual impact on outsiders, it seems much more likely that they were Egyptians themselves, doing their best to retain their traditional practices. It may be significant that while the inside of the tomb was consciously Egyptian, the outside, as far as can now be judged, had no particular Egyptian features and would not have differed from other nearby tombs. It was of course possible for a tomb to convey one message to the general public who passed by and a different one to the private group which actually went inside,[183] but I have found no other comparable cases where this was done in the context of 'national' burial customs.

A very different sort of foreign influence can be seen on the tomb of the second-century Norican *eques singularis* T. Aurelius Genetivus, which has a Pannonian-style depiction of a groom holding three horses.[184] The *equites singulares* developed their own distinctive style of stelae which are unlike any other type of Roman tomb, and may owe something to the artistic influences of their German and Balkan home-lands.[185] Speidel (1994a, 145) points out that the scene of 'the long-reining of the horse by a groom, often with a coil of line in his hands, proves unmistakably that the guardsmen brought these images from Lower Germany'. Others show the 'Thracian rider' scene of a rider and his dog rushing a boar, which came from the lower Danube region.[186] Most of the tombs of *equites singulares* come from a burial area near the Via Casilina, where the SS. Pietro e Marcellino catacomb subsequently developed; many tombstones were reused in the catacomb.

The existence of a cemetery which was apparently exclusive to the *equites* no doubt encouraged the development of burial practices reflecting the military identity of the group, but regional differences within the group were not completely obliterated.

Immigrants did not necessarily preserve the funerary customs of their homelands, however. Nock notes a number of cases where people whose names suggest that they were immigrants to Rome from the East (Egypt, Syria, Parthia) were cremated during the early Empire, even though it was not their native custom.[187] The epitaph of two envoys from Termessus who died at Rome specifically says that 'fire burned both our bodies'.[188] Thus some foreigners are clearly shown to have adopted Roman practices. In general, there is relatively little evidence of provincial burial customs or tomb-types at Rome, although this may to some extent be the result of a lack of preserved sites, or of impracticability: tumuli and tombs with rock-cut façades were not really feasible there.

One way of ensuring burial according to traditional local custom was to have your remains sent home from Rome after you died. There were obvious practical difficulties in this: it would require either someone to accompany the remains throughout the journey (perhaps coming from the home area specially to collect them), or at least someone to send them off from Rome by ship and someone else to receive them and give them a proper burial. Where cremation was the preferred rite, the body could be burnt at Rome and the ashes shipped home; where cremation was excluded on religious grounds, and when inhumation became normal during the second century AD, the practical difficulties became greater. The exiled Judaean ruler Aristobulus II, poisoned at Rome in 49 BC, had his body embalmed in honey so that it could be sent back to the family tomb of the Hasmoneans.[189] This indicates another general requirement: a tomb would need to be available at home. Avraméa (1995, 5) suggests that some people prepared their tomb at home before leaving, and Ricci (1994a, 20–1) gives a number of examples of soldiers serving at Rome who had tombs built at home during their lifetimes. However, most of the migrants to Rome are unlikely to have been in a financial position to do this, or to have left home at the time of life when they would have been thinking about their tombs, so they more probably relied on an existing family tomb.[190]

The desire to be buried at home is unlikely to have been prompted by religious considerations, except perhaps in the case of rabbinic Jews from the third century AD onwards.[191] It implies instead an emotional attachment to home, and perhaps also a feeling that the tomb was more likely to be cared for at home than at Rome. In the *Acta Pauli et Antonini*, the Alexandrian Paulus, who finds himself in trouble at Rome, says, 'My only concern is for the grave in Alexandria which I expect to have',[192] and another Greek writer comments on how, for a Greek, it is a terrible thing 'to lie after death in a foreign land'. [193] Some of the considerations are illustrated in an anecdote about Euodianus of Smyrna, who held the chair of rhetoric at Rome, and whose son had died and been buried there:[194]

> When he was at the point of death in Rome, all his most intimate friends were by his bedside and were consulting about his body, whether they ought to bury it there or embalm it and ship it to Smyrna, when Euodianus exclaimed in a loud voice: 'I will not leave my son behind alone'. Thus did he clearly enjoin on them that he should be buried in the same grave as his son.

There was clearly nothing unusual about someone of that level of society, for whom neither money nor helpers were lacking, wishing to be buried at home, but in this case there was a personal reason for having a stronger attachment to Rome. Another sophist who did have his body taken home by his relatives was Philiscus of Melos.[195] Christians as well as pagans could feel a desire for burial at home. Monica originally made arrangements for her body to be sent back from Italy to Africa to be buried with her husband, but on her deathbed she lost interest in where she was buried, which, Augustine notes, people found surprising.[196]

An alternative for people who died at Rome was to have their remains buried there but to be commemorated at home as well, presumably on the wall of a family tomb. M. Antonius Turbo, aged 65, died at Rome and was buried in a tomb in the Vatican area, but he was also given an epitaph at home at Sicca in Africa.[197] P. Lucanius Reburrinus was buried at Rome, and also commemorated by his mother at Conimbriga in Lusitania.[198] M. Iulius Serenus from the same city died while on a journey to Rome and was buried there, but also commemorated at home by his mother.[199]

Sometimes epitaphs explicitly say that the remains of someone who died at Rome were taken home and buried there. The person who provided the epitaph was usually the same person who had gone to Rome to collect the ashes or body, and made sure that such a pious deed was commemorated. That is the situation in the following inscriptions. The fact that they are all pagan may result from the greater tendency of pagan epitaphs to give details of the commemorator,

rather than from the practice dying out altogether among Christians:
- Q. Cadius Fronto, aged 35; his remains were placed in the family tomb in Hispania by his father.[200]
- Iulia Helias, priestess of the imperial cult, aged 25; her two sisters arranged for her body to be brought back from Rome to Lyon and placed in a sarcophagus in a 'mausoleum'.[201] This was clearly an inhumation not a cremation.
- Antonius Vecetinus, aged 25, buried at home in Gaul by his father.[202]
- Papirius Proculus, aged between 11 and 19, killed at Rome by a falling roof-tile; his mother buried him at Salona in the family tomb along with his sister.[203]
- Principius, a student at Rome aged 22; his body was taken home to Dalmatia by his father.[204]
- L. Postumius Paemulus Pius, aged 21, died at Rome and was buried in Africa.[205]
- Rufinus of 'Nilopolis'; although commemorated at Rome, his remains were taken back to Egypt by his wife, and placed in the tomb where his children were later buried.[206]
- Salome, aged 11 months, was to have her remains taken home, presumably to Syria or Palestine, by her mother.[207]

In a slightly greater number of cases, the deceased was commemorated at home, but it is not explicitly said that the remains were taken there from Rome. No doubt some of the following epitaphs record cases similar to the list above, but others may indicate that the actual remains stayed in Rome.
- A man whose name is lost; commemorated by his *adsidua* Sulpicia Quinta in Hispania.[208]
- Ti. Claudius Pius, died at Rome on an embassy and was commemorated by his parents at Lyon.[209]
- A. Vitellius Valerius, a student at Rome, was commemorated by his parents at Lyon.[210]
- L. Maecius Maelon, died at Ostia aged 50; commemorated at home in Gaul by his sons.[211]
- Proximus, died at Rome; commemorated in Aquitania by his brother.[212]
- C. Maximius Iunianus, aged 30, died on an embassy; commemorated in a family tomb in Noricum.[213]
- Successianus, aged 20; commemorated by his parents in Noricum.[214]
- Ti. Iulius Ingenuus, an *urbanicianus*; commemorated by his parents (both ex-slaves) in Noricum.[215]
- A man whose name is lost, aged 22; commemorated in Dalmatia by his wife.[216]

- Si<th?>a, aged 45; commemorated in Moesia.[217]
- Praetorianus, a *notarius* who died at Rome aged 17 in AD 225, was commemorated at Sitifis in Mauretania with his father, along with his sister who died the following year aged 8.[218]
- L. Caecilius Fronto of Volubilis died at Rome aged 25; the city-council of Volubilis, to which his family presumably belonged, decreed him a statue and a funeral at public expense, but his stepmother accepted only the honour and commemorated him herself.[219]
- L. Senius Flaccus, aged 30; commemorated at Thamugadis in Numidia by his brother.[220]

The predominance of men in their twenties and thirties is hardly surprising, as they appear to have formed the largest part of the immigrant population. Neither is the prevalence of areas fairly close to Rome: western and central Europe and North Africa. The evidence shows that the desire for burial or commemoration at home was widespread geographically and lasted for several centuries. On the whole in these cases, unlike in the literary evidence, the desire of parents to bring their deceased sons' remains home may have been of more importance than the immigrants' own wishes about where to be buried. People who died at Rome while they still had a parent alive were clearly much more likely to be commemorated at home than those who outlived their parents.[221]

The vast majority of epitaphs at Rome follow fairly standard formulae, and some of the more original ones have no parallels anywhere outside Rome. However, in some cases the wording of Greek epitaphs can be linked with forms of expression which were used elsewhere, in areas from where immigrants came to Rome. The foreign wording may be combined with typically Roman formulae like Θ(εοῖς) Κ(αταχθονίοις), or the epitaph may be entirely in a 'non-Roman' style. In these cases it is very likely that the deceased or commemorator came from the area where the non-Roman style was used, or at least had close connections with that area. These epitaphs may have been deliberate attempts to retain the commemorative practices of home, or just unconscious reproductions of what were considered to be 'normal' epitaphs.

There are some examples of a person who is explicitly said to be a foreigner using a formula from the homeland. One of these is IGUR 413. The epitaph of the Bithynian M. Aurelius Xenonianus Aquila calls his tomb τὴν πύαλον, a very unusual term which seems to be used otherwise only at Nicomedia in Bithynia.[222] Another Bithynian whose epitaph has a local formula is C. Hostilius Agathopus of Nicaea; his tomb carries the curse 'if anyone despoils (the tomb), may the sea not be navigable for them nor the earth passable', which was used most commonly at Nicaea.[223] Agathopus was commemorated by a woman who was probably his wife, while Aquila appears to have composed his own epitaph. People who wrote their own epitaphs, or who were commemorated by spouses or siblings from the same place, must have had a much greater chance of receiving a local-style epitaph than those who were commemorated by their children.

The formula χρηστὸς καὶ ἄμεμπτος was largely restricted to Sicily.[224] It occurs twice at Rome, in the feminine form, for Claudia Soteris and Minucia Sicula (Μινουκία Σικελή).[225] Nothing is said about the origin of Soteris. In the case of Minucia, since her husband who commemorated her has only a single name, it seems safe to assume that Σικελή is an ethnic rather than a name, 'Minucia the Sicilian'.[226] Soteris was probably a Sicilian too, or at least commemorated by one.

These clear links between epitaphs written at Rome and styles used in the homeland show that customers must in some cases have composed the epitaphs themselves rather than relying on the stone-cutter to provide a stock one. This was perhaps more likely to happen in Greek, where there was less standardization at Rome and, presumably, considerably fewer competent stone-cutters, than in Latin. It implies that, in some cases where epitaphs have a particularly unusual style, it may be possible to associate them with a home region, either when there is no explicit reference to migration, or in cases where the deceased is evidently an immigrant but it is not stated where from. An example of the latter comes in IGUR 367. Liberalis commemorated his brother Eutactus, aged 14, who had 'lived abroad with him' (συν-ξενειτεύσαντα, an otherwise apparently unknown word) for five years. It is not stated where they came from, but the epitaph calls the tomb τὴν καμάραν, a term which was mainly used in a small part of Asia (Teos, Smyrna, Ephesus). It is therefore very likely that that was the home area of the two brothers.[227]

Agaklytos commemorated his father, whose name is largely lost, using the following wording:[228]

τὸ μνημεῖον κατεσκεύασεν μνήμης χάριν, ζήσαντι ἔτη λ΄.

He built the monument as a memorial, for the man who lived 30 years.

Although the individual elements of this are all common, the combination is very unusual, but reproduces almost exactly the wording of an epitaph from Prusa in Bithynia for a soldier named Nicomedes:[229]

ζήσαντι ἔτη κθ΄, [τὸ μ]νημεῖον κ[ατε]σκεύασεν μνήμης χάριν.

Agaklytos and his father therefore seem likely to have been Bithynians.[230]

There is also an unusual combination of elements in the epitaph which Asclepiodote put up for her husband Stratonicus:[231]

Ἀσκληπιοδότη Στρατονίκῳ γλυκυτάτῳ ἀνδρὶ τὴν στήλην ἐκ τῶν ἰδίων κατεσκεύασα ζήσαντι ἔτη λε΄. χαῖρε παροδεῖτα.

Asclepiodote built the stele from her own resources for her sweetest husband Stratonicus, who lived 35 years. Farewell, passer-by.

Again the individual elements are not unusual but the way they are combined is. At Cius/Prusias, close to Prusa, Aurelia Chreste daughter of Apollonides commemorated her husband Chrestus in a virtually identical way:[232]

Αὐρ. Χρήστη Ἀπολλονίδου τῷ γλυκ[υ]τ[ά]τῳ ἀ[νδ]ρὶν (sic) Χρήστῳ ἐκκ (sic) [τ]ῶ[ν] ἰδίων κατεσκεύασα τὴν στήλην, ζήσαντι ἔτη ν΄. χαίραιται (sic) παροδ[ῖται].

Aurelia Chreste, daughter of Apollonides, built the stele from her own resources for her sweetest husband Chrestus, who lived 50 years. Farewell, passers-by.

Asclepiodote may well have come from the same area.

A Greek inscription denotes a tomb as the property of Cn. Octavius Bassillus, heir of Octavia Hygeia.[233] The practice of indicating ownership of a tomb was in itself unusual at Rome. The formula used to describe tomb and ownership reproduces exactly one found in several epitaphs at Ephesus,[234] and Bassillus, despite his Latin name, was probably an Ephesian too. Similarly, the epitaph of the Jewish trader P. Catilius Hermias and his family uses formulae which are completely unlike anything else known for the Jews at Rome, imposing a fine on anyone who violates the tomb and threatening them with the wrath of God.[235] The style is typical of Jewish epitaphs from Asia, and Hermias almost certainly came from there. He is particularly likely to have been an immigrant in view of his profession.

At Portus, a praetorian named Aurelius Aphrodisius commemorated Lucius Aelianus, probably his father-in-law. He forbade anyone else to use the sarcophagus and imposed a fine if they did, payable to the 'most sacred treasury' and to the heirs.[236] The general wording is typical of Asia Minor, and the fact that the inscription is in Greek, which is extremely unusual for a praetorian, almost certainly indicates that the people involved had come from somewhere in the East. The closest parallel which I have found to the language used is in an epitaph from Nicomedia.[237]

The same process could happen in reverse, with a formula from Rome spreading outwards. The clearest case of this is probably the Jewish formula ἐν εἰρήνῃ ἡ κοίμησις (in peace the sleep). This was extremely common in Jewish epitaphs at Rome, but outside Rome it is only found five times in the early part of the Jewish catacomb at Venosa, once at Portus and once at Taranto.[238] It was almost certainly spread outwards from Rome by Jews who moved from the city.

Epitaphs are thus one aspect of burial practice which foreigners could bring to Rome with them. They do not, however, show anything more than the preferences of a few individuals – and the small number of examples given above shows how unusual foreign epitaphs were at Rome. Other than the Jews, there is little evidence for any foreign group (as opposed to individuals) at Rome making strong communal efforts to retain its separateness after death, despite the claims which have sometimes been made.

Notes

[1] Many people in the inscriptions are identified as Alexandrians, but very few as Egyptians; see p. 247.

[2] In comparable circumstances, Feissel (1995, 372) notes that none of the soldiers with 'barbarian' names in epitaphs at Constantinople gives an ethnic.

[3] La Piana 1927, 203–4.

[4] Faist 1997, 198; Boyle, Halfacree and Robinson 1998, 72; Jones 1993, ch. 3.

[5] Hall is largely concerned with indigenous groups living in 'their' territory, whereas Panayi is dealing with immigrants and their descendants.

[6] IGUR 1287. Cf. Mark 7.26: 'a Greek woman, Syro-Phoenician by birth' (γυνή...Ἑλληνὶς Συροφοινίκισσα τῷ γένει); Lib.Pont., *Euaristus*: 'a Greek by nationality, an Antiochene' (*natione Grecus Antiochenus*).

[7] Cf. Solin 1983, 601–2; Matthews 1999, 16.

[8] Hall 1997, 33: 'Ethnic identity can only be constituted by opposition to other ethnic identities.'

[9] Matthews 1999, 29.

[10] McCormack (1984, 357) notes the emergence of a pan-British identity among immigrants to Canada in the face of competition from other ethnic groups. He also (p. 371) refers to the formation of local societies such as the 'Aberdeen, Banff and Kincardine Association' among British immigrants at Winnipeg.

[11] CIL vi 342 = 30742.

[12] Kaimio 1979, 67: '...we cannot, therefore, compare them to the door plates of consulates of foreign states in modern capitals'.

[13] Moretti 1958, 115–16.

[14] Pliny, *H.N.* 16.236; Moretti 1958, 115–16. However, Moretti believes that these were different from the overseas *stationes*.

[15] Moretti 1958, 105–7.

[16] *Statio*-manager?; the word can also mean the users of, or contributors to, a *statio*.

[17] The same man made a dedication to *Nomioi Theoi* (IGUR 163).

[18] IGUR 80 = CIL vi 31128.

[19] IG xiv 830.

[20] Meiggs 1960, 283–6; Pohl 1978, 333–4; Bakker et al. 1999. They are not necessarily all of the same date; the tenants of some of the rooms no doubt changed. The identity of the users of many of the rooms has not been preserved.

[21] CIL xiv 4142.

[22] Meiggs 1960, 285; he dates it no later than the reign of Hadrian.

[23] Meiggs 1960, 286.

[24] I.Porto 2. Cf. ibid.3, the ἐπιμελητής of the whole Alexandrian fleet.

[25] Meiggs 1960, pl. XXIIIb.

[26] I.Porto 5.

[27] CIL xiv 4620.

[28] Meiggs 1960, 286.

[29] Meiggs 1960, pl. XXIIId.

[30] Meiggs 1960, 287, pl. XXIIIa. A dedication to Diva Sabina by the *Sabrathenses*, found in Caesar's Forum and dated to AD 138, may suggest that there was a *statio* at Rome as well: AE (1934) 146.

[31] Meiggs 1960, pl. XXIVb.

[32] CIL xiv 477.

[33] Loane 1938, 56.

[34] La Piana 1925, 259.

[35] Suetonius, *Nero* 37.

[36] Meiggs 1960, 287.

[37] BGU ii 423; Winter 1933, 41–2.

[38] Martial 1.49. 1.61, 10.103–4.

[39] P.Mich. viii 487; cf. viii 465–6 and 486, probably concerning the same man. Sempronius may not actually have been at Karanis when he received the letter. The use of family terminology in such letters does not necessarily indicate a real family relationship.

[40] P.Mich. viii 490–1 (ed. H.C. Youtie and J.G. Winter).

[41] P.Mich. viii 500–1 (ed. H.C. Youtie and J.G. Winter).

[42] BGU i 27; Winter 1933, 38–9.

[43] CIL vi 2425; CIL iii 1479; Ricci 1993b, 189, 206.

[44] CIL viii 2890.

[45] CIL vi 9677; CIL ii 1971; Ricci 1992b, 111.

[46] CIL vi 16247; CIL ii 3624; Ricci 1992b, 111.

[47] Saller 1982, 191.

[48] Talbert 1984, 42.

[49] SHA, *Sev.* 2.

[50] Digest 50.7.13 Scaevola refers to an ambassador coming to Rome from Nicopolis (it does not say which one), and buying a house at Nicopolis before he had completed the business of the embassy.

[51] Morley 1996, 175.

[52] R. Harder, *Didyma* II (Berlin, 1958) no. 296 ll. 6–11 (quoted from Talbert).

[53] Talbert 1984, 95.

[54] Pliny, *H.N.* 29.5.7–9; Bowersock 1969, 65; Talbert 1984, 413; Jackson 1988, 56–7. Further bibliography in Nutton 1986, n. 20.

[55] Millar 1981, 158–9; the son was also a patron of Tibur.

[56] PIR² C1637.

[57] Talbert 1984, 40.

[58] Martial 10.96.1–4.

[59] Lucian, *My Native Land* (*Patriae Laudatio*) 8 (tr. A.M. Harmon).

[60] Doblhofer 1987, 47, 63–4; Edwards 1996, ch. 5.

[61] Athenaeus 1.3b (tr. C.B. Gulick).

[62] CIL vi 31066. A word written at the end in the Greek alphabet is probably a name: perhaps Ariphilos.

[63] Guarducci 1951–2; Gager 1992, no. 79; SEG xiv 615. It was found in a grave near the Porta Ardeatina; such curses were normally left at tombs.

[64] This is how it is understood by Guarducci (1951–2, 63–4). Gager translates: 'who has worked as his assistant'.

[65] Perhaps 'Do not allow him (i.e. the doctor) (to prevent the departure)', as suggested by Gager.

[66] Guarducci (1951–2, 66), takes this as a reference to the mouth of the Tiber, which she thinks the speaker is asking to be blocked with sand. She goes on to suggest (p. 69) that this idea would be most likely to occur to someone from the coast of Syria or Palestine. However, asking for the exit route to be blocked would be rather strange for someone so anxious to leave Rome.

[67] Stevens 1994, 181–2.

[68] Kajanto 1980, 85.

[69] Or in Greek (MacMullen 1990, 51). Slaves at Rio de Janeiro used Portuguese to each other if they did not share an African language (Karasch 1987, 215).

[70] This would probably not apply if the native language was Greek. Cf. Karasch 1987, 215.

[71] SHA, *Sev.* 19.9: 'sed Afrum quiddam usque ad senectutem sonans'.

[72] SHA, *Had.* 3.1. Spanish accents seem to have attracted particular comment (Balsdon 1979, 130), but regional Italian accents were also mocked (Talbert 1984, 37). Lucian, *On Salaried Posts* (*De Mercede*) 24 refers to the 'villainous accent' of highly educated Greeks.

[73] Quintilian 1.1.4; Soranus, *Gyn.* 2.19.

[74] La Piana 1925, 223; Bardy 1948, 81–94.

[75] Kajanto 1980, 93.

[76] Moretti (1989, 6) rather oversimplifies the issues by claiming that there was no need for Greek-speakers to use Latin because everyone at Rome understood Greek.

[77] Despite the predominance of Greek in Moesia Inferior itself, noted by Kaimio (1979, 89).

[78] Ricci 1994a, 18–19. See below, p. 190.

[79] MacMullen 1993, 48–9.

[80] Juvenal 3.62 ff.; Kajanto 1980, 87.

[81] Kaimio 1979, 166.

[82] Philostratus, *V.S.* 491 (tr. W.C. Wright).

[83] Philostratus, *V.S.* 589 (tr. W.C. Wright).

[84] IG xiv 1440; IGUR 1317. Cf. IGUR 1171, a bilingual Latin and Greek inscription for a charioteer family, and 1350, a Greek epitaph for a girl of 'Ausonian family'.

[85] Moretti 1989, 7.

[86] Solin 1983, 721.

[87] His figures are rather different from those given in the table below, due largely to new publications since his study, but the overall picture remains similar.

[88] Kajanto 1980, 91–2.

[89] Kajanto 1980, Tab. 2. Lombardi (1997) gives a full list of those now in the Musei Vaticani. ICUR was incomplete at the time of Kajanto's study.

[90] Kajanto 1980, 98. This date is somewhat later than the probable date of the Roman church's change from Greek to Latin as the main liturgical language (see above).

[91] Bardy 1948, 87.

[92] Cf. Kajanto 1980, Tab. 3.

[93] Either Latin and Greek, or Latin/Greek and another language (Hebrew, Palmyrene, Nabatean).

[94] Solin 1983, 721.

[95] Noy 1997, 309.

[96] CIL vi 30925 = 374 = IGUR 6.

[97] CIL vi 1508 = IGUR 71.

[98] Noy 1997, 307.

[99] Kajanto 1980, 95; CIL vi 18175, 20548, 33976.

[100] Cf. Noy 1997, 307–8.

[101] Kajanto 1980, 96.

[102] Noy 1997, 308.

[103] Edwards 1995, 83; Boyancé 1956, 125.

[104] Jones 1993, 106–15.

[105] Noy 1997, 308–9.

[106] Solin 1983, 720.

[107] Suetonius, *Aug.* 43. The reference *might* be to other Italian languages.

[108] Suetonius, *Nero* 13. Rochette (1996) finds very little evidence for any sort of interpreters of languages other than Greek at Rome.

[109] Kaimio 1979, 320.

[110] Bardy 1948, 89.

[111] CIL vi 19134, 34196 (CIS ii 159).

[112] Noy 1999.

[113] JIWE ii 58; see p. 283 n. 486.

[114] Noy 1999; Equini Scheider 1988, 64.

[115] IGUR 166; see p. 241.

[116] ICUR 5693.

[117] ICUR 1861.

[118] ICUR 4891.

[119] JIWE ii 562.

[120] IGUR 119–20.

[121] IGUR 122: 'Ares the ancestral god who listens to prayer'.

[122] In the following discussion, I shall refer to names which are not Greek or Latin as 'local', in the absence of any standard terminology – writers such as Kajanto tend to refer to them as 'barbarian' or 'barbaric'.

[123] The most obvious example of this is the use of Semitic names by Christians.

[124] Solin 1977b. They were much commoner in Greece: 4.8% out of 3,530.

[125] Solin 1977b, 210.

[126] Kajanto 1963a, 57; 1997, 106. The same proportions apply in both Latin and Greek inscriptions.

[127] Solin 1977a, 163; Kolb 1995, 460.

[128] Kaimio 1979, 183; Solin 1977a, 164.

[129] Includes one case where the father has both a Latin and a Greek name.

[130] Includes one case where the child has both a Latin and a Greek name.

[131] Kajanto (1963a, 59–60), surveying cognomina of fathers and sons in Christian inscriptions from Rome, produced similar results with a much larger sample (N=212). He found that 48% were Latin in both generations, 24% Greek in both, 12% Latin father Greek son, 16% Greek father Latin son.

[132] As interpreted by Ricci (1993b, no. P3). The father was a veteran.

[133] Solin 1983, 722. If the new recruit was not previously a Roman citizen, he would take on a complete Latin name.

[134] BGU ii 423; Winter 1933, 41–2.

[135] Solin 1983, 722; cf. p. 169.

[136] Cf. Kajanto 1963a, 28.

[137] IGUR 118–19. Cf. p. 243.

[138] On Semitic names at Rome and in the West, see Solin (1983), esp. 633–47.

[139] Cf. Kajanto (1963a, 56): 'it is often impossible to decide the particular provenance of a barbaric name'. Some names can have two different provenances, e.g. Simon can be both Greek and Semitic.

[140] Solin 1983, 723, 782. Cf. for example CIL vi 8653, where the father is called Belambelus (a slave of Tiberius) and the son Primus, evidently named after his mother Prima.

[141] CIL vi 9276. It is not certain that these people were slaves.

[142] Zevi 1973.

[143] See p. 239.

[144] See p. 238.

[145] See p. 248.

[146] Solin 1983, 635. As he notes, the Jews of Rome were an exception (see p. 262).

[147] Solin 1977b, 211–12.

[148] McCormack 1984, 358.

[149] Dion.Hal. 2.19.3 = Beard, North and Price 1998, vol. 1, no. 8.7a.

[150] Beard, North and Price 1998, vol. 1, p. 300: 'It is easy enough to imagine how a rootless immigrant, lost in a great city, might have found attraction in the community or worshippers of Isis. But there is no reason to suppose that such people made up the majority of the cult's adherents or explain its success.'

[151] La Piana 1927, 286.

[152] Dahya 1973, 246.

[153] La Piana 1927, 265.

[154] Karasch 1987, 254–66.

[155] Cf. McCormack 1984, 370.

[156] Augustine, *Ep.* 53.2.

[157] Frend 1952, 164, 169–70.

[158] His no. 72 (ICUR 4437). No. 74 (ICUR 4441) has a Galatian immigrant who might be a Montanist. No. 93 (IGCVO 134) has a Montanist doctor named Alexander. Although there is nothing to connect him with Asia except the use of Greek in his epitaph, Tabbernee writes (p. 546): 'Presumably Alexander was a member of the thriving Montanist congregation of immigrants from Asia Minor resident in Rome... This community was centered around the Via Aurelia.'

[159] La Piana 1925, 213–16; Bardy 1948, 97.

[160] Bardy 1948, 81–94.

[161] Apart from the prevalence of Greek names in some cases, which is not in itself necessarily a sign of foreignness (cf. p. 180 above). The possibility of a link between foreigners and particular burial societies is not even considered by Patterson (1992b).

[162] AE (1972) 14.

[163] In the Jewish catacombs, the designation *Ioudaios* seems largely to have been reserved for those who were somehow on the fringes of the Jewish community (Williams 1997).

[164] Bardy (1948, 274) suggests that Pope Victor may have got from Carthage the idea of establishing corporate ownership of the Christian cemeteries of Rome.

[165] Nuzzo 1997, 707.

[166] La Piana 1925, 229, quoting Marucchi.

[167] Bardy 1948, 96.

[168] Bertolino 1997.

[169] Feissel 1982a, 371–7.

[170] ICUR 4437 (following Feissel 1982a, 371), 4439 (Feissel 1982a, 373–4), 4441, 4442, 4443=4444.

[171] 4434 uses χωρίου with an otherwise unknown village name (*contra* Avraméa (1995, no. 259), who tentatively attributes it to Syria). Ferrua 1939, p. 148 no. 10, uses χωρίου with an unknown village. ICUR 4271b+4452a, joined by Nuzzo 1997, refers to κωρίῳ Μικρᾶς Κώμης, previously assumed to be Egyptian (Avraméa 1995, no. 294, IGCVO no. 100), but on no firm grounds. As the 4452a piece comes from Octavilla, that is further evidence for thinking that Mikra Kome was really a Galatian village.

[172] ICUR 5064 (Avraméa 1995, 322), 5658 (Feissel 1982a, 375), 5661, 5669+5675 (Feissel 1982a, 375–6), 5676 (Feissel 1982a, 374), 5679 (Avraméa 1995, 332).

[173] The same word for village is used in inscriptions in Galatia itself, meaning village, estate or district, although otherwise these inscriptions do not obviously reproduce Galatian patterns. None of them names the commemorator or gives the year of death, as Christian inscriptions from Galatia commonly do.

[174] Cf. Noy 1998a, 75–6.

[175] Turcan 1958.

[176] Toynbee 1971, 127–8; Tacitus, *Ann.* 16.6.

[177] Toynbee 1971, 41–2.

[178] Counts 1996.

[179] IGUR 1288, according to Sacco's interpretation cited by Moretti ad loc.

[180] Lucretius 3.890–3; Statius, *Silv.* 5.1; Toynbee 1971, 41.

[181] IGUR 1333, with comments ad loc.

[182] Toynbee and Ward Perkins 1956, 54.

[183] Cf. D'Ambra (1988) on tombs at Ostia which depicted the deceased's occupation on the outside and were decorated with mythological scenes on the inside.

[184] Speidel 1994c, no. 165, with comments ad loc.

[185] Speidel 1994a, 25. The German bodyguards of the 1st century, on the other hand, borrowed the gravestone style of the praetorians.

[186] Speidel 1994a, 145.

[187] Nock 1932, 329–30. The Egyptians may, however, have been Egyptian Greeks and therefore not departing from their native custom. Audin (1960, 526) notes that initiates of Mithras, Isis and Cybele used cremation at this time.

[188] IGUR 1204.

[189] Josephus, *B.J.* 1.184; *Ant.* 14.124.

[190] Ricci (1994a, 23) also gives examples of veterans who had served at Rome being buried at home in family tombs.

[191] Gafni 1997, ch. 4; Noy 1998a , 78–9; see also p. 267. There does not seem to be any evidence of Jews from Rome being sent for burial in the land of Israel during this period, although burial there was represented as theologically desirable.

[192] Musurillo 1954, 58 col. 6.

[193] Lucian, *My Native Land* (*Patriae Laudatio*) 9.

[194] Philostratus, *V.S.* 597 (tr. W.C. Wright).

[195] Philostratus, *Ap.T.* 8.15.

[196] Augustine, *Conf.* 9.11.

[197] CIL viii 15930. The epitaph is shared with a woman of the same family who is probably an aunt, cousin or niece.

[198] CIL ii 382; 1st–2nd century according to Ricci 1992b, no. a12.

[199] CIL ii 379.

[200] CIL ii 6271.

[201] CIL xiii 2181.

[202] CIL xii 155.

[203] CIL iii 2083.

[204] CIL iii 6414; 3rd–4th century according to Ricci 1993b, no. De4.

[205] CIL viii 27532.

[206] IGUR 1321; 3rd–4th century according to Moretti.

[207] IGUR 1323.

[208] CIL ii 3035. In the context, the Latin word probably means something like 'constant companion'.

[209] CIL xii 1750 (1st century according to Ricci 1992a, no. A7). The surviving

part of the epitaph does not specifically say that the remains were sent home.

210 CIL xiii 2040. He was either aged 10 or a student for 10 years.

211 CIL xii 2211.

212 CIL xiii 260.

213 CIL iii 5031.

214 CIL iii 5667.

215 CIL iii 4845.

216 CIL iii 9713.

217 IMS ii no. 218; 3rd–4th century according to Ricci (1993b, no. Mo7).

218 CIL viii 8501.

219 Inscr.Lat.Mar. 93 = Inscr.Ant.Mar. 457.

220 CIL viii 2402.

221 Charmos at Rome commemorated his mother Chiliarchis, 'dead in the land of Egypt' (IGUR 1357); in this case, it could be that Charmos had come to Rome as an immigrant and, when he heard news of his mother's death, commemorated her at Rome as he was unable to return to Egypt to do it. However, it is equally possible that Chiliarchis had gone to Egypt from Rome. Charmos has not been counted as an immigrant for the purposes of ch. 4.

222 TAM iv 295, 306.

223 IGUR 837 and Robert (1978), with the examples quoted there.

224 Ferrua 1941, 180.

225 IGUR 646, 794.

226 She has been counted as a Sicilian in ch. 4.

227 As they were certainly immigrants from *somewhere*, they have been counted under Asia in ch. 4.

228 IGUR 271.

229 I.K.Prusa ad Olympum 145.

230 These and the following examples have *not* been counted as foreigners in ch. 4.

231 IGUR 379.

232 I.K.Kios 40.

233 IGUR 824: τούτου τοῦ μνημείου καὶ τῶν κατεπικειμένων σορῶν κήδεται Γνάι(ος) Ὀκτάουιος Βάσσιλλος κληρονόμος Ὀκταουίας Ὑγείας. ('The owner of this memorial and of the surrounding sarcophagi is Cn. Octavius Bassillus, heir of Octavia Hygeia').

234 I.K.Ephesus 2344c–d, 2558 use τούτου τοῦ μνημείου, σοροῦ, κήδεται.

235 JIWE ii 360.

236 I.Porto 33: Αὐρήλιος Ἀφροδίσιος ‹σ›τρατιώτης πραιτωριανὸς Λουκίῳ Αἰλιανῷ τῷ κηδεστῇ μου τὴν σορόν· καὶ βούλομαι μηδένα ἕτερον ἀνῦξαι· ‹ε›ἰ δ‹έ› τις τολμήσει, δώσει προστίμου τῷ ἱ‹ε›ρωτάτῳ ταμ‹ε›ίῳ (δην.) ͵ε κ‹α›ὶ τοῖς κληρονόμοις (δην.) σ΄. χαίρ‹ε›τε.

237 TAM iv 1.267: Αὐρ. Μαρκιανὸ[ς κ]ατεσκεύασα τὴν προγονικήν μου πύελον ἐμαυτῷ κὲ [τέκ]νοις [κὲ τῇ π]αρηκούσῃ μου συνβίῳ Διονυσιάδι· βούλομε δὲ μετὰ τὸ κατατεθῆνε τοὺς προγεγραμμένους μηδίνα τεθῆνε· εἰ δέ τις τολμήσει ἐπανῦξε τὴν σορόν, δώσει τῇ πόλι προστίμου (δην.) αφ΄ κὲ τῇ κώμῃ Κυπρινῶν (δην.) ͵α. χέρετε.

238 Noy 1997, 310.

Chapter 8

FOREIGN GROUPS AT ROME

Each section of ch. 8 focuses on one of the main areas from which
foreigners came to Rome. There will be an overview of the basic points
of the history of migration from that area to Rome: dates, political
background, principal reasons. The various ways of referring to the
homeland which are used in inscriptions by people from the area will
be analysed and, in some cases, the occurrences of distinctive local
names at Rome will be studied. Finally, an attempt will be made to
trace any evidence for people from that region acting as a group, for
example through shared institutions or shared religious practices. The
Jews have been treated separately in the final section since, although
they were in some respects seen as a 'geographical' group, their connection with their 'homeland' was much more tenuous than that of
Spaniards or Syrians. There is also literary evidence from rabbinic
sources available for the Jews which is unlike anything which exists for
other groups.

i. Gaul and Hispania

Overview

The first Gauls at Rome were presumably those who captured the city
in 390 BC. After that, for a period of over two centuries, Gauls[1] would
probably have come to Rome only as slaves. On the instructions of the
Sibylline Books, two Gauls and two Greeks (presumably slaves) were
buried alive in the Forum Boarium in 228, 216 and 113 BC, which
must imply that they were a recognized presence in the city at those
dates.[2] Marseille, as a Greek city, may have sent migrants in the same
way and for the same reasons as Greek cities in the East (e.g. as
doctors[3]); the pattern of migration from there later appears to have
been similar to that from Asia Minor.[4] Gallia Narbonensis became
a Roman province in 121 BC, and, as a rapidly romanized area, probably began to send free migrants to Rome. It was heavily settled by
Italian colonists, and also became an important area for military
recruitment. The slave trade also continued: Cicero was taught by
M. Antonius Gnipho, who had been brought up as a slave in Gaul

although originally freeborn, and a grammarian of the first century AD, P. Valerius Cato, was said by some to be a freedman from Gaul.[5] Julius Caesar's campaigns in Gaul in the 50s BC, which created what ultimately became the three provinces (Tres Galliae) of Aquitania, Belgica and Lugdunensis, would have created huge numbers of prisoners, some of whom reached Rome as slaves. The Gauls expelled from Rome after the Varus disaster (see p. 44) would have been only those from the northern part, not from Narbonensis.

Early migration from Hispania to Rome is likely to have followed the same pattern as that from Gaul. People from Hispania probably appeared at Rome first as slaves, perhaps in the late third century BC, but there seems to be no direct evidence for Spaniards there before the time of Augustus. Roman military involvement in Hispania began as a consequence of rivalry with Carthage and the Second Punic War. There was prolonged military activity for most of the second century BC, no doubt creating many captives, and Baetica, like Narbonensis, became a highly romanized area. The conquest of the north-west of the peninsula was only completed under Augustus. Slaves continued to come from the area: Augustus' freedman C. Iulius Hyginus was probably *natus Hispanus*, although Suetonius records some doubts about his origins.[6] Pamphilus *Asturconarius*, commemorated in the Monument of the Statilii from the early first century AD, was presumably a slave or ex-slave.[7] Corinthus, a slave from Collippo in Lusitania, was commemorated by his two brothers.[8]

Both Gauls and Spaniards had a bellicose reputation at Rome.[9] Julius Caesar and Augustus had a band of Spanish bodyguards, probably from Calagurri.[10] Hispania was an important recruitment area for the Roman army, and a substantial number of Spanish praetorians are recorded from the late first and second centuries.[11] *Equites singulares* were recruited in Gaul at the same period. Some people had successful army careers: e.g. P. Valerius Priscus from Urci, who was buried at Rome aged 65, was a military prefect in postings from Mauretania to Cappadocia, and also seems to have his name stamped on a lead pipe from the Via Casilina.[12] Rebels from Gaul and Spain under the bandit-leader Maternus came to Rome to try to murder Commodus.[13] Recruitment of praetorians and *equites singulares* in the West declined substantially in the third century.

Ambassadors to Rome from Hispania are poorly attested; the only one recorded in an inscription at Rome is a man from Clunia.[14] Q. Caecilius Rufinus of Saguntum was honoured at home for undertaking an embassy to Hadrian at his own expense.[15] There are, however, literary references to embassies coming to Rome with business concerning the imperial cult.[16] Presumably the numerous dedications by individual Spanish cities to emperors (Augustus and Aurelian), provincial governors and other patrons also represent the fruits of embassies to Rome.[17]

Some of the people of high rank in their own Gallic communities who died at Rome may have been there on embassies, although this is not specified, e.g. Sex. Attius Atticus of Vienne, *flamen* of the province of Narbonensis.[18] Verus (the rest of his name is lost) took part in an embassy which obtained the juridical separation of Aquitania, probably in the late second or third century.[19] Ti. Claudius Pius, a decurio of Lyon, is specifically said to have died on an embassy.[20] Atticus, a slave owned by the Three Provinces of Gaul, was presumably at Rome on official business when he died there, but the reason for his presence is not stated.[21] P. Claudius Abascantus, who commemorated his *alumnus* at Ostia, was a freedman of the Three Gauls.[22]

Cornelius Balbus from Cadiz became the first provincial consul, in 40 BC.[23] The families of Trajan and Hadrian were from Italica, and represent the most successful of the large number of people from Spain who established themselves in the senatorial class from the first century AD, although they would no doubt have seen themselves as ethnically Roman. Ricci (1992b, 107) notes that the vast majority of known senators are from Baetica rather than from Tarraconensis or Lusitania.[24] Gaul, especially Narbonensis, also produced numerous senatorial families from the first century AD onwards.[25] Leaders of the Aedui and other tribes from Tres Galliae requested Claudius for permission to stand for senatorial office in AD 48, and Claudius commented that there were already senators from Vienne;[26] Julius Vindex who led the revolt against Nero in 68 was the son of a senator and the descendant of a royal family in Aquitania.[27] However, from the second half of the second century, there is little evidence of men from Gaul or Hispania reaching senatorial rank.[28] Others followed an equestrian career which would have taken them to Rome temporarily.[29] People from Hispania and Gaul are also recorded at Rome as *iudices selecti ex quinque decuriis*.[30] A man commemorated at home in Tarraconensis by his sister was *apparitor* of the curule aedile at Rome, probably in the second century.[31]

At the same time that the area was producing senatorial families, it also made an impact on the world of Latin literature. A number of high-profile figures in literature and education came from Hispania: the Elder Seneca (whose sons came with him to Rome as part of a family migration), Columella, Martial, Quintilian, Pomponius Mela.[32]

Martial and the Elder Seneca refer to several otherwise unknown Spaniards from the same milieu.[33] Cordoba and Cadiz recur most frequently as home cities.[34] Narbonensis also produced distinguished orators and writers in the first century AD.[35]

Some products in big demand at Rome came from Gaul and Hispania, notably olive oil, wine and fish-products such as garum (see p. 114).[36] Most of the amphorae fragments from the Monte Testaccio, dating from the late second and early third centuries, are from Spain.[37] Baetica was probably the most important supplier of oil, but it came from Narbonensis too.[38] The trade in these commodities clearly brought a number of reasonably affluent people to Rome, and probably the less affluent too. The businesses operated in the area of the Emporium and the Aventine.[39] There was a *corpus negotiantium Malacitanorum* with its own *quinquennalis* in the second century: P. Clodius Athenio, *negotians salsarius*, who is thought by Ricci (1992b, 137–9) to have originated from Malaga himself.[40] There was also an organization of dealers in oil, *negotiatores olearii ex Baetica*.[41] Wine, especially from Tarraconensis, was imported in large quantities from the Augustan period at least until the end of the second century.[42] Narbonensis was also an important supplier of wine to Rome,[43] but there do not seem to be any Narbonese wine-traders recorded in inscriptions at Rome. There is, however, an epitaph for a man who seems to have had business interests in both Hispania and Gaul; the exact interpretation is not certain because of abbreviations:[44]

> Sacred to the *Di Manes*.
> For C. Sentius Regulianus, *eques Romanus*, dealer in oil (*diffus. olearius*) from Baetica, *curator* of the same corporation, wine-dealer (*negot. vinarius*) of Lyon, operating in the settlements (*canabae*), *curator* and patron of the same corporation, sailor of the River Saône, patron of the same corporation, patron (and) *sevir*[45] of those operating at Lyon. L. Silenius Reginus his grandfather and Vlattia (sic) Metrodora and the sons of the same (man?) arranged for this to be placed. It was carried out by Dionysius and Bellicianus and...

Other products imported from Spain, such as precious metals and minium,[46] cannot be linked directly with any of the known Spaniards at Rome.

Another area in which there is a little evidence for people from Gaul playing an important role is the supply of clothing and footwear. Dio has a story about a cobbler from Gaul who insulted Caligula and got away with it.[47] An inscription records a freedman from Narbonensis who was a *vestiarius* (dealer in clothing).[48] Stanley (1990, 250) detects

Celtic names among some freedman *sagarii* (dealers in woollen clothing).[49]

Female dancers from Cadiz are mentioned by a number of sources from the late first and early second centuries, and seem to have become a proverbial form of erotic entertainment; the 'shameful master from Cadiz' mentioned by Martial probably organized a troupe of them.[50] It is not clear whether they should be envisaged as slaves (which is probably the implication), or whether Cadiz was a training-school for women of all origins. A woman commemorated as Carpime *Gaditana*, apparently the slave of an imperial freedman, may have been one of them.[51] The Lusitanian charioteer C. Appuleius Diocles (see p. 119),[52] the *retiarius* M. Ulpius Aracinthus (*natione Palantinus*)[53] and the *emboliaria* (interlude-actress) Phoebe *Vocontia*[54] are representative of other aspects of entertainment in which people from Hispania and Gaul were prominent.

Ausonius lists many rhetors from Bordeaux (and literary figures from all over Gaul) who spent at least part of their careers at Rome in the fourth and fifth centuries. Eventius of Vienne, who died in AD 407, is described as *causidicus consularis*.[55] Leading church figures moved from Gaul to Rome and its surroundings in the fourth and fifth centuries, notably Paulinus (eventually of Nola).[56] The letters of Sidonius show the continued importance of travel between Gaul and Rome, and of holding office at Rome, for the elite of Gaul in the fifth century AD. The latest dated epitaph for Gauls at Rome (a brother and sister) is from AD 442.[57] There are fewer Christian inscriptions mentioning people from Hispania, or literary references, although Spaniards certainly came to Rome for ecclesiastical reasons (see p. 125). The latest dated inscription is from 388, when Nicetus commemorated his son Rapetiga, a doctor and *civis Hispanus*.[58]

References to the homeland
The way in which a foreigner's place of origin was designated in an inscription may show something about where his or her primary loyalty lay: to province, city, tribe, region or village (although the wording was no doubt also influenced by epigraphic convention as well as personal preference). People could be described by others as *Hispani* in literature without any implication for how they defined themselves, but if they are labelled *Hispani* in inscriptions, it must carry a message about how they defined themselves or were defined by their commemorators. Below, and in the equivalent parts of the other sections of ch. 8, some of the areas which have furnished the most

inscriptions are analysed for their use of 'ethnic' labels.[59] There are many fragmentary inscriptions where the exact form used is uncertain (hence the disagreement with the totals of ch. 4); only those inscriptions where the relevant words are complete, or where the restoration/expansion is certain, have been used here. 'City' includes towns and villages.

TABLE 14. Designation of people from Hispania.

Province	27		
		Hispanus	4
		Hispanus + city	2
		Hispania /ex Hispanis	3
		ex Espanis + city	1
		(ex) Hispania Citerior(e)	2
		Hispania Citerior + city	4
		ex (provincia) Baetica	3
		Baetica + city	3
		ex Hisp. Ult. Lusitania	1
		Hispanus Lusitanus	1
		Lusitania + city	3
Region/tribe[60]	3		
		Arava	1
		Callaeca	1
		Cantaber	1
City[61]	36		

People from Spain were identified by a reference to the whole province or peninsula (rather than a part of it) more often than those from most other areas. It is notable that identification with Hispania as a whole is commoner than with one of the three Augustan provinces, and that the Citerior/Ulterior division is almost as common as that between the three provinces (although the inscriptions are nearly all later than the establishment of the Augustan system). Cities are mentioned more often than Hispania as a whole, but that is normal for all the areas studied; for pagan civilians it is in fact slightly commoner to mention Hispania than just a city. The implication of the inscriptions is that 'Spanish' identity was fairly important (in a way that, for example, 'Asian' identity was not), something which is also implied by the Spanish writers of the first–second centuries AD.

TABLE 15. Designation of people from Gaul.

Province	12		
		Gallus[62]	4
		Gallus + city	1
		III provinciae Galliae	3[63]
		Aquitania + city	1
		Belgica + city/tribe	2
		provincia Lugdunensis	1
Region/tribe	8		
		Aeduus	2
		Ambianus	1
		Novempopulanus	2
		Treveri	2
		Tunger	1
City	47[64]		

Cities and tribes seem to have played a rather more important role in the self-definition of people from Gaul than they did for people from Hispania. The ethnic *Gallus* was certainly much less used than *Hispanus*. This might be attributable to the negative image of the Gaul in traditional Roman history, or to the other meanings which *gallus* could have in Latin.[65] However, since references to the names of the provinces are also much rarer for people from Gaul than for those from Hispania, the implication may be that any form of 'Gallic' identification was seen less positively than the 'Spanish' equivalent.

Community and religion

There are few signs of any communal organizations among the Spaniards at Rome. The corporation of the Malacitani appears to have been a business association, although it may have had social functions too. The seats at the Colosseum which in the third/fourth centuries were reserved for people from Cadiz (see p. 117) imply that there was a substantial Gaditane presence in the city, but they could have been for visitors to Rome rather than for residents.[66] There is no evidence for any shared religious practices. Martial and the Elder Seneca give the impression of some links between Spaniards of similar social background, but these appear to be based entirely on personal connections, not on institutions.

There is also little trace of linguistic or onomastic practices coming to Rome from Spain. 'Phoebus also called Tormogus', born at Segisama in AD 143 and commemorated by his parents at Rome in 163, apparently had a Spanish name as well as a Graeco–Latin one,[67] but he is an isolated case as far as inscriptions are concerned.

The evidence from Gaul is slightly more substantial. Narbonne maintained a *statio* at Ostia, and Arles may have done so as well (see pp. 162–3). There are also dedications by groups of people from a specific city to their patrons or benefactors (or to people who they hoped would become benefactors). These can usually be associated with embassies, but may in some cases have been made by people actually resident in Rome. The *Sextani Arelatenses* (from Arles) made dedications both in the time of Tiberius and to Diva Faustina.[68] The Lugdunenses (from Lyon) made two honorific dedications in the mid-second century.[69] The Three Provinces of Gaul honoured P. Licinius Cornelius Saloninus in 259/260.[70] People living at Rome would no doubt hope that the good offices of the patrons of their home communities would continue to be available to them as individuals at Rome.

One deity from Gaul had her own shrine at Rome: the horse-goddess Epona.[71] Speidel (1994a, 141) associates the spread of her worship with the stationing of cavalrymen from Gaul, and there is certainly no evidence for her being worshipped by civilians at Rome; the bringing to Rome by military personnel of local deities is also well attested for Thracians (see p. 222). Praetorians from the province of Belgica made a dedication to their *Dii Sancti Patrii*.[72] A praetorian named M. Quartinius M.f. Cives Sabinus Remus (which Ricci understands as M. Quartinius Sabinus, *civis Remus*) made a dedication to Arduinna (a goddess from the Ardennes region) and Camulus, along with some more conventional Roman divinities.[73] There is also a dedication to the *numen* of Dea Vienna by a magistrate from Lyon, not necessarily a resident of Rome.[74]

However, none of this amounts to clear evidence that people from Hispania or Gaul acted together outside the very restricted worlds of military worship and trade organization. If there was anything which could be defined as a 'Spanish community' or 'Gallic community' among civilians living at Rome, it has left no trace.

ii. Central and Eastern Europe

Overview

The European provinces from Germany to Moesia, including Raetia, Noricum, Pannonia, Dacia and Dalmatia, have similar histories of contact with the Roman Empire and similar patterns of migration to Rome. Macedonia and Thrace, although their relations with the Empire were rather different, also produced similar migration patterns (see p. 59). The first contacts with the Rhine–Danube region, apart from embassies and cross-border slave trading, were military, and the first migrants to Rome were prisoners of war. With the possible exception of Thracians and Macedonians,[75] these would usually have been considered more useful for farm work than for urban life, although their military qualities also made them desirable as bodyguards and for other security purposes. The influx of slaves in large numbers lasted longer from Central Europe than from anywhere else: German prisoners were led in triumph by Domitian,[76] and the last major influx of captives was probably when Trajan auctioned off 50,000 Dacians.[77] Individual slaves were still coming from the area much later, however: there is an epitaph at Rome from the late second or third century for a freedman from Ovilavis in Noricum. [78]

Germans first came into military contact with the Roman Empire in the invasion of Narbonensis and Italy by the Cimbri and Teutones (defeated in 102–101 BC). It would have been during the campaigns in Germany under Augustus, until the defeat of Varus in AD 9, that they came to Rome in the largest numbers as prisoners, although ongoing conflict on the northern frontier presumably continued to produce sporadic supplies of captives.[79] Ricci (1993c, 223) believes that the Germans always remained on the margins of Roman society, and were seen as more foreign than other geographically remoter peoples such as the Thracians. Germans were both admired and feared as 'fierce barbarians', valuable as fighters as long as they were kept on the right side but viewed with suspicion in other circumstances. The people from the Danube region seem, on the whole, to have attracted less admiration and more contempt, being seen as pure barbarians.[80]

Immigrants from the other future Central European provinces do not seem to have made any impression at Rome before the first century BC. The time of Augustus is when immigration is likely to have begun seriously.[81] The areas which became Raetia and Noricum were brought under direct Roman control in 15 BC. Dalmatia, Pannonia and Moesia were also conquered under Augustus, not without considerable difficulty and therefore, presumably, large numbers of prisoners. Dacia was annexed in AD 106. All these provinces contained a number of cities founded as Roman colonies or which later acquired civic status, and it seems to have been through these that migration to Rome was channelled.

Macedon's first dealings with Rome were rather different from those of the area further north, since it was initially viewed very much as part of the Greek rather than the barbarian world. Rome's interference in

Illyria in the late third century BC led to potential conflict with Macedon, and to an alliance with the Aetolian League against Philip V in 211 BC. After Perseus of Macedon was defeated at the Battle of Pydna in 168, both Illyrians and Macedonians were paraded in the triumph, and 150,000 Epirotes were enslaved.[82] However, the epigraphic evidence for Macedonians at Rome is very similar to that for people from further north, i.e. almost entirely in Latin[83] and heavily dominated by soldiers and their associates. Some of the Macedonian soldiers at Rome have distinctly Thracian cognomina, e.g. Aurelius Mucapor from Beroe,[84] and very few have Greek ones. The population of the Roman province of Macedonia must have been very mixed, partly no doubt as a result of the severity of the treatment given to the area by the Romans in the second century BC, but the romanized and Thracian elements seem to predominate among Macedonians at Rome. The implication may be that the Greek-speaking part of the population tended not to migrate to Rome, or that its migration has been made invisible by lack of references to Macedonia in its inscriptions.

The epigraphic evidence suggests that Thracians were more prominent among civilians at Rome than the other Central/Eastern European groups in the first century AD.[85] Although Thrace only became a Roman province in AD 46, it was an important source of slaves before then;[86] 'Thracian' slaves could, however, have come from a wider area than what became the Roman province of Thrace. Thracian slaves were certainly well known at Rome by the time of Augustus, although there is no direct evidence of Thracians at Rome before then.[87] Thracians often used distinctive local names, and are therefore often easier to identify in inscriptions than many others.

As Central and Eastern Europe came under firm Roman control, it became an important military recruiting ground: initially for such specialized units as the emperors' German bodyguard (an idea begun by Mark Antony), and later for general recruitment to the legions. The Statilii had their own band of Germans, one of whom is described as 'the German of Taurus', and another as 'the German *armiger* of Taurus'.[88] Other leading families may have kept similar private security guards. There was a temporary expulsion of Germans (and Gauls) after the Varus disaster of AD 9 (see p. 44), but this had no long-term effect. The area was always the main source of *equites singulares*, and, after the change of recruitment policy by Septimius Severus, it became the main source of praetorians too.[89] The Urban Cohorts apparently recruited heavily in Noricum and Pannonia.[90] Bessans from the southern coast of Thrace[91] and Dalmatians[92] were important in the fleet. There were also German *frumentarii* at Rome from the end of the second century.[93] The German tribes most heavily represented in military units at Rome are the Batavi, Ubii and Frisii.[94]

Leading figures from independent German tribes came to Rome as hostages or refugees, e.g. Maroboduus of the Marcomanni in AD 19.[95] So did Thracians in the time of Augustus and afterwards;[96] the first seems to be Bithus son of Cotys in the late first century BC.[97] Two ex-slaves of King Rhoemetalces left inscriptions.[98] There is a brief reference to a visit to Domitian by the King of the Semnones and a German virgin priestess.[99] Some Dacian royalty were at Rome at the end of the second century.[100]

Otherwise, there is little literary evidence for free civilians coming from the area to Rome before the fourth century. Trade between Rome and the area was probably less significant than with most of the other parts of the empire, although still substantial. A *negotians* from Moesia was commemorated with his wife by a soldier of the Urban Cohorts.[101] Other jobs attested for Central and Eastern Europeans at Rome seem to be a fairly random selection, with no indication of any particular specialization. A Bessan slave was a dealer in oil, probably at the Porticus Pallantiana; he was not dealing in the produce of his home area.[102] A free Bessan was a *nummularius* (coin-changer or money-lender) at the Basilica Julia.[103] Two Dardanians who are probably slaves are described as masseur (*unctor*) and spinner (*quasillaria*).[104] T. Aurelius Primus, a Norican, was a *librarius*.[105]

Germans are shown in literature to have worked as gladiators at Rome,[106] but there are no inscriptions for German gladiators. Thrace was also an important supplier of gladiators, notably Spartacus,[107] but *Thraex* in gladiatorial inscriptions is a type of fighter rather than an ethnic.[108] There was a Ludus Dacicus in Regio II or III, according to the descriptions of Rome given by the fourth-century regionaries, which may (but need not) imply that Dacian gladiators were important in that period.[109] The charioteer Avillius Teres has a probably Thracian cognomen.[110]

Soldiers at Rome from Germany and elsewhere, particularly those who required grooms for their horses, could apparently bring their own slaves with them. A number of *equites singulares* commemorated their slaves and recorded their place of origin: a Marsacian named Miles;[111] a Norican called Tertius;[112] a Raetian called Mercator;[113] a Dacian freedman, Aurelius Primus[114] (n.b. the Latin names). The place of origin of the commemorator is never stated, but could be the same as that of the slave in each case.[115] Other German soldiers certainly had family members with them (see p. 70).

Central and Eastern Europe produced very few people who achieved advancement other than through the army, at least until the legalization of Christianity opened up another path through the church. Apart from the coastal cities of Dalmatia, almost no senators are known, and very few civilian equestrian officials;[116] this may be attributable to the relative lack of prosperity of the area, which made it difficult for civic leaders to build up the financial base necessary to achieve senatorial or even equestrian rank.[117] However, from the third century, men from Central and Eastern Europe started to appear in positions of prominence at Rome through the army (as officers and sometimes as emperors, from Maximinus Thrax to Gratian) and the church.[118] Pannonians in particular seem to have protected their local interests and exerted influence on the centre,[119] and they were prominent in the administration at Rome in the fourth century (see p. 99). Flavius Ursicinus, a Pannonian, worked for the *magister officiorum*.[120] The *vir clarissimus* Simplicius commemorated in an epitaph of 375 is probably Flavius Simplicius of Emona, *vicarius urbis* in 374–5.[121] There is more evidence for Pannonians in the Christian inscriptions than for people from any other part of the area, and some indication of a Christian Pannonian community at Rome in the fourth century (see p. 188).[122]

References to the homeland[123]

TABLE 16. Designation of people from Germany.

Province	40		
		Germanus[124]	17
		Germanus + tribe	3
		provincia Germania Inf.	1
		Germania Superior	1
		Germania + tribe + city	1
		Germana tellus	1
		ex collegio Germanorum	16
Region/tribe	67		
		Batavus	28
		Batavus + Noviomagum	3
		Frisi(ae)us/Frisaevo	10
		Su(a)ebus	5
		Helvetius	6
		Marsacus/-quius	6

		Ubius	3
		Canonefas	4
		Baetesius	1
		regio Bisentinae	1
City	19		
		Colonia Claudia Ara Ag.	15
		Noviomagum	3
		Mogontiacum	1

The designation German, or a reference to Germany, was very rarely used by regular soldiers at Rome, although it was the normal designation for the Julio-Claudian *corporis custodes* and for private body-guards.[125] The concept of *Germanus/Germania* appears to have been of considerably less importance than *Gallus/Gallia*, and less still than *Hispanus/Hispania*. Most Germans were recorded by their tribe. Very few referred to a city; nearly all those who did came from Cologne. This is a very significant difference from almost every other area: it appears that the recruitment of German soldiers and the migration of German civilians were not channelled through cities as they were for people from elsewhere. It was tribal rather than civic or provincial identity which was important.

TABLE 17. Designation of people from Noricum.

Province	27		
		Noricus	17
		Noricus + city	9
		provincia Noricum	1
City	15[126]		

For the rest of central Europe, however, the vocabulary was very different. Raetians are virtually always designated by *Raetus/Raetia*,[127] and Noricans very commonly use *Noricus*, showing the importance of the province (or of the single tribe on which it was based) in their self-identity. Noricans were, however, more likely than Raetians or Germans to be associated with a city.

TABLE 18. Designation of people from Pannonia.

Province	79		
		Pannonius/a	44

		(provincia) Pannonia	3
		Pannonius/a + city	10
		Pannonius/a + village	4
		Pannonia Superior	6
		Pannonia Superior + city	1
		Pannonia Superior+village	3
		Pannonia Inferior	4
		Pannonia Inferior + city	2
		Pannonia Inferior + village	2
Region/tribe	2		
		Boius	1
		Varcianus	1
City	37[128]		

There is a similar picture for Pannonians, although cities are more significant at least for soldiers. 'Pannonia', whether referring to the province or the tribe on which it was based, was an important self-designation. The one substantial difference between Pannonia and the areas mentioned before is the number of references to the home village; this is always given very carefully after the province and sometimes the nearest city. It will be discussed further below.

Dacia follows the same pattern as Raetia: 29 out of 33 designations contain some form of *Dacus/Dacia*, and only 4 give the city without the province. One man is described as *natione Dacisca regione Serdic<a>*, i.e. 'ethnically' Dacian but from an area in the province of Thrace.[129] This shows the possible disjuncture between official boundaries and locally perceived ones. The same pattern occurs among Dalmatians: 11 out of 16 use a form of *Dalmatus/Dalmatia*. Moesians, however, are very different: 11 out of 21 use some form of *Moesius/Moesia*, but this includes 6 where the city or village is also mentioned; 6 are designated 'Dardanians', and 4 refer only to the city. The 3 which refer to the village follow the same practice as some Pannonians and, as will be seen below, Thracians. Macedonians show even less interest in the province: only 5 out of 18 are designated 'Macedonian', while the others refer to their city only.

TABLE 19. Designation of people from Thrace.

Province	31		
		Thra(e)x	19[130]
		(provincia) Thracia	2

		Thrax/Thracia + city	7[131]
		Thrax/Thracia + village	3
Region/tribe	35		
		Bessus	28
		Bessus + city	4
		Bessus + village	1
		region + village	2
City	12[132]		

Thrace shows a very different pattern from the other provinces considered here, largely because of the frequency of the designation *Bessus*, which is mainly (but not exclusively) used for sailors. It had no connection with any Roman administrative unit, and shows that pre-Roman distinctions (or unofficial distinctions existing alongside the Roman system) could retain considerable importance.[133]

Another feature of the Thracian, Pannonian and Moesian inscriptions is the frequency of references to the home village (rather than the home city). This is shared with some, but only some, of the eastern provinces: particularly Galatia, but also Syria and Egypt. Any casual reader of an epitaph could probably be expected to know what an Alexandrian or a Pannonian was, but was unlikely to have much knowledge of, or interest in, an obscure village (*vicus*, κώμη, χωρίον). Nevertheless, home villages are mentioned in some religious dedications by soldiers (where it is explicitly part of a *self*-designation) and in epitaphs for soldiers and civilians.

In the case of the soldiers' dedications, it is used when a group of soldiers from the same village or from several different villages joined together to erect an inscription. This seems to be exclusively a third-century Thracian custom. Four praetorians from the same village who between them were serving in three different cohorts co-operated in one dedication.[134] In a dedication by twenty praetorians from the Philippopolis area to the *domus divina* and Asclepius Zimidrenus, each one gave his *vicus*, and fifteen different *vici* are named; between them, they were members of eight different cohorts.[135] The village name was invariably preceded by a reference to the area or tribe, e.g. *ex Dardania ex vico Perdica et ex vico Titis*.[136] On one occasion the village name was accidentally omitted.[137] There is also an example of the village formula being given in Greek.[138] In one case, a very odd word is used where *vico* should have been written: *cives prov. Tracie reg. Serdicens. MIDNE Potelense*. The most probable explanation is that *MIDNE* was a Thracian word for village.[139]

These Thracian votive inscriptions use the name of the village in a context where it would mean something to other contributors to the inscription, either because they came from the same village or because they came from other similar villages, presumably nearby. Some attempt was also made to make the names more generally meaningful by associating the village with a region or city which other readers might have heard of. It seems likely that similar circumstances existed when villages were mentioned in epitaphs: a group of people from the same place joined together to commemorate one of their number. Most of the villages are otherwise completely unknown. Inscribing the village names may have been a way of preserving a sort of local identity.[140] The Latin epitaphs which name villages all concern praetorians or *equites singulares*. They appear to be contemporary with the votive inscriptions, but cover a wider geographical area: Pannonia and Moesia as well as Thrace. Thracians and Moesians always used the term *vicus*, and nearly always gave a city or region as well as province and village.[141] Pannonians used *vicus*,[142] *pagus*[143] or *pedes*,[144] and one inscription has all three.[145] Thus there seems to be a clear attempt to preserve some sort of shared local identity, and at the same time there is perhaps a survival of distinctive local terminology.

Language and names

As has already been noted (p. 171), the inscriptions for people from all the Central and Eastern European provinces are almost exclusively in Latin, even though Moesia, Thrace and Macedonia themselves all had a high proportion of Greek inscriptions. This can be explained by the military context of the vast majority of the inscriptions; Latin was the natural epigraphic language for soldiers. Thracian and other local languages had no epigraphic tradition of their own, and, with the possible exception of the one Thracian word discussed above, there is no evidence for any of the local languages being inscribed at Rome. This does not, however, necessarily mean that Greek, Thracian and other languages were not spoken among the Eastern Europeans resident there.

Thracians (not only those from the province of Thrace) often had distinctive names which are easily recognizable in inscriptions. Some Thracians used alternative local and Roman names, e.g. the veteran Aurelius Marcellinus *qui et* Diza.[146] Since a thorough survey of occurrences of Thracian names is beyond the scope of this work,[147] only the best-documented one will be studied here.

'Bithus' (occasionally written Bitus or Vitus) was a common

Thracian name which occurs many times at Rome.[148] The status of the bearers of the name is as follows:

TABLE 20. Status of people called *Bithus*.[149]

Slave	6	Duo/tria nomina	9
Freedman	11	Uncertain	1
Single name	5	Soldier	18

The associations of the name seem to be rather different from those of the predominantly servile 'eastern' names discussed later in this chapter. Although at least 34% of the people called Bithus, and potentially considerably more, are of servile origin, at least 36% are soldiers. This probably prevented Bithus from being seen as a typical slave name. It had the advantage of being very similar to the Latin name Vitus. The slave and military context of the inscriptions means that no named children are recorded for any of the Bithi at Rome,[150] but their brothers all have Graeco–Latin, not Thracian cognomina: A. Mucius A.l. Bithus, brother of Attalus and Philotimus;[151] M. Livius Bithus, brother of Aratus;[152] Aurelius Vitus, a praetorian, brother of Aurelius Lucius;[153] M. Aurelius Bithus, brother of M. Aurelius Surus.[154] This also suggests that the name was quite acceptable in families whose naming practices were otherwise Graeco–Roman.

Community and religion

Noricum is the only province known to have maintained its own *statio* at Rome.[155] The *stationarius*, a civilian, honoured the *Genius Noricorum*. This is unusual because other local deities from Central and Eastern Europe are only known to have been worshipped at Rome by soldiers. Eight Norican *civitates* combined to make a dedication to a curule aedile, presumably their patron or benefactor, in the third century, but this is likely to have been done by a special delegation rather than by residents of Rome.[156] There is no other evidence of any specifically Norican or Raetian organization at Rome.

The importance for some Thracians of their home village, and the implications for shared local identity, were discussed above. There is another indication of this. When in 238 the villagers of Scaptopara in Thrace wanted to present a petition to the emperor about the impositions they suffered from people attending a nearby market, they used a villager who also happened to be a praetorian serving in Rome to do it, Aurelius Purrus.[157] This was clearly a case where a city would have sent its own ambassadors but a smaller community had to make do with whomever it could find. It shows, however, that Purrus must have maintained his links with his home, something which is consistent with the other Thracian evidence.

A number of specifically Thracian divinities had cults at Rome, such as the Thracian Hero, who was worshipped at Rome and Ostia.[158] Some of them seem to be extremely local gods, whose worship at Rome was probably part of the same outlook which emphasized the home village. For example, an inscription honoured, in Greek, 'the most manifest god Zberthourdos and Iambadoules'.[159] Several forms of Apollo (*Cicanos, Vergulesis, Raimullos*) which are probably derived from Thracian toponyms were honoured by praetorians.[160] Thracian gods were probably honoured in a Greek inscription put up by the praetorian Aurelius Bouris and his father Aurelius Pouris; the beginning is lost apart from 'to the gods'.[161] Moretti thinks that a Thracian god was also honoured by a *frumentarius* of Legio II Italica on a third-century altar.[162] The occasional use of Greek at Rome for Thracian religious inscriptions probably illustrates that the altars were sometimes inscribed in an in-group context, to be read only by other Thracians.

The following rather odd inscription was put up by a group of *equites singulares* for Caracalla in 219:[163]

> To Hercules Magusanus, for the return of our lord M. Aurelius Antoninus Pius Felix Augustus, his *equites singulares Antoniniani*, Batavian or Thracian citizens, recruited from the province of Germania Inferior, willingly discharged their vow, deservedly.

These may have been Batavians recruited to a Thracian unit while it was stationed in Germany; as the deity they honoured was a German one, they must have retained their own religious practices.[164] It was not unusual for a group of soldiers from the Balkan provinces, describing themselves as *cives* of a certain area, to join together for a dedication to a god or emperor, for example the *cives Dalmatas* (sic) who honoured Jupiter Optimus Maximus Capitolinus,[165] the *Marcianopolitani cives* who honoured Juno,[166] the *cives Philippopolitanorum* who honoured Asclepius Zimidrenus,[167] and the *cives Cotini ex provincia Pannonia inferiore* who erected several praetorian discharge inscriptions.[168]

The *collegium Germanorum* formed by the Julio–Claudian bodyguard was in itself an unusual institution since regular soldiers were not allowed to form similar associations.[169] It evidently gave Germans of varied tribal backgrounds a formal organization with its own officers which presumably, in view of its frequent occurrence in epitaphs, arranged burials. It came to an end under Galba, and there is no evidence of any equivalent institution later, although Germans still co-operated for religious purposes: a fragmentary dedication dated to AD 223 seems to have been put up by *cives* of Germania Inferior,[170] and the worship of the Matres Suleviae (a Celtic name) was brought by the *equites singulares* from Lower Germany to Rome.[171]

For Pannonians, there is some circumstantial evidence for at least informal activity as a community in late antiquity. The evidence for a Pannonian burial area in the S. Sebastiano catacomb, perhaps patronized by the Pannonian Urban Prefect Viventius and encour-aged by the transfer to Rome of the relics of the Pannonian saint Quirinus, was discussed at p. 188. The importance of Pannonian of-fice-holders at Rome in the fourth century was mentioned above, and there may have been some sort of support network which encouraged Pannonians to work for the advancement of their compatriots. In the Christian period a sense of solidarity could not be expressed by dedica-tions to local gods, so there is no epigraphic evidence of it, but it probably existed nevertheless.

iii. Greece

Overview

A history of Rome's contacts with Greece (in the sense of what became the province of Achaea, including the Aegean islands) is beyond the scope of this work. The establishment of direct Roman rule over much of the area in 146 BC, and the creation of the province of Achaea in 27 BC, were the culmination of a long involvement in the political manoeuvres of the various leagues and monarchs who competed with each other in the third century, but the cultural influence was of course of much longer standing. The attempt made by Dionysius of Halicarnassus to prove that Rome was really a 'Greek' city is perhaps indicative of the desire of some highly educated Greek-speaking immigrants to capitalize on it.[172]

The first Greeks from the future area of Achaea recorded in reliable literature at Rome are prisoners-of-war such as Polybius, ambassadors and slaves. There must have been a Greek presence in the city by the end of the third century BC, since, as mentioned above, on the instruc-tions of the Sibylline Books, two Gauls and two Greeks (presumably slaves) were buried alive in the Forum Boarium in 228, 216 and 113 BC.[173] The rationale behind the choice of nationalities is unclear because although the Gauls were enemies of Rome at the time, the Greeks were not. Rome's direct involvement in Greece began with the anti-Macedonian alliance with the Aetolian League in 211, an alliance which gradually expanded to include various Greek cities.[174] Numerous leading Greeks suspected of being pro-Macedonian were taken back to Rome for trial or imprisonment after the defeat of Macedon in 168.[175] In the second century BC, enslavement and manumission was a regular route by which Greeks with sought-after skills came to prominence at Rome. Fighting, and therefore presumably capture and enslavement, continued sporadically in Greece for much of the first century BC,[176] when there was still a plentiful supply of slaves born in Greece (although much of this may have come from those born in slavery). L. Ateius Philologus, a grammarian and rhetorician active in the late Republic, was a freedman born at Athens; Pompey's freedman Lenaeus was allegedly kidnapped from there as a boy.[177]

The supply of Greek slaves may have dried up later, since Philostratus makes Apollonius of Tyana remark, when accused of murdering an Arcadian boy, that 'slaves from Pontus or Lydia or Phrygia can be bought in Rome, because you may see droves of them being sent here', but that Greeks, and especially Arcadians, were not available in the slave market;[178] the point might be applicable to Apollonius' time in Rome (late first century AD) or Philostratus' (early third century). Inscriptions show that there were still Greek-born slaves at Rome in Apollonius' time, e.g. Eutyches, *natione Graecus*, whose epitaph is from the Flavian period or later.[179] Iulia Laudice, a freeborn woman from Same on Cephallenia, where she left her family in unspecified circumstances, was married to an imperial freedman, T. Flavius Alcimus, who may have been of the same origin, judging from his Greek cognomen, although this is not stated.[180]

Greece under Roman rule had the image of being an area suffering from depopulation and economic decline, although this picture was probably some way removed from reality. The Greeks themselves could be depicted as responsible for their own decline, at least when it suited Roman propaganda purposes.[181] The difficulty for someone based in Greece to establish the necessary capital may be a reason for the relative lack of senators from the area, although it was possible, as Herodes Atticus showed in the second century, to be extremely rich while retaining local links. The economic stagnation of Greece would, if genuine, have been a significant push factor in encouraging emigration, and there was certainly a demand at Rome for some of the skills which educated Greeks were likely to possess. Nevertheless, evidence for migration to Rome by free Greeks outside certain specific professions is fairly limited.

The taste for Greek culture among Roman aristocrats in the second and first centuries BC created a demand for philosophers, poets and private tutors in great houses. The geographical origin of these people was less significant than their command of Greek culture, but many of them came from Greece itself. Rome continued to have an attraction for them in the imperial period, encouraging some to come independently, even if it periodically reacted against them, e.g. with expulsions of philosophers (see p. 44). As discussed at p. 94, the Greek chair at Rome was apparently considered a promotion over the equivalent chair at Athens. The attractions were still there in late antiquity: Palladius of Athens taught rhetoric at Rome before being summoned to court in 379.[182]

Greece was an important source of doctors for Rome, including Claudius' doctor C. Stertinius Xenophon, from Cos (see p. 167). Cos itself was a training centre for doctors who later worked at Rome. Craftsmen also came to Rome from Greece, such as Cn. Arrius Stratocles, a sculptor from Athens,[183] and Euboulos, a Corinthian goldsmith.[184] Corinth had a particularly high reputation for metalwork although, since the city was a Roman colony, Corinthians could be of Italian ancestry.

Greece was not an important military recruitment area, although Greek freedmen were prominent as naval commanders in the civil wars at the end of the Republic. Only three military figures from Greece have epitaphs at Rome, all of whom served in the fleet.[185] This is consistent with the low estimation of Greek military prowess which is found in many Roman sources.

References to the homeland
The ethnic *Graecus*, in Latin or Greek form, seems to be confined largely to military and Christian inscriptions. It is also used for a small number of people who are probably slaves or ex-slaves.[186] In graffiti from the Palatine Paedagogium, the labels *Graecus* and Ἕλλην are both used for imperial slaves.[187] Pagan civilians from Greece are usually labelled according to their home city (Athenian, Lacedaemonian, Corinthian, etc.) or region (Boeotian). A 'Hellene' certainly did not need to come from Greece itself, so it is possible that a *Graecus* did not either, but it seems likely that it would imply Greek geographical origin, especially in the absence of any alternative terminology – *Achaicus* is never used as an ethnic, and there is only one inscription where Achaea is given as the name of the homeland.[188]

It is slightly surprising to find that in TABLE 1, Greece is one of the

'Type C' areas where a substantial proportion of the epigraphic evidence for migration is Christian/Jewish, since it would seem more natural for people to move from Greece to Constantinople than to Rome in the fourth century. It is even more surprising to find that in the pagan inscriptions for people from Greece (TABLE 12) Latin is used as often as Greek is, in contrast to areas like Asia and Egypt, for which Greek is used far more often than Latin. The explanation may be that migration from Greece is *under*-represented in the pagan inscriptions: people from Greece tended not to record that they were 'Greeks', perhaps because they were commemorated as doctors or rhetoricians instead, or because the Greek label was so widespread that it was of little use in identifying homeland, or, for those who did not qualify as Athenians or Lacedaemonians, because the connotations of 'Greek' were felt to be too negative in a Roman environment where anti-Greek prejudice was strong.

Community and religion

The cultural position of Greece made it virtually impossible for there to be any local gods who were not worshipped by people from elsewhere too. Thus there is no clear evidence for any religious organization exclusive to those from Greece. A long Greek-language inscription of *c.* AD 150 shows the existence at Rome of a Dionysiac cult organized and aided financially by Pompeia Agrippinilla, a woman of senatorial background whose family traced its ancestry back 200 years to Lesbos, where there was a local Dionysus cult.[189] The members, who numbered over 400, were slaves and ex-slaves of her family and a related one, who were taking part in the cult because of their ties to Agrippinilla, not through religious choice.[190] Although many of the names are Greek, this is only to be expected among slaves, and there is no reason to suppose a direct association between the cult and people of one particular geographical origin, despite the claims which have sometimes been made.[191]

There is no other evidence for any sort of community at Rome of people from Greece. Doctors and rhetoricians were more likely to associate with other doctors and rhetoricians than with people from the same place (although of course other doctors might happen to come from the same place). The indications in literature of solidarity among 'Greeks', not necessarily just those from Greece, are from a hostile perspective which only reflects the xenophobic prejudices behind it, not any real behaviour (see p. 34).

iv. Asia Minor

Overview

Direct Roman involvement in Asia Minor[192] began when Antiochus III came into conflict with Rome in the 190s BC; he was defeated at Magnesia in 189 and forced to withdraw to the east of the Taurus Mountains. Rome was then dominant in the area, but without any direct territorial control until the kingdom of Pergamum was bequeathed to the Roman people by Attalus III in 133 BC and turned into the province of Asia. Direct rule spread only gradually, more by peaceful absorption of client kingdoms than by conquest, until the province of Lycia et Pamphylia was created by Vespasian, bringing the whole area under Roman administration. On the eastern frontier, Armenia's status varied between province and client kingdom.

Roman expansion in Asia Minor did not, therefore, produce large quantities of enslaved prisoners in the way that expansion in Europe did. However, the slave trade was extremely active in the area, and the plentiful supply of Asian slaves is made clear in Roman literature. These varied from Greek inhabitants of the west coast to 'barbarians' from the interior. Juvenal refers to slaves who are the 'flower of Asia', and to Phrygians and Lycians as good quality slaves.[193] Slaves from Pontus, Lydia and Phrygia were supposedly in plentiful supply at Rome in the Flavian period.[194] According to Catullus, Bithynia was a good source of litter-bearers; i.e. the sort of job considered to need strength rather than intelligence or education.[195] Evidently not all the inhabitants of Asia Minor were regarded as attractive. Cicero insults someone by saying that he looks as uncouth as 'a Cappadocian just grabbed from the flock of slaves for sale', a comment which also illustrates the automatic association between the area and slavery in some Roman minds.[196]

Domitian's eunuch cupbearer Earinus came from Pergamum.[197] After Domitian prohibited castration, eunuchs would, at least theoretically, have had to be imported from outside the empire, normally via Asia Minor. Another source of slaves was kidnapping: Hierax, one of the companions of Justin Martyr at Rome, was a Phrygian who had been orphaned and kidnapped.[198] Asian slaves attested in inscriptions from the imperial period include Hector, Mygdonian slave of Domitilla;[199] Eutychas (sic), Phrygian slave of an *eques singularis* who is unlikely to have been from Asia Minor himself;[200] Primitivus, Cappadocian slave of another *eques singularis*.[201] The numerous imperial slaves and ex-slaves who originated in Asia Minor may have been born on imperial estates in the area.

Although literature emphasizes the significance of Asian slaves at Rome, inscriptions present a rather different picture. The large number of epitaphs in Greek, especially for people from the province of Asia (see TABLE 12), is consistent with the large number of recorded *peregrini* (see TABLE 10) in suggesting that the migration of people of free status was particularly significant for this area. The evidence is, however, almost exclusively concerned with the Greek population of Asia Minor, and there is very little sign of people of non-Greek background coming to Rome except as slaves.[202] This is consistent with the general predominance of the most romanized/hellenized section of their home society among free migrants to Rome. One exception is the introduction of the cult of Magna Mater to Rome in 205–4 BC, which brought Phrygian priests with it, both then and later. The strangeness of the rites led to the initial segregation of the priests, and to a prohibition on 'native-born Romans' participating in the ceremonies.[203]

Cities in Asia Minor seem to have had the greatest fondness of any part of the empire for sending embassies to Rome (see p. 100). This may also help to explain the number of people of high status at home who are commemorated at Rome although not specifically said to have been there on embassies: L. Antonius Hyacinthus, an asiarch;[204] Aurelia Tatia, probably high-priestess of Asia;[205] Lucius, an *athlothetes* from Smyrna and son of a high-priest.[206] Hortensius Pedon of Laodicea appears to have been an ambassador;[207] Chrysippus is specifically called a Cilician ambassador.[208] Two of the three members of one embassy from Termessos died at Rome.[209] Nicias from Xanthus in Lycia is explicitly said to have been both high-priest and ambassador.[210]

Senators from Asia Minor started to appear in significant numbers from the Flavian period, although individuals reached senatorial rank under the Julio-Claudians.[211] Some came from Roman colonies or Greek cities with Italian settlements; some were descendants of local rulers. According to Millar (1981, 203):

> Most came from the landed bourgeoisie of the cities, whose families combined office in the cities and provincial *koina* with posts in the equestrian order and the Senate.

Others who did not achieve senatorial rank could still find a comfortable lifestyle at Rome. Socrates from Tralles was able to boast in his Latin epitaph about enjoying the delights of Baiae and spending HS 50,000 on his tomb.[212] The fact that a description of a dispute at the Circus Maximus in 217 has the senators and equites shouting in Greek is probably a reflection of the importance of the eastern elite at Rome by that date.[213]

People from Asia Minor, especially Bithynia, are associated with the marble trade, and with building, sculpting and painting (see p. 114). There is enough evidence to assume that there was an established pattern of Bithynian marble-workers moving to Rome, something which is likely to have created a distinctive Bithynian community at Rome, linked by occupation as well as origin. This is, however, hypothetical, since there is no direct evidence for such a community.

There is some evidence for Asian involvement in entertainment. Alcimas the *tubocantius* was from Smyrna.[214] There may be a Bithynian actor in a fragmentary inscription.[215] There is a Cappadocian charioteer, and another from somewhere in the Diocese of the Orient.[216] However, it is in athletics that Asians are best attested. People from Asia dominate the list of victors at the Capitoline Games (see TABLE 11), and the athletes' association at Rome had a secretary from Philadelphia in Lydia and met in a building provided by a man from Ephesus in the second century AD (see p. 121).

Most of the foreign doctors whose place of origin is known came from Asia Minor.[217] The prominence of Asians in the world of literature is also reflected in inscriptions: there are several sophists;[218] Septimius Nestor of Laranda, a poet;[219] Alexander of Tarsus, a philosopher;[220] Cn. Artorius Apollo of Perge, a Stoic philosopher.[221] The lengthy epitaph of Philetus from Limyris in Lycia suggests that he was a philosopher too.[222]

Trade between Asia Minor and Rome was certainly important: some Asian cities maintained *stationes* at Rome (see p. 160), and Nicomedian merchants at Portus may have collectively honoured Caracalla,[223] but there is little evidence for individual traders.[224] A man from Phrygia was a banker in partnership with someone from Antioch, probably in the second century AD.[225] Two freedmen were involved in the sale of cloaks: L. Arlenus L.l. Demetrius, a Cilician *negotiat(or) sagar(ius)* is commemorated with L. Arlenus L.l. Artemidorus, a Paphlagonian *mercator sagarius*.[226] However, there is no reason to think that these occupations were connected with the places of origin of the people involved.

Asia Minor was not a significant area of military recruitment. Neither the Greek nor the indigenous populations had much of a military reputation among the Romans, although there are individual examples of soldiers from nearly all the Asian provinces serving at Rome (see p. 59). The numbers are similar to those from Greece, e.g. four from Bithynia, three from Cilicia.

There is substantial evidence that migration to Rome from Asia

Minor continued in late antiquity, despite the foundation of Constanti-nople. Galatians are particularly well attested (see p. 188), although the evidence for them may have been distorted slightly by the preser-vation of one distinctive group of epitaphs, discussed further below. The latest dated Asian inscription is for a Galatian, from AD 534.[227]

References to the homeland[228]

TABLE 21. Designation of people from Asia.

Province	24		
		Asiaticus	1
		Asia	2
		Asia/Asiaticus+city	10
		Phryx/Phrygius	8
		Phrygia	1
		Phrygia + city	1
		Phrygia + village	1
Region	3		
		Maeander	1
		Mygdonia	1
		Maeonia	1
City	43		
		Laodicea[229]	6
		Cyzicus	4
		Aphrodisias	4
		Miletus	3
		Smyrna	3
		Ephesus	3
		others[230]	20

For people from the province of Asia, the province itself seems to have had little significance unless it was associated with the name of a city – which in some cases was probably done simply to avoid confusion with another city of the same name. The recurrence of the designation 'Phrygian' probably reflects the importance of Phrygia as a pre-Roman entity rather than its revival as an administrative unit in late antiquity, since only 2 of the 11 relevant inscriptions are Christian. It was the home city which was important for people from Asia, and this is consistent with the high proportion of *peregrini* among them, people who had citizenship of an Asian city which they wished to emphasize in their inscriptions. Thus there is unlikely to have been any community of people from Asia at Rome, although there may have been communities of Ephesians, Aphrodisians, etc. Laodicea is indicated by the inscriptions to have been the most important city in sending Asians to Rome.

TABLE 22. Designation of people from Bithynia.

Province	11		
		Bithynius/icus	4
		Bithynia + city	2
		Ponticus	2
		Paphlago	3
City	22		
		Nicomedia	12
		Constantinople[231]	4
		others	6

The Bithynian inscriptions show a similar picture to those from Asia (although the evidence is much less plentiful): the province was less important than the city in people's self-identity. Nicomedia is mentioned more often than all other Bithynian cities combined. Lycia, on the basis of very little evidence, seems to follow the same pattern: there are only 2 references to the province, both accompanied by the name of a city, while 5 inscriptions refer to the city only. On the other hand, for Cappadocia, the provincial designation (usually *Cappadox*) is of great importance, accounting for 14 of the 16 relevant inscriptions, and Cilicia is similar: 8 out of 13 inscriptions use some form of *Cilix*, and 4 of the others refer to one city, Tarsus.

TABLE 23. Designation of people from Galatia.

Province	17		
		Galata/-es	8
		Galatia	1
		Galata + city	1
		Galates + village	7
Region/tribe	5		
		Gallograecus	2
		Solymius + city	3
City	6		
Village	7		

For Galatians, the picture is somewhat different. In their identity, the city has less importance, and the province (or at least the ethnic) more.

This probably reflects the predominance of Christian inscriptions for the Galatians; by the fourth century, with universal Roman citizenship, civic identity was of less significance than provincial or regional identity. Additionally, *Galata* did not have the negative implications at Rome which *Gallus* had for Celts from Gaul.

The habit of recording the home village occurs in Christian epitaphs in Greek for people from Galatia as well as, less often, from Egypt and Syria. The few precisely dated ones are fifth or sixth century. The implications of naming villages for the attempted preservation of local identity have already been discussed in the context of Thracian military inscriptions (see p. 219). The same considerations apply for the Galatians: there must have been others present at Rome for whom the village also had significance.[232] In keeping with usual Christian epigraphic practice, the commemorator is never identified in these epitaphs, so it is not clear if the commemoration was done by family members. The Galatians show less concern for making the villages identifiable than the Thracian soldiers and their commemorators – they do not specify the nearest city, or give the region.[233] Instead, the intended readership was probably people who already knew all about the villages, something which would be consistent with Galatians predominating in an area of one catacomb (see p. 188).

The Galatian epitaphs use formulae which are rather different from those referring to Syrian and Egyptian villages.[234] Only one uses κώμη for village,[235] and the normal expression was the genitive χωρίου followed by the name of the village;[236] occasionally the dative was used instead.[237] Some form of the word Galatia or Galatian was often attached. In view of this distinct regional usage, it seems that several epitaphs which use χωρίου and mention otherwise unknown villages should be attributed to Galatians rather than to Syrians or Egyptians, as has been done previously.[238]

Community and religion

There is considerable evidence for the importation of deities from Asia Minor to Rome, which may be connected with Asian life at Rome. By far the best documented Asian cult is that of Magna Mater/Cybele, but its history is rather different from that of most originally local cults, since it first came to Rome officially, at the order of the Senate. However, besides the 'official' temple on the Palatine, several other shrines appeared in Rome, in Regions XI and XIII and the Vatican.[239] The priests, including the eunuch *galli*, were almost certainly immigrants from the cult-centre in Phrygia,[240] since Roman citizens were for a long time prohibited from taking part in the 'Phrygian ceremonies', at least until the period when Dionysius of Halicarnassus was writing. One priest, a man from Pessinus, was expelled in the late Republic (see p. 44). They may, however, have been partially recruited among immigrants who were already in Rome, rather than all being brought to Rome specifically to serve as priests.[241] Some were imperial ex-slaves,[242] and La Piana (1927, 296) suggests that it was the influence of Asian freedmen which led Claudius to remove the legal curbs on the priesthood.

Vermaseren (1977) lists 57 Latin, 4 Greek and 2 bilingual inscriptions from the Cybele/Attis cult at Rome. They date from the first to the late fourth century AD. The earliest Greek inscription is from 244 (his no. 245) and the others (nos. 237, 239, 271) are fourth-century; the bilingual ones (nos. 236, 238) are both from the 370s. This suggests that the association of Greek with the cult is late, but since many of the earlier Latin inscriptions are epitaphs for freedmen and others who would tend to use Latin anyway in such a context, they do not *necessarily* indicate that Latin was the main language of the cult before the fourth century. There is little direct association with immigrants, but the epitaph of Hector, a 'Mygdonian' (i.e. Phrygian) and apparently a slave or freedman of Domitilla, is addressed in Latin to 'You who worship Cybele and mourn Phrygian Attis.'[243] People of high status in Roman society who were not immigrants themselves also patronized the cult, at least in late antiquity. For example, an elaborately carved altar dated to 370 has an inscription in Latin and Greek: the Latin part gives details of the donors Petronius Apollodorus and his wife Rufia Volusiana, and the Greek part has a poem about Magna Mater and Attis.[244] This shows that the use of Greek need have no connection at all with immigrants.

The worship of the healing god Asclepius was brought to Rome officially, from Epidaurus, on the instructions of the Sibylline Books in 293 BC. However, new institutions for the cult continued to be founded over a long period. A *Collegium Aesculapii et Hygeae*, with a constitution of AD 153,[245] has officers with foreign names, and in view of the prevalence of immigrant doctors may well have been dominated by people from Asia, but it was apparently not exclusive to one geographical area. The doctor Nicomedes of Smyrna erected a very long Greek inscription honouring Asclepius.[246] Asclepius was also honoured in Greek by P. Aelius Isidorus.[247] The cult is more likely to be connected with the collective identity of doctors than of people from Asia.

There are two dedications to 'the Virgin Goddess of the Sardians' by imperial freedmen, L. Aurelius Satyrus and M. Aurelius Symphorus, presumably Sardians themselves.[248] Other Asian deities worshipped were Artemis of Ephesus,[249] Aphrodite of Aphrodisias,[250] and Sabazius.[251] A very specific local deity was honoured in Greek by the *stator* Aurelius Marcus: 'Zeus Olybrius of the nation of the Cilicians of the most honourable city of Anazarbus'.[252] Apart from Sabazius, who may have acquired wider appeal, these are all deities who can only have interested people from the city with which the deity was associated. They may therefore indicate the existence of cult organizations which were exclusive to people from that city, but there is unfortunately no evidence of how such organizations operated, or even any proof that the worshippers were permanent residents of Rome rather than just temporary visitors.

The other communal organization known to have existed at Rome for people from Asia is the *statio* (see p. 160). The majority of known *stationes* at Rome are for Asian cities. They indicate that trade between these cities and Rome was thriving, but the lack of evidence about exactly what the functions of the *stationes* were makes it impossible to say whether they were focal points for communities of Ephesians, Tarsians, etc. at Rome.

The clearest evidence for an Asian 'community' at Rome concerns the Galatians in late antiquity. The recurrence of references to Galatian villages was discussed above, and the concentration of Galatian burials in the Octavilla catacomb was examined at p. 188. The evidence does not show that there was a specific Galatian residential area, as Ricci (1997a, 190) claims, but it is enough to indicate that the Galatians at Rome had sufficient communal feeling to be buried near to each other and to refer in their relatives' epitaphs to their home villages. The fact that this was happening in late antiquity, when Constantinople might be expected to be a more attractive destination for Galatians, is surprising. The most likely explanation is that there was a pattern of chain migration, in which the success of one or two Galatians at Rome[253] encouraged more people from the same area to join them; the pattern could have continued for several generations. There is no obvious reason why this should apply to Galatians more than to others from Asia Minor, so it may just be an accident of the survival of evidence that there is no equivalent material for Cappadocians or Cilicians.

v. Syria

Overview

Roman annexation of Syria took place in 63 BC, but Syrians were already familiar at Rome – Phoenicians may even have been there as early as the sixth century BC.[254] Some prisoners would have been taken during Rome's conflicts with the Seleucids in the second and first centuries BC, and there were also Seleucid hostages at Rome at various times (see p. 107).[255] However, most Syrians arrived at Rome through the workings of the slave trade. Syrus was a common slave name, although not necessarily given only to Syrians, since the association Syrian = slave seems to have been very widespread: it is exemplified by Cicero's notorious comment, 'Jews and Syrians, nations born for slavery', and by a passage of Livy where M. Acilius talks about 'Syrian and Asiatic Greeks, most worthless races of men and born for slavery'.[256] Plautus refers to 'a Syrian or Egyptian' slave girl, and Ap. Claudius Pulcher had a Syrian freedman in 72 BC.[257] Cicero comments that there were many eunuchs from Syria and Egypt.[258] Slaves who had been brought to Rome from overseas for sale had their feet marked with white chalk or what the Elder Pliny calls silversmiths' earth. He goes on to list some of the famous people whose lives at Rome had begun in this way, including Publilius of Antioch (Publilius Syrus), his cousin Manilius of Antioch and Staberius Eros, who came on the same ship in the early first century BC and founded, respectively, mime-writing, astronomy and grammar-teaching at Rome.[259] He continues with a list of those who achieved political influence as the freedmen and -women of people like Sulla and Pompey. Slaves still came from Syria in the imperial period, for example Strato, 'by birth Syrian, Antiochene', freedman of the Augusti, must be late second century AD (or later); as with Asia Minor, slave-breeding and cross-border trading maintained the supply.[260]

Voluntary migration from Syria to Rome would probably have begun in the late Republic. Most of the evidence, however, is from the second century AD or later. There is a clear implication that some of the slaves and ex-slaves labelled Syrians in the literary sources were thoroughly imbued with Greek culture, whether their ancestry was Syrian, Greek or mixed. Solin (1983, 722) notes that Syrian immigrants in general tended to be of Greek descent or at least to be from the most hellenized part of Syrian society. When Juvenal's Umbricius complains about 'the filth of the Orontes' at the same time as complaining about Greeks, he clearly equates the two (see p. 34). However, a distinction between 'Syrian' and 'Syrian Greek' appears to be made in some sources, e.g. Pope Evaristus (*c.* 97–105) is described in the *Liber Pontificalis* as *natione Grecus Antiochenus*, whereas Anicetus (*c.* 155–166) is *natione Syrus*.[261]

Even after the demise of the Seleucids, there were still local dynasts in Syria. The presence of a freedman of King Sampsiceramus of Emesa (either from the time of Julius Caesar or of Caligula and Claudius) may indicate that the king himself came to Rome.[262] Syria gradually produced its share of senators, almost exclusively men from the large cities.[263] The influence of Julia Domna under Septimius Severus, and the reigns of Elagabalus and Alexander Severus, were presumably stimuli for members of the Syrian elite to come to Rome, but there may have been a corresponding reaction against them after the end of the Severan dynasty.

Syria was not a major recruitment area for the military units at Rome, although Syrian praetorians, *equites singulares* and sailors are all recorded. A number of people from Syria with specialized skills are known at Rome: Archias the poet, Apollodorus the architect, Probus the grammarian.[264] These are all the sorts of work carried out at Rome by people from the Greek-speaking world. In general, people from Syria seem to have their work mentioned in inscriptions much more rarely than people from Asia Minor.[265] A banker from Antioch was in partnership with one from Phrygia.[266] Auge (probably a slave), commemorated in the Monument of the Statilii, was a spinner.[267] A man described as 'both traversing the land and crossing the waves in ships' was probably a trader.[268] Syrians had a reputation as slave-traders, and the epitaph of 'L. Valerius Aries, freedman of the slave-trader Zabda' probably refers to one of them in view of the Semitic name.[269] With this exception, there is no evidence for any concentration of Syrians at Rome in any particular sort of work in the classical period.

This seems to have changed in late antiquity, however, when trade in the West was regarded as being so dominated by Syrians that *Syrus* was used by some writers as an equivalent of merchant and money-lender, in addition to being an ethnic label.[270] The evidence only really shows that Syrians were dominant in luxury goods and the slave trade, however.[271] On the possibility of emigration from Syria in late antiquity being encouraged by changing conditions in Syria itself, see p. 88. Syrians are particularly well attested in Christian inscriptions at Rome (see table 1); there are more than twice as many Syrian Christians recorded as Christians from any other province. Augustine admired the Syrian rhetor Hierius, who taught Greek rhetoric at Rome first but became accomplished in Latin too.[272] Diogenes, who died in AD 414, was the nephew of Anatolius, *praepositus thesaurorum*; the family came from a village near Apamea.[273] As with Galatia, a substantial number of Syrians decided to come to Rome in late antiquity rather than make the shorter migration to Constantinople.

References to the homeland

TABLE 24. Designation of people from Syria			
Province	49		
		Syrus	24
		Syria	2
		Syrus/Syria + city	13
		Syria + village	2
		Surisca	2
		Coele Syria	2
		Phoenix	1
		Phoenicia + city	1
		Phoenicia + village	2
Region/tribe	3		
		Arab(ic)us	2
		Arabus + city	1
City	35		
		Antioch	8[274]
		others	27
Village	9		

The designation *Syrus* is very common at Rome, numerically commoner than any other ethnic. It was used for nearly all Syrian soldiers, and for the majority of civilians. It was rare, however, among Syrian Christians and Jews, something which may be the result of the tendency in late antiquity to identify 'Syrian' with 'trader' noted above. Christians were normally designated by their home city or, in at least 12 cases, village. The practice of referring to the home village has already been discussed for Galatian Christians (232) and Thracian soldiers (219), and it is found among groups of Syrians elsewhere in late antiquity, e.g. at Corycus[275] and Aquileia.[276] Where the locations of the villages mentioned at Rome can be identified (fewer than half the inscriptions give the region as well as the village), they are all from the Apamea area.[277] The term used for village is nearly always κώμη, either in the genitive or after ἀπό. There is also one Latin inscription for a Syrian, using *vicus*.[278] In two cases where the name of the village following ἀπό κώμης has been lost, Syrian origin is most likely.[279] There were clearly some Syrians at Rome for whom the recording of the home village was important, but it appears that they were predominantly those from the Apamea area. The fact that they referred to each other by the village rather than just as Apameans is significant, and the presence of a substantial community of villagers from the area is probably implied, presumably the consequence of a process of chain migration.

Names and language

Syrians, like Thracians, often had distinctive local names which are identifiable in inscriptions from Rome. Solin (1983) gives a magisterial survey of the occurrences of such names. There are, as would be expected, some examples of people using both a Syrian and a Graeco–Latin name, e.g. Xanthias *qui et* Adudas.[280] Below, two names are studied in an attempt to discern their implications when used at Rome.

'Malchio' (and latinized variant Malchus) was a common Syrian name.[281] It occurs in many inscriptions at Rome, mainly Latin but including several Christian ones of which most are in Greek:[282]

TABLE 25. Status of people called *Malchio*

Slave	4	Duo/tria nomina	10
Freedman	18	Uncertain	6
Freeborn	1	Christian	4
Single name	2		

The association with servile status is clear: at least 22 of the pagan bearers of the name were slaves or ex-slaves, and only one definitely was not. However, two of the four Christians are explicitly free immigrants,[283] and one of the others is aged 4 and commemorated by his father (who has a Latin name);[284] the fourth has a son named Petrus.[285] Of all the non-Christian people called Malchio, only one has his children named in the inscription:[286]

> For Sabidia Ɔ.l. Fusca who lived 18 years.
> [an 8-line verse epitaph follows]
> L. Faenius Malcio her father, Faenia L.Ɔ.l. Hilara her mother, P. Sabidius Fortunatus her brother.

This man's children and his wife all had Latin cognomina. The name Malchio appears not to have been passed on to children because of its Syrian and/or servile connotations (which might be the same thing; see above). However, among Christians, Malchio, like many Semitic names, was apparently viewed rather differently, and was given to a child presumably born at Rome.

'Pharnaces' was a name which must have sounded distinctively 'oriental' (although not particularly Syrian). It is of Iranian origin, and was much used by the Parthian and Armenian royal family, as well as in Syria and around the Black Sea. It is well attested as a personal name at Rome, always in Latin inscriptions.[287] It occurs for people with the following statuses:

TABLE 26. Status of people called *Pharnaces*.

Slave	2	Duo/tria nomina	11
Freedman	14	Uncertain	1
Single name	3		

Not a single bearer of the name is certainly freeborn, and at least half are definitely from a slave background. None of the inscriptions has any reference to the parents of the person called Pharnaces. Few of the men called Pharnaces are recorded with children, but where children are named they have Latin names in three cases,[288] Greek names in two,[289] and both types of name in the following inscription:[290]

> P. Ostorius Scapulae l. Pharnaces made this for himself, and for his freedwoman Ostoria P.l. Amma, and for his sons C. Sallustius Calvinae l. Utilis and Phosphorus, and for his freedmen and freedwomen and all his descendants.

Since this Pharnaces' children were born slaves, he may not have decided their names anyway; his wife had a name which is probably Syrian. One of the wives of an imperial slave called Pharnaces had a probably Thracian name, Claudia Paezusa.[291] The name Pharnaces was apparently not one which people who had settled in Rome wished to pass on to their children. That could be because it was oriental, or because of its connotations of slavery.

In pagan inscriptions for Syrians, Latin is commoner than Greek, largely because of the slave background of many of the Syrians recorded. In Christian inscriptions, the picture is completely different, with nearly all the inscriptions in Greek, a clear consequence of the possibility of using the in-group language in the catacombs whereas the out-group language was required in pagan burial areas (see TABLE 12). Some Syrians had to make further linguistic choices, however, since a few chose to use Palmyrene or Nabataean; presumably others who could have used those languages decided not to. The Palmyrene inscriptions come from the Palmyrene sanctuary, and will be discussed below. Nabataean is used alongside Latin in two epitaphs.[292] The original contexts of these are not known, but they are likely to have been in some sort of private or semi-private burial area where an in-group language could be used along with the out-group one. The fact that only two are known may be due to the rarity of the appropriate burial arrangements, the difficulty of finding someone competent to inscribe Nabataean (see p. 178), or to a general lack of interest in the language among commemorators (who are likely to have been born at Rome).

Community and religion

There is more evidence about the religious activities of Syrians than of any other pagan group at Rome. The evidence has been studied in considerable depth recently, and an attempt will be made below to summarize the relevant findings. The important question here is the extent to which Syrian cults remained the preserve of Syrians, something which is not easy to answer. It is likely that the Janiculum sanctuary and the Palmyrene cult, at least, were only of interest to people with Syrian connections in the second and third centuries.

The Syrian Sanctuary on the Janiculum

The building now referred to by this title, containing a number of *cellae* around a courtyard, was found on the Janiculum in Trastevere at the beginning of the twentieth century.[293] It may have been dedicated to the Heliopolitan triad, but this is not certain;[294] Lombardi thinks it is more generally Syro-Phoenician rather than specifically Heliopolitan, although Calzini Gysens takes it as Heliopolitan with some external influence.[295] Jupiter Heliopolitanus was certainly worshipped there, but numerous finds show that various other local deities were too: Hadad,[296] Dea Syria (a.k.a. Atargatis, Venus Heliopolitana),[297] Jupiter Maleciabrudes ('lord of Iabruda'),[298] Zeus Keraunios.[299] A relief of the Palmyrene gods Aglibel and Iarhibol was also found there, dated approximately to the 230s.[300] The sanctuary flourished (on a site with previous religious associations, the Lucus Furrinae) at least between the mid-second and mid-third centuries; it may subsequently have undergone an 'egyptianizing' process.[301] Its users were probably workers in the Horrea Galbiana, just across the Tiber, and people living in Trastevere itself.[302]

The most important benefactor there was M. Antonius M.f. Gaionas, who was active in the time of Marcus Aurelius and Commodus. His background is not known: he was clearly a freeborn Roman citizen (although he is referred to just as Gaionas in most of the inscriptions), but, despite the assumptions which have sometimes been made, there is no direct evidence about whether he was an immigrant or a native of

Rome.[303] The inscriptions show that he felt a strong attachment to Commodus, and he was able to write (or commission) Homeric verse.[304] He occurs in six inscriptions, of which four are definitely associated with the sanctuary, and another is his epitaph. Those found in the sanctuary all have a uniform style of lettering.[305]

1. CIL vi 36793, dated 176, from the Janiculum: a marble plaque from a table for offerings, later reused as a threshold.

> [Latin] For the safety and return and victory of the Emperors Augusti Antoninus and Commodus Caesar Germanicus *princeps iuventutis* Sarmaticus, Gaionas, *cistiber*[306] of the emperors, gave (this) as a gift.

2. CIL vi 420 = 30764 = 36749 = CIL xiv 985 = IGUR 166, dated 186, from the Janiculum; a marble column which probably carried a statue of Commodus. [307]

> [Latin] To Jupiter Optimus Maximus Heliopolitanus.
> [Greek] To the most kingly man, shielder (*aspistes*) of the world.
> [Latin] To the Emperor Caesar M. Aurelius Commodus Antoninus Pius Sarmaticus Germanicus (etc.), M. Antonius M.f. Gaionas, Claudialis, Augustalis, Quirinalis, *eg[regi]us*,[308] *cistiber*, dedicated this in the year A.U.C.939, in the fifth consulship of Commodus Antoninus Pius Felix Augustus, and second consulship of M. Acilius Glabrio, November 9th.

3. CIL vi 36804 = IGUR 109, from the Janiculum; carved on a plaque which was perforated to serve as a fountain-mouth[309] or, according to the recent suggestion of Scheid (1995, 311–14), held a ring to which a sacrificial animal was tethered.

> [Greek] A strong *desmos* which Gaionas the *deipnokrites* erected so that it might supply sacrifice to the gods.[310]

4. Duthoy and Frel 1996, 294: a limestone column base from the Janiculum.

> [Latin] [To Jupiter Optimus Maximus Heliopolitanus, for L. Aurelius Commodus] Antoninus Augustus Pius Imperator, M. Antonius Gaionas, *cistiber* of the emperors, gave (this) as a gift.

5. CIL xiv 24 from Portus, on a 'granitello' column, dated 176–180.[311]

> [Latin] To Jupiter Optimus Maximus Angelus Heliopolitanus, for the safety of the emperors Antoninus and Commodus Augusti, Gaionas gave (this) as a gift.

6. CIL vi 32316 = IGUR 1157: Gaionas' epitaph.

> [Latin] Sacred to the *Di Manes*.
> [Greek] Here I lie in death, Gaionas, who was once *cistiber* in Rome, and

judged many things in banquets with cheerfulness, owed nothing.
[Latin] Gaionas, little soul.

The Heliopolitan cult was not a widespread one at Rome, and the number of cult objects connected with it found outside the sanctuary is small.[312] Ciceroni (1996, 363) writes that the finds follow 'le mode figuratif oriental', and suggests:

> ...on ne peut exclure que la réalisation des monuments 'héliopolitains' de Rome puisse être expliquée, mieux que par la circulation de modèles iconographiques, par des descriptions détaillées fournies par les commanditaires.[313]

This would suggest that the devotees were themselves people who had been to Heliopolis, and therefore most probably Syrian immigrants. There is no reason to think that the cult was deliberately exclusive, but it may have been attractive only to people with Syrian connections. Gaionas had a Semitic cognomen which is otherwise attested at Rome only for one freedman, a citizen of uncertain status, and two men for whom it appears as a single name.[314] If he were not explicitly said to be freeborn, he would seem likely to be a freedman himself. He is most likely to have been a free immigrant, given the apparent rarity of Semitic names for immigrants' children (see above, and p. 181) and also the rather strange dating in inscription no. 2 above (discussed at p. 178) which suggests someone not fully at home with the Roman dating system. Nevertheless, he was very well integrated, with status in the imperial cult and (probably) the city police as well as within the Heliopolitan cult. His nomen, Antonius, may suggest that he came from a family which had had Roman citizenship for a long time (although it could, of course, have been acquired from a freedman ascendant). Devotion to some of the indigenous institutions of the city could co-exist happily with devotion to some imported institutions. In his epitaph, both his police and his cult functions were mentioned, although the latter was done rather cryptically. There may, however, have been a deliberate omission of his place of origin.

Palmyrenes

There was a sanctuary of the Sun God and other Palmyrene deities in Trastevere.[315] This too may have been used by workers at the docks and warehouses, as well as people from Trastevere. Solin (1983, 683) notes that the users may not have been permanent residents, but this seems unnecessarily sceptical; there is nothing to suggest that the dedicants were only temporary visitors.[316] In a Latin/Palmyrene inscription of the first or second century AD, Ti. Claudius Felix, his wife and son made a dedication which differs notably between the two languages:[317]

> [Latin] To the most holy Sun. Ti. Claudius Felix and Claudia Helpis and Ti. Claudius Alypius their son fulfilled their vow willingly and deservedly. The Galbienses from block 3.[318]
> [Palmyrene; tr. Teixidor 1979] This is the altar (which) Ti. Claudius Felix and the Palmyrenes offered to Malachbel and the gods of Palmyra. To their gods. Peace.

The people involved may be (but need not be) imperial ex-slaves from the end of the Julio–Claudian period, as supposed by Turcan (1996, 175–6). Felix used the same name in both languages; presumably he did not have a Palmyrene name, which suggests that he may not have been an immigrant himself. The Latin text uses the standard vocabulary of Latin votive inscriptions, and names all the dedicators. The Palmyrene version, which no doubt says what was considered appropriate in that language, names different gods, and specifies none of the individual dedicators other than Felix; they are presumably included among "the Palmyrenes".

A fragmentary Greek/Latin inscription records the building of a temple, perhaps the same one, to some local deities: [319]

> [Latin] For the safety of the Emperor [-------------], C. Licinius [N---- and Heliodorus] the Palmyrene built [the temple for Bel, Iaribol, Malachbel with their own money?]
> [Greek] Heliodorus the [Palmyrene and C. Licinius N---- built] the temple for Bel, [Iaribol, Malachbel and the gods] of Palmyra [with their own money?]

Heliodorus is found again in a bilingual Greek/Palmyrene inscription dated to 236,[320] where he dedicates a silver statue and other offerings to Bel, Aglibel and Malachbel: this time he gives his full name as Aurelius Heliodorus Hadrianus son of Antiochus in Greek, but as Iarhai, with filiation going back to his great-great-grandfather, in Palmyrene (see p. 182). Another Greek/Palmyrene inscription marks a dedication to Bel, Iaribol and Malachbel by Makkaios Male (common Palmyrene names) and So'adu (also the name of Heliodorus' great-great-grandfather).[321]

The change of language accompanied by a complete change of onomastic practice shows someone at home in both linguistic codes. Heliodorus/Iarhai was presumably an immigrant from Palmyra. The use of Palmyrene in the inscriptions implies that the language had some role in the cult. Equini Schneider (1988, 63–4) sees its use as the result of traditionalism and a desire to emphasize links with Palmyra, not of linguistic necessity. The use of a minority language and imported religious practices can go hand-in-hand, and a decline in one may accompany a decline in the other, as occurred in the Welsh-language Nonconformist chapels in Pennsylvania in the late nineteenth and early twentieth centuries; the children of immigrants rejected the use of Welsh and founded their own English-language chapels which rapidly displaced the Welsh-language ones.[322] It is impossible to know if the Palmyrene sanctuary at Rome had a similar experience, but it is quite plausible; the children of Palmyrene immigrants would perhaps generally (although not in the case of Felix) have preferred to use Latin or Greek only.

Jupiter Dolichenus

The worship of Jupiter Dolichenus at Rome is shown by the existence of a building called the Dolocenum on the Aventine, where a large number of altars with Latin dedications have been found, and another shrine on the Esquiline. His cult was widespread, and not restricted to people with a Syrian connection, although there clearly were Syrians among the participants. The users of the Aventine shrine were civilians from a wide variety of backgrounds; Bellelli suggests that they, and the military users of the Esquiline shrine, were *mainly* orientals, but even this is not clear.[323] Both shrines seem to have flourished from the mid-second to early-third centuries.[324] She writes (p. 325):

> Certaines formes de culte (procession de la statue), tout comme les mobiliers (petites statues d'offrants égyptiens, antefixes avec *uraei*, décorations zoomorphes) semblent vouloir recréer l'atmosphère de la patrie d'origine pour célébrer les rites qui la rappellent. L'organisation du sanctuaire, les fidèles, les bienfaiteurs étaient surtout orientaux.[325]

Sorrenti (1996, 424) offers a similar explanation for the orientalizing style of Dolichenian iconography at Rome:

> ...elle s'explique sans doute par la présence stable d'individus d'origine orientale, notamment syrienne, dans les sanctuaires de la capitale, soucieux de maintenir leurs liens avec les traditions culturelles de leur terre natale.[326]

This is equivalent to the comments on the Heliopolitan and Palmyrene cults. Since Dolichenus had a wider appeal, however, it is possible that emphasizing the 'Syrian-ness' of the cult is different from the cult actually being dominated by Syrians; Egyptian elements of the Isis cult were also emphasized because they were attractive to people who had no Egyptian connections of their own. At least, the cult did not have the exclusively Syrian nature which would have been necessary if it was to play a part in the maintenance of Syrian group identity.

Other deities

A variety of other local deities from Syria were also worshipped at Rome, but in most cases there is little evidence about how their cults operated. The 'paternal god of Commagene', another title for Dolichenus, was honoured by a Syrian sailor from the Misenum fleet, his sons and a priest.[327] The cult of Elagabal, from Emesa, received official sponsorship by the emperor of that name, but was already established at Rome by the late second century AD, probably in Trastevere.[328] Other Syrian deities were also honoured: Jupiter Bellefarus (Baal of 'Efârâ);[329] Jupiter Damascenus;[330] Jupiter Turmasgada, another form of Baal;[331] Jupiter Balmarquodes and Neotera, from Berytus.[332] Marnas from Gaza had a shrine at Portus.[333]

Thus, there is clear evidence that a large number of Syrian deities were worshipped at Rome. Jupiter Dolichenus is the only one whose appeal clearly went beyond the part of the population with Syrian connections. The cults of Jupiter Heliopolitanus, the Palmyrene gods, and the other local divinities are likely to have been the preserve of Syrians, but it is unfortunately impossible to distinguish first-generation immigrants from their descendants among the worshippers who left inscriptions. The nearest parallel is the worship of local Thracian deities by Thracian soldiers serving at Rome (see p. 222), but the Thracians were at Rome for a limited period before they went home. The Syrians, on the other hand, must have included many permanent immigrants. Their cults are likely to have been an important feature of community life, providing a form of institution not usually available to pagan civilian groups, but one which would have been lost in the fourth century with the spread of Christianity.

vi. Egypt
Overview

Egypt became a Roman province in 30 BC, but had already been closely entwined with Roman history for a long time. The sorts of Egyptians recorded as coming to Rome in the Republic fall into three categories: members of the Ptolemaic family, priests of Egyptian cults (discussed at the end of the section), and slaves. Several Egyptian rulers spent time at Rome: Ptolemy VI Philometor in the second century BC and Ptolemy XII Auletes in the first when they were driven from their thrones, and Cleopatra VII during her relationship with Julius Caesar (see p. 109).

Egyptian slaves are mentioned as early as the time of Plautus. At first they would only have reached Rome through the slave trade, but large numbers were probably brought back for Octavian's triumph in 29 BC, and more after the revolt of 25 BC.[334] By the first century AD, Egyptian slaves and ex-slaves had allegedly achieved great influence at Rome, e.g. Caligula's Egyptian chamberlain Helicon who is said to have used his influence on behalf of the Alexandrian Greek delegation against the Jews.[335] The association between Egyptians and slavery found in literature of the late first and early second centuries AD suggests that Egyptian slaves were still coming to Rome in significant numbers,[336] although Ricci (1993a, 85) notes that none of the Egyptians recorded in inscriptions are specifically said to be slaves (cf. TABLE 10).

Most references to Egyptians at Rome concern Alexandrians, apparently of Greek extraction, rather than 'indigenous' Egyptians. On the other hand, the stereotyped Roman image of Egyptians concentrated on the aspects of their behaviour perceived as most outlandish, particularly the worship of animal-gods,[337] and largely ignored the Greek component of their culture. There seems to be something of a contradiction between image and reality which may be due at least in part to anti-Cleopatra propaganda and its legacy.

The Egyptian elite was never really incorporated into the senatorial class, and the province did not produce any senators until the second century. Both of those recorded then are certainly not representative of the elite of the province: Ti. Iulius Alexander Iulianus, from the ex-Jewish family of Philo's nephew, and P. Aelius Coeranus, probably descended from a freedman of Hadrian.[338] Crispinus, a pickled-fish seller from Canopus mentioned frequently by Martial and Juvenal, allegedly reached at least equestrian rank at Rome under Domitian.[339]

Alexandrians were active at Rome in the world of literature, from the time of Augustus until Claudian came to Rome in 394.[340] Egyptian doctors, who may not all have been Alexandrian, are well documented (see p. 111). Astrologers from Egypt were also prominent.[341]

The Roman fleet recruited in Egypt, no doubt among the same pool of people who manned the grain fleet (see p. 165). Service in the fleet (or legions) was a reason for leaving Egypt which was specifically allowed in the Gnomon of the Idios Logos.[342] A small number of Egyptian praetorians are recorded, but praetorian recruitment appears to have been unusual there.[343] The corn trade also brought Alexandrian merchants to Rome,[344] although their activities were not only concerned with grain. According to Suetonius, Augustus was honoured while sailing through the Bay of Puteoli by the passengers and crew of an Alexandrian ship, who thanked him for making the seas safe, and he responded by giving his staff money to spend on Alexandrian goods.[345] Two *peregrini* with Egyptian-sounding names are recorded as members of the *corpus fabrum navalium* of Ostia.[346] Someone known from a papyrus may have been dealing in cotton. [347] Other products of Egypt, notably papyrus, linen and stone, must also have brought traders to Rome, although there is no direct evidence for Egyptians dealing in them.

Egyptian slaves are recorded in literature as entertainers, such as the dancer Bathyllus (a freedman of Maecenas),[348] one of the actors named Paris,[349] and Verus' actor freedman Apolaustus (see p. 118). Egypt was also a source of gladiators (see p. 118),[350] and there is an epitaph for a *citharoedus*.[351] The pancratiast M. Aurelius Asclepiades Hermodorus came from a rather different social background, an office-holding Alexandrian family.[352]

Egypt remains a fairly well-attested source of immigrants to Rome in Christian inscriptions. The latest dated one is from 589.[353] Church politics brought some Alexandrian exiles to Rome: Athanasius in the fourth century and John Talaïa in the fifth.

References to the homeland

TABLE 27. Designation of people from Egypt.

Province	13		
		Aegypt(i)us	12
		Egypt+Alexandria	1
Alexandria	21		
Other cities	3		
Villages	4		

The predominance of Alexandrians in the evidence is clear, and there is a distinct lack of references to any other Egyptian cities. The people designated with the ethnic *Aegyptus* are mainly but not entirely military. This suggests either a genuine shortage of non-Alexandrian Egyptians at Rome or, perhaps more plausibly, a reluctance to identify themselves as such in view of the strong hostility to Egyptians noted above. The label 'Alexandrian' may sometimes indicate not only a native of Alexandria but also someone who moved there from somewhere in the Egyptian *chora* and then moved on to Rome, a pattern of migration which is certainly to be expected on the basis of modern evidence (see p. 55).

There are three references to the otherwise undistinguished village of Koprithis in Christian inscriptions.[354] The practice of naming the home village also occurs in ICUR 12883: κώμη Μεγάλης Ποτθεως in the territory of Heracleopolis Magna. For Egypt, as for Syria, the term used for village is always κώμη, either in the genitive or after ἀπό. The province or nearest city is never given for Egyptians. The significance of naming home villages has already been discussed (see p. 237 for the Syrian villages). There appears to have been a community of people from Koprithis at Rome in the fifth century.

Names, language and calendar

Few distinctly Egyptian names are recorded in inscriptions at Rome. The commonest seems to be Horus, but that occurs only five times, all in Latin inscriptions.[355]

TABLE 28. Status of people called *Horus*.

Slave	2
Freedman	2
Duo/tria nomina	1

The same association with servile status applies for this as for many other local names (see pp. 179, 238). The one bearer of the name with a recorded child (a freedman of Galba) had a daughter named Basilia, which is consistent with the general reluctance of the bearers of local names to pass them on to their children.[356]

Greek is commoner than Latin for Egyptians in pagan inscriptions, something which reflects the fact that free immigrants, especially Alexandrians, predominate and slaves are absent. The Christian inscriptions are almost entirely in Greek. There is no trace of the use of any form of the Egyptian language; hieroglyphics might have been used for the same sort of visual effect which some Jews achieved with Hebrew, but apparently they were not – this may be a consequence of the lack (apart from the tomb of the Egyptians at the Vatican; see p. 189) of separate Egyptian burial areas.

One other epigraphic way of showing Egyptian identity was by using the Egyptian calendar, the only non-Roman calendar which was regularly inscribed at Rome (see p. 178). This is something for which there is substantial evidence. It was only used in inscriptions written largely or entirely in Greek, and it seems to have been commonest in the fifth century. Three Christian epitaphs use it for people who are stated to be immigrants: Paulus of Alexandria died on Phaophi 24;[357] a man from Koprithis died on Payni 22;[358] Ammon from Alexandria died on Mecheir 21.[359] There is also a Christian epitaph in which the details of the deceased are almost entirely lost but a date in Phaophi is given;[360] another very fragmentary one which seems to use both Greek and Latin has a date in Pharmouthi;[361] and both give the year by consular dating (471 and 458 or 474). Someone whose name is largely lost died on Hathyr 7,[362] and there is another fragmentary date in Pharmouthi.[363] An epitaph which may be Jewish records the death of [Theo]dosia on Tybi 20.[364] An inscription dated to 589 which seems to record a benefaction has a date in Pharmouthi.[365]

Egyptian dates were not restricted to a Christian context, although that is where most occur. In two inscriptions concerning the cult of Serapis, the date is carefully given according to both systems: '1 day before the Nones of May, which is according to the Alexandrians Pachon 11',[366] and '6 days before the Kalends of April, Pharmouthi 1';[367] both give the year by the normal consular dating. The mainly (but not exclusively) Egyptian practice of writing L for 'year(s)', either in a date or in someone's age, is also found in several Greek inscriptions at Rome.[368]

On the other hand, Aurelius Apion of Hermopolis died on the Kalends of December.[369] The important difference is that Apion's epitaph is in Latin, whereas all those which use Egyptian dates are in Greek. It was evidently felt that a Latin epitaph required a date according to the Roman system, but that the Egyptian dating system and the Greek language went together naturally. It is not clear if the people commemorated with Egyptian dates were all immigrants from Egypt themselves, although some clearly were. While non-Egyptians might adopt the Egyptian calendar for religious reasons, the fact that the large majority of the examples given above are Christian shows that this was not usual. More probably, the inscribing of dates from their own calendar was a small statement of Egyptian identity made by Egyptians themselves and perhaps also (although this is not provable) by people of Egyptian ancestry.[370]

Community and religion

The cult of Isis at Rome was probably established by the early first century BC (see p. 43). It was repressed repeatedly from the 50s BC, although the triumvirs set up a temple of Isis and Serapis in 43 BC.[371] Despite some further setbacks up to and including the reign of

Tiberius, the cult achieved such prominence that one of the regions of Rome came to be known as *Isis et Serapis*.

Although the cult was not exclusive to, or even dominated by, Egyptians, there is some evidence that Egyptians usually held the priesthoods.[372] Embes, described as *prophetes* and *pater* of the college of Paeanistai of Serapis in AD 146, was almost certainly an Egyptian.[373] The *neokoros* of the temple of Serapis at Portus in *c.* 200 was an Alexandrian.[374] Even as late as the third century, Plotinus met an Egyptian priest who had come to Rome and conjured up a spirit in the temple of Isis.[375]

The Greek language seems to have been obligatory for dedications to Isis and Serapis. The Egyptian calendar was occasionally used (see above). The cult was very attractive to some upper-class Romans, and the role of Egyptians seems to have been fairly limited beyond supplying the priests. When it was temporarily suppressed by Tiberius after a scandal, the priests were crucified, which indicates that they must have been slaves or *peregrini*. However, the lack of any associated expulsion of Egyptians then or in any of the previous suppressions may indicate that it was not thought to be limited to one national group (see p. 43). At Ostia, where Isis' popularity was no doubt increased by her patronage of sailing and by the regular arrival of the grain fleet from Alexandria, the same man was priest of both 'Ostian Isis and Mater Deorum of Trastevere'.[376]

According to the epigraphic evidence, most of those involved in the cult do not appear to be immigrants. This is demonstrated by the inscriptions for Serapis. The priest Vibius made a dedication to him, 'on the god's orders'.[377] The Arellii Severus and Fuscus (very Latin names) and the 'holy order of *paianistai* in Rome' also honoured him in Greek.[378] The *prophetes* Embes who appears to have been Egyptian, with a group of *paianistai* who probably were not, associated him with the imperial cult.[379] The *hierodoulos* C. Avidius Trophimianus made a vow to him for the safety of the emperor (probably Caracalla).[380] He was identified with Zeus Helios in a thanksgiving inscription.[381] At Portus, he was honoured by a father and son from Alexandria.[382] The cosmopolitan nature of the cult means that it cannot have functioned as a communal focus for Egyptians at Rome.

Egyptian gods other than Isis and Serapis were also worshipped, and in these cases there are some clearer connections with people who came from Egypt. 'Antinous the companion of the gods in Egypt' was honoured with a dedication from the *prophetes* M. Ulpius Apollonius.[383] An Alexandrian councillor honoured 'the ancestral gods' at Portus.[384]

The epitaph of a girl named Isias commemorated by her parents Antinous and Panthia suggests the influence of Egyptian worship on naming practice, but does not necessarily indicate that the people were themselves Egyptians.[385]

The inevitable conclusion is that Egyptians at Rome lacked any form of communal organization. Isis- and Serapis-worship could have united Alexandrians with other Egyptians, but only along with people from a variety of other backgrounds. There is no evidence of any other institution which provided a focus for Alexandrians or other Egyptians, and only the people from fifth-century Koprithis seem to have been anxious to preserve a form of local identity.

vii. North Africa[386]
Overview

Rome's dealings with Carthage would have brought people to Rome from there as ambassadors and as prisoners of war during the third century BC. There was also a thriving slave trade between Rome and Africa. The playwright Terence, born at Carthage, is an example of someone coming to Rome through the slave trade; he was not a war captive.[387] Cicero comments on the high number of Carthaginian and Macedonian prisoners in slavery at Rome.[388]

Direct Roman rule was established in Africa after the destruction of Carthage in 146 BC. Cyrene was annexed in 74 BC and joined with Crete to form a province. Numidia came under Roman control in 46 BC, although it was not made a separate province until AD 196. Mauretania, previously a client kingdom, was incorporated into the empire in AD 42/3 after fierce resistance. North Africa contained some cities which were Greek, Libyan or Phoenician foundations, but many of the main population centres began as Roman colonies (notably the re-established Carthage) or military settlements. Ricci (1994b, 198) believes that the colonization programme of Julius Caesar and Augustus in North Africa also stimulated a population flow from there to Rome. The inhabitants of the area came from a wide variety of ethnic backgrounds (Italian, Greek, Punic, Libyan, Berber, Jewish), but, as with other areas, it is likely to have been the most romanized/ hellenized section of the population which provided most of the free migrants to Rome.

Various members of North African ruling families are recorded as spending time at Rome. Juba II, client king of Mauretania, lived at Rome in the time of Julius Caesar and Augustus, and there are epitaphs for two of his slaves: a *structor*, subsequently owned by Augustus,[389] and

251

a mime-actress. [390] There are also two freedmen of 'King Ptolemaeus', meaning Juba's son. [391] Even after Mauretania was incorporated into the empire, other minor dynasts remained outside direct rule, and at the end of the second century AD an inscription mentions the son of Canartha, assigned by the Romans as *princeps* of the tribe of the Baquates. [392]

Senators from North Africa became numerous from the second half of the second century AD, and the influence of Fronto and, later and more significantly, Septimius Severus no doubt encouraged them. Over a hundred African senators are known in all. [393] Mauretania and Numidia produced their first senator in the Flavian period; Numidians, mainly from Cirta, heavily outnumbered Mauretanians. [394] The extent of North African influence became so great that: 'In the third century perhaps one in eight of the Roman Senate was of African origin.' [395] This can be attributed in part to the prosperity of the area, which enabled large numbers of men to achieve the level of wealth necessary for senatorial status.

Ricci (1994b, no. A1) reconstructs the family of L. Aelius Perpetuus, an ambassador [396] from Thamugadis who died at Rome in the late second century AD. His brother Sex. Aelius Victor was a *scriba quaestorius* at Rome, and his grandson L. Aelius Tertius, a *causidicus*, was born at Rome and commemorated at Piacenza. The family illustrates the possibility of people slightly below the senatorial elite migrating from North Africa to Rome. They are not the only people from North Africa who worked at Rome in connection with the law: there is also an *advocatus* from Tripolitania. [397] Praetextatus was a *iuris peritus*. [398] L. Septimius Severus, a city magistrate from Lepcis, was a *iudex inter selectos* at Rome. [399] Several African jurists who were active at Rome are known from literary sources. [400]

Since the province of Africa was one of the main sources of Rome's grain supply, trade must have been an important reason for Africans to come to Rome. The numerous African cities which had *stationes* at Ostia (see p. 162) were involved in the corn trade, although they may have sent other commodities too. [401] L. Caelius Aprilis Valerianus, *curator* of the Carthaginian ships and probably a Carthaginian himself in view of his voting tribe, built his family tomb at Ostia. [402] So did L. Caecilius Aemilianus, a praetorian veteran, magistrate of Aelia Ulizibbira and member of the corporation of wine-importers. [403] Iulius Credentius, 'who sailed from the region of Vaga', may have been a trader (although the reference could simply be to his moving to Rome). [404] There was a boom in the olive oil trade from North Africa to

Rome in the second-third centuries, although no inscriptions explicitly record individuals settling at Rome because of it.[405]

The city of Volubilis remained loyal to Rome throughout the conquest of Mauretania, and Valerius Severus son of Bostar, one of the leading men of the city who commanded auxiliaries in the war, is recorded as going on an embassy to Claudius and obtaining Roman citizenship for the city and immunity from tribute for ten years.[406] Soldiers were subsequently recruited throughout North Africa, but particularly in Mauretania. North Africans are recorded as members of all the military units at Rome: praetorians, *equites singulares*, *vigiles*, *urbanicianii*, *classiarii*. Many of the recruits are likely to have been children of soldiers stationed in the area, who intermarried with other soldiers' families much more than with the native population.[407]

Africans are well attested as charioteers at Rome. M. Aurelius Liber and his son Aurelius Caecilius Planeta Protogenes were both *Afri*,[408] and Crescens was a *Maurus*.[409] Claudius Aurelius Polyphemus, *dominus et agitator* of the Red faction, is described as a Caesarean, which is likely to mean Caesarea in Mauretania.[410] North African horses were also popular,[411] and grooms may have come to Rome with them.

The slave trade remained significant in late antiquity. Augustine comments on both kidnapping and the sale of children by their parents as important sources of slaves for the overseas market in early fifth-century Africa.[412] Voluntary migration remained important too: epitaphs for people from all the North African provinces include substantial proportions of Christians and Jews (see TABLE 1). The early success of Christianity in Africa and the importance of African Christians in the church hierarchy would have boosted the number of Christian migrants and, for people whose *lingua franca* (if not always their first language) was Latin, Constantinople would have been a much less attractive alternative destination.

References to the homeland

Africans had a wider choice of self-designation than almost anyone else, since, in addition to using forms based on 'Africa', they could also use versions of 'Punic' or, as Fronto did, 'Libyan'. The significance of the terms seems to have varied considerably, since *Afer* could be used for a Carthaginian who was not a Berber or a Berber who was not a Carthaginian.[413] The only occurrence of 'Punic' is for a freedwoman,[414] and it may have been a term deliberately avoided at Rome because of its historical connotations. Carthage itself is mentioned only twice, perhaps for the same reasons.

253

TABLE 29. Designation of people from Africa and Numidia.

Province	33		
		Afer/Afra	14
		Africanus/a	2
		(provincia) Africa	5[415]
		Afer/Africa + city	10[416]
		Numidus	1
		Numidia + city	1
Region/tribe	3		
		regione + name	2
		Punica	1
City	19[417]		

Libya was not a Roman administrative unit until the time of Diocletian, but the ethnic 'Libyan' is used twice in Greek Christian inscriptions (Λυβεικόν, Λυβυκή).[418] The exact significance of the term is unclear: Moretti thought it designated Greeks from Cyrene, but it could equally well designate people who specifically did *not* consider themselves Greek.[419] The Latin *Libycus* is used once as the designation of a man from the Misenum fleet.[420] Fronto may have called himself a Libyan because he had ancestors who were of indigenous (i.e. non-Greek, Italian or Punic) stock, or simply as a geographical label.

Community and religion

There was certainly no formal organization of senators from North Africa, but the extent to which people from the same home area who achieved political influence felt any sympathy with each other is a matter of some dispute. According to Barnes (1967, 89):

> ...there is no evidence of an African patriotism or of African senators' regarding themselves as thereby joined by any common bond.

Champlin (1980, 14–15), however, believes that there was a distinct Cirtan aristocratic community at Rome in the second century, with Fronto acting as patron of younger senators.[421] There need be no contradiction between the two statements if Fronto was, as Champlin indicates, interested only in Cirtans, and felt no solidarity with other Africans. Aristocratic solidarity with fellow-citizens might largely be based on family connection, as the leading families in a city like Cirta were no doubt related to each other by blood or marriage. The branch of the Septimii who moved to Rome evidently gave help to those who remained at Lepcis.[422]

There was a corporation of *mercatores frumentarii et olearii Afrari* in the second century AD.[423] They made a dedication to the *praefectus annonae*, with whom they must have had regular professional dealings. This is the only evidence for an organization of Africans as a whole (assuming that they were Africans themselves rather than just dealers in African products), but nine groups of *navicularii* from African ports had *stationes* at Ostia, and also seem to have co-operated in one joint inscription (see p. 162). P. Aufidius Fortis, a magistrate at Ostia and Hippo Regius, was *quinquennalis* of the *corpus mercatorum frumentariorum*, which may in the context be another African organization, but this is not made clear.[424]

The existence of an African community among Christians (orthodox or Donatist) has been discussed already (p. 186). Africans may have been responsible for Latin replacing Greek as the liturgical language of Christians at Rome in the third century. The Donatist bishop at Rome was regarded by Augustine as the leader of a group of Africans there in the fourth century, and the Donatist movement was primarily associated with Africans. There may be a parallel with the Syrian cults. The worship of Jupiter Heliopolitanus at Rome was not formally restricted to Syrians, but in practice was probably largely or entirely exclusive to them; however, not all the Syrians at Rome were participants. Similarly, Donatism at Rome was not officially exclusive to Africans but was dominated by them; however, not all the Africans at Rome were Donatists. It seems that, whereas for Syrians Christianity abolished the main communal focus which they had, for Africans it unintentionally created a new focus.

viii. Jews

Overview

There is a fundamental difference between the evidence for Jews and for other foreign groups: 'Syrian', 'African', etc. were ethnic/geographical labels, but 'Jew' was a religious one as well. No-one 'became' a Syrian however fervently they worshipped Jupiter Dolichenus, but people who publicly adopted the Jewish religion became Jews, whatever their original background. Thus it was possible to be an African Jew or a Syrian Jew, and such double labels are occasionally found in the inscriptions. Jewish identity could be passed down the generations at Rome or anywhere else in the Diaspora, in a way which was very unlikely to happen for African or Syrian identity. While all Jews at Rome (except proselytes) must have assumed like other Jews that their ancestors ultimately came from the land of Israel, their *known* ancestors need have no connection with anywhere outside Rome. Rutgers (1995, 48–9) writes:

> Jews, not only in Rome but throughout the Roman Empire, formed a religious community, one which derived its internal coherence not merely from the fact that they upheld the same religious beliefs and practices, but also from the knowledge that they shared in the same history. In other words, in ancient Rome Syrian immigrants never had nor could have the sense of belonging that many Jews in this city must have felt. The Jews of Rome were a *people* in the sense that their Syrian neighbors were not.

Nevertheless, when Rome first came into contact with the Jews, they formed a separate political and geographical unit, the Maccabean state. In the period from the 160s to the 140s BC, the Maccabean leaders Judas, Jonathan and Simon are all said to have sent embassies to Rome to obtain support against the Seleucids.[425] Some Jews must have established themselves in the city at around this time if the report of the expulsion of 139 BC is correct (see p. 41).

Philo attributes the origin of Rome's Jewish community to prisoners who were brought to Italy and then emancipated.[426] This is likely to have been the tradition of the Roman Jews themselves, whom Philo would have met when he took part in the embassy to Caligula. Large numbers of prisoners were captured by Pompey during his war in Judaea in 63 BC and brought to Rome for his triumph in 61, but this does not explain the existence of the second-century BC community, which may have consisted of a small number of free immigrants and individuals who reached Rome through the slave trade.[427] The Jews, acting collectively, were a significant factor at public gatherings (*contiones*) in 59 BC, which seems too early for substantial numbers of Pompey's prisoners to have been manumitted.[428] The politically active Jews of 59 were presumably Roman citizens,[429] which implies that they were themselves freedmen or the descendants of freedmen; at this date few free immigrants from the East would have had citizenship. It seems therefore that Jewish slaves must have been reaching Rome in the late second and early first centuries BC, achieving manumission (which implies that they were doing skilled work rather than being used as forced labour) and establishing themselves as a significant and recognizable presence in the city. Pompey's prisoners would have added to the numbers of the existing community.[430]

Smaller numbers of Jewish slaves may have continued to reach Rome after smaller-scale wars such as Sosius' in 37 BC and Varus' in 4 BC, disturbances like the anti-census protests of AD 6, and Herod's policy of selling brigands into slavery.[431] In addition, enslaved Diaspora Jews could be sent to Rome by the slave trade in exactly the same circumstances as any other slaves. Livia had a female Jewish slave named Acme who was not necessarily a prisoner-of-war,[432] and the Jewish rhetor of the Augustan period, Caecilius of Calacte, was a freedman from Sicily. [433] Further waves of prisoners would have arrived after the revolts of the first and early second centuries AD.[434] Enormous numbers of Jews were captured in 66–70: e.g. after the fall of Tarichaeae in 67, 6,000 prisoners were sent to work on the Corinthian Canal and another 30,400 were sold as slaves.[435] Even if only a small proportion were eventually sent westwards, the numbers could still have been quite considerable. The religious duty for Jews to try to ransom enslaved fellow-Jews[436] may have meant that slavery lasted a shorter time for Jewish slaves at Rome than for others: for example, during his visit to Rome in AD 95, R. Joshua is said to have ransomed a Jewish child, who returned to Palestine with him and became R. Ishmael b. Elisha.[437] If Ishmael was one of the prisoners taken back to Rome after the fall of Jerusalem in 70, he was hardly a 'child' in 95. Nevertheless, the story may illustrate a real possibility for a few involuntary migrants (not only Jews): that they might be rescued by their compatriots and returned to their homeland.

The Jewish community of Rome probably numbered somewhere in the region of 20,000–60,000 in the early first century AD; Solin takes 40,000 as a likely maximum.[438] The estimates are based on two figures in the ancient sources: Josephus says that 8,000 Jews turned out to oppose Archelaus when he came to Rome to claim his father Herod's throne in 4 BC,[439] and Tacitus says that 4,000 Jews descended from freedmen (i.e. male citizens of military age) were conscripted and sent to Sardinia in AD 19 (see p. 42). The Jews therefore composed something between 2% and 6% of Rome's population up to AD 19.[440] The expulsions by Tiberius and Claudius would have reduced this temporarily, but probably made little long-term difference. It is, however, unlikely that the Jews of Rome would have been self-reproducing, since most of the factors inhibiting the reproduction rate in the city would have applied to them as much as to the rest of the population (see p. 18).[441] Conversions to Judaism could have helped to maintain the size of the community, but they were surely not happening to the same extent as they later did for the Christians; Solin (1983, 616) thinks it unlikely that there were 'many' proselytes.[442] As there is no evidence of whether the number of Jews or the proportion of the population which they formed remained stable, increased or decreased after the Julio-Claudian period,[443] there are no grounds for estimating how much Jewish immigration there was after the early first century. Epitaphs and rabbinic literature show that there was certainly some.

It is also impossible to know what proportion of the Jewish community at Rome held Roman citizenship before 212. Ex-slaves would normally be citizens; other immigrants from the East were more likely to be *peregrini*. If the two groups intermarried, the extent of citizenship may have diminished rather than increased within the community, since citizenship could only be inherited by the children of marriages between citizens.[444]

Literary sources about Rome from the Jewish perspective are limited. Some rabbinic first impressions of Rome were mentioned at p. 145. Philo makes some observations in the *Legatio* based on information he must have acquired when he had dealings with the Jews of Rome during his stay there. Josephus says very little about them despite being one of their number after AD 70; it is unlikely that he was on very friendly terms with most of them.

The only evidence surviving from Jews themselves which gives any real insight into their life in the city is epigraphic: the epitaphs from the Jewish catacombs and other places of Jewish burial. This material has many shortcomings: the difficulty of differentiating Jewish from non-Jewish records; the lack of any Jewish epitaphs from before the end of the second century AD. Nevertheless, it is informative about some aspects of the life of the community, such as the number of different synagogues and the titles held within them. It provides information about a small number of Jews who are specifically said to be immigrants: from Aquileia, Catania, Achaea, Laodicea, Caesarea in Palestine, Sepphoris, Tiberias, Arca Libani, Thabraca in Numidia, Tripolis (which one is uncertain); there is a notable predominance of places in Syria-Palaestina in the list.[445] One epitaph has a curse formula about the 'wrath of God' which is also attested at Acmonia in Asia, suggesting an immigrant from there.[446] Inscriptions also show the various terms of self-identification which were available, such as *Ioudaios* and *Hebraios* (see below), as well as the visual symbols by which the Jews identified themselves.

The state saw the Jews as an identifiable group which received special treatment in certain circumstances. The fact that there were three expulsions of Jews from Rome up to the time of Claudius (see p. 41) shows that they were perceived as 'foreign' at least until that date, since expulsions were only practised against groups which were in some sense foreign. However, their treatment as a special case had some advantages too, such as the permission they were given to make their own collections of money for the Temple even while Jerusalem was outside Roman jurisdiction, and the special arrangements made by Augustus to save Jews from having to collect their corn dole on the sabbath.[447] Jews were likely to be objects of suspicion but, unlike the treatment of the Germans after the Varus disaster, they were not penalized for the behaviour of their co-religionists elsewhere against Roman armies. Whatever the exact motivation of the expulsions, they were related to local causes in Rome rather than events in Judaea, and they were not repeated during AD 66–70 or the subsequent revolts. There is no evidence that reprisals were taken against the Jews of Rome then, or even that they suffered any particular restrictions during the revolts, although like all Jews they subsequently became liable to the Jewish Tax.[448]

Two Roman Jews who became Christians, Prisc(ill)a and Aquila, have one of the most complete surviving migration histories of any individuals of similar status, and show the distances it was possible for migrants to travel and the range of contacts they could make. Aquila was a native of Pontus; Prisca's place of origin is not stated (but may well have been the same). Nothing is said about their legal status, but they were probably *peregrini*. The Latin names which are recorded for them may not have been their original names. They were victims of the expulsion from Rome under Claudius and went to Corinth, where they met Paul, probably in AD 51.[449] While living at Corinth, they sailed with Paul from Cenchreae to Ephesus, and stayed there for long enough to convert the Alexandrian Jew Apollos. They were tentmakers (σκηνοποιοί) at Corinth like Paul, and presumably practised the same trade at Rome. They had returned to Rome by the time Paul wrote *Romans*.[450] Their story illustrates two points about being expelled from Rome: the expelled did not necessarily return to their original homes, and they could return to Rome after the initial problem had died down. Some of the other Jews expelled at the same time seem to have gone only as far as Aricia.[451]

Jewish migration to Rome was probably demographically similar to that of other groups: dominated by males in their teens and twenties. Ages are given in the epitaphs too rarely to confirm this, but there are a number of cases where Jewish immigrants seem to have had their children at Rome. Justus, son of Amachius of Catania, who died at 22 was evidently not an immigrant himself; he was probably commemorated by his father, who emphasized his own place of origin.[452] In the epitaph of Alypius of Tiberias and his sons Justus and Alypius, the sons are also implied to have been born at Rome.[453] Symmachus, *gerusiarch* of Tripolis, may have been commemorated at Rome aged 80 with the title he held at home, but if so he would have been an immigrant of fairly advanced age, since gerusiarchs usually seem to have been at least in their forties.[454]

A number of members of the Herodian family, sons and grandsons of Herod the Great, had at least part of their upbringing at Rome.[455] This was probably more for Herod's convenience than at Rome's demand, giving them education and contacts and keeping them out of his way. It had the advantage for Rome of creating a number of suitable actual and potential client-rulers, but came to an end with Agrippa II. He and Josephus were effectively exiles at Rome after the end of the revolt in AD 70.[456]

Numerous Jewish embassies to Rome are recorded, including those sent by the Maccabees to secure an alliance (see above), the pro- and anti-Archelaus embassies of 4 BC, the embassy of the Alexandrian Jews to Caligula (see p. 104), and various rabbinic delegations in the first and second centuries AD (see below). In this respect the Jews acted like many other groups within or around the Empire, and the subjects of the embassies were usually matters affecting only one city or area, rather than the Jews of the Empire as a whole. Some ambassadors, such as Philo, could find themselves staying at Rome for much longer than they expected.

The defeat of the Bar Kokhba revolt created some voluntary exiles, as well as people who were enslaved. One of the former was R. Matthia b. Ḥeresh, who eventually founded a *yeshivah* at Rome.[457] On his first voyage there, however, he allegedly reached Puteoli but then turned back because of longing for the land of Israel.[458] Todos or Theudas (Theodosius?) of Rome, who was active at a similar time, was presumably also a Hebrew scholar, in view of his high prestige among the sages of Palestine;[459] he was also a figure of influence among the Jews of Rome, to whom he introduced the practice of eating a 'helmeted kid' (or possibly a lamb) roasted whole on Passover night (implying that there were large gatherings to celebrate the occasion).[460]

The visit to Rome in AD 95 by a group of rabbis (Gamaliel II, Eleazar b. Azariah, Joshua b. Ḥananiah and Aqiba) is mentioned frequently in rabbinic literature (see p. 145); the real purpose of the trip is not clear. In the Antonine period, R. Simon b. Yohai and R. Eleazar b. Yose visited Rome to ask for the repeal of anti-Jewish legislation (probably, therefore, in the reign of Antoninus Pius);[461] their visit thus fits into the general tradition of embassies to Rome. While there, Eleazar saw some of the spoils of the Temple: the curtain from the Holy of Holies, the High Priest's vestments,[462] and fragments of Solomon's throne.[463] They met Matthia b. Ḥeresh while in Rome, and evidently had dealings with the Jewish community there, since Eleazar is recorded as delivering a ruling in Rome.[464] One third-century rabbi, R. Joshua b. Levi, is also recorded as visiting Rome, probably as part of a delegation.[465] In the late third or early fourth century, R. Ḥiyya b. Abba went to Rome as well as travelling around the eastern Diaspora.[466] The exact purpose of this and most other rabbinic visits to Rome is not stated, but they must have served (intentionally or not) to strengthen the links of the Roman Jewish community with the land of Israel.[467]

Jewish attitudes to migration

Jewish literature provides some insights into how migration was viewed which are unavailable from any other ancient literary source. Although they are not directly related to people moving to Rome, the ideas they express would have applied as much to those going to Rome as to anywhere else, and are therefore worth some brief consideration here. They are all from the perspective of Jews living in the land of Israel.

Moving from Israel to the Diaspora is treated with a variety of attitudes; it could be seen as a mission sent by God to extend the Jewish religion, or as a punishment for the sins of the people.[468] Most pseudepigraphical, apocryphal and rabbinic literature tends towards the latter view, while Philo and Josephus are more sympathetic to the positive interpretation. To some extent, the cause of the migration could be taken into consideration: voluntary migration was more likely to be seen positively than forced migration. There was an increasing hostility on the part of the Palestinian rabbis after the Bar-Kokhba revolt, i.e. at exactly the time when both voluntary and involuntary emigration from Israel are likely to have increased. According to them, living in the land of Israel could confer atonement for sins and speed messianic resurrection; i.e. emigrants would lose these benefits.[469]

The Jews were aware that there were other diasporas than their own, but felt that their own problems were greater because of the religious obstacles to full assimilation in their host communities:[470]

'Judah has gone into exile' (Lam.1.3) – do not the nations of the world go into exile? [The fact is, however, that] though they go into exile, their exile is not really exile. The heathen nations who eat their [local] bread and drink their wine, their exile is not real exile, but Israel – who do not eat their bread or drink their wine – do experience real exile.

This consciousness of a fundamental difference between being a Jewish immigrant and a gentile immigrant shows awareness of something which, it will be suggested below, seems to have been very real in the lives of the Jews of Rome. For theological reasons, they maintained institutions and practices which preserved a separate identity for them, even though most of them were no doubt fully integrated into the life of the city in other respects.

Jewish migration in general may have been facilitated by contacts between Jewish communities in different parts of the Diaspora, or between the Diaspora and the land of Israel. The existence of synagogues also made it relatively easy for Jews to seek out their co-religionists; this was how Paul and his companions made contact with other Jews while they were travelling, and it enabled Jews newly arrived at Alexandria to find others in the same line of work.[471]

Names

According to the epigraphic evidence, the Jews of Rome had Latin names more often than Greek ones, and Greek ones more often than Semitic ones. Semitic names occur in 13.1% of the epitaphs.[472] Most people are recorded with only one name, or with a nomen and cognomen, as is usual in inscriptions from the third century and later. While it might be expected that Roman Jews would have a Jewish name in addition to a standard Roman one, there is little evidence of this. There are only four cases where both a Greek or Latin name and an additional Jewish name (*agnomen* or *signum*) are recorded: Monimus Eusabbatis, Cocotia Iuda, Hermione Barsheoda, Veturia Paulla Sarah.[473] The last of these was a proselyte who took on the name of Sarah after her conversion. Since the context of the evidence is the Jewish catacombs, Jewish names would naturally be used there if they existed (unlike Thracian or Syrian names in mixed pagan burial areas). It is, however, clear that Latin, Greek and Semitic names all occurred within the same family, and (on the basis of very limited evidence) that parents with Latin or Greek names were as likely to give their children Semitic names as parents with Semitic names were to give their children Latin or Greek names.[474] This is a clear contrast with the Syrians, for whom most Semitic names disappeared in the first generation of immigrants. It was presumably the biblical connotations of Semitic names which made them acceptable to the descendants of Jewish immigrants when they were not acceptable to the descendants of Syrian immigrants.

Self-identification and language

Two labels were available to identify Jews, used by both themselves and others: *Ioudaios* and *Hebraios*, which both existed in Greek and Latin versions. There has been much debate about the exact significance of the two words, and whether they were primarily religious or ethnic descriptions.

Various interpretations of *Ioudaios* are summarized by Williams (1997, 249). Kraemer (1989) argues for a range of meanings, geographical ('Judaean') as well as religious ('Jew'), but Williams (1997, 251–2) shows that there is no evidence of *Ioudaios* ever being used in the geographical sense in inscriptions. Roman writers such as Dio were certainly aware that the term was originally a geographical one, but also that it had lost its geographical significance, and that the existence of proselytes meant that Jews were no longer a distinct racial group.[475] Using the label in a predominantly Jewish context such as a Jewish catacomb would normally be superfluous. Hence it is rarely found in Roman Jewish inscriptions; when it is, it is usually emphasizing the Jewishness of people who, as proselytes or immigrants, were on the fringes of the Jewish community.[476]

The imposition of the Jewish Tax in AD 70 meant that the state had to define who was (and was not) a Jew in a more systematic way than ever before. Goodman (1989) argues that Nerva's reform of the *Fiscus Iudaicus* transformed 'Jew' from an ethnic label which people were born with to a religious one which they could acquire or lose through proselytism or apostasy. However, I have suggested at p. 43 that the state was already capable of defining Jews either ethnically or religiously in the early first century AD. Nerva's reform would have set up a fixed definition, where previously the more convenient one had been used in different contexts.

Hebraios in epigraphic usage simply signifies an adherent of the Jewish religion, although its literary usage was rather more complex.[477] It seems to have superseded *Ioudaios* gradually as the preferred form of self-identification, because of the negative associations which *Ioudaios* had with the tax and the revolts. Hebrews were 'good Jews' who could claim piety, tradition and orthodoxy.[478] The term does not have any particular association with the use of the Hebrew language, or any direct connection with the land of Israel.[479]

Another possible label, Israelite, is much rarer in literature[480] and almost unknown in Roman inscriptions. The one occurrence, in the epitaph of a three-year-old girl described as both *Ioudaia* and Israelite, seems to be an attempt to emphasize the Jewishness of someone whose family were proselytes.[481] There are also epigraphic occurrences of 'Israel', either as an individual word written in Hebrew characters[482] or as part of the Hebrew formula 'peace upon Israel' (*salom 'al yisra'el*).[483] The significance is almost certainly the whole Jewish 'nation' rather than the land of Israel as a geographical concept.[484]

The fact that 'Israel' is only written in the Hebrew alphabet is connected with the symbolic importance of the Hebrew language for Jews at Rome. With one exception, Hebrew (or Aramaic) is only used for a concluding formula in an otherwise Greek or Latin epitaph (see p. 178). Whereas immigrants apparently used Nabataean and Palmyrene, there is no reason to associate the use of Hebrew with immigrants. Instead it seems to have been inscribed as much for its symbolic and visual effect as for any linguistic reason.[485] All Semitic languages lacked competent inscribers at Rome. There is one exception to this: JIWE ii 58, from the Monteverde catacomb. This is entirely in the Hebrew alphabet, with no Greek or Latin. The standard of the lettering is much higher, with reasonable alignment (although the letters become slightly smaller to the left) and some use of serifs. It appears to be in Aramaic, but no satisfactory interpretation has been suggested, and it is completely exceptional among the Roman inscriptions, almost certainly inscribed for someone with close connections to the land of Israel.[486]

The important language of the synagogues and Jewish catacombs at Rome was Greek. These were both contexts in which the in-group language could be used, so there is no doubt that Greek (rather than Latin, Hebrew or Aramaic) *was* the primary in-group language. The titles held within the synagogues were all basically Greek, even if occasionally latinized (never hebraized). Title-holders were in fact slightly more likely than other Jews to have an epitaph in Greek.[487] The vast majority of epitaphs for the Jews as a whole are in Greek: 74%, as opposed to 17% in Latin, 6% in a mixture of Greek and Latin, and 3% using some Hebrew or Aramaic.[488] The Jewish community was probably largely diglossic, using Greek or Latin in different circumstances; the important difference from other groups at Rome is that this seems to have remained a permanent situation rather than dying out within one or two generations after immigration.[489]

Community

The Jewish synagogues of Rome were a form of organization without parallel among other foreign groups. By establishing communal institutions which took on a life of their own, the Jews had the means to pass on a separate identity from one generation to the next, irrespective of immigration.[490] Other groups which were probably more numerous than the Jews had no equivalent, perhaps because they had no similar ideological imperative to create such institutions. The Syrian cults were not in principle exclusive to one group, whether defined on religious or ethnic grounds, although in practice they may have been confined to people of the same ethnic and geographical background. They produced few people who held titles within them of sufficient importance to be recorded in their epitaphs: Gaionas (see p. 240) is very much an exception.[491] For the Jews, on the other hand, the holding of titles seems to have been remarkably common. Over 20% of the Roman Jews known from inscriptions as deceased, commemorators or relatives are recorded with titles.[492]

Nothing is known about the foundation of any of the individual synagogues beyond what can be inferred from their names. Other large cities had several synagogues, but none except Jerusalem is known to have had as many as Rome:[493] at least eleven different names of synagogues are known there,[494] and there may well have been more which are not recorded. There was certainly no overall planning behind them, and various processes of splitting, merger, new foundations and closures can be imagined. Some may have been influenced by practices brought from elsewhere in the Diaspora, since their names suggest that they had regional origins (Tripolitans, perhaps the Secenians and El(a)ea).[495] It may be significant that no synagogues are known for people from, for example, Tiberias or Sepphoris. Only Jews from more obscure places in the Diaspora seem to have wanted to preserve their identity in this way, perhaps paralleling the Galatian villagers in the Christian epitaphs (see p. 232). The synagogue of the Vernaculi may have been originally for natives of Rome as opposed to immigrants.[496] The synagogue of the Hebrews has often been claimed to be the first synagogue founded at Rome, but it would have been more natural to call the first synagogue the *Ioudaioi*;[497] Harvey's interpretation (1998, 146–7) that they used the label to identify themselves as 'good Jews' is more plausible. Of the other synagogues, the Agrippesians and Augustesians appear to have been named after famous people;[498] the Calcaresians, Campesians and Siburesians after areas of Rome where the synagogues were situated or their members lived;[499] the origin of the name of the Volumnesians is very uncertain.[500] The synagogues appear to have been treated in some respects like *collegia* under Roman law, but were apparently exempt from the legislation against *collegia* enacted by Julius Caesar and Augustus.[501]

Because of the proliferation of synagogues and lack of evidence for any joint organization, it has usually been assumed that the Jews of Rome (unlike those of Alexandria) did not have a *gerousia* or other city-wide body to represent their interests; Botermann (1996, 69) sees this as a factor in minimizing conflict between Jews and non-Jews in the city. However, Williams (1998) claims that there was a centralized communal structure for the Jews of Rome. One of her arguments is that this would have reflected the practice of the Jews in Alexandria and elsewhere. However, it may be more relevant to note that it would have gone against the practice of all other foreign groups at Rome. There is no evidence for any city-wide organization of any religious, geographical or ethnic group at Rome beyond what emerged around particular shrines. There is no doubt that the Roman Jews did act collectively on occasions, as she points out,[502] and could be treated as a unit by the authorities (although all the evidence for this comes from the period from Augustus to Claudius), but the same could be said of Egyptians or astrologers, groups which certainly did not have a central council.

The synagogues do not seem to have been involved in the organization of the Jewish catacombs. Williams (1994a) notes the impossibility of linking where the Jews were buried with where they lived or which synagogue they belonged to; the same is true for the Christians, as shown by Pietri (1976). She suggests (p. 181) that the catacombs were run by separate burial consortia, but the nature of these is not known.

The synagogues appear to have flourished until the fourth century, judging from the epitaphs. There is some evidence that they may have not lasted much longer, at least in the same form. Christians destroyed one of the Roman synagogues in 388, and its rebuilding was ordered by the 'usurper' Maximus, something which apparently cost him Christian support.[503] There was probably another incident of synagogue-burning in 395,[504] but the fate of individual synagogues after that is unknown. Since there certainly were still synagogues in the sixth and seventh centuries, they were not all destroyed, but the number of separate institutions, and the size of the Jewish community as a whole, is likely to have contracted as the total population of the city contracted.

Links with the land of Israel

There is evidence for direct links between the Jews of Rome and the land of Israel of a rather different nature from the sorts of link discussed at p. 164. According to Acts 28.21, it was normal practice for the Temple authorities in pre-70 Jerusalem to correspond with the Jewish community in Rome, at least to warn them about travellers between the cities:

And they said to him [Paul], 'We have received no letters out of Judaea about you, and none of the brethren coming here has reported or spoken any evil about you.'

Cicero and Josephus show that money was being sent from Rome to the Temple in the first centuries BC and AD.[505] In the second century, according to rabbinic sources, Todos' introduction of the Passover kid or lamb at Rome (see above) was permitted by the rabbis in the land of Israel, because they held him in such high regard, although supposedly it would have been condemned if it had been anyone else's idea. The story shows rabbinic authorities claiming some power at Rome (just as the Temple authorities had done in the first century), whether it reflects the real position in the second century or not.[506] The Patriarch (Nasi) must have undertaken fund-raising in the West, since the legal text of AD 399 which abolishes his right to send out *apostuli* to collect money is addressed to the Praetorian Prefect of Italy and Africa.[507] Thus it seems that religious leaders in the land of Israel always claimed some sort of suzerainty over the Jews of Rome. How far they were able to enforce it is much less clear. Burial in the land of Israel was strongly encouraged by rabbis from the third century, but the only known case of a Jew who died at Rome being sent back to Israel for burial is much earlier: Aristobulus II in 49 BC (see p. 191).

The links could be political as well as theological. When Archelaus came to Rome to plead for Herod's throne in 4 BC, huge numbers of Jews turned out to oppose him.[508] A man claiming to be another of Herod's sons, Alexander, won support among Jews at Puteoli and Rome – the real Alexander had earlier lived at Rome and presumably built up his popularity.[509] At this stage, there was clearly a lively interest among the Jews of Rome in events in Judaea.[510] The revolts appear to have changed this, and largely to have severed the political links. Nevertheless, the land of Israel remained the focal point for the Roman Jews, something which is graphically illustrated by the way in which the synagogue at Ostia was reorientated, probably in the fourth century, so that people would face Jerusalem when praying.[511] Jews born at Rome no doubt regarded the city as their homeland, just as Philo regarded Alexandria,[512] but would still have felt an overriding loyalty to Jerusalem.

Notes

[1] Other than those from Cisalpine Gaul, who are not under consideration here.

[2] Beard, North and Price 1998, vol. 2, no. 6.6b.

[3] Ricci 1992a, 304.

[4] The three Massiliotes mentioned in epitaphs all appear to be *peregrini:* CIL

vi 24057; IGUR 820, 940.

[5] Suetonius, *Gramm.* 7, 11; an alternative version said that Gnipho was educated at Alexandria.

[6] Suetonius, *Gramm.* 20.

[7] CIL vi 6238.

[8] CIL vi 16100: 1st–2nd century according to Ricci (1992b, no. a34).

[9] Ricci 1992b, 105.

[10] Suetonius, *D.J.* 86 ('armed Spaniards'), *Aug.* 49 ('men from Calagurri').

[11] Ricci 1992b, 121–2.

[12] AE (1974) 226, AE (1993) 388.

[13] Herodian 1.10.3.

[14] Ricci 1992b, 108; CIL vi 1454.

[15] RIT 331.

[16] Tacitus, *Ann.* 1.78, 4.37. A priest of the imperial cult for the *conventus Asturum* apparently died at Rome: CIL vi 29724.

[17] Ricci 1992b, 125–6. There are also dedications by Arles, Lyon and the Three Provinces of Gaul (Ricci 1992a, 314–15).

[18] CIL vi 29688.

[19] CIL xiii 412, add. p.4; Ricci 1992a, no. A41. 'He obtained for the nine peoples (the right) to separate (from) the Gauls'.

[20] CIL xii 1750.

[21] CIL vi 29687; Ricci 1992a, no. A34.

[22] CIL xiv 327.

[23] Millar 1981, 147; García Martinez 1991, 270.

[24] This is not the case with the civilians in the inscriptions, among whom both Lusitania and Tarraconensis outnumber Baetica (Ricci 1992b, 128). García Martinez (1993, 325) gives an extensive bibliography on Spanish senators.

[25] Ricci 1992a, 305. A. Annius Camars of Arles, tribune in the Flavian period, was probably one of the first office-holders from Gaul, if Ricci's identification (no. A2) is correct.

[26] Tacitus, *Ann.* 11.23–5; CIL xiii 1668.

[27] Millar 1981, 149.

[28] Millar 1981, 159.

[29] Ricci 1992b, 108. M. Vibius Maternus, who describes himself as *Ilurensis*, put up a dedication to the Urban Prefect L. Fabius Septiminus Cilo, whose 'candidate' he was (CIL vi 1410).

[30] Spain: Ricci 1992b, nos. a13, a16; Rodriguez Neila 1978. There is one from Lyon (CIL xiii 1798) who is explicitly said to have served at Rome. There may also be one from Gaul (CIL xiii 5007–8; Ricci 1992a, no. A20), but the text is heavily restored.

[31] RIT 230 = CIL ii 4180.

[32] Ricci 1992b, 105.

[33] Ricci 1992b, 106.

[34] Ricci 1992b, 129.

[35] Ricci 1992a, 303–4.

[36] Ricci 1992b, 139–40. *Salsarii/salsamentarii* were dealers in salted fish products. Strabo (3.1.8, 3.5.3) refers to *salsamentarii* from Cadiz.

[37] Millar 1981, 128; García Martinez 1991, 268; Remesal and Revilla 1999.

[38] CIL vi 9717, an *olearius* from Aix-en-Provence.

[39] Ricci 1992b, 137.

[40] CIL vi 9677.

[41] CIL vi 1625. Ricci (1992b, 135) notes that an *olearius ex Baetica* did not necessarily come from Baetica personally, but there is little evidence that any of the people supplying Baetican products were *not* Baeticans themselves. However, I have not counted as Baetican (*contra* García Martinez 1993, 325) L. Marius Phoebus, who is described in CIL vi 1935 as both *viator tribunicius decuriae maioris* and *mercator olei Hispani ex provincia Baetica*: he may have been a Spanish merchant who had a career change after coming to Rome, but more probably he was someone from a wealthy Roman background who also made money from trade with Baetica.

[42] Ricci 1992b, 137.

[43] Ricci 1992a, 316.

[44] CIL vi 29722; cf. Panciera 1980, 241.

[45] According to Panciera (1980, 241), 'patron of the *seviri*'.

[46] Ricci 1992b, 129.

[47] Dio 59.26.8–9; it is not certain that this happened at Rome.

[48] AE (1979) 75 (CIL vi 9962+21053).

[49] CIL vi 7971 L. Salluius L.l. Nasta; CIL vi 37378 L. Salluius L.l. Theuda.

[50] Ricci (1992b, 105 n. 4) gives a full list of references; Martial 1.41, 6.71.

[51] CIL vi 9013.

[52] CIL vi 10048 (dated AD 146); CIL 2884.

[53] CIL vi 10184. CIL vi 10177 = 33977 is the epitaph of a Tungrian (*natione Tunger*) man who is described as *mimillonis veterani* – possibly a veteran myrmillo, although *mimillonis* could be part of his name.

[54] CIL vi 10127.

[55] AE (1953) 200.

[56] Ricci 1992a, 305.

[57] ICUR 20819.

[58] ICUR 17495 = CIL vi 9597.

[59] Inscriptions such as dedications which are not treated in ch. 4 or the Appendix as showing immigrants (because they may have been made by people who were only in Rome very briefly) but which show the sort of self-designations available have sometimes been used in this chapter; references are given in the footnotes.

[60] The 'tribal' designations used by Martial for 'his' people, *Celtae et Hiberi* (6.52, 10.65) do not occur in the inscriptions.

[61] No city occurs more than three times. All but one of the Spanish soldiers takes his designation from city not province.

[62] Ricci (1992a, 317) believes that *Gallus* is used for someone from Tres Galliae not from Narbonensis. However, no other label appears to have been available to someone from Narbonensis (unless *Narbonensis* is an ethnic from the province rather than, as assumed in this table, the city).

[63] Including AE (1934) 161.

[64] Including AE (1930) 70, CIL vi 1400, CIL vi 36835. The city mentioned

most often is Vienne (7).

65 Since it was also a title for the castrated priests of Magna Mater, and was used by them (in the forms *gallus* and *archigallus*) in their epitaphs, there was potential for confusion in epigraphic usage. *Gallus* also means a cockerel in Latin.

66 Ricci 1992b, 130.

67 CIL vi 24162.

68 BCAR 56 (1928), pp. 318–20; CIL vi 1006.

69 CIL vi 1400, 1526; Ricci 1992b no. C2.

70 NS (1933) pp. 505–6 no. 226 = AE (1934) 161.

71 Beard, North and Price (1998), vol. 1, pp.270–1. She was the only western deity to get her own shrine.

72 CIL vi 32550. 32551 includes *omnibus diis patriensibus* in a list of gods beginning with I.O.M.

73 CIL vi 46; Ricci 1992a, no. B21; RE ii 616. Arduinna and Camulus are depicted as Diana and Mars.

74 CIL vi 36835. According to Bang, quoted as 'più che attendibile' by Ricci (1992a, 306), this may be evidence of a *statio* for Vienne at Rome, but this seems an unnecessary conclusion, and would be inconsistent with the other *stationes*, where magistrates from the home city are not mentioned.

75 Cicero, *Tusc.* 3.53, mentions the large number of Macedonian slaves at Rome.

76 Ricci 1993c, 223.

77 Carcopino 1941, 75.

78 CIL vi 12304; Ricci 1993b, no. N1.

79 Martial (11.96) complains about a German slave elbowing someone out of the way to drink from the Aqua Marcia.

80 Ricci 1993b, 144.

81 Ricci 1993b, 144.

82 Hammond and Walbank 1998, ch. XXVI.

83 The only ones in Greek are ICUR 15000 and IGUR 1312.

84 CIL vi 2386 = 32625, a.i.9.

85 Ricci 1993b, 161.

86 Ricci 1993b, 165–6.

87 Palmer 1981, 374; Mateescu 1923, 74–5. A number of slaves commemorated in the Monument of the Statilii have Thracian names (Mateescu 1923, 78).

88 CIL vi 6221, 6229–37.

89 Dio 75.2.4 says that before 193 the praetorians were recruited 'exclusively from Italy, Spain, Macedonia and Noricum'. Inscriptions show that this was not actually the case, but it was perhaps how it seemed to an onlooker.

90 Ricci 1993b, 176.

91 Kolendo 1988–9.

92 According to Tacitus, *Hist.* 3.12, the fleet at Ravenna in 69 was mainly manned by Dalmatians and Pannonians; the inscriptions show the importance of Dalmatians but not of Pannonians.

93 Ricci 1993c, 219.

94 Ricci 1993c, 206.

95 Ricci 1993c, 206.

[96] Ricci 1993b, 145; CIL vi 26608.

[97] Mateescu 1923, 114.

[98] CIL vi 20718; NS (1922) 417 nos. 51+53. Mateescu (1923, 80) thinks that the latter is associated with a 2nd-century AD Bosporan king, not a Thracian ruler, but Ricci (1993b, no. T7) links him with a Thracian king from the time of Augustus.

[99] Dio 67.5.3.

[100] CIL vi 1801. According to Mateescu (1923, 100), they were probably captured by the Asdings in 171–2 and handed over to the Romans.

[101] CIL vi 2933; Ricci 1993b, no. Mo.2.

[102] CIL vi 9719; Ricci 1993b, no. T12. The main products exported from the area to Rome were metals, amber, animals, skins (Ricci 1993b, 163–4).

[103] CIL vi 9709–10; Ricci 1993b, 164–5. 9709, the inscription from the tomb which T. Flavius Genethlius prepared for himself and his family, ends with the mysterious comment: 'He never drove a chariot in the four stables'. Other *nummularii* are recorded at Aquincum and Poetovio.

[104] CIL vi 6343.

[105] CIL vi 33036. This may be a military post, as it is in CIL vi 2638 (a man possibly from Serdica), and Ricci 1993b, 198–200 no. 1 (a Dacian), but could also refer to a civilian transcriber or seller of books.

[106] Dio 51.22; Ricci 1993c, 207.

[107] Mateescu 1923, 76: presumably there were other Thracians in his revolt. Horace, *Sat.*1.7.20 mentions a gladiator with the Thracian name Bithus.

[108] In CIL vi 10187, the gladiator is a Samnite from Thrace.

[109] Petolescu 1992.

[110] Mateescu 1923, 86, 214.

[111] AE (1989) 30. The same man also had a slave 'from the shores of the Black Sea'.

[112] CIL vi 3229.

[113] CIL vi 32796.

[114] CIL vi 3227.

[115] Other *equites singulares* were commemorated by their freedmen: e.g. M. Ulpius Victor from Cologne (CIL vi 3311); T. Aurelius Impetratus, a Raetian (CIL vi 32845; Speidel 1994c, no. 133); T. Aurelius Iucundus, another Raetian (CIL vi 3208). In these cases, the freedmen's place of origin is not given.

[116] One exception is C. Vallius Scribonianus, a magistrate from Carnuntum who was a judge (*inter selectos*) at Rome. CIL iii 14359.3; Ricci 1993b, no. P.14.

[117] Millar 1981, 235; Ricci 1993b, 146–7; Ricci 1993c, 207–8, 223.

[118] Ricci 1993b, 145–8.

[119] Ricci 1993b, 206.

[120] CIL vi 32978; Lega and Orlandi 1997.

[121] ICUR 13109; Bertolino 1997, 119; PLRE i 844.

[122] ICUR 1480 is a dedication by the *gens Carnuntum* to their bishop; this has usually been taken to refer to the Pannonian city of Carnuntum, but Di Stefano Manzella (1997a) argues that it means the *Carnutes* from Gaul.

[123] There is some general discussion of the nature of these tables at p. 209.

[124] Someone with this designation is almost invariably a German bodyguard.

[125] For them, *Germanus* was both an ethnic and a job title (Ricci 1993c, 220).

[126] Including 6 from Celeia.

[127] 25 out of 28 refer to the province; 3 are designated by city only.

[128] Including 17 from Savaria.

[129] CIL vi 2605.

[130] Including CIL vi 31147.

[131] Including CIL vi 32546.

[132] Including CIL vi 32543 = 2799.

[133] Fol (1967, 9) notes that Roman administrative divisions did not replace earlier ones in Thracian thinking.

[134] CIL vi 32582 = 2807.

[135] CIL vi 32543 = 2799.

[136] CIL vi 32605 = 2845.

[137] CIL vi 32589=2818: '*nationem Mesacus vic.*'

[138] IGUR 134: ἐκ δὲ χωρίης Τήσεος. One of the men who erected this dedication was himself commemorated with a Latin epitaph (CIL vi 2732).

[139] CIL vi 32567 = 2819, dated 266; Ricci 1993b, no. T17; Mateescu 1923, 133.

[140] I owe this idea to Stephen Mitchell.

[141] Thrace: AE (1993) 332, CIL vi 2772+32660, ICUR 23627. Moesia: CIL vi 2730, 2736 (both by wives for praetorian husbands).

[142] CIL vi 3300; one of the commemorators is the deceased's wife.

[143] CIL vi 37224, 3297.

[144] CIL vi 2494a.

[145] CIL vi 37213.

[146] CIL vi 2694.

[147] See Mateescu 1923 for an exhaustive survey; however, subsequent comments on his work show the scope for disagreement about exactly what constitutes a Thracian name.

[148] The following table is largely based on the list of occurrences compiled by Mateescu (1923, 77). Vitus is assumed to be a form of Bithus only when there is a Thracian ethnic with it.

[149] The status criteria used are the same as those outlined at p. 76, with the addition of the category of 'soldier'.

[150] In CIL vi 3165, the *classiarius* C. Caecilius Valens was the son of a Bithus, presumably a *peregrinus*.

[151] CIL vi 9166.

[152] CIL vi 20216.

[153] CIL vi 2570. The brother's cognomen is suggestive of someone who took up a Latin name on enlistment and did not understand the difference between a praenomen and a cognomen.

[154] CIL vi 3195.

[155] CIL vi 250=30723; see p. 161.

[156] CIL vi 1569; Ricci 1993b, no. N10.

[157] CIL iii 12336, corrected in AE (1994) 1552; Millar 1981, 228–9. Mateescu (1923, 148) suggests that the village of Omurovo thanked the

praetorian Aurelius Mucianus for a similar reason (IGR i 738).

[158] Turcan 1996, 249–50; Mateescu 1923, 159–62, 188, 243; CIL vi 30912 = 3691, 32582 = 2807. Floriani Squarciapino (1962, 67) suggests a link between his cult at Ostia and the presence of Bessan sailors there.

[159] IGUR 132, found on the Esquiline. The first divinity is well attested in Thrace, but the second is otherwise unknown.

[160] CIL vi 32546 = 2797, 32570 = 2798, 32571; Mateescu 1923, 143–4.

[161] IGUR 134.

[162] IGUR 135.

[163] CIL vi 31162; Ricci 1993c, no. C1; Mateescu 1923, 186.

[164] RE viii 611.

[165] CIL vi 32588 = 2817.

[166] CIL vi 2808.

[167] CIL vi 32543 = 2799.

[168] CIL vi 32542, 32544, 32557. According to Mateescu (1923, 137), the Cotini were a Celtic tribe allowed to settle in Pannonia Inferior.

[169] Speidel 1994a, 26.

[170] CIL vi 2835.

[171] Speidel 1994a, 142.

[172] Dion.Hal, *Ant.Rom.* 1.89–90.

[173] Beard, North and Price 1998, vol. 2, no. 6.6b. These Greeks *could* be from Magna Graecia rather than from Greece itself.

[174] Hammond and Walbank 1998, 403.

[175] Hammond and Walbank 1998, 567.

[176] Alcock 1993, ch. 1.

[177] Suetonius, *Gramm.* 10, 15.

[178] Philostratus, *Ap.T.* 8.12.

[179] CIL vi 17448.

[180] CIL vi 20548 = IGUR 1239.

[181] Alcock 1993, 24–32. The ambivalent attitudes of the Roman elite to Greek culture in the late Republic are discussed by Erskine (1997).

[182] PLRE i 660.

[183] IGUR 370.

[184] CIL vi 18175 = IGUR 1210.

[185] CIL vi 3102, 3136, 3168 (all described as *natione Graecus*).

[186] CIL vi 8142, 9906, 17448 (definitely a slave).

[187] Solin and Itkonen-Kaila 1966, nos. 121, 329.

[188] JIWE ii 503.

[189] McLean 1993 gives the text.

[190] Beard, North and Price 1998, vol. 1, 271 (IGUR 160); Scheid 1986. She was the daughter and wife of 2nd-century consuls, but, as often in this type of inscription, her full name was omitted, and she is referred to only as Agrippinilla.

[191] e.g. McLean 1993, 252: 'The fact that parents bearing Greek names tended to give their sons Latin cognomina suggests that most of these slaves and freedmen bearing Greek names on the Agrippinilla inscription are first-generation immigrants'; 254: 'Since I have established that many of those bearing Greek names had only recently immigrated from Lesbos as the slaves

and freedmen of the Gallicanus household...' Many of McLean's comments in the article are based on misunderstandings about onomastic practices in Roman epigraphy.

[192] In this section, 'Asia Minor' will be used to refer to the area which eventually contained the provinces of Asia, Bithynia et Pontus, Galatia, Lycia et Pamphilia, Cilicia and Cappadocia. In the absence of any other available terminology, 'Asian' refers to someone from Asia Minor, not just from the province of Asia.

[193] Juvenal 5.56, 11.147.

[194] Philostratus, *Ap.T.* 8.12; cf discussion at p. 224.

[195] Catullus 10. CIL vi 6311 is an epitaph for a Paphlagonian litter-bearer. Carrying sedan chairs in 18th-century London was a job associated with Irish immigrants.

[196] Cicero, *Post Red. in Sen.* 14.

[197] PIR² F262.

[198] *Acts of Justin & Companions* 4.

[199] CIL vi 10098.

[200] CIL vi 3173.

[201] Speidel 1994c, no. 697.

[202] In IGUR 846, a woman with the local (cf. Palmer 1981, 386) name Ouddas commemorates her husband; both have only a single name. In AE (1983) 50, a woman named Iulia Ma is commemorated by her son, a praetorian from Germanicopolis in Bithynia. The same name occurs (Ramia M.l. Maa) in AE (1966) 51. In Väänänen 1973, 79, the imperial slave Tilles has a Cappadocian name according to Robert.

[203] Beard, North and Price 1998, vol. 1, p. 97; vol. 2, no. 8.7a (Dion.Hal., *Ant.Rom.* 2.19). See further below.

[204] IGUR 352.

[205] IGUR 433, with Moretti's comments ad loc. A high-priest from Laodicea may be commemorated in the very fragmentary IGUR 1063.

[206] IGUR 1260.

[207] IGUR 1288 (heavily restored).

[208] IGUR 1361.

[209] IGUR 1204.

[210] IGUR 815.

[211] The first known Bithynian senator was advanced under Claudius (Jones 1978, 4).

[212] CIL xiv 480.

[213] Dio 79.20.2.

[214] CIL vi 10149.

[215] BCAR 51 (1923), p. 74 no. 16.

[216] ICUR 10549; ICUR 5688 as understood by Feissel 1982a, no. I.

[217] IGUR 607, 682, 1283, 1355; CIL vi 9580; Jones 1978, 1. See also p. 111.

[218] AE (1947) 162; IGUR 872; IGUR 626 = CIL vi 6048.

[219] SEG xxvii 678.

[220] IGUR 320.

[221] IGUR 371.

222 IGUR 1351, with Moretti's comments ad loc.

223 I.Porto 1, according to the interpretation by Mazzoleni cited ad loc.

224 But see I.Porto 45, as interpreted by Ebert 1985.

225 Bevilacqua 1978.

226 CIL vi 9675.

227 ICUR 5064, as restored by Avraméa 1995, 322.

228 There is some general discussion of the nature of these tables at p. 209.

229 In addition, there are 6 references to some version of 'Laodicea in Asia', counted above under province.

230 These are all cities which are mentioned once or twice only.

231 Including one reference to 'Byzantium'.

232 Villages were of great importance in communal life throughout Asia Minor, not just in Galatia (Mitchell 1993, vol. 1, 170, 178), so there is no obvious reason why only Galatian villages are named at Rome.

233 Cf. Mitchell 1993, vol. 1, 179.

234 Cf. the discussion by Feissel 1982a.

235 ICUR 4441, with the spelling κόμη; the name of the village seems to have been omitted accidentally. The restoration in ICUR 5679 of [ἀπὸ κώμης] is almost certainly wrong; in a Galatian inscription, it is much more likely to be [χωρίου].

236 ICUR 4437, 4444 (where just [χ]ωρίου rather than [ἀπο χ]ωρίου should probably be restored), 5661, 5676.

237 ICUR 5669+5675.

238 ICUR 4041: χωρίου Πιαμ[– –]. ICUR 4271b: κωρίῳ Μικρᾶς Κώμης. ICUR 4434: χωρίου Τουγουτέων. ICUR 5833: χωρίου Κνηκνων. Ferrua 1939, p. 148 no. 10: [χ]ωρίου Ξιτων. Cf. p. 188.

239 La Piana 1927, 219–20; Richardson 1992, 290 on the Phrygianum in the Vatican under St Peter's.

240 Dion.Hal. *Ant.Rom.*2.19.4: 'her priests are a Phrygian man and a Phrygian woman'.

241 La Piana 1927, 289.

242 e.g. Livia Briseis Aug.lib. in CIL vi 496.

243 CIL vi 10098.

244 IGUR 129.

245 CIL vi 10234.

246 IGUR 102, probably the same man for whom IGUR 1283 is the epitaph (they are assumed to be the same man in ch. 4).

247 IGUR 104.

248 IGUR 86–7; they are probably connected with the Sardian *statio* (see p. 161). They have not been counted as Sardians in ch. 4.

249 IGUR 146; Turcan 1996, 254.

250 Turcan 1996, 257. Floriani Squarciapino (1962, 69) notes that at least seven statues of her were found at Rome and one in Ostia, probably for private use in *lararia*. She suggests a link with Aphrodisian sculptors at Rome (cf. p. 113).

251 IGUR 185–6; Turcan 1996, 323–4. Cf. p. 41 on the possible expulsion of Sabazius worshippers in the 2nd century BC.

252 IGUR 131 = CIL vi 32591 = 2823.

253 ICUR 4441 (Philip the *domesticus*); perhaps ICUR 23743 (Eustathius the merchant).

254 Rebuffat 1966.

255 The background of the Syrian prophetess Martha who advised Marius is not clear (Plutarch, *Marius* 17).

256 Cicero, *de Prov.Cons.* 10; Livy 36.17.5.

257 Plautus, *Merc.* 415; Plutarch, *Luc.* 21.

258 Cicero, *Orat.* 232.

259 Pliny, *H.N.* 35.58.199.

260 CIL vi 26883.

261 Solin 1983, 671. Cf. IGUR 1287: 'my race was Greek (Ἕλλην), my homeland was Apamea'.

262 CIL vi 35556a.

263 Solin 1983, 666–70.

264 Solin 1983, 671.

265 Cf. Solin 1983, 722.

266 Bevilacqua 1978.

267 CIL vi 6431.

268 IGUR 1334.

269 CIL vi 33813.

270 Ruggini 1959, 188.

271 Ruggini 1959, 189.

272 Augustine, *Conf.* 4.14.21.

273 AE (1982) 74 = Feissel 1982b, no. II.1.

274 There are also 4 inscriptions, counted under province, which use both 'Syria(n)' and 'Antioch(ene)'.

275 MAMA iii 240, 248, 408, 436, 443, 445, 500, 507, 563, 642, 733. The expression used for 'village' in these inscriptions is nearly always χωρίου; only one uses κώμης.

276 The names of a number of donors from Syrian villages were recorded in the mosaic floor of the 4th–5th century basilica at Monastero in Aquileia; see JIWE i, p. xiv, with the bibliography there.

277 ICUR 4004: ἀπὸ κώμης Μ[-- ὅρων Ἀπα]μέων τῆς Κύλη(ς) ‹Σ›υρίας. ICUR 4891: ἀπὸ κώμης Λατ[--] ὅρων Ἀπαμέ(ων). ICUR 9319: ἀπα (sic) κ(ώ)μη(ς) Ὀρ(ά)γων χώ(ρας) Ἀπαμ(έων). AE (1982) 74 (dated 414): κώμης Μαγαρατων κατωτέρας τῆς Ἀπαμέων παροικίας.

278 ICUR 5175.

279 ICUR 5706, 8404. However, I have argued above (pp. 188, 232) that some inscriptions which have previously been assigned to Syrians actually belong to Galatians.

280 ICUR 12896.

281 The suggestion by Solin (1977b, 210) that it was such a common slave name that it may have been given to non-Syrian slaves seems unnecessary, given that so many slaves were of Syrian origin.

282 In addition to occurrences in CIL vi and ICUR, the following are included: NS (1916), p. 107 no. 119 = BCAR 43 (1915), p. 308; NS (1923), p. 360; NS (1969), p. 104; BCAR 51 (1923), p. 107 no. 153.

283 ICUR 1861, 2636.

284 ICUR 6467.

285 ICUR 20608.

286 CIL vi 25703.

287 All the relevant inscriptions are in the index of CIL vi except Väänänen 1973, no. 36.

288 CIL vi 16851, 19118, 28635.

289 CIL vi 21548, 29636.

290 CIL vi 23601.

291 CIL vi 20564.

292 CIL vi 19134, 34196 (CIS ii 159). The latter was found in the Tiber.

293 Palmer 1981, 370–2; Turcan 1996, 188.

294 Turcan 1996, 188–93; he suggests, apart from the Syrian element, a link with the cult of Osiris and a late, clandestine use by pagans during the ascendancy of Christianity.

295 Lombardi 1996, 62; Calzini Gysens 1996a, 262; 1996b, 277–82. Ciceroni (1996, 364), in the same volume, regards it as established that it was *not* a Heliopolitan shrine.

296 CIL vi 36803 = IGUR 110; Lombardi (1996, 61–2) dates it to the late 2nd century. One of Hadad's epithets is *Libaneotes*, i.e. of Lebanon.

297 Cellini 1996, 29; Calzini Gysens 1996a, 263–4.

298 CIL vi 36792. Duthoy and Frel (1996, 296) state that the name of Jupiter Heliopolitanus was erased in order to inscribe this one. Iabruda was near Damascus (Calzini Gysens 1996c, 54).

299 CIL vi 36802 = IGUR 111; Lombardi 1996, 58–61. The inscription, which also mentions the Nymphae Furrinae, is by a woman from Cyprus; the god was worshipped in both Cyprus and Syria (Calzini Gysens 1996c, 54). Lombardi dates it to the first half of the 2nd century.

300 Duthoy and Frel 1996, 299. It therefore appears that Palmyrenes did not worship entirely in their own sanctuary (see below), which was also active at this time.

301 Calzini Gysens (1996b, 285) thinks that 'phase II' lasted until the mid-4th century, but Duthoy and Frel (1996, 298) link its destruction by fire with a fire of AD 242.

302 MacMullen 1993, 62–3.

303 Hajjar (1977, no. 288) sees him as probably Syrian and possibly from Heliopolis. Duthoy and Frel (1996, 293) call him 'a Heliopolitan, whose family was well established at Rome for at least one generation', but they do not appear to have any grounds for being so definite. Meiggs (1960, 216) and Lampe (1989, 42) even call him 'a Syrian trader'.

304 Duthoy and Frel (1996, 295), on the assumption that the very fragmentary CIL vi 36805 = IGUR 112, a Greek metrical inscription of at least three lines, was also by Gaionas.

305 Duthoy and Frel (1996, 295); they suggest that some other inscriptions, including one from the Dolichenum on the Aventine, were produced by the same *officina*.

306 This is usually taken as a nocturnal police function descended from the

republican *quinqueviri cis Tiberim*. An alternative view that it is a cult title derived from κιστοφόρος has not received much support, but has recently been revived by Scheid (1995, 314). See Lombardi 1996, 67.

[307] Duthoy and Frel 1996, 294.

[308] Restored by Goodhue, quoted by Duthoy and Frel (1996, 294 n. 28).

[309] Turcan 1996, 190; Lombardi 1996, 64–7; Duthoy and Frel 1996, 295.

[310] Greek: δεσμὸς ὅπως κρατερὸς θῦμα θεοῖς παρέχοι. The exact significance of *desmos* in this context is unclear; the Liddell & Scott definition is 'a band, bond, fetter: a halter: a mooring cable: a door-latch'. The fountain interpretation involves seeing the *desmos* as a 'bond' for the water. *Deipnokrites*, 'judge of banquets' (ὃν δὴ Γαιωνᾶς δειπνοκρίτης ἔθετο), appears to be a cult title, and is also alluded to in Gaionas' epitaph (see below). According to Duthoy and Frel (1996, 295), quoting the interpretation of Montesi, the words should be understood as spoken by the monument: '(I am) a strong...' According to Bianchi (1982), *desmos* is an installation for the water supply, and the *deipnokrites* was in charge of banquets held at the sanctuary in honour of Jupiter. Lombardi suggests that channelling the water into a basin would have provided somewhere for people to leave ex-voto lead figurines, as they did in the temple at Heliopolis.

[311] Pellegrino 1996, 565.

[312] I.O.M. Heliopolitanus received an altar from a unit of Ituraeans: CIL vi 421.

[313] 'It cannot be excluded that the creation of "Heliopolitan" monuments at Rome can be explained, rather than by the circulation of iconographic models, by detailed descriptions provided by the commissioners.'

[314] Solin 1983, 677, 680; AE (1975) 101; CIL vi 21235; IGUR 451, 569.

[315] The site has been variously known as Vigna Crescenzi/Bonelli/Mangani (Palmer 1981, 372).

[316] It is the use of the Palmyrene language which led to the suggestion, also made by Kajanto (1980, 85), but it does not seem very logical, since the language was quite appropriate in the context.

[317] CIL vi 710 = 30817 = CIS ii 3.3903; Teixidor 1979, 47; Palmer 1981, 370–2; Rutgers 1995, 70; Turcan 1996, 176. Malachbel is shown as a little child carrying a kid, riding a sun chariot, with a youth with a radiate halo.

[318] This is how the Latin *Calbienses de coh(orte) III* is understood by Houston (1990), taking it as a reference to residents of the Horrea Galbiana.

[319] CIL vi 50 = IGUR 117. CIL vi 51 = IGUR 118, which seems to have the same text, gives a consular date (AD 116).

[320] IGUR 119 = CIS ii 3.3902. It is not absolutely certain that he is the same man. The inscription is from an aedicula in which Aglibel and Malachbel are depicted in very romanized fashion (Rutgers 1995, 70).

[321] IGUR 120 = CIS ii 3.3904; Equini Schneider 1988, 62. Dated to the late 2nd century by Savage 1940, 54.

[322] Jones 1993, 106–8.

[323] Bellelli 1996, 305–36; Cellini 1996, 21, 32, 35; Lombardi 1996, 71–7; Zappata 1996, 87–228; Calzini Gysens 1996a, 262. There may have been other Dolichenian shrines on the Caelian and in Trastevere. Bellelli (1996, 311) says that the names of the people on the Aventine altars 'are most often

greco-oriental, Egyptian, oriental'. However, some are not, e.g. Chaibio, probably Germanic (Zappata 1996, 99); Semnus, mainly known in Venetia (ibid., 113); Bacradis, probably African (ibid., 121). M. Ulpius Chresimus was a Parthian (CIL vi 31187); Bellelli (1996, 315) associates him with the Caelian shrine. On the other hand, the priest Aquila Barhadados (Zappata 1996, 104) has a very Syrian name along with a Latin one; Teatecnus is probably a latinization of the Syriac Baralaha (ibid., 193).

[324] Bellelli 1996, 314–15, 321.

[325] 'Certain forms of cult (processions of the statue), just like the furnishings (small statues of Egyptians making offerings, antefixes with *uraei*, zoomorphic decorations) seem to try to recreate the atmosphere of the original homeland to celebrate rites which recall it. The organisation of the sanctuary, the faithful and the benefactors were primarily oriental.'

[326] 'It is probably explained by the lasting presence of individuals of oriental, especially Syrian, origin in the sanctuaries of the capital, anxious to maintain their links with the cultural traditions of their native land.'

[327] Hörig and Schwertheim, CCID 433 = AE (1953) 26 (the base of a statue of Jupiter Dolichenus); Zappata 1996, 195; Bianchi 1996, 599–603. There is also a reference to the 'great god of the Commageni' in another Dolichenus inscription: Hörig and Schwertheim, CCID 376; Zappata 1996, 125.

[328] Turcan 1996, 178; Calzini Gysens 1996a, 270–1.

[329] Calzini Gysens 1996a, 266–7.

[330] Calzini Gysens 1996a, 267–8.

[331] CIL vi 39050a; Turcan 1996, 172; Calzini Gysens 1996a, 269–70.

[332] Calzini Gysens 1996a, 271–2.

[333] I.Porto 10–11; Turcan 1996, 171; Pellegrino 1996, 562.

[334] Ricci 1993a, 76.

[335] Philo, *Leg.* 166–78. He may have been an Alexandrian rather than an Egyptian, since Philo would naturally use the most pejorative (in his view) term available; cf Pearce 1998.

[336] Ricci 1993a, 76.

[337] Ricci 1993a, 71–3.

[338] Ricci 1993a, 77; Kolb 1995, 458. Ricci classes them only as 'possible senators'.

[339] Ricci 1993a, 78.

[340] Ricci 1993a, 75.

[341] Ricci 1993a, 75.

[342] Vidman 1990, 259; Gnomon 55.

[343] Ricci (1993a, 87) counts six, all from the 3rd century. Three were from Ptolemais and only two from Alexandria.

[344] I.Porto 2–3; IGUR 393.

[345] Suetonius, *Aug.* 98.

[346] CIL xiv 256; Ricci 1993a, 90.

[347] P.Mich. viii 500–1; cf. p. 165.

[348] Ricci 1993a, 76.

[349] Martial 11.13.

[350] CIL vi 10194, 10197; IGUR 939 = ICUR 4032; AE (1988) 24.

[351] IGUR 1034.

352 IGUR 240.

353 ICUR 3974.

354 ICUR 4973, dated AD 474; 4957, dated 471; 9307. Cf. Feissel 1982a, 377–8: it is the modern Kôm Kabrît.

355 Vidman 1990, 261.

356 CIL vi 26959.

357 ICUR 12856.

358 ICUR 4957; the year is given by consular dating.

359 ICUR 6415.

360 Ferrua 1939, p. 148 no. 11; SEG xxx 1215; cf. Avraméa 1995, 296.

361 IGCVO 1066.

362 ICUR 12864.

363 ICUR 19855c.

364 JIGRE 141.

365 ICUR 3974.

366 IGUR 77.

367 IGUR 191 = Vidman, SIRIS 398, dated 299.

368 IGUR 333, 452, 644, 884.

369 ICUR 1170.

370 Lombardi (1997) considers that the people who used Egyptian dates and gave no place of origin are more likely to be from Cyrene than from Egypt, but I can see no reason for thinking that Cyrene is *more* likely, in view of the small number of known immigrants from there.

371 La Piana 1927, 291; Turcan 1996, 85–7.

372 Beard, North and Price 1998, vol. 1, 294.

373 IGUR 77; Ricci 1993a, no. A12; Vidman 1990, 263.

374 Vidman 1990, 262.

375 Porphyry, *V.Plot.* 10.

376 Floriani Squarciapino 1962, 15, 30; CIL xiv 429.

377 IGUR 100.

378 IGUR 188, 77.

379 IGUR 77; Ricci 1993a, no. A12; Vidman 1990, 263.

380 IGUR 190.

381 IGUR 193. IGUR 187, 189, 191, 192, 194 are also Serapis inscriptions.

382 I.Porto 16.

383 IGUR 98.

384 I.Porto 21.

385 CIL vi 19716; *contra* Ricci 1993a, no. A16.

386 In this section, 'North Africa' means the provinces of Mauretania, Numidia, Africa and Cyrene. 'Africa' will be used for the province only.

387 Suetonius, *Terence* 1.

388 Cicero, *Tusc.* 3.53.

389 CIL vi 9046.

390 CIL vi 10110.

391 CIL vi 4078, 20409; Ricci 1994b, 193.

392 CIL vi 1800; Ricci 1994b, 203.

393 Ricci 1994b, 203.

[394] Ricci 1994b, 203–4.

[395] Millar 1981, 178.

[396] The numerous dedications by North African cities which must have been placed at Rome by ambassadors are listed by Ricci (1994b, 198).

[397] CIL vi 33829 = ICUR 6537.

[398] CIL vi 33867.

[399] Ricci 1994b, no. A17. Ibid., 205: 35 African *iudices ex quinque decuriis* are known altogether.

[400] Ricci 1994b, 203.

[401] Cf. Ricci 1994b, 202. Other North African products exported to Rome included wine, figs, dates and Numidian marble.

[402] CIL xiv 4626; Meiggs 1960, 214.

[403] AE (1940), 64; Meiggs 1960, 214–15. However, Ricci (1994b, 202) argues that he was of Italian origin; this seems unnecessary in view of the similar case of Valerianus.

[404] ICUR 20100; Ricci 1994b, no. A13.

[405] Ricci 1994b, 201.

[406] AE (1916) 42; Millar 1981, 172.

[407] Cherry 1998, 133.

[408] CIL vi 10058; AE (1979) 155.

[409] CIL vi 10050.

[410] CIL vi 10060, dated AD 275.

[411] For example, one of the horses depicted in CIL vi 10058 is called Garamantinica.

[412] Augustine, *Ep.*10*.2.

[413] Ricci 1994b, 197.

[414] AE (1972) 14, dated 47 BC.

[415] Including CIL vi 1366.

[416] Including CIL vi 1401, xiv 4620.

[417] Including AE (1934) 146, CIL vi 1010.

[418] Libya (Λιβύη) could be used in Greek as Africa was in Latin, to indicate the province, North Africa or the whole continent (Fruyt 1976, 235).

[419] ICUR 1891, 19797; Ricci 1994b, 194.

[420] CIL vi 3134. *Libys* is used in CIL viii 12792, where a woman from Rome died at Carthage: 'Rome was your nation (*genus*); it was your fate to be a Libyan'. It is also used in a verse epitaph, Gk.Anth. 7.185: 'Italian dust covers me, a Libyan'.

[421] Cf. Saller 1982, 181.

[422] Saller 1982, 177–8; Barnes 1967, 88.

[423] CIL vi 1620.

[424] CIL xiv 4620.

[425] 1 Macc. 8.17–32, 12.1–4, 14.24.

[426] Philo, *Leg.* 155.

[427] As noted by Leon (1960, 2), the victims of the first expulsion were not *necessarily* permanent residents of Rome.

[428] Cicero, *Pro Flacco* 66.

[429] This is not certain, however, as *contiones* were not voting assemblies, so

attendance was not restricted to citizens.

430 Leon 1960, 4–5.

431 Kasher 1987, 50–1; Rutgers 1995, 168.

432 Josephus, *Ant.* 17.5.7; *B.J.* 1.32.

433 Leon 1960, 15.

434 Fuks 1985. Jerome, *In Hieremiam* 31.15.6 (CCSL 74, 307), refers to huge numbers of prisoners in both revolts, but only mentions their reaching Rome under Vespasian.

435 Josephus, *B.J.* 3.540.

436 Williams 1994a, 176.

437 b. Giṭṭ. 58a = Midrash Lam.R. 4.4; JE ix 83–6.

438 Various estimates (or guesses) are collected by Solin (1983, 698–701) and Botermann (1996, n. 132). Two contributions to a recent volume show the lack of consensus: 'These figures allow for a guess that there were around twenty thousand Jews at Rome in the time of Nero' (Brändle and Stegemann 1998, 120); 'About forty thousand to fifty thousand Jews lived in the city of Rome by the first century CE' (Jeffers 1998, 129).

439 Josephus, *B.J.* 2.80; *Ant.* 17.300. Botermann (1996, n. 132) is sceptical about the basis of the figure.

440 Solin 1983, 700. If the total population was less than 1,000,000, the Jewish proportion would be correspondingly greater, since the Jewish figures are independent of the total population figures.

441 However, their aversion to family limitation and their use of charity (Goodman 1994, 84) may have made them nearer to being self-reproducing than the rest of the population.

442 Antoninus Pius forbade circumcision for non-Jews and Septimius Severus forbade conversion (Digest 48.8.11.pr Modestinus; SHA, *Sev.* 17.1), which would certainly have restricted the number of proselytes in the late 2nd century AD if the law was enforced.

443 Solin 1983, 700–1. Even his assumption of the proportion remaining stable cannot be confirmed, any more than the statement by Williams (1994a, 180) that the Jewish community must have grown by the 2nd century.

444 Or, outside the *Familia Caesaris*, by the children of (technically) unmarried citizen women.

445 JIWE ii, p. 537. First-generation immigrants would have formed only a small proportion of the Jewish community by the 3rd century AD.

446 JIWE ii 360.

447 Josephus, *Ant.* 14.215–16; Cicero, *pro Flacco* 66; Philo, *Leg.* 158.

448 Rutgers 1998, 112–13; Walters 1998, 185 (noting that the Jews at Rome, like those at Antioch, would have *feared* reprisals even though they did not materialize). Admittedly, Josephus might be unlikely to mention such measures if they did exist, and the sources for the other two revolts are very scanty anyway.

449 Levinskaya (1996, 175) points out that they did not necessarily go directly from Rome to Corinth.

450 Acts 18.1–3, 18.18, 18.24–6; Romans 16.3–4; 1 Cor. 16.19.

451 Scholion to Juvenal 4.117 (= Stern, GLAJJ 538).

452 JIWE ii 515.

[453] JIWE ii 561.

[454] JIWE ii 113. It is also possible to understand 'gerusiarch (and) of Tripolis', or to take Tripolis as a reference to the Tripolitan synagogue at Rome rather than to the original city.

[455] Leon 1960, 14.

[456] Vismara 1986, 354.

[457] b. Sanh. 32b; Levi 1970; Segal 1992; Rutgers 1995, 203–4.

[458] JE xi 1132, quoting Sifre Deut. 80; this could well be an addition for the purposes of anti-emigration propaganda. b. Yoma 86a has Matthia meeting R. Eleazar b. Azariah at Rome, but that is apparently an anachronism.

[459] b. Bezah 23a; t. Yom Ṭov 2.15; y. Moed Qatan 3.1. It is not stated that he was an immigrant to Rome, but his prestige seems more plausible in someone born in the land of Israel than in a native of Rome.

[460] y. Pesaḥim 7.34a; Bokser 1990; Rutgers 1995, 204.

[461] JE vi 599–600.

[462] b. Yoma 57a; b. Sukk. 5a; b. Me'il. 17b; Midrash Ex.R. 1.4.

[463] Midrash Esth.R. 1.12.

[464] b. Me'il. 17a; b. Nidd. 58a. The story that Eleazar was in Rome at the time of Titus' death (Midrash Eccl.R. 5.8.4) is another anachronism.

[465] Midrash Gen.R. 33.1, 78.5; Midrash Lev.R. 27.1; JE x 282–4.

[466] y. Ma'as.Sh. 4.1.54d; JE viii 796.

[467] Solin 1983, 625, 660.

[468] The points made in this paragraph are all based on Gafni (1997, passim).

[469] Babylonian rabbis developed a view of Babylonia as a moral equivalent of Israel, where it was equally commendable to live.

[470] Midrash Lam.R. 1.28, quoted from Gafni (1997, 30).

[471] y. Sukk. 5.1.55a–b.

[472] Rutgers 1995, 150 tab.4.

[473] JIWE ii 108 (the second name appears to be Semitic with a Greek prefix), 217 (since the person in question is male, Cocotia cannot be a nomen), 551, 577.

[474] Noy 1999.

[475] Williams 1997, 252–3.

[476] Williams 1997, 254.

[477] Williams 1997, 253; Harvey 1996, passim.

[478] Harvey 1998, 132, 145–6.

[479] Harvey 1998, 135–6 and Noy 1998b, 112–13, refuting various theories.

[480] Harvey 1996, 47.

[481] JIWE ii 489; Williams 1997, 254; Noy 1998b, 113–14.

[482] JIWE ii 186.

[483] JIWE ii 193, 529.

[484] Noy 1998b, 116.

[485] Noy 1999.

[486] The text reads:

אניה חתנה

דכר כולכריה

The words are divided by small spaces on the stone.

[487] Noy 1997, 306–7.

[488] Noy 1997, 301.

[489] Noy 1997, 307–8.

[490] Marett (1989, 21) comments, in the context of Asians in East Africa: 'this exclusiveness and concern with perpetuating communal traditions were interpreted as racial arrogance and superiority'. The Jews may well have been viewed in the same way.

[491] The 'Agrippinilla inscription' (see p. 226) lists a wide range of titles held by members of a Bacchic association, but none of these seem to occur in epitaphs from Rome.

[492] Rutgers 1995, 199; Noy forthcoming. This does not, of course, mean that 20% of the Jewish community held titles; the community leaders are certain to be heavily over-represented in the evidence.

[493] The Great Synagogue of Alexandria implies a more centralized organization of the Jewish community there, consistent with the existence of a Jewish *gerousia*. Rome had no equivalent.

[494] Williams 1994a, 166–8; JIWE ii, pp. 539–40.

[495] Williams 1994b, 137. It is not clear which of the cities called Tripolis the Tripolitans came from. The Seceni may have come from (I)Scina in North Africa (see JIWE ii 436). On Elea, which may be a place name, see JIWE ii 406 and Levinskaya (1996, 183).

[496] Vismara 1986, 358.

[497] Noy 1998b, 112, *contra* Richardson 1998, 20.

[498] Cf. Richardson 1998, 20–1. However, his attempt to revive the argument that there was a synagogue of the Herodians (pp. 23–8) is unconvincing, and requires both a forced reading of the surviving part of the inscription (JIWE ii 292) and an improbable reconstruction of the missing part; cf. my comments ad loc. (not taken into account by him).

[499] Although Philo states that the Jews of Rome lived in Trastevere, this does not necessarily mean that they all lived there, or that they always remained as concentrated there as they were in the time of Augustus to which he is referring.

[500] Richardson (1998, 22) identifies it with the Volumnius known from Josephus as a Roman official in Syria, but he seems too peripheral a figure to be honoured by the Jews of Rome.

[501] Richardson 1998, 18; Rutgers 1998, 94. Slingerland (1997, 46–7, 93 n. 12) expresses some doubt about the collegial status of synagogues.

[502] Cf. Botermann 1996, n. 136.

[503] Ambrose, *Ep.* 40.23.

[504] Ruggini 1959, 207 n. 54.

[505] Cicero, *pro Flacco* 66; Josephus, *Ant.* 18.81–4.

[506] Noy 1998b.

[507] C.Theo. 16.8.14.

[508] Josephus, *B.J.* 2.80; *Ant.* 17.300.

[509] Josephus, *B.J.* 2.101–10; *Ant.* 15.342–3, 17.324–38.

[510] However, Botermann (1996, 65) points out that there is no reason to assume that messianism spread from Judaea to Rome in this period.

[511] White 1998, 50.

[512] Pearce 1998, 101–5.

CONCLUSION

The people whose epitaphs were quoted in the Introduction exemplify some of the trends which have been discussed in the previous chapters.

• Basileus came from Bithynia to be a teacher at Rome and was commemorated with an epitaph in Greek. He shows the attraction of the city to people with marketable skills, even if they had to travel very long distances to get there, and the importance of the Greek language to immigrants from Asia Minor.

• The Theban, Phrygian, Smyrnan and Carthaginian ex-slaves who were all recorded in the same inscription show how slavery could bring together people of very different origins, and how the use of Latin could be part of their acculturation at Rome.

• P. Papirius Proculus, killed in an accident at Rome and buried at home in Salona, is a reminder of how people who came to Rome did not necessarily lose contact with their homelands, at least while they still had family members there.

• Flavia Viventia, commemorated by her mother, shows that Rome attracted female immigrants as well as males, and that it was still drawing newcomers in late antiquity. Viventia and her mother may have been members of a Pannonian community at Rome.

• The Egyptians Fuscinus and Taon commemorated their young son, who had probably been born at Rome and had a Latin name. Fuscinus was a gladiator, one of the many people brought to Rome from all parts of the empire to work in the world of entertainment.

• The Thracian Aurelia Marcia, whose epitaph was put up by her sister and by her husband, a member of the Praetorian Guard, shows that not only the praetorians themselves but also the relatives who came to Rome with them formed an important element of the foreign population.

The nature of the evidence means that it is impossible to draw a complete picture of the lives of foreigners at Rome. Nevertheless, there is enough epigraphic and literary source material to form a clear background for some parts of a picture, and to sketch in other parts rather more tentatively, bearing in mind the tendency of the sources to convey most information about the people whose 'foreignness' was most obvious.

Immigration was essential to Rome both demographically, to increase or at least maintain the size of the city's population, and socially, to provide skilled workers and soldiers. The slave trade met some of the requirements, but free immigrants were always needed. Provincials probably began to outnumber Italians among newcomers to Rome in the first centuries BC and AD. The third century AD, when all recruitment for the Praetorian Guard was done in the provinces, may have seen the numerical peak of Rome's foreign population. It is plausible to suppose that at least 5% of the city's inhabitants were born outside Italy in that period; the reality could be much greater.

Foreigners who did not have Roman citizenship were always liable to summary expulsion from the city, and by the fourth century the possession of citizenship was no longer protection against such treatment. Although there was a certain amount of xenophobia within the Roman literary class, expulsion was only used in certain circumstances: to deal with the actual or potential misdeeds or alleged bad influence of specific groups (which could be defined by nationality, religion or occupation), or to counteract the effect of food shortages by reducing the number of mouths to feed. Expulsions were probably not carried out very efficiently, and were always short-lived.

Information from inscriptions can be used to answer many questions about the people who came to Rome as free immigrants. They came from all parts of the empire (and beyond), but civilians usually came from the provinces around the Mediterranean, whereas soldiers were mostly from Central and Eastern Europe. Immigration continued into late antiquity even from places as remote as Galatia and Syria. Males outnumbered females substantially, probably in a ratio of three or four to one. Males in their teens and twenties predominated, and they were more likely to come to Rome as individuals than as part of a family unit.

A wide variety of reasons for free civilians to come to Rome are recorded, although the relative importance of the different reasons cannot be assessed. Rome as a centre of education attracted both teachers and students. As the centre of government, it drew aspiring politicians and civil servants, lawyers, ambassadors, hostages and refugees. As it was by far the largest single market in the Ancient World, people wishing to provide goods and services came there: doctors, craftspeople, builders, traders, entertainers. Others came to the city to accompany or join family members, or, especially if they were Christians, in pursuit of religious fulfilment.

The experiences of newcomers when they first arrived in the city are poorly documented. They might get there by land or sea, and the journey was potentially hazardous by either method. On arrival, they would certainly have been struck by Rome's size and noise. They would usually seek out family, friends, compatriots or potential patrons who would help them to find work and accommodation.

Once they were settled at Rome, foreigners could try to integrate or to retain at least some aspects of their 'foreign' identity; they might also try to pass this on to their children. People could keep in touch with their homelands, through the *stationes* organized by traders from some cities, by letter, personal visits and, ultimately, by being buried or commemorated at home. At Rome, they might continue to speak their native language, although if it was not Latin or Greek they were unlikely ever to have it inscribed. Many immigrants were bilingual, but their children and grandchildren were much more likely to be monoglot Latin-speakers. Foreigners might have names which were typical of their homeland, but they almost never passed these on to their children, and may often have adopted Latin or Greek names themselves. They could participate in religious cults which were imported from their homelands, and use the burial practices and types of epitaphs which were normal at home.

The group which made the greatest effort to retain a separate identity was the Jews. In their religious and communal institutions, their use of separate catacombs, their epigraphic and liturgical use of Greek, and even their naming practices, they behaved differently from others and were able to pass on a Jewish identity, so that people whose ancestors had lived at Rome for generations and who were otherwise well integrated into Roman society were still identifiably Jewish. Other people had only very limited equivalents. Syrians practised cults which were exclusive to them. Thracians, Pannonians, Galatians and Syrians retained loyalty to their home villages and were in close contact with others who came from the same places. Asians and Alexandrians were proud of their citizenship of their original cities, and Germans emphasized their native tribes. Egyptians used their own calendar. The oil trade was dominated by Spaniards and the marble trade by Bithynians. African senators offered hospitality to each other, and Pannonians helped their compatriots to important administrative posts in late antiquity. Yet all these practices seem to have been relevant only to first-generation immigrants. Their children may have continued some, but it is unlikely that any were used by their grandchildren. Only Jewish identity was strong enough to be passed that far down the family tree.

APPENDIX

A LIST OF INDIVIDUAL IMMIGRANTS RECORDED IN INSCRIPTIONS[1]

Reference[2]	Name[3]	Role in inscription[4]	Reason for inclusion[5]
Africa and Numidia (Military)			
2431	Decimius Augurinus	comm	nat. Afer
2564	Q. Aurelius Q.f. Quir. Gallus	dec	Uszali
2663	[---]ius L.f. Arn. [---]	dec	domo Carthagin.
2987	Q. Iulius Q.f. Galatus	dec	Thysdro
3171	L. Surdinius Saturninus	dec	nat. Afer
3212	Aurelius Masculinus	dec	nat. Afer
32757	C. Iunius C.f. Quir. Fortunatus	dec	Curzesis
32802	T. Flavius Fortunatus	dec	nat. Afer
viii 2890	Iulius Modestus	comm	brother
xiv 4488	Q. Gargilius Q.f. Iu[lia]nus qui et Semeliu[s]	dec	Karthago
Speidel 1994a, 208	T. Aur. V[---]	dec	[nat.] Afe[r]
Africa and Numidia (Pagan Civilian)			
1803[6]	L. Aelius Perpetuus	dec	coloniae Ulpiae Thamugadis ex Numidia
2564	Aurelius Saturninus	dec	brother (see above)
	Q. Aurelius Maximus	comm	brother
3171	Clodia Secunda	comm	mother
6507	Preima	dec	Afra
10058[7]	M. Aurelius Liber	dedicatee	natione Afri
	Aurelius Caeciliius Planeta Protogenes	dedicator	
11496	Allia Urbica	dec	Numidi
12281 = 34055	Venus	dec	Afra
13327–8	Numida	comm	Medauriani/
	Catulus	comm/ dec	oriundi ex Africa
	Aemilia Primitiva	comm	col. Theveste
25917	Saturninus	dec	[co]loniae Milevitan.

29539	L. Volussius Saturninus	dec	na. Afro Neapolitano
31652	Faustinus	comm	ex Africa
33867	Praetex[tatus]	dec	[ex] Africa
36277	P. Rutilius Saturninus	dec	Gurzensis ex Africa
viii 2402	L. Senius Flaccus	dec	commemorated at home
viii 15930	M. Antonius D.f. Turbo	dec	commemorated at home
viii 27532	L. Postumius Paemulus Pius	dec	commemorated at home
xiv 477	P. Caesellius Felix	dec	civis Sullecthinus
xiv 481	Valerius Veturius	dec	civis Afer
xiv 4626	L. Caelius L.fil. A[rn.] Aprilis Valerian[us]	builder	curator navium Kartha[g.]
AE (1928) 9	Phryne qua(e et) Sillaria	dec	Africana
AE (1940) 64	L. Caecilius Aemilianus	builder	duovir Aeliae Uliz-ibbirae Africae
AE (1972) 14	Numitoria C.l. Erotis	dec	natio. Punica
AE (1974) 143	Q. Sextius C.f. Pap. Martialis	dec	Ricci 1994b, A18 & 19
	C. Sextius Martialis	comm	

Solin and Itkonen-Kaila 1966,

65	Tertius	graff	Hadrumetinus
73	Saturus	graff	Afer Hadrumetinu[s]
78, 198	Marinus	graff	Afer
118	Venustus	graff	[A]fer
281	Umanus	graff	Af.
297, 332–3	Nikaensis	graff	Af. Hadrimetinus/ Ἄφ. Ἀδρυμητι[νος]
298	Fortunatus	graff	Afer
322–3	Eugamus	graff	Af. Kartha.

Africa and Numidia (Christian/Jewish)

2444[8]	Vernaclus	dec	Carpitanus
6151	Balsamius	dec	Tenitanus
8596	Ulpius Festus	dec	Afer
9517	(name lost)	dec	Ves[ce]ritanu[s]
12632	Felix	dec	Africanus
15451	Considius Lucius	dec	ex provincia Africa
	(name not given)	comm	brother
17166	Victoria	dec	de regione{m} Admederensium
19659	(names lost)	parent(s)	Ammedarenses
	commemorate children		
20100	Iulius Credentius	dec	ex Bagense regione
32054a	(name lost)	dec	provinc. Afri[cae]
JIWE ii 508	Maximus	dec	Θαβρακενός

Armenia/Bosporan Kingdom/Parthia (Civilian)

1797	Abgar Prahates	dec	PIR² A11
1799	Seraspadanes	dec	Parthus
	Rhodaspes	dec	Parthus
8972	[---]s Aug.l. Narcissus	dec	natione Parthus
9431	C. Pettius Celer	dec	Gaunacarius⁹
20537D	Iulia Irena	dec	natione Armin.
29694¹⁰	L. Cornificius Telemastes	dec	leg(atus) Bospor[anorum]
	P. Cornelius Serapio	comm	father
32264 = IGUR 602	C. Iulius C.f. Artabasdes	dec	Pani 1979–80
IGUR 415	Aurelius Merithas	dec	Moretti, ad loc.
	Aurelius Pacorus	comm	
IGUR 567	Hedykos	dec	πρεσβευτὴς Φαναγ- ορειτῶν τῶν κατὰ Βοὸς πόρον
	Aspourgos	dec	ἑρμηνεὺς Σαρματῶν Βωσπορανός
IGUR 763	Macarius	dec	Βοσπορεανέ
IGUR 1142	Abgaros	dec	PIR² A9 & 10
	Antoninus	comm	brother
IGUR 1151	Amazaspus	dec	Moretti, ad loc.
AE (1979) 78	(name lost)	builders	opses Parthorum
	Ulpia Axse		
Speidel 1994a, 692	(name lost)	dec	[nat. P]ontico
Solin and Itkonen-Kaila 1966, no. 73	Bassus	graff	Graecus Chersonesita
Solin and Itkonen-Kaila 1966, no. 249	Asclepiodotus	graff	ὁ Σκύθης

Armenia/Parthia (Christian)

1441	Quirillus	dec	civem Armeniacum Cappadocem
1942	Eu[---]	dec	[θεο]δοσειοπολίτ[ης]
13443	Aedesius	dec	natione Armenius
16997	Aurelius Theofilus	dec	civis Carrhenus

Asia (Military)

2669	M. Aurelius Hermias	dec	patr. Meonia
3627	M. Sempronius M.f. Col. Celer	dec	domo Pessenunto
32699	M. Tuccius C.f.Col. Maximus	dec	Tiberiopoli

Asia (Civilian)

3173	Eutychas	dec	natione Phryge
4936	Cotinos	dec	Milesios

9907	Timotheus	dec	Laudica Asiatica
10091 = IGUR 1566	Q. Iulius Miletus	dedicatee/ builder	προλιπὼν Ἀσίας Τρίπολιν
10098	Hector	dec	Mygdonis umbra
10149	Alcimas	dec	Zmurneus
10683+21021	L. Aelius L.l. Eros	dec	Asiatico
13139	Aurelius Iustus	dec	natio. Asi[a]
13236	M. Aurelius Sostratianus	comm	Stratoni(cea?)
17130	Egnatuleia Ɔ.l. Urbana	dec	epitaph addressed to: *quem Phrycia* (sic) *edidit tellus*
27264	Terentia M.l. Tyrannion	dec	Cyzicena
27657	Trophimus Aug. lib.	dec	Phrygii
34466	Apollonius	dec	n. Phryg.
	P. Aelius Papias	comm	
	Messia Candida	dec	
xiv 475	Asclepiades	builder	Cnidius
xiv 480	Socrates	dec	natus in egregiis Trallibus ex Asia
IGUR 244	Cl. Rufus ὁ καί Apollonius	dec	Πεισαῖον[11]
IGUR 322	Alcestis	dec	Ἀσίηθεν Ἀφροδισιάς
IGUR 326	P. Alfenus Martialis	dec	Λαοδικεὺς τῆς Ἀσίας
	(unnamed)	comm	father
IGUR 337	Andromenes	dec	Ἰλιεύς
IGUR 352	L. Antonius Hyacinthus	dec	Λαοδικεῖ τῆς Ἀσίας
IGUR 363	Apronias	dec	Λαδικηνῇ
IGUR 367	Eutactus	dec	see p. 195
	Liberalis	comm	
IGUR 433	Aurelia Tatia	dec	Θυατιρηνῆι
IGUR 453	(name lost)	dec	Κυζικηνῷ
	Galenus	comm	brother
IGUR 470	Menippus	dec	brother
	Demetrius	comm	Ἀφροδεισιεύς
IGUR 532	Eudamos	dec	Ἀφροδεισεύς
IGUR 589	Theseus	comm	Περγαμηνός
IGUR 607	C. Iulius Themison	dec	[Τρ]αλλιανός
IGUR 682	Claudius Zosimus	comm	Ἐφέσιος
IGUR 784	Menandros	dec	Ἱεραπολείτης πρὸς Μέανδρον ποταμόν
IGUR 834	Onesimus	dec	Ἰλιεῦ
IGUR 843	Valeria Olympias	dec	Ἀσιανὴ πόλεως Λαοδικείας
	Valerius Menander	comm	father
IGUR 870	Papias	builder	Σαρδιανός
IGUR 891	Pinitas	dec	Σαλάνιος[12]
IGUR 902	Iulia ἡ καί Nana	dec	Εὐμένισσα
IGUR 987	Tryphon	dec	Λαδικὺς τῆς πρὸς Λύκον

IGUR 1141	Flavia Aphrodisia	dec	Τραλλιανή
IGUR 1200	Donata	dec	Τράλλεως ἦν δὲ γένος καὶ γῆς Ἀσίης ἐρατεινῆς
IGUR 1202	Elpis	dec	πατρὶς δ᾽ Ἀσίης προΰχουσα Λαοδίκει᾽
IGUR 1222	Zeno	comm	πατρὶς…Ἀφροδ[ι]σιάς
IGUR 1244	Kosmos	dec	Περγάμου
IGUR 1260	Lucius	dec	πάτρης Σμύρνης ἐρατινῆς
IGUR 1274	Menophilus	dec	ἐξ Ἀσίης ἐλθών
IGUR 1283	Nicomedes	dec	Moretti, ad loc.
IGUR 1288	Hortensius Pedon	dec	[πατρί]δα Λαοδ[ίκειαν ἔλειψα Ἀσίη]ς ἀπὸ γαί[ης]
IGUR 1293	Ulpius Philometor	dec	ἀπὸ χρυσῆς Κεράμου
IGUR 1354	Flavianus	dec	πάτρης ἀπάνευθε Μυρίνης
	Dorus	comm	father
IGUR 1355	Fonteius Fortis Asclepiades	dec	τῷ γένει Ἐφέσιον
IGUR 1395	Nymph[---]	dec	πατρὶς ‹γ›εῖα Μεανδρείας
IGUR 1425	(name lost)	dec	Λαοδίκια πάτ[ρη]
IG xiv 938	Phileros	comm	Μειλήσιος
SEG iv 132	Hyginus	dec	Μειλήσιος
SEG xxxv 1039	(name missing)	dec	comments ad loc.[13]
AE (1972) 14	Numitoria C.l. Philumina	builders	natione Prugia
	P. Opitreius C.l. Butas		natione Smurnaeus
AE (1979) 24	Antiochis	dec	Prygiae
AE (1984) 49	L. Sedatius Celsus Artemas	dec	Laudiceni
Bevilacqua 1978	Synnadeus	uncertain	Φρύξ[14]

Asia (Christian/Jewish)

1857= 9767	Anthesthius	dec	Εὐκαρπεὺς ἀπὸ Φρυγίας
1883	Metricius	dec	Κυζικηνός
11691	Gaies	dec	πατρὶς Ἔφεσ[ος][15]
12182	Anatolius	comm	Κυζικηνός
	Heliodorus	dec	brother
12204	[---]lakios	dec	Ἀφροδισιεύς
12473	Constantius	comm	Ladiciae
12841= IGUR 404	Aurelius Herodes	dec	γεννηθεὶς ἐν Φιλαδελφίᾳ
CIL vi 37072	Q. Pompeius Callistratus	dec	Dareno
JIWE ii 183	Ammias	dec	ἀπὸ Λαδικίας
Avraméa 1995, 318	(name lost)	dec	[ὅρ]ων τῆς Φρυ[γίας]

Bithynia (Military)

2780	L. Musius Q.f. Pol. October	dec	Nicom.
3094	T. Amydius Severus	dec	n. Ponticus
3143	C. Veratius Maximus	dec	n. Ponticus
AE (1983) 50	Aurelius Tau(rus)	comm	Germanicopolis in B(ithynia)

Bithynia (Civilian)

5639	L. Lutatius Paccius	dec	de familia rege Mitredatis
6311	Philiros	dec	LAPLAGO (l. Paph-lago?)
9675	L. Arlenus L.l. Artemidorus	dec	nat. Paphlago
27053	Synforus	comm	gen. Bythynus
IGUR 299	Q. Aelius Tertianus	comm	foster-brother
	Q. Aelius Archelaus	dec	Νεικο[μ]ηδεῖ
IGUR 377	Asclepiodotus	dec	Νικομηδεύς
IGUR 378	Asclepiod[---]	dec	[Ν]εικομηδε[ῖ]
IGUR 413	M. Aurelius Xenonianus Aquila	dec?	Βειθυνὸς γενεῆ
IGUR 418 +708	M. Aurelius Proclus	dec	Νι[κ]ομηδεύς
IGUR 837	C. Hostilius Agathopus	dec	Νεικαεύς
IGUR 956	Sympherousa	dec	Βειθυνή
IGUR 1175	Barbarianus	dec	Ἄμαστρις ἔθρεψε
IGUR 1176	Basileus	dec	Νικαίης προλιπὼν Βιθυνίδος
IGUR 1196	Domitianus	dec	[Ἀστα]κίδην[16]
IGUR 1205	Hermione	dec	[Ἀστ]ακί[ης γ]αίης
IGUR 1255	Cornoution	dec	ἐκπρολιπὼ[ν] [δὲ π]άτραν Σινώπην
IGUR 1263	Maximus	dec	πατρίδος Ἀστακίης
IGUR 1383	(name lost)	dec	Πόντος πέλει
BCAR (1923), p. 74 no. 16	M. Volcius M.f. E[---]	comm	Bithynicus
AE (1947) 162	P. Aelius Samius Isocrates	dec	Νεικομηδεύς καὶ Ἐφέσιος
AE (1983) 50	Iulia Ma	dec	mother
I.Porto 26	L. Aelius Flavius Diodorus	dec	Προυσαεύς ἀπ' Ὀλύμπου
I.Porto 38	Gorgias	dec	Νεικομηδεύς

Bithynia (Christian)

2052	Pan[---]	dec	[Κωνσταν]τινοπ-[ολίτη](ς)[17]
2092	(name lost)	dec	Κ[ω]νσταντινου-πολίτι[σσα]
4002	Zosimus	dec	Νεικομηδεύς

4009	(name lost)	dec	Avraméa 1995, 305
4731=IGUR 573	Eris	dec	Βυζάντιος
4849	Hypatia	dec	Κωσταντινοπολίτισσα
9287	Aurelius Aelianus	dec	Παφλαγών
10541	Aggaros	dec	Χαλκε‹δ›όνις
12183	Anicetus	dec	Νεικο[μηδ]εύς

Britain (Military)

3279	Nig. Marinianus	dec	natione Britanicianus
3301	M. Ulpius Iustus	dec	natione Britto
32861	(name lost)	dec	natione Brit[---]

Cappadocia (Military)

3092	Afranius Zoilus	dec	nat. Cappadox

Cappadocia (Civilian)

2171	L. Antistius L.l. Eros	dec	Cappadoxs
6510	Prima	dec	Cappadoca
10636[18]	Aelius Aelinus	dec	n. Καπ.
11188	C. Aeteius C.l. Eros	dec	Cappadox
14968	Ti. Claudio Chilon	dec	Kappadoci
37552	L. Arruntius Castor	dec	n. Cappadoces
	Pollux	comm	
IGUR 872	Papirius Heraclitus	dec	Λαρανδεῖ
IGUR 1186	Gordius	dec	Καππαδό[κην]
IGUR 1338	Spinther	dec	Τυανῆος
Speidel 1994a,697	Primitivus	dec	na. Cappadoc.

Cappadocia (Christian)

10549	Acacius	dec	Καππάδοκος
12201	Paulus	dec	πωλείτης Καπα[δοκίας]
13397	(name lost)	dec	civis Cap[padox?]
19478	Bibianus	dec	Kappados

Cilicia (Military)

3113	L. Germanius Asclepiades	dec	natio. Cilix
3123	C. Mucius Valens	dec	n. Cilix
3129	Publicius Messor	dec	natione Cilix

Cilicia (Civilian)

6483	Laudica	dec	Cilicissa
9675	L. Arlenus L.l. Demetrius	dec	nat. Cilix
13066	M. Aurelio Di[---]	dec	nation. Cilix
IGUR 320	Alexander	dec	Ταρσεύς
IGUR 1166	Pompeia	dec	Ταρσογενῆ
IGUR 1206	Hermocrates	dec	[γε]νεῆ πάτρης ἀπὸ Τάρσ[ου]

IGUR 1278	Mousaios	dec	Ταρσέα
IGUR 1286	Athenaeus[19]	comm	Κίλιξ
IGUR 1361	Augustanus	dec	Κίλιξ

Cilicia (Christian)

12186	Aurelius Silvanus	dec	κώ(μης) Εὐανδρείας ὅρων Γερμανεικίας

Corsica/Sardinia (Military)

3101	Atilius Modestus	dec	nat. Sard.
3105	Q. Catius Firminus	dec	nat. Sardus
3121	M. Marius Pudens	dec	nat. Sardus
3172	(name lost)	dec	na. Corsus
32766	Cossu[tius?] Nepot[---]	dec	nat. Sa[rd.]
37251	(name lost)	dec	[n]at. Sard.
xiv 242	(name lost)	dec	n. Sardus
xiv 4496	M. Marius Nepos	dec	n. Cor.
AE (1916) 52	L. Tarcunius Heraclianus	dec	na. Sardus

Corsica/Sardinia (Civilian)

29152=	M. Ulpius Augg.l. Chariton	dec	τίκτε δὲ Σαρδονίη με
IGUR 1294	Ulpia Charitine	comm	sister
	P. Aelius Augg.l. Africanus	comm	cognatus

Crete/Cyrene/Cyprus (Military)

3115	C. Iulius Aristianus	dec	Cyr.
3134	T. Turranius Pollio	dec	n. Libycus

Crete/Cyrene/Cyprus (Civilian)

IGUR 508	Epaphrys	dec	Κρὴς Πολ‹υ›ρήνιος ὁ καὶ Κισάμις
	Antipolios	comm	father
IGUR 512	Episkeuos	dec	Κυπρίου
IGUR 1262	Lyca	dec	ἀπὸ Κρήτης

Crete/Cyrene/Cyprus (Christian)

1891	Rufinus	dec	Κρὴς Πολυρήνιος ὁ καὶ Κισάμις
6537	Aemilius Pollio	dec	[e regi]one Tripolit<a>n<a>
14510	Nicolaus	dec	Creticum
15752	Epaphroditus	dec	Κυπ(ρίῳ)
17297	Chresimus	dec	Κυπρίος
19258	Romana	dec	nationis Tripolitanae
19797	Thallousa	dec	Λιβυκή [ἀ]πὸ Βερνεικίδο[ς]

Dacia (Military)

2403=32642	Ulpius M.f. [---]	dec	Sarm(izegetusa)
2425	Aurelius Ingenuus	dec	nat. provinc. Dacia
	Aurelius Petronianus	comm	brother
2495	Iulius Secundinus	dec	nat. Dacus
2602	M. Aurelius Lucianus	dec	ex provincia Dacia
2696	Aurelius Domitianus	dec	nat. Dacus
2698	Aurelius Passar	dec	domo Daciae regione Scodrihese
3191	Aurelius Antonius	dec	nat. Dacus
3200	T. Aurelius Dexter	dec	nat. Dacus
3234	Aurelius Victor	dec	nat. Dacus
3236	Aurelius Victorinus	dec	natione Daqus domum coloni Zermiegete
3238	Aurelius Vitalis	dec	nat. Dacus
3277	C. Marius Gemellinus	dec	nat. Dacus
	Aurelius Emeritus	comm	brother
	Marius Marcellinus	comm	brother
3288	Septimius Sacretius	dec	nat. Dacus
3296	M. Ulpius Avitus	dec	Ulpia Traiana
3320	(name lost)	dec	[D]aciscu[s]
3419	Aurelius Iulianus	dec	nat. Dacia
3456	(name lost)	dec	nat. Dacia
32786	Iulius Quintianus	dec	na. Dac.
32791	(name lost)	dec	[natio]ne Da[cus?]
32845b	Aurelius Super	dec	natione Da[cus?]
37252	Aureliu[s ---]	dec	[n.] Dac[us]
37258a	(name lost)	dec	[ex provi]nc. Da[cia]
AE (1983) 82	Aurelius Fro[---]	dec	nat. Da[cus?]
AE (1993) 333[20]	(name lost)	dec	Col. Ulpia Traiana
Mateescu 1923, 194	Aurelius [---]	dec	Dac[us]
Speidel 1994a, 151	(name lost)	dec	[nat. D]ac. [domo colonia U]lpia [Sarmizegeth]usa
Speidel 1994a, 254	(name lost)	dec	[Ulpia Tra]iana

Dacia (Civilian)

1801	Zia	dec	Dacae
3227	Aurelius Primus	dec	nat. Dacus
3236	Aurelius Longinus	comm	paganus
	(name lost)	comm	grandparent
3456	Aurelius Aurelianus	comm	brother
4230	Nunnia Tyche	dec	Dac[---]
16903	Diuppaneus qui et Euprepes	dec	Dacus
AE (1993) 331	Munatia Procula	dec	nat. pr. Dacia

Dacia (Christian)

23076	Alexander	dec	Dacia quem genuit

Dalmatia (Military)

2451	M. Valerius M.f. Ser. Quintianus	dec	Seni[21]
3108	M. Domitius Nepos	dec	n. Dalmat.
3126	P. Plotius Celer	dec	n. Dalmata
3149	Antonius [---]	dec	nat. Delm.
3261[22]	[--- G]emellinus	dec	n. [Da]lm.
3663	(name lost)	dec	[D]almat[---]
32895	L. Statilius L.f. Secundus	dec	Salonas
39472	M. Baebius Celer qui et Bato	dec	Delma.
AE (1984) 64	M. Sestius M.f. Ser. Clemens	dec	Aenona
AE (1988) 1138	D. Annius Rufus	dec	natione Dalmati.
Speidel 1994a, 366	(name lost)	dec	nat. Dalmat[us]

Dalmatia (Civilian)

2633	Septimia Secunda	dec	ex provincia Dalmatia
20012	C. Iulius H[---]	comm	Liburnus
	C. Iulius Fla[---]	dec	father
28053b	Vibia Euplia	dec	n. Da<l>m.
iii 2083	P. Papirius Proculus	dec	commemorated at home
iii 6414	Principius	dec	commemorated at home
iii 9713	(name lost)	dec	commemorated at home

Dalmatia (Christian)

3421	Erotia	dec	Dalma(ta?)
ILCV 1178	Caelestinus (Pope)	dec	Illyrica de gente

Egypt (Military)

3093=7463	C. Ammonius Montanus	dec	n. Alex.
3096	C. Antestius Longus	dec	nat. Alexandrinus
3110[23]	T. Flavius Maximus	dec	n. Aegyp.
3112	Germanus	dec	nat. Alex.
3117	C. Iulius Priscus	dec	nat. Aeg.
3127	T. Plotius Maximus	dec	n. Aegyp.
3133	L. Sulpicius Artemidorus	dec	natione Aegyptius
3159	L. Septimius Amonianus	dec	na. Aegy.
3162	[---]clisis	dec	nati[one Aegy]ptus
32670	M. Aurelius Gaius	dec	d[omo A]lexan[dria]
xiv 239	Q. Lusius Rufus	dec	[n. A]egyptius
IGUR 312a	M(?). Cornelius Pr[---]	dec	[n]ation. Aegy.
AE (1916) 109	T. Flavius Flavianus	dec	nat. Al[---]
NS (1916) p. 100 no. 44	M. Pinnius Vales	dec	n. Aegyp.

Egypt (Civilian)

10117	L. Aurelius Augg.lib. Apolaustus[24]	dedicatee	Memphio
10194	M. Antonius Exochus	dec	nat. Alexandrinus
10197	Macedo	dec	Alexandrin.
xiv 478	T. Flavius Apollonius	dec	Alexandrino
xiv 479	Aphrodisius	dec	Alex.
IGUR 77	Embes	dedicatee	Ricci 1993a, A12
IGUR 240	M. Aurelius Asclepiades Hermodoros	dedicator	Ἀλεξανδρεύς
IGUR 393	M. Aurelius Asklas ὁ καί Zenon	dec	πλοίου Ἀλεξανδρείνου
IGUR 395[25]	Aurelia Boubastous	dec	Ἀλεξανδρίνη
IGUR 610	Iulius Hilarus	dec	Ἀλεξανδρῖ
	Iulia Pia	comm	mother
IGUR 858	M. Ulpius Heron	builder	Ἀλεξανδρεύς
IGUR 875	Pappus	dec	Ἀλεξ[ανδρεύς]
IGUR 1034	Flavius Terpnus	dec	Ἀλεξανδρεύς
IGUR 1060	(name lost)	dec	εὐθηνιάρχην τῆς λαμπροτάτης πόλεως τῶν Ἀλεξανδρέων καὶ βουλευτήν
IGUR 1191	Dikaiosyne	dec	θρέψε μ' Ἀλεξάνδρεια
	(name not given)	comm	sister
IGUR 1233	I[---]	dec	πρεσβευτής[26]
IGUR 1321	Rufinus	dec	Νείλου πόλιν
IGUR 1358	Epaphras	comm	Ἀ⟨λ⟩εξάνδροιο πολείτης
AE (1916) 57	Thermitarion	dec	Alexandrin.
AE (1988) 24	Pardus	dec	nat. Aegyptus
I.Porto 23	[---]us Lupus	comm?	[Ἀλεξα]νδρείας τῆ[ς Αἰγύπτου]

Egypt (Christian)

1170	Aurelius Apion	dec	Ermopoli[s]
4032 = IGUR 939	Fuscinus Taon	comm	Αἰγύπτιοι
4957[27]	[---]onna	dec	ἀπὸ κώμης Κωβρη(θ)έων
4973	Ammonius	dec	Κοπριθ[έως]
6415	Ammon	dec	Ἀλεξανδρέως
9307	Ioannes	dec	ἀπὸ κώμης Κοβρ[ί]θεος
12856	Paulus	dec	Ἀλεξανδρεύς

12883	Flavius Paulus	dec	Ἡρακλείδου ἀπὸ Ἐγύπτου κώμης Μεγάλης Ψότθεως τῆς Μεγάλης Ἡρα(κλεου- πόλεως)
15868	Bassus	dec	πάτρη πόλις Βαβυλῶνος

Galatia (Military)

2455	L. Annius L.f.Cla. Valens	dec	Iconio
2964	C. Iulius C.f.Cla. Sossianus	dec	Iconio
3271	C. Iulius Vales	dec	natione Nysius[28]

Galatia (Civilian)

4351	Diocles	dec	natione Gallograe[c.]
5188	Alexander	dec	Pylaemenianus[29]
12495	Asclepi[---]	dec	nati[one Ga]lata
33777	Hilarus	dec	Gallograeci
IGUR 527	Euangelis	dec	γένει Γαλάτισσα
IGUR 535	Exeteon	dec	[Ἀ]μασεύς
IGUR 789	Mettius Nicephorus	dec	Σελγέ‹ω›ς
IGUR 797	(name lost)	dec	Γαλά[τη]ς ἀπὸ Πα[---]
IGUR 1204	[---]nes	dec	Τερμησσὸν ναίων Σολύμοις
	Hermaios	dec	
	Konon	comm	
IGUR 1341	Telesistratus	dec	Γέρμης ἐξ Ἱερῆς

Galatia (Christian)

870[30]	Eustathius	dec	Γαλάτων Πιτερμηνων
4041[31]	(name lost)	dec	χωρίου Πιᾶμ
4271b	Alexander	dec	κωρίῳ Μικρᾶς Κώμης
4434	Callinicus	dec	χωρίου Τουγουτέων
4437[32]	Ablabes	dec	Γαλάτης χωρίου Μουλίκο(υ)
4439[33]	Sumeonis	dec	Ἀπουκώμης
4441	Philippus	dec	πατρίς μοι Γαλατία‹ς› κόμη
4442	(name lost)	dec	Γαλάτη[ς]
4443	(name lost)	dec	Γαλάτης
5064= IGCVO 32	Calonymus	dec	[Γαλά]της
5658	Antiochus	dec	Γαλ[άτης]
5661	Docimus	dec	χωρίου Φολόης Μικρᾶς Γαλατίας
5669+5675[34]	Ioannes	dec	[Γ]αλάτης χωρίῳ Ἀμνίων
5676[35]	Saloukina	dec	χωρίου Παπουκώμη
5679[36]	Nessi[---]	dec	‹Γ›αλ[άτης ἀπὸ κώμης] Γο[λόης]
5833	Sozomenus	dec	χωρίου Κνήκνων
27335	(name lost)	comm	de Galatia
23743	Eustathius	dec	Γάλατα Ἀνκυρανός/ Galata cibis Anquira

23748	(name lost)	dec	[Γ]αλάθης
AE (1988) 30	Hypatius	dec	Galata
Ferrua 1939, 10	(name lost)	dec	[χ]ωρίου Ξιτου

Gaul (Military)

2549	Sex. Valerius C.f.Vol. Firminus	dec	Viennae
2623	C. Acilius C.f.Vol. Martialis	dec	Vasione
2714	T. Lucconius Quartinus	dec	domo Reis
	T. Lucconius Paternus	dec	Apollinarib.
2763	L. Aucilius L.f.Vol. Secundus	dec	Vienna
3328	M. Orbius M.f. M[---]	dec	Aquis Sex(tis)
3339	L. Gratius L.f. Cla. Verinus	dec	Cemeneli
3607	C. Iulius C.f.Vol. Silvanus	dec	domo Vienna
3639	M. Valerius M.f. Ani. Saturninus	dec	Foro Iuli
32799	Aurelius Paternus	dec	[nat.] Trever.
32872	T. Aurelius Cla. Certus	dec	Cemeneli
33977	M. Ulpius Felix Mimillo	dec	natione Tunger
x 6230	C. Licinius C.[f.] Ani. Fuscus	dec	Foro Iuli
xii 65	Quartinius Maternus	dec	commemorated at home
AE (1934) 139	L. Terentius L.f.Ani. Secundus	dec	Foro Iuli
	C. Terentius L.f.Ani. Fronto	comm	Foro Iuli
AE (1954) 82	M. Ulpius Gal. Verecundus	dec	Lugduno
AE (1984) 59	Q. Valerius Q.f.Cla. Verus	dec	Cemeneli
AE (1984) 62	C. Iulius C.f.Vol. Verecundus	dec	Tolosa
AE (1984) 69	L. Octavius L.f.Vol. Saturninus	dec	Reis
AE (1984) 70	C. Primius C.f.Vol. Proclus	dec	Vasione
NS (1917) p. 303 no. 44	D. Valerius Feroxs	dec	Nemausi

Gaul (Civilian)

1625a	Iulius Lupercus	dedicator	ex Belgica
	Clau[dia] Victorina	dedicator	Treveri
2497=32651	Valeria Iustina	dec	nata Convena Aquitania
2714	Iulia Quartia	comm	mother
6974	Q. Hortensius Q.f.Vol. Secundus	dec	Nemausies
7760	L. Vetilius L.l. Primus	dec	Gall[---]
9717	L. Iulius M.f.Vol. Fuscus	dec	Aquensis
9998	L. Faenius Telesphorus	dec	Lugdunensis
10127	Phoebe	dec	Vocontia
15493	Claudia Lepidilla	dec	ex provincia Belgica Ambianae
17555	Q. Fabius Pompeianus	dec	Viennensis
17643	C. Fabricius C.f.Vol. Proximus	dec	Tolosensis
20121/2[37]	C. Iulius Marcellus	dec	Narbonesi

	[G]lyco	comm	father
21921	L. Manilius L.f.Vol. Silanus	dec	Viennensi
24057	Phaeder	dec	Massalitanus
27344	[---]us Tharsus	dec	Narbonensi
27477	A. Titinius A.l. Scymnus	dec	Corda
27741	T. Tullius Syntropus	dec	nati. Gal.
28278	Valeria L.f. Successa	dec	Narboniensis
29687	Atticus	dec	III provinciarum Galliarum servo
29688	Sex. Attius Sex.f.Vol. Atticus	dec?	Vienn.
29692	Ti. Claudius Honoratianus	dec	Castrensis Morini
29709	P. Manlius Vitalis	dec	decurioni Lugudunensium
29718	Sex. Sammius Sex.f.Vol. Aper	dec	domo Nemauso
29722	C. Sen[ti]us Regulianus	dec	see p. 208
34037	Aemilius Morvinnicus	dec	Aeduo
34676	Belliciola	dec	natione Galla in cibitate Triberis
xii 155	Antonius Vecetinus	dec	commemorated at home
xii 1750	Ti. Claudius Ti.f.Gal. Pius	dec	decurioni Luguduni, commemorated at home
xii 2211	L. Maec(ius) Terti(i) f. Maelo	dec	commemorated at home
xiii 260	Proxumus Danna	dec	commemorated at home
xiii 2040	A. Vitellius Valerius	dec	commemorated at home
xiii 2181	Iulia Helias	dec	commemorated at home
xiv 327	P. Claudius Abascantus	comm	trium Galliar. lib.
IGUR 820	Nymphon	dec	Μασσαλιῶτα
IGUR 940	(name lost)	dec	Μασσαλιῆτα
AE (1953) 56	T. Iulius T.f.Vol. Lentinus	dec	ex civitate Tricassium
	T. Iulius C.f.Vol. Couribocalus	dec	ex civitat<e> Tricassium
AE (1979) 75	M. Licinius M.l. Laetus	dec	N[a]rbone[n(sis)]
AE (1984) 102	Ti. Claudius Sextinus	dec	ex provincia Lugdunensi
AE (1984) 121	Caprilia Severa	dec	civis Aeduae
Thylander 1951-2, A13	C. Annaeus Atticus	dec	Pict. ex Aquitanica

Gaul (Christian)

5568	Bon[osus?]	dec	cibis Triberensis
	(name not given)	comm	mother
5967	(name lost)	dec	stirpe Novempo[pulana--] Gallica terra
11104[38]	(name lost)	dec	Salicenis
20819	Remus	dec	natione Galla
	Arcontia	dec	

22694	Victoria	dec	civi Galle
25968	[---]centia	dec	Novempop[ulana]
ILCV 4443	Aurelia Theudosia	dec	nat. Ambiana
AE (1953) 200	Eventius	dec	Viennae

Germany (Military – including Julio–Claudian bodyguard)

2514	Q. Vetius Ingenuus	dec	ex provincia Germania Inferiore
	Felicius Marcus	comm	cives
2548	Sanctinius Probinus	dec	nat. Batavs
	Sanctinius Genialis	comm	brother
3175=xiv 208	Aelius Aventinus	dec	Col. Cl. Ara
3203	T. Aurelius Felix	dec	nat. Canonefas
3220	T. Aurelius Probus	dec	nat. Batavs
3223	T. Aurelius Scribonius	dec	natione Batavs
3230	Aurelius Verus	dec	nat. Friseo
3237	T. Aurelius T.f. Vindex	dec	Ulp. Noviomag.
3240	Candidinius Verax	dec	natione Badavs
	Candidinius Spectatus	dec	nat. Badavs
3260	T. Flavius Verinus	dec	nat. Frisaevone
	T. Flavius Victor	comm	brother
3263	T. Hortensius Mucro	dec	nat. Marsaquio
	Aelius Verinus	comm	brother
3280	Paulinius Abentinus	dec	n. Ger.
3284	[---] Saturninus	dec	[Ulp. Noviom]agi[39]
3289	Superinius Peregrinus	dec	nat. Ba[tavo]
3290	T. Tertinius Marcianus	dec	natus in Ger. Sup.
	Iulius Iulianus	comm	municeps
3298	M. Ulpius Faustus	dec	Cl. Ara
3299	Ulpius Flavinus	dec	Cl. Ara
3302	M. Ulpius Liberalis	dec	natione Helvetius
3311	M. Ulpius Victor	dec	nat. Cl. Ara
3315	[------]inus	dec	[nat.] German.
3321a	(name lost)	dec	[nat.] Frisi[avoni]
3343	[.] Aelius P.f. [---]	dec	[M]ogont[iaco]
3348	C. Acutius Cla. Severus	dec	Ara
3360	M. Aemilius M.f. Cla. Nigrinus	dec	Ara
3458[40]	Q. C[......]s [T]ere[ntia]nus	dec	na. <C>l. Ara
4337	Bassus	dec	Germanus
4338	Bassus	dec	Germanus
4339	Macer	dec	Germano natione Vein.
4340	Macer	dec	Germanus
4341	Valens	dec	Germanus natione ATAEVS
4342	Bassus	dec	natione Frisius
4343	Hilarus	dec	natione Frisiaeo
4344	Nereus	dec	nat. German. Peucennus

4345	Proculus	dec	decurio Germanorum
8802	Alcimachus	dec	nat. Batavs
	Batavus	comm	ex coll. Ger.
8803	Ti. Claudius Chloreus	dec	natione Batavs
	Ti. Claudius Diadumenus	comm	ex collegio Germanorum
	Censor	comm	
8804	Epagathus	dec	natione Batavus
	Macer	comm	ex collegio Germanorum
8805	(name lost)	dec	nation. U[bius]⁴¹
	Marsus	comm	ex collegio Germanorum
8806	Nobilis	dec	nat. Batavs
8807	Paetinus	dec	nat. Batavs
	Virus	comm	ex col. Germa[norum]
8808	Phoebus	dec	nat. Baetesius
	Gnostus	comm	ex colleg. German.
8809	Postumus	dec	nat. Ubius
	Capito	comm	ex col. Germ.
8810	Severus	dec	natione Sue[bus]⁴²
8811	Ti. Claudius Aug.l. Ductus	dec	dec. Germanorum
32789	P. Aelius Pom[---]	dec	[nat.] Helvetius
32806	[.] Secundinius Verus	dec	natione Suaebo
32812a	(name lost)	dec	[nat.] Batavs
32834	(name lost)	dec	[nat.] Batavs
32843	[.] Aurelius A[---]	dec	Ulpia Novioma[go]
32850	(name lost)	dec	[natio]ne Fr[isaevo]
32866	(name lost)	dec	[nat. Fr]isiavo
32869a	(name lost)	dec	[nat. Ma]rsac[us]
33016	Certin[---]	dec	Batavo
37299	(name lost)	dec	Agrippinensis
AE (1952) 145	Fannius	dec	nation. Ubius
	Corinthus	comm	ex colleg. German.
AE (1952) 146	Ter[...]	dec	nat. Batavs
	Sollemnis	comm	ex collegio Germanorum
	Reginus	comm	
AE (1952) 147	Gamo	dec	nat. Batavs
	Hospes	comm	brother, ex collegio Germanorum
AE (1952) 148	Indus	dec	natione Batavus
	Eumenes	comm	brother, ex collegio Germanorum
AE (1952) 149	[...]nus	dec	nat. Batavs
	Calyx	comm	ex col. Germ.
AE (1968) 32	Saturni[nus]	dec	natione Ba[tavs]
	La[---]	comm	ex [coll.] Germanor[um]
AE (1983) 55	Divius Tau[rus]	dec	n. Bad.
AE (1983) 56	Septimi[us ---]dus	dec	n. B(atavus)
AE (1983) 58	Vetus	dec	n. Ba[tavus?]

AE (1984) 58	C. Valerius C.f.Cla. Flaccus	dec	Ara
AE (1993) 385	[. Si]mplicinius Serenus	dec	natione Ulp. Novimagi Batavs
NS (1922) 142 no. 6	(name lost)	dec	nat. Hel[vet.]
Speidel 1994a, 87	[.] Iulius Messor	dec	nat. Hel[vet]io
Speidel 1994a, 103	T. Flavius Genialis	dec	[nat.] Frisaoni
Speidel 1994a, 137	(name lost)	dec	[nat.] Marsacus
Speidel 1994a, 144	[--- Simp]lex	dec	[nat. Ba]tavs Ulpia [Novioma]gi
Speidel 1994a, 170	M. Ulpius Quartio	dec	C. Ar. A.
Speidel 1994a, 174	[P. A]elius Bassus	dec	natione Mars[aquius]
Speidel 1994a, 175	P. Aelius Cresc[ens]	dec	Cl. Ara
Speidel 1994a, 239	[---] Vindex	dec	n[at. Canno]nef[as]
Speidel 1994a, 245	[---] Aprilis	dec	[nat. Cannone]fas
Speidel 1994a, 275	(name lost)	dec	[nat. Mar]saquio
Speidel 1994a, 277	(name lost)	dec	nat. Bat[avs]
Speidel 1994a, 278	(name lost)	dec	[nat.] Helvet[ius]
Speidel 1994a, 298	(name lost)	dec	[nat.] Cl. Ara
Speidel 1994a, 352	(name lost)	dec	[nat. Ba]tavs
Speidel 1994a, 359	(name lost)	dec	[nat. Fri]saoni
Speidel 1994a, 374	[---]s Avitus	dec	[nat. Bat]avs
Speidel 1994a, 378	Aurelius Dignu[s]	dec	[nat.] Germ.
Speidel 1994a, 555	Aurelius Victor	dec	n. B(atavus)
Speidel 1994a, 703a	[...]ius Ama[ndus]	dec	[na]t. Ba[tavo]
Speidel 1994a, 744	C. Iulius C.f.Cla. Victor	dec	Ara
	C. Valerius Lepidinus	comm	brother
Ferrua 1951, no. 77	(name lost)	dec	[nat. Bat]avo
Ferrua 1951, no. 82	(name lost)	dec	nat. Hel[vetius]
Speidel & Scardigli 1990, 201[43]	[...]bius Vitalis	dec	nat. Suebus Necresis
Speidel & Scardigli 1990, 203	Verecundinius Verus	dec	Suebus

Germany (Civilian – including private bodyguard)

3348	C. Acutius Romanus	comm	brother
3452	Paterna	dec	me Germana creat tellus
6221	Donatus	dec	German.
6229	Felix	dec	German.
6230	Casti	dec	Germ.
6231	Cirratus	dec	Germanus
6232	Clemens	dec	Germanus
6233	Nothus	dec	Germanu[s]
6234	Pothus	dec	Germanus
6235	Strenuus	dec	Germanus
6236	Suebus	dec	Germanus
6237	Urbanus	dec	Germani

17861	Felix	dec	nat. Germanus
22981	T. Nigrius Similis	dec	Triboco ex Germania Superiore Luco Augusti
	Nigrius Modestus	comm	brother
30569	(name lost)	dec?	Suebus
34773[44]	(name lost)	dec	natione Canin.
36324–5	M. Sennius M.f. Verus	dec	nat. Agrippinensi
	C. Valerio C.f. Messeanus	dec	nat. Frisao
	C. Valerius Messor	comm	father
AE (1989) 30	Miles	dec	nat. Marsac.
BCAR (1915), p. 305	M. M(em)mius Saturninus Primus	dec comm	Agrippinensis father
Speidel 1994a, 710	(name lost)	dec	[Ulpi]o Novio[ma]gi, Batavo

Germany (Christian)

18423	Anneus Fortunalis	dec	Bisentinae Se(quanorum)

Greece (Military)

3102	L. Baebius Diogenes	dec	n. Grae.
3136	M. Valerius Bassus	dec	natione Graecus
3168	L. Acc<ius?> Valens	dec	nati. Grae.

Greece (Civilian)

6436	Eros	dec	Boeotiani
8142	L. Abuccius Eros	dec	Graecus
9906	Cornelia Stacte	dec	Graeca
17343=37867	Euhodus	comm	Athenesis
17448	Eutychides	dec	nat. Graecus
IGUR 370	Cn. Arrius Stratocles	dec	Ἀθηναίωι
IGUR 480	Diodora	dec	Ἀθηναία
IGUR 615	Petronius Serenus	comm	Λακεδαιμόνιος
IGUR 771	Martha	dec	Λακεδαιμονία
IGUR 809	Neike	dec	Ἀργεία
IGUR 1161	Artemo	dec	Λακωνίς
IGUR 1210	Euboulos	dec	Κορίνθιος
IGUR 1239	Iulia C.f. Laudica	dec	πατρὶς Σάμη
IGUR 1293	Ulpia [---]	dec	ἀπ' Ἀθηνῶν
AE (1972) 14	C. Numitorius C.l. Nicanor	builder	nationi Tebaeus
Thylander 1951–2, A27	Aristida	comm	Rodi
Solin & Itkonen-Kaila 1966, no. 121	[Peri?]genes	graff	Graecus
Solin & Itkonen-Kaila 1966, no. 329	Zosimus	graff	Ἕλλην

Greece (Christian/Jewish)

1856⁴⁵	Andragathos	dec	Γρέκος
2973	Agathemerion	dec	Γραίκος
3455	Euschemon	dec	Graecus
5098b	Atto	dec	Τενάρ[ου]⁴⁶
13899	Mar[tin]us	dec	Grecus
19820	Nicomachus	dec	Γραίκος
23369	Helene	dec	Κορινθία
JIWE ii 503	I[−−]	dec	Ἀχαϊάς

Hispania (Military)

1410	M. Vibius Maternus	dedicator	Ilurensis
2454	C. Aelius C.f.Gal. Aelianus	dec	Sego[briga]
2490	L. Cornelius Qui. Firmanus	dec	Avila
2536	L. Flavius L.f.Pom. Caesianus	dec	Asturica
2607	C. Fabius C.f.Ser. Crispus	dec	Carthag.
2614	M. Paccius M.f.Iul. Avitus	dec	Scallabi
	L. Valerius	comm	municeps
2629	C. Antonius C.f.Qui. Priscus	dec	Osca
2685	C. Melamus C.f.Gal. Rufinus	dec	Salacia
2728	T. Acilius T.f.Gal. Capito	dec	Bilbili
3349	L. Pontius Gal. Nigrinus	dec	[Br]ac(ara)⁴⁷
32682	M. Iulius M.f. Nevianus	dec	Pace Iulia
ii 2610	L. Pompeius L.f.Pom. Reburrus	dec	commemorated at home
AE (1921) 83	C. Marius C.f. Aemilianus	dec	Calacur.
AE (1974) 226⁴⁸	P. Valerius P.f.Gal. Priscus	dec	Urc[i]tano ex Hisp. Citer.
AE (1984) 65	L. Aemilius L.f.Qui. Candidus	dec	Compluto
AE (1992) 156	(name lost)	dec	[---]briga
BCAR (1915), p. 61	C. Iulius C.f.Pap. Flaccus	dec	Aug. (Emerita)
BCAR (1915), p. 323	C. Proculeius C.f.Pom. Rufus	dec	Asturica

Hispania (Civilian)

1885⁴⁹	D. Caecilius Abascantus	comm	diffusor olearius ex provincia Baetica
3422	Reginia Titula	dec	nat. Arava
3491	C. Vibellius Fortunatus	dec	Emeritus Augustorum
5337	Primulus	comm	Hispanus
6238	Pamphilus	dec	Asturconarius
9013	Carpime	dec	Gaditanae
9677	P. Clodius Athenio	builder	qq. corporis negotiantium Malacitanorum

10048	C. Appuleius Diocles	dec	[nati]one Hispanus Lusitanus
10184	M. Ulpius Aracinthus	dec	Hispano natione Palantinus
13820	Caecilia Graecula	dec	natione Hispana
14234	Calpurnia Ilias	dec	Eborensi ex Lusitania
16100	Corinthus	dec	ex Lusitania municip. Collipponensi
	Victor	comm	brother
	Celer	comm	brother
16247	C. Cornelius C.f. Iunianus	dec	ex Hispania Citeriore Saetabitanus
16310	L. Cornelius Secundus	dec	ex provincia Lusitania Salacensis
18190	T. Flavius Rufus	dec	ex Hispania Ulteriore Lusitania
20768	C. Iunius Celadus	dec	Cordubensis
21569	Lucifera	dec	ex Hispanis Ev(andriana?)
	Atticianus	comm	
21763	[– –]nius C.f. [M]acer	dec	[Hispani]a Cite[rio]re
21956	M. Manlius Saturninus	dec	Segobri.
24162	Phoebus qui et Tormogus	dec	Hispanus natus Segisamoine
	Phoebion	comm	father
	Primigenia	comm	mother
27198	M. Terentius Paternus	dec	ex Hp. Citeriore Aesonensi
27441	Timoteus	dec	Cantabrio
	Arrius Severus	comm	father
	Arria Felicissima	comm	mother
28151	Domitia Clodiana	comm	Ilipensis ex provincia Baetica
28624	Vesonia Cn.f. Procula	dec	ex Hispania Citeriore Iessonensis
28743	P. Veturius P.f. Niger	dec	Saguntinus
29724	[---]us L.f. Quir. Silvanus	dec	conventus Asturum
30430	(name lost)	dec	Gaditan[o]
34664= 37898	Baebia Venusta	dec	domo Cordub[a]
38309	Ephesia	dec	Hisp.
38595	L. Manlius A.f.Cor. Canus	dec	colonia patricia Corduba
38809	C. Pupius Restitutus	dec	ex provincia Baetica civitate Baesarensi
39136	[---]nius Q.f. [---]rnus	dec	[Segob]rigensi
ii 379	M. Iulius Serenus	dec	commemorated at home
ii 382	P. Lucanius [.]f. Reburrinus	dec	commemorated at home
ii 3035	(name lost)	dec	commemorated at home
ii 6271	Q. Cadius Fronto	dec	commemorated at home
xiv 397	L. Numisius L.l. Agathemerus	dec	ex Hispania Citeriore
xiv 4822	M. Caesius Maximus	dec	Aeminiensis
RIT 230	M. Laelius Sabinianus	dec	commemorated at home

AE (1973) 71	(name lost)	dec	[ne]gotiatri. olear. ex provinc. Baetic.
AE (1980) 98	D. Caecilius Onesimus	dec	diffusori [olear(io)] ex Baet[ica]
AE (1992) 152[50]	L. Popilius Dento	dec	Iliberritani
	M. Allius Pudens	dec	
AE (1992) 153	Iunia L.f. Amoena	dec	ex provinci[a] Baetica municipi[o] Italica
AE (1992) 154	L. Valerius L.f. C[---]	dec	Me<i>dubr[igens(i)]
	Valeria C.f. Ma[---]	dec	Sala<c>ens(i)
	L. Valerius [---]	dec	Me<i>dubri[gens(i)]
	Valeria S[---]	comm	sister
AE (1992) 155	Corbulo	dec	nat. Tarracone
	Clodia Ursa	comm	mother
	Helius	comm/dec	father
NS (1915) p. 48 no. 42	Atilia	dec	natione Galliga
Castrén in Väänänen 1973, no. 120	(name lost)	dec?	ex Hispania

Hispania (Christian)

962	Iulius Syrus	dec	ἐν Εἰμερίτῃ πόλι τῆς Εἰσ‹π›ανίας
1748	Saturnalis	dec	ex Espanis, Cartaginese
3402	Contantius Clamerarus	builder	Ilicenis
	Sibirinus	dec	relative
	Silvina	dec	sister
17495	Rapetiga	dec	civis Hispanus
	Niceitus	comm	father
18216a	(name lost)	dec	Spanii[s]
18762	Felicissimus	dec	had wife in provincia Hispanica
18995	Lazarus	dec	had wife in prov. Hispania
	Timoteus	comm	brother
	Pannosus	comm	brother

Lycia (Civilian)

9580	T. Flavius Coelius Severus	comm	Sidensis
28228	Valeria Ɔ.l. Lycisca	dec	epitaph says she is an immigrant
IGUR 371	Cn. Artorius Apollo	dec	Περγαίωι
IGUR 626	Seccius Trophimus	dec	γένει Σιδήτης
IGUR 815	Nicias	dec	Ξάνθιος τῆς Λυκίας
	Aurelius Agesilaus	comm	fellow-citizen
IGUR 1351	Philetus	dec	τῆς Λυκίης Λιμύρων

Appendix

Lycia (Christian)

9316	Onesimus	dec	Περγέε
19808	Aurelia Domna	comm	Περγέα

Macedonia (Military)

2520	T. Aelius T.f.Aem. Marcellus	dec	Dobiro
	T. Flavius Petronianus	comm	municeps
2611	C. Iulius C.f. Verus	dec	Heraclia
2645	C. Iulius Fab. Gemellus	dec	domo Heraclea Sentica
2646	C. Iulius C.f.Cor. Pudes	dec	Thessalonica
2679	L. Cusonius L.f. Proculus	dec	Thessalonic.
2715	[---] Aem. Maximus	dec	Dobero
2767	C. Iulius Fab. Montanus	dec	domo Heraclea Sentica
2886	P. Aelius P.f.Cla. Quintianus	dec	Thess.
2916	C. Iulius C.f.Aem. Rufus	dec	Durraci
32738	P. Herennius P.f. Aem. Macedo	dec	Stobis
32851	(name lost)	dec	[nat.] Macedo
AE (1916) 49	L. Aurelius L.f.Iul. Dignus	dec	Anphipoli
Speidel 1994a, 568	Valerius Mestrius	dec	nat. Macedo

Macedonia (Civilian)

18132a	Flavius Meiovius	dec	nat. Macedo
22178	C. Marius [---]	dec	domo Byllid[---]
IGUR 1312	Publius	dec	Μακεδών

Macedonia (Christian)

188	Claudia Apuleia	dec?	Macedon[---]
15000	Valerius	dec	Τησαλωνικαῖος

Mauretania (Military)

3262	Geminius Pacatus	dec	Cl. Caesaria Mauretania
3312	Umbrius Valerianus	dec	ex provin. Maur. Caesarense
	Umbrius Sedatus	comm	brothers
	Umbrius Secundus	comm	
3365	[Valerius His]panus	dec	natus in provincia Maure[tania Cae]sariensi
	Valerius	comm	brother
AE (1990) 63	A[ur]elius [---]	dec	n. Mau[rus]
Speidel 1994a, 210	T. Aurelius Pompeius	dec	nat. Maurus

Mauretania (Civilian)

1800[51]	Memor	dec	son of princeps gentium Baquatium

4078	Paramonus	dec	ex-slave of King Ptolemy
9046	Chius	dec	slave of King Juba
10050	Crescens	dec	natione Maurus
10060	Claudius Aurelius Polyphemus	dedicatee	Caesareus[52]
10110	Ecloga	dec	slave of King Juba
33032	Ulpia Danae	dec	ex Mauretania Caesariensi
viii 8501	Praetorianus	dec	commemorated at home
viii 9249	Licinio Q.f. Qui. Donatus	dec	patriae Rusguniensum
Inscr.Lat.Mar. 93 = Inscr.Ant.Mar.			
457	L. Caecilius L.f.Cla. Fronto	dec	Volubilitano, commemorated at home

Mauretania (Christian)

5337	Gaudentius	dec	[de prov]<i>ncia Mauritania
	[Fortu?]nata	comm	mother
12780	Valerius Lila	dec	natione Maurus

Moesia (Military)

2525	M. Aurelius M.f.Ael. Gallus	dec	Vivinacio
2736	Aurelius Mucconius	dec	natione Mesacus civis Meletinus vico Perepro
2760	Valerius Victorinus	dec	nat. Mesia Inferiore domo Escum
3199	T. Aurelius Decimus	dec	nat. Mysius
3650	(name lost)	dec	Dardanus
3292	[Val]erius Herculanus	dec	[nat.] Moes. Imp.
3342	T. Flavius Pap. Valerianus	dec	Oesco
3891=32685	L. Licinius L.f.Qui. Paternus	dec	Novia
32559	Aurelius Paetinianus	dec	Dardan[---]
32800	M. Aurelius Paulus	dec	nat. Dardanus
32937	(name lost)	dec	[Nai]sso Darda[niae]
AE (1979) 20	Antonius Paterius	dec	nat. Mysia Superiore reg. Ratiarese vico C[---]nisco
Speidel 1994a, 246	(name lost)	dec	[nat.] Moesus
Speidel 1994a, 427	Aurelius Satur[ninus]	dec	nat. Mo[esus col. Ul]pia Oesci
Ferrua 1951, 102	(name lost)	dec	Mo[esus]

Moesia (Civilian)

2933	Aurelius Diza	dec	natus ex provincia Moesia infer. regione Nico-politane vico Saprisara
3650	Aurelius [---]ianus	comm	brother
	Aurelius [----]	comm	brother
6343	Messia	dec	Dardana
	Iacinthus	comm	Dardanus
13233	Aurelius Silvinus	dec	natione Moesia Inf. civitate Oesci
	Aurelius Severus	comm	brother
29235	[Ul]pius Marcellus	dec	[n]atus Viminacio

Thomasson 1961, p. 185

no. 20	[---]erna[---]	dec	Moesiacus

Moesia (Christian)

IMS ii 218	Si<th?>a	dec	commemorated at home

Noricum (Military)

2482	Aelius Emeritus	dec	ex provincia Norica
2483	P. Aelius P.f.Cla. Fuscus	dec	Viruno
2522	P. Aelius P.f.Cla. Taurus	dec	Ce{l}leia
2534	C. Cornelius Memor	dec	d. Celeia
2543	L. Plenatius L.f. Qui. Senilis	dec	Solva
2547	C. Sabinius C.f. Angulatus	dec	Solva
2619	C. Valerius C.f. Cla. Cupito	dec	Celeie
	C. Quartius Secundus	comm	brother
2712	Iustius Frontinus	dec	nat. Noricus
2751	M. Saturius M.f.Cla. Maximus	dec	Celeia
2914	Ti. Iulius Ti.f.Cla. Ingenuus	dec	Viruno
3206	T. Aurelius T.f. Genetivus	dec	nat. Noricus
3211	T. Aurelius Mansuetinus	dec	nat. Noricus
3225[53]	T. Aurelius Summus	dec	Claudio Viruno nat. Noric.
3253	T. Flavius Iulius	dec	nat. Noricus
3259	T. Flavius Saturninus	dec	Claud. Viruni
3283	Rexpectinus Respectianus	dec	nat. Noricus
3295	Ulpius Angulatus	dec	natione Noricus
3304	M. Ulpius Maturus	dec	nat. Noricus Cl. Viruno
	Aurelius Messor	comm	municipes
	Aurelius Novellus	comm	
3588	L. Cuspius L.f. Cla. Lautus	dec	Iuvai Norico
32681	Cottionius Rusticus	dec	Claudia Iuvao
32797	(name lost)	dec	nat. Noricus
32805	[---] Maturus	dec	[nat.] Noric.
32813	P. Aelius [---]	dec	[nat.] Nor[---]
32822	T. Aur[elius---]	dec	n[at. No]ricus
32844	Aurelius Hon[oratus]	dec	nat. Nori[cus]

37218	C. Iulius Verus	dec	ex civitate Celeiae
	C. Reginius P[---]	comm	comm[uniceps?][54]
37228	(name lost)	dec	Agun[to]
iii 4845	Ti. Iulius Ingenuus	dec	commemorated at home
AE (1924) 107	P. Aelius P.f.Cla. Finitus	dec	Celeia
	P. Aelius Tutor	comm	brother
	P. Aelius Respectus	dec	municipes
	P. Aelius Tutor	dec	
AE (1993) 165	(name lost)	dec	[n]atione Noricus
BCAR (1941) p. 171 no. 4	Ael[ius ---]	dec	na[tione No]rico civita[te ---]o
Speidel 1994a, 89	[--- Re]stitutus	dec	[nat]ione Norico C[l.] Viruni
Speidel 1994a, 186	(name lost)	dec	[nat. Nor]ic. Cl. Iuavo
Speidel 1994a, 233	Aelius Vi[---]	dec	nat. No[ricus civi]s Ovilavis
Speidel 1994a, 236	(name lost)	dec	[natio]ne N[oricus]
Speidel 1994a, 248	[---]inius	dec	Cl. Iuavo
Speidel 1994a, 252	(name lost)	dec	[nat. N]oricus
Speidel 1994a, 285	[--- Am]battus	dec	natione Noricus Cl. [---]o
Speidel 1994a, 574	[--- Ad]namus	dec	[n. Nori]cus
Speidel 1994a, 594	Aurelius Decoratus	dec	nat. Noricus

Noricum (Civilian)

250=30723	L. Iulius Bassus	dedicator	Noricorum stationarius
2482	Aelia Saturnina	comm	sister
2543	L. Plenatius Valens	comm	brother
3229	Tertius	dec	nat. Noric.
12304	Argentonius Martialis	dec	Ovilavis
33036	M. Ulpius Ursinus	dec	natione Norico Aelio Cetio
	T. Aurelius Primus	comm	brother
iii 5031	C. Maximius C.f. Iunianus	dec	decurioni Viruniensium, commemorated at home
iii 5667	Successianus	dec	commemorated at home

Pannonia (Military)

2488	M. Aurelius M.f. Secundinus	dec	nat. Pannonio
2494a	Iulius Nero	dec	Pannonia Superiore pede Faustiniano

2504	C. Poetilius C.f.Cla. Paullus	dec	Emona
2518	M. Ulpius M.f.Iul. Verus	dec	Emona
2521	Aelius Regulus	dec	n. Pannunia Sup.
2544	Pletorius Primus	dec	ex pr[o]vincia Panno.Inferiore natus Castello Vixillo
2552	Ulpius Tertius	dec	natione Petoviensis
2571	P. Barbius P.f. Pap. Maximianus	dec	Poetovione
2579	C. Iulius C.f. Iulianus	dec	Ulpia Petavione
	C. Iulius Glaus	comm	brother
	C. Iulius T(---)	comm	brother
2644	Sex. Iulius Sex.f.Fla. Augurinus	dec	Siscia
2673	Aurelius Tertius	dec	natione Pann.
2689	C. Valerius C.f.Fla. Spectatus	dec	Siscia
2697	Aurelius Iaseir[55]	dec	natio. Pan.
2710	C. Iulius C.f.Cla. Florus	dec	Savaria
2718	L. Optatius L.f.Iul. Secundinus	dec	Emona
	L. Optatius Crispinus	comm	brother
2733	T. Aurelius A.f.Pap. Clemens	dec	domo Altini
2735	Aurelius Muccus	dec	natus [Panno]nia Infer[iore]
2746	C. Iulius Valerianus	dec	natione Pannunius
2758	Valerius Martinus	dec	natione Pannonius
	Valerius Ianuarinus	dec	civis
2877	C. Marcius Proculus	dec	domo Sa[varia?]
3146	[---]eri[us?]	dec	n. Pan[---]
3156–7	C. Iulius Proculus	dec	natione Pannonius
3180	Aelius Lucius	dec	dom. Fl. Siscia
	(unnamed)	comm	
	(unnamed)	comm	
3183	T. Aelius Rufinus	dec	nat. Pann.
3184	P. Aelius Surio	dec	natione Pannonius
3186	C. Arantius Atiutor	dec	nat. Pannonius
3192	T. Aurelius Armenius	dec	nat. Savarie
3204	Aurelius Firmanus	dec	ex provin. Pann. Imf.
3214	T. Aurelius T.f.Ael. Maximus	dec	Mursa, natione Pannonio
3222	T. Aurelius Saturninus	dec	nat. Pann.
3232	T. Aurelius Victor	dec	nat. Pannonius
3235	T. Aurelius Victorinus	dec	Ael. Mursa
3239	T. Aurelius Vitellianus	dec	nat. Pann.
3241	Candidius Valentinus	dec	nation. Pann. civi Faustiano
3256	T. Flavius Reburrus	dec	n. Pannonius
3257	Flavius Respectus	dec	n. Varcianus
3264	Iulius Bonosus	dec	nat. Pann.
3266	Iulius Proculus	dec	nat. ex Pann. Imf.
3267	Iulius Quartus	dec	nat. Pann.
3270	Iulius Serbandus	dec	nat. Pannonius

3272	C. Iulius Victor	dec	nat. Pann. Cl. Savaria
3276	Q. Marcius Q.f.Cla. Rufus	dec	Savaria
3285	Septimius Adiutor	dec	nat. P[anno]n.
3286[56]	Septimin[---]	dec	[nat.] Pann. Sup[eriore]
3287	L. Septimius	dec	[nati]one Cl. Savaria
3291+3310[57]	M. Ulpius Valens	dec	[Sav]aria
3293	Valerius Iustianus	dec	Panonie Superiore
3297	Ulpius Cocceius	dec	ex Pan. Sup. natus ad Aquas Balizas pago Iovista vic. Coc[---]
3300	Ulpius [I]an[u]arius	dec	natione Pannoniae Superiore C. Savaris vico Voleuci[o?]nis
3307	M. Ulpius Speratus	comm	brother
3308	Ulpius Titus	dec	nat. Boius
3336	M. Ulpius M.f. Iustinus	dec	domo Savaria
	M. Ulpius Ingenuus	comm	brother
3411	Albius Moderatus	dec	nat. Pannonius
3431	Iulius Iulianus	dec	domo Sept. Aquinci ex Pannonia Inferiore
3472	Longinius Victor	dec	natus Pannoniae Superiorae
3489	(name lost)	dec	nat. Pann.
3625	Salvinius Valentinus	dec	natus Carnunto
3913=32807	[M. Ul]pius Genetivus	dec	[e]x Pann[onia]
32671	L. Valerius L.f. Fla. Sabinus	dec	Novid.
	L. Valerius Victorinus	comm	brother
32680	M. Aurelius Dasius	dec	nat. Pann. colon. Siscia
	M. Aurelius Candidus	comm	brother
32783	Aurelius Constans	dec	natus in Pa[n]nonia Inferiore domo Briget[i]one
32793	Aurelius Aurelianus	dec	nat. Pannon.
32798	Aurelius Martinus	dec	nat. Pannon. Super.
32804a	(name lost)	dec	ex provincia Pannonia Superiore civitate Poetabionense
32808	Ulpius Quintianus	dec	Pannonia terra creat
32859	[---]us Tert[---]	dec	[natio]ne Pann[---]
32862	(name lost)	dec	[Pa]nnonio d[omo ---]
37206	[---] Cla. Aquilinus	dec	Savaria
37213	Aurelius Verus	dec	nat. Pannon. pede Sirmese pago Martio vico Budalia
37224	Valerius Paternianus	dec	natione Pannonica pago Traiani
xiv 238	L. Licinius Capito	dec	nationae Panonius

315

AE (1946) 148	Germ. Taurinus	dec	brother
AE (1967) 33	L. Helvius L.f.Cla. Victor	dec	Savaria
AE (1983) 48	Aelius Florus	dec	natione Pann.
AE (1984) 68	M. Lucilius M.f.Qui. Proculus	dec	Siscia
AE (1993) 334	C. Iulius [---]	dec	Cl. Sava[ria]
AE (1993) 335	(name lost)	dec	nati. Pan[nonius] Flav. Sirmi.
AE (1993) 336	(name lost)	dec	[S]avaria, nat. [Pannon]io
AE (1993) 337	(name lost)	dec	Cl. Savaria
BCAR (1941) p. 172 no.79	M. Ulpius Vitalis	dec	domo Aelia Mursa
Ferrua 1951, no. 26	(name lost)	dec	nat. Sava[ria]
Ferrua 1951, no. 81	(name lost)	dec	nat. Pan[---]
Speidel 1994a, 128	[---]inus	dec	[Cla]udia [S]avaria [nat. Pa]nn.
Speidel 1994a, 139[58]	[---] Secundus	dec	[n]at. Pannonius Claudia Savaria
Speidel 1994a, 221	C. Iulius [---]	dec	Cl. Sava[ria]
Speidel 1994a, 261	(name lost)	dec	Savaria
Speidel 1994a, 273	Faonius [---]	dec	[nat.] Pannonio
Speidel 1994a, 281	[---] Dextrianus	dec	[nat.] Pann. Ael. S[ept. Aquin]ci
Speidel 1994a, 306	Aurelius Crispinus	dec	nat. Pan[n.]
Speidel 1994a, 335	L. Aurelius [---]	dec	[nat.] Pannon.
Speidel 1994a, 395	(name lost)	dec	[Sava]ria
Speidel 1994a, 415	(name lost)	dec	[na]t. Sava[ri---]
Speidel 1994a, 425	(name lost)	dec	[nat.] Panno[---]
Speidel 1994a, 529	Ulpius Victorinus	dec	natio[n]e Pannonius
Speidel 1994a, 530	[Nata]linius Natalinianus	dec	natione Pan[noni]us
	Natalinius [---]	comm	brother(?)
Speidel 1994a, 563	Aelius Im[---]	dec	nt. Pann. I[nfer.]
Speidel 1994a, 564	(name lost)	dec	[n]at. Pan[nonio]
Speidel 1994a, 623	Septimius Marcianus	dec	nat. Pann.
Speidel 1994a, 624	M. Ulpius Criscentinus	dec	nat.Pann.Inferior. nat.[---]

Pannonia (Civilian)

2488	Aelia Valentina	comm	sister
2501	Aurelia Crescentina	dec	civi Pannoniae
2673	Aurelius Quintus	comm	brother
	Aurelia [---]a	comm	sister
2708	Aurelia Iusta	dec	na. Pann.
3183	Titius Marcellus	comm	brother
3239	T. Aurelius Verus	comm	brother
3307	Ulpius Ianuarius	dec	nat. Pannon.
3411	Flavia Ursa	comm	sister

3454[59]	Aurelia Gorsilla	dec	natione A[q]ui(n)ce(n)sis
13336	Aurelia Iustina	dec	nat. Pannonia
15011	Ti. Claudius E[---]	comm	natione Panon[---]
26478[60]	P. Seberin(us) [---]	dec?	Pann.
32804a	Longinius Paternianus	comm	brother
32808	(name uncertain)[61]	comm	cousin
32755[62]	(name lost)	dec	prata per Inlyrici litora Dannuvii
34408	Q. Annius Q.f. [---]cianus	dec	Iul. Emona
36351	Silvania Cresce[ntina]	dec	nata [Panno]nia Su[pe]r[i]ore ter[ritorio] Arabo[n]e
37271	Iulia Carnuntilla	dec	ex pr. P. Super.
AE (1946) 148	Germ. Super	comm	nat. Savar.
Speidel 1994a, 623	Septimius Romulus	dec	brother
	Aurelius Dubitatus	comm	brother
Bertolino 1997, 124	(name lost)	dec	natio. Pan[---]

Pannonia (Christian)

1480[63]	Mandronius	dec	gens Carnuntum
1619+22460[64]	Flavius Ursicinus	dec	cives Pannonius
3327=20722	Aurelia Marciana	dec	cives Pannonia
13109	Simplicius	dec	Bertolino 1997, 119
13155	Flavia Valeria	comm	mother
	Flavia Vi(v)entia	dec	ex provincia Pannonia
13355	Maximilla	dec	civis Pannonia
	Nunita	dec	mother
19444	Valerius Taurus	dec	natio. natu. Panonius
25130	Euf[---]	dec	Pann[onicus civis] Vindobo[nensis]

Raetia (Military)

3190	T. Aurelius Africanus	dec	nat. Raetus
3208	T. Aurelius Iucundus	dec	nat. Raetus
3210	T. Aurelius M[---]	dec	[nat.] Rae[tus]
3213	Aurelius Masucius	dec	nat. Raet.
3218	T. Aurelius Pacatinus	dec	nat. Raetus
	T. Aurelius Victorinus	dec	brother
3224	T. Aurelius Speratus	dec	natione Raeto
3228	T. Aurelius Tertius	dec	nat. Rae[to]
3233	T. Aurelius Victor	comm	brother
3273	Iustus Ilissa	dec	n. Raetus
3282	Q. Putentinus	dec	na. Ret.
3353	C. Iulius Vettius	dec	Aug. Vindelicum
3430	Iulius Concessus	dec	natione Retus
3576	T. Aurelius Secund(us?)	dec	nat. Raito

32473	Claudius Quintilianus	dec	nat. Raetus
32804	Iulius Saturninus	dec	n. Ret.
32840	(name lost)	dec	Ael. Aug.
32845[65]	T. Aurelius Impetr[atus?]	dec	n[at. Ra]etus
32848	(name lost)	dec	[nat.] Retus
33025	Sabinius Sabinianus	dec	nation. Raet.
Ferrua 1951, p. 115 no. 80	(name lost)	dec	n. Rae.
Speidel 1994a, 88	(name lost)	dec	[Ae]l. Aug., [n]ation. [Raeto]
Speidel 1994a, 164	C. Ann[---]lianus	dec	[Aelia] Augusta
Speidel 1994a, 234	T. Aurelius Em[---]	dec	nat. Raet[---]
Speidel 1994a, 267	(name lost)	dec	natione [Raetu]s Aelia Au[gusta]
Speidel 1994a, 565	(name lost)	dec	n. Reto
Speidel 1994a, 745	C. Iulius Secl[aris]	dec	[nat.] Retus

Raetia (Civilian)

3233	T. Lavinius	dec	nat. Ra[eto]
32796	Mercator	dec	nat. Raeto

Raetia (Christian)

1640	Heraclius	dec	civis Secundus Retus

Sicily (Civilian)

6514	Rufio	dec	Siculi
IGUR 456	L. Gellius Peticianus	dec	Τυνδαρείτου
	Synkamon	comm	brother
IGUR 794	Minucia	dec	Σικελή[66]
IGUR 823	Xenon	dec	Τυνδαρῖτα

Sicily (Christian and Jewish)

2585	Symphorus	dec	Σικε. Πανορμίτης
4209	Helpis	dec	Siculae regionis
	(unnamed)	comm	husband[67]
13858	(name lost)	dec	ἐκ Σικελίης
22815	Callistus	dec	ἀπὸ τῆς Σικελίας
23409	[---]us	dec	Siciliae
27228	Mari(u?)s	dec	Σικελός
ILCV 725	(name lost)	dec	[Sy]racusis
JIWE ii 515	Amachius	comm?	Κατανέου

Syria and Palestine (Military)

2627	M. Antonius M.f. Ianuarius	dec	domo Laudicia ex Suria
2910	A. Curius A.f.Sab. Rufus	dec	domo Beryt.
3114	Iulius Apollinaris	dec	nat. Surus

3138	Valerius Maximus	dec	nat. Syro
3151	M. Aurelius Romanus	dec	n. Sur.
	M. Aurelius Romanus [sic]	comm	brother
3197	T. Aurelius Claudianus	dec	nat. Surus
3251	Domitius Herenianus	comm	brother
3644	C. Vettius C.f.Col. Niger	dec	domo Antiochia Syria
32776	C. Anthestius Niger	dec	natio. Surus
32795	T. Aurelius Gemellinus	dec	na. Surus
33009	T. Aurelius Maximus	dec	nat. Syrus
33039	(name lost)	dec	n. Sur[---]
37254	(name lost)	dec	nat. Syru[s]
IGUR 590	Antoninus	comm	brother
Ferrua 1939, p. 145 no. 4	(name lost)	dec	from Berytus
Ferrua 1951, p. 112 no. 54	[------]sianus	dec	natio. Surus
Speidel 1994a, 206	T. Aurelius Ariscus	dec	nat. Syrus c[o]l. Caesarea
Speidel 1994a,215	T. Aurelius Augu[---]	dec	[nat.] Syrus
Speidel 1994a, 265	(name lost)	dec	[nat.] Arabus Filadelf[ia]
Speidel 1994a, 424	[--- B]enignus	dec	n[at. Sy]rus Damas[c---]
Speidel 1994a, 524	Marius Alexander	dec	n. Sur.

Syria and Palestine (Civilian)

50 = IGUR 117	Heliodorus	dedicator	Palmyrenus
700	C. Ducenius C.l. Phoebus	dedicator	natus in Suria Nisibyn.
3251	Domitius Lucius	dec	nation. Surus
	Domitius Italus	comm	brother
4699	Glapyra	dec	Syra
6338	Prima	dec	Sura
6340	Auge	dec	Sura
6431	Dapnis	dec	Sura
8883	M. Ulpius Castoras	comm	librarius Arabicus
13021	T. Aur. Apollinaris	dec	nat S[y]rus Apamenus
13055	Aurelius Cl(audius?) Aurelius Antipater	builders	natio. Syri
16486	Manneia Ɔ.l. Epistolium	dec	Surisca
17117	Egnatia Ɔ.l. Fortunata	dec	Surisca
17318	Eudem[---]	dec	natione Surus
17356	Eunus	dec	Antioc.
19134	Habibi	dec	Palmurenus
	(name not given)	comm	brother

24898	Postumus L.l. Annaeus	dec	Syrus
26883	Strato Augg.l.	dec	natione Syru Antiocense
27868	Tyche	dec	Phoenicae
32827	Bassus	dec	nationem Surus
33009[68]	T. Ingenus Acceptus	comm	brother
	[---] Iulianus	comm	brother
34196	Abgarus	comm	Petraeus; uses Nabataean
	Abdareta	dec	cognatus
34672	Bathyllus	dec	Syro
35556a	C. Iulio regis Samsicerami l. Glacus	dec	freedman of king of Emesa
38719	Patulcia Truphera	dec	Surae
IGUR 304	Aelius Philocalus	dec	τὸ γένος Τυρίῳ
IGUR 306	Cocceius Iulianus Synesius	comm	Ἀντιοχεὺς τῶν πρὸς Δάφνην
IGUR 590	Iamour	dec	Σύρος Ἀσκαλωνείτης Παλαιστείνη
IGUR 749	L. Lon. Protogenes	dec	Ἀντιοχεὺ‹ς› ‹ἀπὸ› Δάφνης
IGUR 811	Neike ἡ καί Marcellina	dec	Ἀπάμισσα
IGUR 1027	T. Flavius Cassianus	dec	Ἀντιοχῖ τῶν πρὸς Δάφνην
	(name not given)	comm	sibling
IGUR 1243	Callistus	dec	γένος Συρίηθεν
IGUR 1287	Olympia	dec	Ἕλλην μὲν τὸ γένος, πατρὶς δέ μοι ἦτον Ἀπάμεα
	(name not given)	comm	brother
IGUR 1317	Proclus	comm	Συρίης ἀπὸ γαίης
IGUR 1323	Salome	dec	see p. 193
	(name not given)	comm	
IGUR 1334	Soemus	dec	see p. 236
IGUR 1384	(name lost)	dec	ἐξ Συρίης, πόλεω[ς ---]
IG xiv 934	Maros	dec	Σελευκεὺς Πιερίας
SEG xxx 1801	Diodorus	dec	ἀπὸ Συριακῆς Δεκα- πόλεως Γαδάρου
Bevilacqua 1978	(name lost)	uncertain	Σύρος Ἀντιοχεύς
Teixidor 1979, p. 47	Ti. Claudius Felix	dedicator	see p. 243

Syria and Palestine (Christian and Jewish)

330=8721	Megetius	dec	cibes Eliopolit[an]us
731	[---]na	dec	Emisina
868	Emidabous	dec	κώμης Ἀδάνων
1860	Aurelius Agathias	dec	Σύρος
1861	Aurelius Malchus	dec	ἀπὸ κώ(μης) Ἀβνωνορ [τ]ῆς Φυνίκης

1870	Zaoras	dec	κώμ(ης) Καπροκιλλεων
2151	Asclepius	dec	Σιδόνιος τῆ Φυνικῆς
2634	Leonteis	dec	Θρησπολείτης
2636	Malchus	dec	Θελσεη[νός]
2896	Heliodorus	dec	Ἀντιοχεύς
4554	Bassus	dec	civis Arabus[69]
4891	(name lost)	dec	ἀπὸ κώμης Λατ[---] ὅρων Ἀπαμέων
5175	Sosanna	dec	de provincia Syriae ex vico Ravv[...]no
5659[70]	Aurelius Ia[---]s	dec	Κοίλης Συρίας
5688[71]	Heortasius	dec	Ἀνατο‹λι›κ[ός]
6417[72]	(name lost)	dec	ἀπὸ κώμης Βερ‹σ›αβέ
7243	Ginadis	dec	Σύρος Ἐμισηνός
7275a[73]	(name lost)	dec	Κανώθ[ων]
8048[74]	Hermes	dec	κώμ‹η›ης Καπρανανέων
8395[75]	Zenodorus	dec	Σααρηνός
8404[76]	(name lost)	dec	ἀπὸ κ[ώμης ---]
	(name lost)	dec	
9319[77]	Paulus	dec	ἀπὰ κ(ώ)μ(ης) Ὀρ(ά)γων χώρας Ἀπαμ(έων)
12188	Vitalius	dec	Ἀντιοχεύς
12198	Maris	dec	Νισιβανός
12200[78]	Obres	dec	Φενησία
12400	Constantius	dec	ἀπὸ Θίλσης τῆς Φυνίκης
12404a[79]	Stercorius	dec	[Β?]αμβυ[κηνός?]
12516[80]	Heliodorus	dec	Ἐμεσηνόν
12866c	(name lost)	dec	Ῥαφι[ώτης]
13150	Eusebius	dec	Antiocenos
13845	(name lost)	dec?	[Ἀ]ντιοχεί[α], Σύρα
13849	Euetheia	dec	Ἀντιοχ[είας]
17373	Silvanus	dec	Σύρου ἀπὸ πόλεως Ζεῦγμα
	Theodotus	comm	brother
	Merou	comm	brother
19790	Eusebius	dec	κώμης Ἄρρων
22909a	(name lost)	dec	χώρας Ἀντιο[---]
AE (1982) 74	Diogenes	dec	κώμης Μαγαρατων κατωτέρας τῆς Ἀπαμέων παροικίας
JIWE ii 60	Ionios ὁ καί Akone	dec	Σεφωρηνός
JIWE ii 112	Macedonius	dec	Κεσαρεὺς τῆς Παλεστίνης
JIWE ii 113	Symmachus	dec	Τριπολίτης[81]
JIWE ii 459	Gelasius	comm	Κεσαρέως
JIWE ii 561	Alypius	comm	Τιβερεύς
JIWE ii 568	Alexander	comm	Ἄρκ[ης Λιβ]άνου

Thrace (Military)

2461	M. Aurelius Mucianus	dec	nat. Thrax
2486	Aurelius Iobinus	dec	nat. Bessus

2566	Aurelius Mucianus	dec	natus Tremontiae
2570	Aurelius Vitus	dec	natione Trax domu Sergica Asclepias
2601	Aurelius Bitus	dec	natione Trax cives Filopopulitanus
	Valerius Aulusanus	comm	brother
2605	Aurelius Victorinus	dec	natione Dacisca regione Serdic<a>
	Valerius Augustus	comm	brother
2616	[---] Dolens	dec	natus Pautaliae
	[---] Sebastianus	comm	cousin
2638[82]	Aurelius Zinama	dec	Serdicensis (?)
2671	Aurelius Pyrrhus	dec	nat. Pautalia
2699	Aurelius Victor	dec	natione Besus
2732	Aurelius Buris	dec	cf. IGUR 134 (below, p. 324)
	Aurelius Diszairai	comm	convicani
	Aurelius Asclepiades	comm	
2742	Diogenes Gaius	dec	nat. Trax civitate Serdica
	Aurelius Erodes	comm	brother
2772+ 32660[83]	Aurelius Mestrius	dec	nat. vico Bitalcost[---] reg. Pautaliense[---]
	Aurelius Vitupaus	comm	brother
2785	Valerius Sarmatius	dec	civis Filopopuletanus
2954	Firminius Valens	dec	natus in prov.Trhacia civit. Philippopol.
3097	C. Antistius [Secun]dus	dec	n. Bess[us]
3103	Caecilius Celer	dec	natio. Bessus
3107	Ti. Claudius Urbanus	dec	n. Bessus
3128	P. Popilius Maximus	dec	n. Bessus
3139=7466	C. Valerius Modestus	dec	n. Bes.
3141	M. Valerius Proculus	dec	nat. Bessus
3142	Velonius Masclus	dec	nat. Bessus
3145	M. Ulpius Maximus	dec	nat. Bess.
3163	Q. Arruntius Aquila	dec	nat. Bessus
3176	P. Aelius Avitus	dec	Traianopoli, natione Thrax
3177	P. Aelius Bassus	dec	nat. Bessus Claudia Apris
	T. Flavius Marcellinus	comm	municipes
	Aurelius Quintus	comm	
3195	M. Aurelius Bithus	dec	nat. Thrax
	M. Aurelius Surus	comm	brother
3196	Aurelius Brinursius	dec	nat. Trax civis Bero<e>ensis
3201	Aurelius Diso	dec	n. Thrax
3202	Aurelius Dizala	dec	nat. [Thrax?][84]
3205	T. Aurelius Gaius[85]	dec	Fl. Scupis nat. Bessus
3216	Aurelius Mucianus	dec	domo Thracia
	Iulius Valens	comm	municeps
3217	M. Aurelius Optatus	dec	nati. Tra.
3250	[---] M.f. Deciminus	dec	[nat.Thr]ax

3303	M. Ulpius Longinus	dec	natione Bessus
3314	(name lost)	dec	natus Ulpia Serdicae
3447	P. Aelius Severus	dec	nat. Bessus
32714	(name lost)	dec	[S]erdic.
32768 = xiv 236	M. Flavius Valens	dec	natio. Bessus
32836	(name lost)	dec	[Th]raci
32867a	(name lost)	dec	[nat.] Trax
33040[86]	(name lost)	dec	[Heraclea] Senti[ca], [na]t. Bessus
37255	Ulpius Valentinus	dec	nati. B(essus)
xiv 234	L. Carisius Val[ens]	dec	nat. Vessus
xiv 240	C. Valerius Festus	dec	Bessus
AE (1931) 89	Ti. Claudius Dolens	dec	nat. Bes.
AE (1980) 141	Flavius Mucianus	dec	dom. Nicopoli
AE (1981) 94	T. Aurelius Secundus	dec	nat. Thrac[---] Ulpia Tonzo
NS (1906) p. 209 no. 6	(name lost)	dec	Bess[us]
Ferrua 1943–4, no. 93	Sisitianus Clemens	dec	nat. Vessus
Ferrua 1951, no. 22	(name lost)	dec	[nat.] Trax
Ferrua 1951, no. 109	(name lost)	dec	n. Bes[---]
Speidel 1994a, 209	P. Aelius Bellicus	dec	[nat.] Bess[us] civitas U[---]
Speidel 1994a, 216	T. A[urelius ---]	dec	[nati]on. Bessu[s]
Speidel 1994a, 243	[---] Ingenuus	dec	[natio]ne Bes[sus]
Speidel 1994a, 253	[---] Veratius	dec	[nat. B]essu[s]
Speidel 1994a, 545	[---] Apronius	dec	[nat.] Bes.
Speidel 1994a, 546	(name lost)	dec	[nat.] Bes.
Speidel 1994a, 567	Iulius Lucius	dec	n. Tr.
Speidel 1994a, 608	Aurelius Daicosis	dec	nat. Thrax
	Aurelius Daicon	comm	brother

Thrace (Civilian)

2570	Aurelius Lucius	comm	brother
2734	Aurelia Marcia	dec	n[a]tione Trax civitate Promesiana
	Aurelia Zenodora	comm	sister
2785	Sudicentius	comm	brother
2954	Tataza	comm	mother
	Tataza Mucapora	comm	wife[87]
3163	C. Cassius Censorinus	comm	brother
3303	L. Sentius Fortis	comm	father
6519	Secunda	dec	Thraecida
9709	T. Flavius Genethlius	builder	natione Bess.
9719	Crescens	dec	natione Bessus
10187	Thelyphus	dec	natione Traex
18066	Flavius Felix	dec	na[tio]ne Trhax
	[Flavius E]xupergius Fidus	comm	brother

20718	Iulia Tyndaris	builder	freedwoman of K. Rhoemetalces
26608	Sitalces	dec	opses Thracum
	Iulia Phyllis	dec	sister
30584	[---]thus	dec	[na]t. Thrax
32714	[---]ruillio	comm	brother
	Se[---]	comm	brother
33005	Aurelius [---]	dec	nat. T[hrax]
34619	T. Aurelius Bithus	dec	Thrax
34635	(name lost)	dec	nacione Thracia
IGUR 134	Aurelius Puris	dedicator	ἐκ δὲ χωρίης Τήσεος
AE (1980) 141	Iulius Valerianus	comm	cousin
AE (1993) 332	(name lost)	dec	cives Bes[sus regione ---]ese vico Trifon.
NS (1922) p. 417 no. 51	Ti. Iulius Diogenes Remothalcianus	builder	Fabre and Roddaz 1982, 87

Thrace (Christian)

14201	(name lost)	dec	Serdica
16873	Paula	dec	ἀπ[ὸ] Νεικοπόλ[εως]
23627	Valerius Dalat[ralis]	dec	[e pro]vincia Tracia vicu[---]

Unknown (Military)

2740	Ti. Claudius Ti.f. Rufus	dec	Apsoles
2741	C. Commagius Secundinus	dec	commemorated by municeps
2992b	T. Aurelius Salvianus	dec	natio. MINOP[---]
3239a	M. Aurelius [---]	dec	domu I [---]

Unknown (Civilian)

2741	(name not given)	comm	municeps
IGUR 962	Artemidorus	dec	ἐπὶ ξένης
	Socrates	comm	brother
	Dionysis	comm	brother
IGUR 1257	Lacon	dec	πατρὶς δὲ M[---]
IGUR 1313	(name lost)	dec	[ἐ]πὶ ξείνης
SEG xiv 615	Demetrius	dec	see p. 168
	(name not given)	comm	brother

Unknown (Christian)

1491	Aestonia	dec	perecrina
2274	Honoratus	dec	peregrini
13226	Victor	dec	qu\<i> \<ma>ria treiecit
MGR 18 (1994) pp. 177–285 no. 87	Asclepiod[---]	dec	in peregre [obitus/a]

Notes

[1] The criteria for inclusion here are set out at pp. 6–7.

[2] For the 'military' and 'civilian' categories, references are to CIL vi if there is simply an Arabic numeral, or to another volume of CIL if there is a Roman and then an Arabic numeral. For the 'Christian/Jewish' category, references are to ICUR if there is simply a numeral. I have tried to give the most accessible reference rather than the original publication.

[3] Names are given in the nominative case and, as far as possible, in standardized spelling.

[4] 'comm' = commemorator, 'dec' = deceased, 'builder' = builder of tomb, 'graff' = graffiti.

[5] Where the reason for inclusion is quoted directly from the inscription, the exact form and spelling used in the inscription is given here (with restoration or expansion where necessary). I have not used 'sic' to indicate non-standard spellings and grammar, because these are too common.

[6] Ricci (1994a, no. A1) gives a family tree.

[7] Two charioteers who appear to have been working at Rome.

[8] Following Ricci 1997b.

[9] I have assumed that there is a connection with the city in Media called Gauna (RE vii 876).

[10] Ricci (1993b, T4) treats these people as Thracian.

[11] This could be in Asia or Greece.

[12] See Moretti, ad loc.

[13] There is a different interpretation in SEG xliv 822.

[14] The man is described as a banker in the Roman Forum.

[15] Avraméa 1995, 307.

[16] Moretti, ad loc., takes this as an alternative form of 'Nicomedian'.

[17] Restoration by Avraméa 1995, 299.

[18] This is almost certainly military.

[19] The man in the inscription could be Athenaeus the Cilician or Cilix the Athenian; I have assumed the former.

[20] Published independently by Speidel 1994c, 584.

[21] Ricci 1993b, De13, following Vulpe 1925, 143.

[22] Corrected by Ferrua 1951, 135.

[23] Printed as 3109 in CIL.

[24] See p. 118.

[25] Interpretation from Ricci 1993a, A5.

[26] This inscription is very fragmentary; Moretti restores ['Αντινόη πατρίς] in l.1 and 'Αντιν[όη] in l.4; the latter seems more likely to be the beginning of a personal name. However, since the deceased was an ambassador from *somewhere*, Moretti has been followed here.

[27] As interpretated by Avraméa 1995, 291.

[28] Mateescu (1923, 193) takes *Nysius* as a mistake for *Mysius*, and Speidel (1994c, 435) understands it as *Moesius*. It is assumed here to be the ethnic for Nysa.

[29] According to RE xxiii.2 2107–8, the Pylaemenes who was the previous owner was the son of King Amyntas of Galatia.

[30] Interpretation from Avraméa 1995, 319.

[31] For the assumption that this and some other unknown villages are Galatian, see p. 232.

[32] Interpretation from Feissel 1982a, 371.

[33] Interpretation from Feissel 1982a, 373–4.

[34] Feissel 1982a, 375–7.

[35] Interpretation from Feissel 1982a, 373–4.

[36] Interpretation from Felle 1997, 331, 400.

[37] 25249 is probably the same inscription.

[38] Following Ricci 1992a, A44, *contra* Nuzzo 1997.

[39] CIL restores *[nat. Noviom]agi*.

[40] Following Ricci 1993c, B60.

[41] Restoration from Dobó 1975, 585.

[42] Restoration from Granino Cecere 1994b.

[43] This is from a gravestone now at Fiesole but most likely to originate from Rome.

[44] Following Ricci 1993c, A9.

[45] Lega and Felle 1997.

[46] Tainaron in Laconia according to Nuzzo 1997.

[47] Restoration by Ricci 1992b, b19.

[48] Includes CIL vi 3654.

[49] Corrected in AE (1994) 193.

[50] It is unclear if these are two separate people or one person with a double name.

[51] Interpretation from Ricci 1994a.

[52] I have assumed this to be Caesarea in Mauretania as the man in question is a charioteer, and therefore more likely to have been of North African than Eastern origin.

[53] Corrected by Ferrua 1951, 135.

[54] Restoration by Ricci 1993b, N41.

[55] Name interpreted by Vulpe 1925, 146.

[56] Corrected by Ferrua 1951, 135.

[57] Joined by Speidel 1994c, 346.

[58] CIL vi 32830, 32835, 32837d.

[59] Interpretation from Ricci 1993b, P3.

[60] Interpretation from Ricci 1993b, P19.

[61] One of the commemorators, *Valerius Antonius et Aurelius Victorinus*, is the deceased's cousin, but it is not stated which one.

[62] Interpretation from Ricci 1993b, P20.

[63] Different interpretation by di Stefano Manzella 1997a.

[64] Lega and Orlandi 1997.

[65] Corrected by Speidel 1994c, 133.

[66] See p. 195.

[67] Who travelled with her.

[68] AE (1992) 92.109.

[69] The interpretation of the text is uncertain. It reads: *Bassus bixit annus XX[---] | civis Arabus vota Marina vixit [---]*

[70] Feissel 1982a, no. II.3.

[71] Feissel 1982a, no. I; the 'ethnic' could be from anywhere in the East.

[72] Avraméa 1995, 286.

[73] Nuzzo 1997, 706.
[74] Feissel 1982a, 361.
[75] Feissel 1982b, 338–9.
[76] Nuzzo 1997, 706.
[77] Feissel 1982b, 330–1.
[78] Feissel 1982a, 358.
[79] Nuzzo 1997, 706.
[80] Feissel 1982a, 267–9.
[81] It is uncertain which Tripolis is meant.
[82] Ricci 1993b, 206 n. 14.
[83] Joined by Ricci 1993b, T26.
[84] Restoration from Mateescu 1923, 192.
[85] Although commemorated by his brother, someone else acted as *curator*, so
I have assumed that the brother was not present at Rome.
[86] Mateescu 1923, 203.
[87] She has been included because of her Thracian name.

GLOSSARY

Advocatus fisci	A barrister working for the state.
Annona	Rome's corn supply and the administration dealing with it.
Apparitor	The servant of an official.
Assessor	A judge's assistant.
Beneficiarius	A soldier seconded to special duties.
Civis Romanus/a	Someone with the legal status of a Roman citizen.
Classiarius	A soldier serving in the Roman fleet.
Cognomen	The final part of a Roman name, e.g. M. Tullius *Cicero*, Vipsania *Agrippina*.
Collegium	A society or association, usually with a nominal religious function.
Cursus publicus	The state-run system for delivering official correspondence.
Dextrarum iunctio	The joining of right hands symbolizing marriage.
Di Manes	The spirits of the dead, regularly invoked in second–third century AD epitaphs.
Domesticus	Probably a personal assistant to an officer of state such as the urban prefect, but could also be an army officer.
Duo/tria nomina	The name of a Roman citizen, usually with three parts for a man (*M. Tullius Cicero*), two for a woman (*Vipsania Agrippina*).
Equites	People of the rank immediately below that of the senatorial class, normally having to meet a property qualification of HS 400,000.
Equites singulares	The cavalry, normally recruited outside Italy, who formed the imperial bodyguard (see p. 21).
Evocatus	A semi-retired soldier, liable to be called up in an emergency.
Familia	A household, including free members and slaves.
Filiusfamilias	A male whose father was still alive and who was therefore legally under his father's control.
Frumentarius	A soldier whose duties included security and surveillance.
Grammaticus	A teacher of grammar.
Hospitium	The moral right to claim hospitality or the duty to give it.
Iudices quinque decuriarum	Men selected for jury service, who had to meet a property qualification. Only those designated *inter selectos* served at Rome.

Latus clavus	The broad stripe on a toga which denoted someone entitled to seek office of senatorial status.
Loculus	A burial slot in a catacomb.
Magister officiorum	The official in charge of the central bureaucracy from the fourth century.
Mercator	A merchant.
Munera	The financial responsibilities undertaken by city magistrates or other wealthy citizens.
Navicularius	A shipowner.
Negotiator/negotians	A dealer or trader.
Nomen (gentilicium)	The inherited part of a Roman name, e.g. M. *Tullius* Cicero, *Vipsania* Agrippina.
Notarius	A civil servant, originally with secretarial functions but also used for diplomatic and under-cover activity.
Officina	A workshop.
Patria	Someone's home city or country.
Peregrinus/a	Someone who was of free status but not a Roman citizen.
Praenomen	The first part of a Roman man's full name, e.g. *Marcus* Tullius Cicero.
Praeses	A provincial governor.
Praetorian Guard	The main body of troops stationed at Rome to guard the emperor and keep order (see p. 20).
Provocator	A type of gladiator.
Quinquennalis	The leading magistrate in a *collegium* or a city, appointed once in five years.
Sacerdos augustalis	A priest of the imperial cult.
Signum	An additional name (the word is usually found in the ablative case, *signo*).
Stator	An official servant of a provincial governor or general.
Structor	A building worker.
Urbanicianus	A member of the Urban Cohorts, the main law-enforcing body in Rome.
Verna	A home-bred slave.
Viator	A magistrate's attendant and enforcement officer.
Vicarius urbis	A deputy to the Urban Prefect.
Vigiles	The night-watch of Rome, mainly responsible for detecting and fighting fires.
Vir clarissimus	A man of senatorial status.

ABBREVIATIONS

AE	Année Epigraphique
b.	Babylonian Talmud
BCAR	Bullettino della Commissione Archeologica Comunale di Roma
BGU	Aegyptische Urkunden aus den Staatlichen Museen zu Berlin, Griechische Urkunden
CCSL	Corpus Christianorum, Series Latina
CIG	Corpus Inscriptionum Graecarum
CIL	Corpus Inscriptionum Latinarum
CIS	Corpus Inscriptionum Semiticarum
CSEL	Corpus Scriptorum Ecclesiasticorum Latinorum
EE	Ephemeris Epigraphica
ICUR	Inscriptiones Christianae Urbis Romae
IG	Inscriptiones Graecae
IGCVO	Inscriptiones Graecae Christianae Veteris Occidentis
IGR	Inscriptiones Graecae ad Res Romanas Pertinentes
IGUR	Inscriptiones Graecae Urbis Romae
IK	Inschriften griechischer Stadte aus Kleinasien
ILCV	Inscriptiones Latinae Christianae Veteres
ILS	Inscriptiones Latinae Selectae
IMS	Inscriptiones Moesiae Superioris
JE	Jewish Encyclopaedia
JIWE	Jewish Inscriptions of Western Europe
m.	Mishnah
MAMA	Monumenta Asiae Minoris Antiqua
MGH	Monumenta Germaniae Historica
NDIEC	New Documents Illustrating Early Christianity
NS	Notizie degli Scavi
PG	Patrologia Graeca
PIR	Prosopographia Imperii Romani
PL	Patrologia Latina
PLRE	Prosopography of the Later Roman Empire
RE	Real-Encyclopadie der classischen Altertumswissenschaft
RIT	Die römischen Inschriften von Tarraco
SB	Sammelbuch griechischer Urkunden aus Aegypten
SEG	Supplementum Epigraphicum Graecum
SHA	Scriptores Historiae Augustae
SIG	Sylloge Inscriptionum Graecarum
TAM	Tituli Asiae Minoris
t.	Tosefta
y.	Jerusalem Talmud

Other abbreviations which are not self-explanatory follow the *Année Philologique* system.

BIBLIOGRAPHY

Affortunati, M.
    1994   'Ambasciatori germanici in Italia dal II sec. a.C. al II sec. d.C.', in
                B. and P. Scardigli (eds.) *Germani in Italia*, Rome, 105–15.

Ahmed, I.
    1997   'Exit, voice and citizenship', in T. Hammar, G. Brochmann,
                K. Tamas and T. Faist (eds.) *International Migration, Immobility and*
                Development. Multidisciplinary perspectives, Oxford/New York, 159–85.

Alcock, S.
    1993   *Graecia Capta*, Cambridge.

André, J.M. and Baslez, M.F.
    1993   *Voyager dans l'Antiquité*, Paris.

Audin, A.
    1960   'Inhumation et incinération', *Latomus* 19, 312–22, 518–32.

Avraméa, A.
    1995   'Mort loin de la patrie. L'apport des inscriptions paléochrétiennes',
                in G. Cavallo and C. Mango (eds.) *Epigrafia medievale Greca e Latina.*
                Ideologia e funzione. Atti del seminario di Erice (12–18 sett. 1991),
                Spoleto, 1–65.

Bacher, W.
    1896   'Rome dans le Talmud et le Midrasch', *REJ* 33, 187–96.

Bagnall, R.S. and Frier, B.W.
    1994   *The Demography of Roman Egypt*, Cambridge.

Bakker, J.T. et al.
    1999   *Ostia, Harbour of Ancient Rome*, http://www.ncl.ac.uk/ostia/

Balsdon, J.P.V.D.
    1979   *Romans and Aliens*, London.

Barclay, J.M.C.
    1996   *Jews in the Mediterranean Diaspora from Alexander to Trajan*, Edinburgh.

Bardy, G.
    1948   *La question des langues dans l'église ancienne*, Paris.
    1949   'Pèlerinages à Rome vers la fin du IVe siècle', *AB* 67, 224–35.

Barnard, L.W.
    1967   *Justin Martyr: His life and thought*, London.

Barnes, T.D.
    1967   'The family and career of Septimius Severus', *Historia* 16, 87–107.

Barnish, S.J.B.
    1987   'Pigs, plebeians and *potentes*: Rome's economic hinterland *c.* 350–
                600 AD', *PBSR* 55, n.s. 42, 157–85.

Beard, M., North, J. and Price, S.
    1998   *Religions of Rome*, 2 vols., Cambridge.

Bellelli, G.M.
1996 'Les sanctuaires de *Iuppiter Dolichenus* à Rome', in G.M. Bellelli and U. Bianchi (eds.) *Orientalia Sacra Urbis Romae. Dolichena et Heliopolitana*, Rome, 307–30.

Beloch, J.
1886 *Die Bevölkerung der griechisch-römischen Welt*, Leipzig. Repr. New York, 1979.

Bertolino, A.
1997 ' "Pannonia terra creat, tumulat Italia tellus". Presenze pannoniche nell'area di S. Sebastiano', *RivAC* 73, 115–27.

Bevilacqua, G.
1978 'Due trapeziti in un'iscrizione di Tivoli', *ArchClass* 30, 252–4.

Bianchi, U.
1982 'Per la storia dei culti nel sito del "santuario siriaco" sul Gianicolo', in M. Mele and C.M. Carpano (eds.) *L'area del «santuario siriaco del Gianicolo». Problemi archeologici e storico-religiosi*, Rome, 89–105.
1996 '*I.O.M. et Deo Paterno Comageno*', in G.M. Bellelli and U. Bianchi (eds.) *Orientalia Sacra Urbis Romae. Dolichena et Heliopolitana*, Rome, 601–6.

Bjerén, G.
1997 'Gender and reproduction', in T. Hammar, G. Brochmann, K. Tamas and T. Faist (eds.) *International Migration, Immobility and Development. Multidisciplinary perspectives*, Oxford/New York, 219–46.

Blackman, E.D.
1948 *Marcion and his Influence*, London.

Bokser, B.M.
1990 'Todos and rabbinic authority in Rome', in J. Neusner et al. (eds.) *New Perspectives on Ancient Judaism I: Religion, literature and society in ancient Israel, formative Christianity and Judaism*, Brown Judaic Studies 206, Atlanta, 117–30.

Bollmann, B.
1997 'La distribuzione delle *scholae* delle corporazioni a Roma', in *La Rome impériale. Démographie et logistique. Actes de la table ronde (Rome, 25 mars 1994)*, CEFR 230, Rome, 209–25.

Bonner, S.F.
1977 *Education in Ancient Rome*, London.

Botermann, H.
1996 *Das Judenedikt des Kaisers Claudius*, Hermes Einzelschriften 71, Stuttgart.

Bowersock, G.W.
1969 *Greek Sophists in the Roman Empire*, Oxford.

Boyancé, P.
1956 'La connaissance du grec à Rome', *REL* 34, 111–31.

Boyle, P, Halfacree K. and Robinson V.
1998 *Exploring Contemporary Migration*, Harlow.

Bradley, K.R.
1994 *Slavery and Society at Rome*, Cambridge.

Brändle, R. and Stegemann, E.W.

1998　'The formation of the first "Christian congregations" in Rome in the context of the Jewish congregations', in K.P. Donfried and P. Richardson (eds.) *Judaism and Christianity in first-century Rome*, Grand Rapids, 117–27.

Brown, P.

1982　'Dalla "plebs romana" alla "plebs Dei": aspetti della cristianizzazione di Roma', in P. Brown, L. Cracco Ruggini and M. Mazza, *Governanti e intellettuali, popolo di Roma e popolo di Dio (I–VI secolo)*, Passatopresente 2, Turin, 123–45.

Brunt, P.

1980　'Free labour and public works at Rome', *JRS* 70, 81–100.

Caldelli, M.L.

1992　'*Curia athletarum, iera xystike synodos* e organizzazione delle terme a Roma', *ZPE* 93, 75–87.

1993　*L'agon Capitolinus*, Studi pubblicati dall'Istituto Italiano per la Storia Antica 54, Rome.

Calzini Gysens, J.

1996a　'Dieux ancestraux et Baals syriens attestés à Rome', in G.M. Bellelli and U. Bianchi (eds.) *Orientalia Sacra Urbis Romae. Dolichena et Heliopolitana*, Rome, 261–76.

1996b　'La localisation du temple de Jupiter Héliopolitain au Janicule', in G.M. Bellelli and U. Bianchi (eds.) *Orientalia Sacra Urbis Romae. Dolichena et Heliopolitana*, Rome, 277–90.

1996c　'Il *Lucus Furrinae* e i culti del cosidetto «Santuario Siriaco»', in E.M. Steinby (ed.) *Ianiculum–Gianicolo. Storia, topografia, monumenti, leggendi dall'antichità al rinascimento*, Acta Instituti Romani Finlandiae 16, Rome, 53–60.

Calzini Gysens, J. and Duthoy, F.

1992　'Nuovi elementi per una cronologia del santuario siriaco del Gianicolo', *Ostraka* 1, 133–5.

Canali de Rossi, F.

1997　*Le ambascerie dal mondo greco a Roma in età repubblicana*, Rome.

Carcopino, J.

1941　*Daily Life in Ancient Rome*. Penguin, tr. E.O. Lorimer, ed. H.T. Rowell, Harmondsworth, 1991.

Castagnoli, F.

1980　'Installazioni portuali a Roma', in J.H. d'Arms and E.C. Kopff (eds.) *The Seaborne Commerce of Ancient Rome: Studies in archaeology and history*, MAAR 36, Rome, 35–42.

Cellini, G.A.

1996　'Les sources littéraires sur *Iuppiter Dolichenus* et *Iuppiter Heliopolitanus*', in G.M. Bellelli and U. Bianchi (eds.) *Orientalia Sacra Urbis Romae. Dolichena et Heliopolitana*, Rome, 19–56.

Champlin, E.

　　　　Fronto and Antonine Rome, Cambridge, Mass.

Bibliography

Chauvot, A.
1998   *Opinions romaines face aux barbares au IVe siècle ap.J.-C.*, Paris.
Cherry, D.
1998   *Frontier and Society in Roman North Africa*, Oxford.
Chevallier, R.
1988   *Voyages et déplacements dans l'empire romain*, Paris.
Ciceroni, M.
1996   'L'iconographie de la triade héliopolitaine à Rome', in G.M. Bellelli
       and U. Bianchi (eds.) *Orientalia Sacra Urbis Romae. Dolichena et
       Heliopolitana*, Rome, 359–68.
Clark, P.
1979   'Migration in England during the late seventeenth and early
       eighteenth centuries', *P&P* 83, 57–90.
Counts, D.
1996   '*Regum externorum consuetudine*: the nature and function of embalming
       in Rome', *CA* 15, 189–202.
Cracco Ruggini, L.
1997   'Spazi urbani clientelari et caritativi', in *La Rome impériale. Démographie
       et logistique. Actes de la table ronde (Rome, 25 mars 1994)*, CEFR 230,
       Rome, 157–91.
Dahya, B.
1973   'Pakistanis in Britain: transients or settlers?', *Race* 14, 241–77.
       Repr. in C. Holmes (ed.) *Migration in European history*, vol. 2,
       Cheltenham, 1996,
D'Ambra, E.
1988   'A myth for a smith: a Meleager sarcophagus from a tomb in Ostia',
       AJA 92, 85–99.
Dauge, Y.A.
1981   *Le barbare: recherches sur la conception romaine de la barbarie et de la
       civilisation*, Coll. Latomus 176, Brussels.
Di Stefano Manzella, I.
1976–7 'Il riordinamento del Lapidario profano ex lateranense', *RPAA*
       49, 249–93.
1997a 'Il venerando Mandronius (benefattore o santo?) nella dedica
       votiva del popolo gallico dei Carnutes presso Lione (355–363?)', in
       I. di Stefano Manzella (ed.) *Le iscrizioni dei Cristiani in Vaticano*,
       Inscriptiones Sanctae Sedis 2, Vatican City, 294–6 no. 3.7.5.
1997b 'Roma: società, presenze etniche e religiose', in I. di Stefano
       Manzella (ed.) *Le iscrizioni dei Cristiani in Vaticano*, Inscriptiones
       Sanctae Sedis 2, Vatican City, 338–9.
Doblhofer, E.
1987. *Exil und Emigration: zum Erlebnis der Heimatferne in der römischen
       Literatur*, Darmstadt.
Dobó, A.
1975   *Inscriptiones extra fines Pannoniae Daciaeque repertae ad res earundem
       provinciarum pertinentes*, 4th edn, Amsterdam.
Dudley, D.
1967   *Urbs Roma*, London.

Dunand, F.
1980   'Cultes égyptiens hors d'Égypte. Essai d'analyse des conditions de leur diffusion', in *Religions, pouvoir, rapports sociaux*, Annales Litteraires de l'Université de Besançon 237, 71–148.

Duncan-Jones, R.
1990   *Structure and Scale in the Roman Economy*, Cambridge.

Duthoy, F. and Frel, J.
1996   'Observations sur le sanctuaire syrien du Janicule', in G.M. Bellelli and U. Bianchi (eds.) *Orientalia Sacra Urbis Romae. Dolichena et Heliopolitana*, Rome, 291–306.

Dyson, S.L and Prior, R.E.
'Horace, Martial and Rome: two poetic outsiders read the ancient city', *Arethusa* 28, 245–63.

Ebert, J.
1985   'Ein alter Name des Mäander. Zu IG XIV 933 und I. Magn. 17', *Philologus* 129, 54–63.

Edwards, C.
1996   *Writing Rome*, Cambridge.

Edwards, J.
1995   *Multilingualism*, London.

Elton, H.
1996   *Warfare in Roman Europe, AD 350–425*, Oxford.

Equini Schneider, E.
1988   'Palmireni a Roma e nell'Africa del nord. Tradizionalismo linguistico e religioso', in E. Campanile, G.R. Cardona and R. Lazzeroni (eds.) *Bilinguismo e biculturalismo nel mondo antico*, Pisa, 61–6.

Erskine, A.
1994   'Greek embassies and the city of Rome', *Classics Ireland* 1, 47–53.
1997   'Greek gifts and Roman suspicion', *Classics Ireland* 4, 33–45.

Evans, J.K.
1991   *War, Women and Children in Ancient Rome*, London.

Fabre, G. and Roddaz, J.M.
1982   'Recherches sur la «familia» di M. Agrippa', *Athenaeum* 60, 84–112.

Faist, T.
1997   'The crucial meso-level', in T. Hammar, G. Brochmann, K. Tamas and T. Faist (eds.) *International Migration, Immobility and Development. Multidisciplinary perspectives*, Oxford/New York, 187–217.

Feissel, D.
1982a   'Contributions à l'épigraphie grecque chrétienne de Rome', *RivAC* 58, 353–82.
1982b   'Remarques de toponymie syrienne d'après des inscriptions grecques chrétiennes trouvées hors de Syrie', *Syria* 59, 319–43.
1995   'Aspects de l'immigration à Constantinople d'après les épitaphes protobyzantines', in C. Mango and G. Dagron (eds.) *Constantinople and its Hinterland*, Aldershot, 366–77.

Felle, A.
1997   'Manifestazioni di bilinguismo nelle iscrizioni cristiane di Roma', *XI*

Congresso Internazionale di Epigrafia Greca e Latina. Preatti, 669–76.

Ferrua, A.
1939　'Antiche iscrizioni inedite di Roma', *Epig* 1, 142–50.
1941　'Epigrafia sicula pagana e cristiana', *RivAC* 18, 151–243.
1943–4　'Analecta romana II – S. Sebastiano', *Epig* 5–6, 3–26.
1951　'Nuove iscrizioni degli equites singulares', *Epig* 13, 96–141.
1967–8　'Antiche iscrizioni inedite di Roma', *Epig* 29, 62–100.

Finlay, R.
1981　*Population and Metropolis: The demography of London 1580–1650*, Cambridge.

Fischer, P.A., Martin, R. and Straubhaar, T.
1997　'Should I stay or should I go', in T. Hammar, G. Brochmann, K. Tamas and T. Faist (eds.) *International Migration, Immobility and Development. Multidisciplinary perspectives*, Oxford/New York, 49–90.

Floriani Squarciapino, M.
1962　*I culti orientali ad Ostia*, EPRO 3, Leiden.

Fol, A.
1967　'Les thraces dans l'empire romain d'occident (Ier–IIIe s.). Deuxième partie: documentation épigraphique', *Ann.Univ.Sof.Fac.Lett.* 61, 1–17.

Frend, W.H.C.
1952　*The Donatist Church*, Oxford.

Friedländer, L.
1907–13　*Roman Life and Manners under the Early Empire*, 4 vols., tr. A.B. Gough, London.

Frier, B.
1980　*Landlords and Tenants in Imperial Rome*, Princeton.

Fruyt, M.
1976　'D'*Africus ventus* à *Africa terra*', *RevPhil* 3e sér. 50, 221–38.

Fuks, G.
1985　'Where have all the freedmen gone?', *JJS* 36, 25–32.

Gafni, I.M.
1997　*Land, Center and Diaspora: Jewish constructs in late antiquity*, Sheffield.

Gager, J.G.
1992　*Curse Tablets and Binding Spells from the Ancient World*, New York.

García Martínez, M.R.
1991　'Caracteres y significación socio-económica de los movimientos de población hispana hacia las provincias imperiales en época romana', *HAnt* 15, 263–97.
1993　'Aspectos socio-profesionales y onomasticos del proceso migratorio hispano hacia las provincias imperiales en época romana', *HAnt* 17, 321–8.

Gardner, J.F.
1993　*Being a Roman Citizen*, London.

Garnsey, P.
1988　*Famine and Food Supply in the Graeco–Roman World: Responses to risk and crisis*, Cambridge.

Gilfoyle, T.J.
  1992   *City of Eros. New York City, prostitution and the commercialization of sex, 1790–1920*, New York.

Ginzberg, L.
  1925–38   *The Legends of the Jews*, 7 vols., tr. H. Szold, Philadelphia.

Giorgetti, D.
  1977   'Castra Ravennatium: indagine sul distaccamento dei classiari Ravennati a Roma', *CCAB* 24, 223–53.

Goodman, M.
  1989   'Nerva, the *Fiscus Iudaicus* and Jewish identity', *JRS* 79, 40–4.
  1994   *Mission and Conversion*, Oxford.

Gorce, D.
  1925   *Les voyages, l'hospitalité et le port des lettres dans le monde chrétien des IVe et Ve siècles*, Paris.

Gordon, M.L.
  1924   'The nationality of slaves under the early Roman Empire', *JRS* 14, 93–111.

Granino Cecere, M.G.
  1994a   'D. Caecilius Abascantus, diffusor olearius ex provincia Baetica (CIL vi 1885)', in *Epigrafia della produzione e della distribuzione*, CEFR 193, Rome, 205–19.
  1994b   'Suebi nelle iscrizioni di Roma', in B. and P. Scardigli (eds.) *Germani in Italia*, Rome, 199–207.

Guarducci, M.
  1951–2   'L'Italia e Roma in una "tabella defixionis" greca recentemente scoperta', *BCAR* 74, 57–70.

Hajjar, Y.
  1977   *La triade d'Héliopolis-Baalbek*, 2 vols., EPRO 59, Leiden.

Hall, J.M.
  1997   *Ethnic Identity in Greek Antiquity*, Cambridge.

Hammond, N.G.L. and Walbank, F.W.
  1998.   *A History of Macedonia. Vol. III, 336–167 BC*, Oxford.

Harris, W.V.
  1980   'Towards a study of the Roman slave trade', in J.H. d'Arms and E.C. Kopff (eds.) *The seaborne commerce of ancient Rome: Studies in archaeology and history*, MAAR 36, Rome, 117–40.

Harvey, G.
  1996   *The True Israel. Uses of the names Jew, Hebrew and Israel in ancient Jewish and early Christian literature*, AGAJU 35, Leiden.
  1998   'Synagogues of the Hebrews: "good Jews" in the Diaspora', in S. Jones and S. Pearce (eds.) *Jewish local patriotism and self-identification in the Graeco–Roman period*, Sheffield, 132–47.

Hörig, M. and Schwertheim, E.
  1987   *Corpus cultus Iovis Dolicheni*, EPRO 106, Leiden. [CCID]

Hopkins, K.
  1978   *Conquerors and Slaves*, Cambridge.

Horbury, W. and Noy, D.

1992   *Jewish Inscriptions of Greco-Roman Egypt*, Cambridge. [JIGRE]

Horsfall, N.

1993   'Empty shelves on the Palatine', *G&R* 40, 58–67.

Houston, G.W.

1990   'The altar from Rome with inscriptions to Sol and Malakbel', *Syria* 67, 189–93.

Huttunen, P.

1974   *The Social Strata in the Imperial City of Rome*, Oulu.

Jackson, R.

1988   *Doctors and Diseases in the Roman Empire*, London.

Jeffers, J.S.

1998   'Jewish and Christian families in first-century Rome', in K.P. Donfried and P. Richardson (eds.) *Judaism and Christianity in first-century Rome*, Grand Rapids, 128–50.

Jones, A.H.M.

1964   *The Later Roman Empire 284–602*, 3 vols., Oxford.

Jones, C.P.

1978   *The Roman World of Dio Chrysostom*, Cambridge, Mass.

Jones, W.D.

1993   *Wales in America. Scranton and the Welsh, 1860–1920*, Cardiff.

Joshel, S.R.

1992   *Work, Identity, and Legal Status at Rome: A study of the occupational inscriptions*, Norman, Okla.

Kaimio, J.

1979   *The Romans and the Greek Language*, Commentationes Humanarum Litterarum 64, Helsinki.

Kajanto, I.

1963a   *Onomastic Studies in the Early Christian Inscriptions of Rome and Carthage*, Acta Instituti Romani Finlandiae 2.1, Rome.

1963b   *A Study of the Greek epitaphs of Rome*, Acta Instituti Romani Finlandiae 2.3, Rome.

1980   'Minderheiten und ihre Sprachen in der Hauptstadt Rom', in G. Neumann and J. Untermann (eds.) *Die sprachen im römischen Reich der Kaiserzeit*, Beihefte der Bonner Jahrbucher 50, Cologne, 83–101.

1997   'Roman nomenclature during the late Empire', in I. di Stefano Manzella (ed.) *Le iscrizioni dei Cristiani in Vaticano*, Inscriptiones Sanctae Sedis 2, Vatican City, 103–11.

Karasch, M.C.

1987   *Slave Life in Rio de Janeiro 1808–1850*, Princeton.

Kasher, A.

1987   'The nature of Jewish migration in the Mediterranean countries in the Hellenistic–Roman era', *MHR* 2, 46–75.

Kelly, A.J.D.

1989   'Ethnic identification, association and redefinition: Muslim Pakistanis and Greek Cypriots in Britain', in K. Liebkind (ed.) *New identities in*

Europe, Aldershot, 77–115.

Kennedy, D.L.
1978 'Some observations on the Praetorian Guard', *AncSoc* 9, 275–301.

Klein, S.
1940 'Bar-Yohannis of Sepphoris at Rome', *Bulletin of the Jewish Palestine Exploration Society* 7, 47–51.

Kolb, F.
1995 *Rom. Die Geschichte der Stadt in der Antike*, Munich.

Kolendo, J.
1988–9 'Les Besses dans la flotte romaine de Misène et de Ravenne', *Puteoli* 12–13, 77–86.

Kraemer, R.S.
1989 'On the meaning of the term "Jew" in Graeco–Roman inscriptions', *HTR* 82, 35–53.

Lampe, P.
1989 *Die stadtrömischen Christen in den ersten beiden Jahrhunderten*, 2nd edn, Wissenschaftliche Untersuchungen zum Neuen Testament 2, Reihe 18, Tübingen.
1991 'The Roman Christians of Romans 16', in K.P. Donfried (ed.) *The Romans Debate*, rev. edn, Edinburgh, 216–30.

Lane, E.N.
1979. 'Sabazius and the Jews in Valerius Maximus: a re-examination', *JRS* 69, 35–8.

La Piana, G.
1925 'The Roman church at the end of the second century', *HTR* 18, 201–77.
1927 'Foreign groups in Rome during the first centuries of the Empire', *HTR* 20, 183–401.

Laurence, R.
1996 'Writing the Roman metropolis', in H. Parkins (ed.) *Roman Urbanism. Beyond the consumer city*, London, 1–19.
1998 'Territory, ethnonyms and geography. The construction of identity in Roman Italy', in R. Laurence and J. Berry (eds.) *Cultural Identity in the Roman Empire*, London, 95–110.

Le Bohec, Y.
1994 *The Imperial Roman Army*, London.

Lee, A.D.
1993 *Information and Frontiers: Roman foreign relations in late antiquity*, Cambridge.

Lega, C. and Felle, A.
1997 'Epitaffio del catecumeno Andragathos di origine greca', in I. di Stefano Manzella (ed.) *Le iscrizioni dei Cristiani in Vaticano*, Inscriptiones Sanctae Sedis 2, Vatican City, 287 no. 3.6.7.

Lega, C. and Orlandi, S.
1997 'Epitaffio di Flavius Ursicinus funzionario Pannone della burocrazia imperiale', in I. di Stefano Manzella (ed.) *Le iscrizioni dei Cristiani in Vaticano*, Inscriptiones Sanctae Sedis 2, Vatican City, 276 no. 3.5.12.

341

Lega, C. and Ricci, C.

1997 'Epitaffio di Cyrillus Armeno di Cappadocia', in I. di Stefano Manzella (ed.) *Le iscrizioni dei Cristiani in Vaticano*, Inscriptiones Sanctae Sedis 2, Vatican City, 350–1 no. 3.12.25.

Leon, H.J.

1960 *The Jews of Ancient Rome*, Philadelphia.

Levi, A.J.

1970 'Gli ebrei in Roma antica nel ricordo della Haggadà', in D. Carpi, A. Milano and U. Nahon (eds.) *Scritti in memoria di Enzo Sereni*, Jerusalem, 75–87.

Levinskaya, I.

1996 *The Book of Acts in its First Century Setting. Vol. 5. Diaspora setting*, Grand Rapids.

Lichtenberger, H.

1996 'Jews and Christians in Rome in the time of Nero: Josephus and Paul in Rome', *ANRW* II.26.3, 2142–76.

Lightfoot, J.B.

1889–90 *The Apostolic Fathers*, 5 vols., London.

Lintott, A.

1994 'Political history, 146–95 BC', in J.A. Crook, A. Lintott and E. Rawson (eds.) *The Cambridge Ancient History*, 2nd edn, Vol. IX, Cambridge, 40–103.

Loane, H.J.

1938 *Industry and Commerce of the City of Rome (50 BC–200 AD)*, Baltimore.

Lo Cascio, E.

1997 'Le procedure di *recensus* dalla tarda repubblica al tardoantico e il calcolo della popolazione di Roma', in *La Rome impériale. Démographie et logistique. Actes de la table ronde (Rome, 25 mars 1994)*, CEFR 230, Rome, 3–76.

Lombardi, P.

1996 'Les sources épigraphiques grecques du sanctuaire du Janicule et de Jupiter Dolichénien à Rome', in G.M. Bellelli and U. Bianchi (eds.) *Orientalia Sacra Urbis Romae. Dolichena et Heliopolitana*, Rome, 57–86.

1997 'Le iscrizione greche cristiane nei Musei Vaticani', in I. di Stefano Manzella (ed.) *Le iscrizioni dei Cristiani in Vaticano*, Inscriptiones Sanctae Sedis 2, Vatican City, 45–51.

McCormack, A.R.

1984 'Networks among British immigrants and accomodation [sic] to Canadian society: Winnipeg, 1900–1914', *Histoire Sociale/Social History* 17, 357–74. Repr. in C. Holmes (ed.) *Migration in European history*, vol. 2, Cheltenham, 1996.

McGinn, T.A.J.

1998 *Prostitution, Sexuality and the Law in Ancient Rome*, New York.

McLean, B.H.

1993 'The Agrippinilla inscription: religious associations and early church formation', in *Origins and Method: Towards a new understanding of Judaism and Christianity: Essays in honour of John C. Hurd*, JSNT s.s. 86, Sheffield, 239–70.

MacMullen, R.
  1990   *Changes in the Roman empire: Essays in the ordinary*, Princeton.
  1993   'The unromanized in Rome', in S.J.D. Cohen and E.S. Frerichs
          (eds.) *Diasporas in Antiquity*, Brown Judaic Studies 288, Atlanta, 47–64.
McNeill, W.H.
  1978   'Human migration: a historical overview', in W.H. McNeill and R.S.
          Adams (eds) *Human Migration: Patterns and policies*, Bloomington,
          Ind., 3–19.
Malmberg, G.
  1997   'Time and space in international migration', in T. Hammar,
          G. Brochmann, K. Tamas and T. Faist (eds.) *International Migration,
          Immobility and Development. Multidisciplinary perspectives*, Oxford/New
          York, 21–48.
Marett, V.
  1989   *Immigrants Settling in the City*, Leicester.
Mateescu, G.G.
  1923   'I Traci nelle epigrafi di Roma', *EphDacor* 1, 57–290.
Matthews, J.
  1989a   *The Roman Empire of Ammianus*, London.
  1989b   'Hostages, philosophers, pilgrims and the diffusion of ideas in the
          late Roman Mediterranean and Near East', in F.M. Clover and R.S.
          Humphreys (eds.) *Tradition and Innovation in Late Antiquity*, Madison
          Wis., 29–49.
Matthews, K.J.
  1999   '*Britannus/Britto*: Roman ethnographies, native identities, labels,
          and folk devils', in A. Leslie (ed.) *Theoretical Roman Archaeology and
          Architecture. The Third Conference proceedings*, Glasgow, 14–32.
Meiggs, R.
  1960   *Roman Ostia*, Oxford.
Millar, F.
  1977   *The Emperor in the Roman World*, London.
Millar F. et al.
  1981   *The Roman Empire and its Neighbours*, 2nd edn, London.
Miranda, E.
  1990   *Iscrizioni greche d'Italia: Napoli 1*, Rome. [I. Napoli]
Mitchell, S.
  1993   *Anatolia. Land, men and gods in Asia Minor*, 2 vols., Oxford.
Moretti, L.
  1958   'Sulle «stationes municipiorum» del Foro Romano', *Athenaeum*
          n.s. 36, 106–16.
  1968–90 *Inscriptiones Graecae Urbis Romae*, 4 vols., Rome. [IGUR]
  1989   'I greci a Roma', *Opuscula Instituti Romani Finlandiae* 4, 5–16.
  1990   'Sui traci nelle iscrizioni pagane e cristiane di Roma', in *Tra epigrafia
          e storia*, Vetera 5, 205–9. First published in *Pulpudeva* 2 (1978), 36–40.
Morley, N.
  1996   *Metropolis and Hinterland: The city of Rome and the Italian economy, 200
          BC–AD 200*, Cambridge.

Musurillo, H.A.

    1954   *The Acts of the Pagan Martyrs: Acta Alexandrinorum*, Oxford.

    1972   *The Acts of the Christian Martyrs*, Oxford.

Namias, J.

    1978   *First Generation*, Boston.

Nock, A.D.

    1932   'Cremation and burial in the Roman Empire', *HTR* 25, 321–59.

Noy, D.

    1993–5 *Jewish Inscriptions of Western Europe*, 2 vols., Cambridge. [JIWE]

    1997   'Writing in tongues: the use of Greek, Latin and Hebrew in Jewish inscriptions from Roman Italy', *JJS* 48, 300–11.

    1998a 'Where were the Jews of the Diaspora buried?', in M. Goodman (ed.) *Jews in a Graeco–Roman World*, Oxford, 75–89.

    1998b ' "Letters out of Judaea": echoes of Israel in Jewish inscriptions from Europe', in S. Jones and S. Pearce (eds.) *Jewish Local Patriotism and Self-identification in the Graeco–Roman Period*, Sheffield, 106–17.

    1999   ' "Peace upon Israel": Hebrew formulae and names in Jewish inscriptions from the Western Roman Empire', in W. Horbury (ed.) *Hebrew Study from Ezra to Ben-Yehuda*, Edinburgh, 133–44.

  (forthcoming) 'Jewish inscriptions of Western Europe: language and community', in S. Panciera (ed.) *Atti del XI Congresso Internazionale di Epigrafia Greca e Latina*.

Nutton, V.

    1973   'The chronology of Galen's early career', *CQ* 23, 158–71.

    1986   'The perils of patriotism: Pliny and Roman medicine', in R. French and F. Greenaway (eds.) *Science in the Early Roman Empire: Pliny the Elder, his sources and influence*, London, 30–58.

Nuzzo, D.

    1997   'Provinciali a Roma nelle testimonianze dell'epigrafia sepolcrale tardoantica', *XI Congresso Internazionale di Epigrafia Greca e Latina. Preatti*, 705–12.

Pack, R.

    1953   'The Roman digressions of Ammianus Marcellinus', *TAPhA* 84, 181–9.

Pagnoni, A.

    1942   'Sul reclutamento degli «urbaniciani»', *Epig* 4, 23–40.

Palanque, J.R.

    1931   'Famines à Rome à la fin du IVᵉ siècle', *REA* 33, 346–56.

Palmer, R.E.A.

    1981   'The topography and social history of Rome's Trastevere (southern section)', *PAPhS* 125, 368–97.

Panayi, P.

    1994   *Immigration, Ethnicity and Racism in Britain, 1815–1945*, Manchester.

Panciera, S.

    1980   'Olearii', in J.H. d'Arms and E.C. Kopff (eds.) *The Seaborne Commerce of Ancient Rome: Studies in archaeology and history*, MAAR 36, Rome, 235–50.

    1993   'Soldati e civili a Roma nei primi tre secoli dell'impero', in W. Eck (ed.) *Prosopographie und Sozialgeschichte*, Cologne, 261–76.

Pani, M.
1979–80 'Documenti sulle relazioni fra Augusto e i re d'Armenia', in *Miscellanea di studi classici in onore di Eugenio Manni*, 5 vols, Rome, vol. 5, 1679–84.

Parkin, T.
1992 *Demography and Roman Society*, Baltimore.

Patterson, J.R.
1992a 'The city of Rome: from Republic to Empire', *JRS* 82, 186–215.
1992b 'Patronage, *collegia* and burial in imperial Rome', in S. Bassett (ed.) *Death in Towns*, Leicester, 15–27.

Pearce, S.
1998 'Belonging and not belonging: local perspectives in Philo of Alexandria', in S. Jones and S. Pearce (eds.) *Jewish Local Patriotism and Self-identification in the Graeco–Roman period*, Sheffield, 79–105.

Pellegrino, A.
1996 'Les cultes de Jupiter Dolichénien et de Jupiter Héliopolitain à Ostie', in G.M. Bellelli and U. Bianchi (eds.) *Orientalia Sacra Urbis Romae. Dolichena et Heliopolitana*, Rome, 563–82.

Perler , O.
1969 *Les voyages de saint Augustin*, Paris.

Petolescu, C.C.
1992 'Varia Daco-Romana (XV–XVI)', *Thraco-Dacica* 13, 121–3.

Pietri, Ch.
1976 *Roma Christiana*, Rome.
1987 'D'Alexandrie à Rome: Jean Talaïa, émule d'Athanase au Ve siècle', in ΑΛΕΞΑΝΔΡΙΝΑ. *Hellénisme, Judaïsme et Christianisme à Alexandrie. Mélanges P.C. Mondésert, S.J.*, Paris, 277–95.

Pleket, H.W.
1973 'Some aspects of the history of the athletic guilds', *ZPE* 10, 197–227.
1993 'Rome: a pre-industrial megalopolis', in T. Barker and A. Sutcliffe (eds.) *Megalopolis: The giant city in history*, Basingstoke, 14–35.

Pohl, I.
1978 'Piazzale delle Corporazioni ad Ostia. Tentativo di ricostruzione del Portico Claudio e la sua decorazione', *MEFRA* 90, 331–47.

Polomé, E.
1983 'The linguistic situation in the western provinces of the Roman Empire', *ANRW* II.29.2, 509–53.

Purcell, N.
1994 'The city of Rome and the *Plebs Urbana* in the late Republic', in J.A. Crook, A. Lintott and E. Rawson (eds.) *The Cambridge Ancient History* 2nd edn, Vol. IX, Cambridge, 644–88.

Quilici, L.
1974 'La campagna romana come suburbio di Roma antica', *PdP* 29, 410–38.

Rapport, N. and Dawson, A.
1998 'The topic and the book', in N. Rapport and A. Dawson (eds.)

Migrants of Identity, London/New York, 3–17.

Rebuffat, R.
  1966   'Les phéniciens à Rome', *MEFRA* 78, 7–48.
Remesal, J. and Revilla, V.
  1999   *Le anfore betiche: un vuoto a perdere*, http://www.ub.es/CEIPAC/
         MOSTRA/expo.htm
Reynolds, J.
  1982   *Aphrodisias and Rome*, JRS Monographs 1, London.
Ricci, C.
  1992a 'Dalle Gallie a Roma', *RAN* 25, 302–23.
  1992b 'Hispani a Roma', *Gérion* 10, 103–43.
  1993a 'Egiziani a Roma', *Aegyptus* 73, 71–91.
  1993b 'Balcanici e Danubianii a Roma', in L. Mrozewicz and K. Ilski (eds.)
         Prosopographica, Poznan, 141–208.
  1993c 'Germani a Roma', *Polis (Universidad de Alcalá de Henares)* 5, 205–25.
  1994a *Soldati delle milizie urbane fuori di Roma. La documentazione epigrafica*,
         Opuscula Epigraphica 5, Rome.
  1994b 'Africani a Roma. Testimonianze epigrafiche di età imperiale di
         personaggi provenienti dal Nordafrica', *AntAf* 30, 189–207.
  1997a 'Presenze italiche e multietniche a Roma fra IV e VI secolo', in I. di
         Stefano Manzella (ed.) *Le iscrizioni dei Cristiani in Vaticano*, Inscriptiones
         Sanctae Sedis 2, Vatican City, 189–91.
  1997b 'Epitaffio di Vernaculus originario di Carpis sul golfo di Cartagine',
         in I. di Stefano Manzella (ed.) *Le iscrizioni dei Cristiani in Vaticano*,
         Sanctae Sedis 2, Vatican City, 347–8 no. 3.12.18.
Richardson, L. jr
  1992   *A New Topographical Dictionary of Ancient Rome*, Baltimore.
Richardson, P.
  1998   'Augustan-era synagogues at Rome', in K.P. Donfried and P. Rich-
         ardson (eds.) *Judaism and Christianity in First-century Rome*, Grand
         Rapids, 17–29.
Rigsby, K.J.
  1997   'Graecolatina 5. A Roman address', *ZPE* 119, 249–50.
Robert, L.
  1978   'Malédictions funéraires grecques', *CRAI*, 241–89.
Robinson, O.
  1992   *Ancient Rome: City planning and administration*, London.
Rochette, B.
  1996   '*Fidi interpretes*: la traduction orale à Rome', *AncSoc* 27, 75–89.
Roda de Llanza, I.
  1970   'Lucius Licinius Secundus, liberto de Lucius Licinius Sura', *Pyrenae*
         6, 167–83.
Rodriguez Neila, J.F.
  1978   'Los jueces de las cinco decurias oriundos de la Hispania romana.
         Una contribucion prosopografica', *HAnt* 8, 17–65.
Ruggini, L.
  1959   'Ebrei e orientali nell'Italia settentrionale fra il IV e il VI secolo

d.Cr.', *SDHI* 25, 186–308.

Rutgers, L.V.

1995 *The Jews of Late Ancient Rome*, Leiden.

1998 'Roman policy towards the Jews: expulsions from the city of Rome during the first century CE', in K.P. Donfried and P. Richardson (eds.) *Judaism and Christianity in first-century Rome*, Grand Rapids, 93–116.

Sacco, G.

1984 *Iscrizioni greche d'Italia: Porto*, Rome. [I.Porto]

Saller, R.P.

1982 *Personal Patronage under the Early Empire*, Cambridge.

Saller, R.P. and Shaw, B.D.

1984 'Tombstones and Roman family relations in the principate: civilians, soldiers and slaves', *JRS* 74, 124–56.

Savage, S.M.

1940 'The cults of ancient Trastevere', *MAAR* 17, 26–56.

Scarborough, J.

1969 *Roman Medicine*, London.

Schäfer, P.

1997 *Judeophobia*, Cambridge, Mass.

Scheid, J.

1986 'Le thiase du Metropolitan Museum, (IGUR i 160)', in *L'association dionysiaque dans les sociétés anciennes*, CEFR 89, Rome, 257–90.

1995 'Le *desmos* de Gaionas. Observations sur une plaque inscrite des Dieux Syriens à Rome, (IGUR 109)', *MEFRA* 107, 301–14.

Scheidel, W.

1994 'Libitina's bitter gains: seasonal mortality and endemic disease in the ancient city of Rome', *AncSoc* 25, 151–75.

1996 *Measuring Sex, Age and Death in the Roman Empire: Explorations in ancient demography*, JRA s.s. 21, Ann Arbor.

Scobie, A.

1986 'Slums, sanitation and mortality in the Roman world', *Klio* 68, 399–433.

Segal, L.

1992 'R. Matiah ben Ḥeresh of Rome on religious duties and redemption: reacting to sectarian teaching', *PAAJR* 58, 221–41.

Sharlin, A.

1978 'Natural decrease in early modern cities: a reconsideration', *P&P* 79, 126–38.

Slingerland, H.D.

1997 *Claudian Policymaking and the Early Imperial Repression of Judaism at Rome*, SFSHJ 160, Atlanta.

Smallwood, E.M.

1981 *The Jews under Roman Rule*, Leiden.

Solin, H.

1977a 'Zu den griechischen Namen in Rom', in *L'onomastique latine*, Colloques internationales du Centre Nationale de la Recherche Scientifique 564, Paris, 161–75.

1977b 'Die Namen der orientalischen Sklaven in Rom', in *L'onomastique latine*, Colloques internationales du Centre Nationale de la Recherche Scientifique 564, Paris, 205–20.

1983 'Jüden und Syrer im westlichen Teil der römischen Welt.', *ANRW* II.29.2, 587–789.

Solin, H. and Itkonen-Kaila, M.

1966 *Graffiti del Palatino I. Paedagogium*, Acta Instituti Romani Finlandiae 3, Rome.

Sorrenti, S.

1996 'Les représentations figurées de Jupiter Dolichénien à Rome', in G.M. Bellelli and U. Bianchi (eds.) *Orientalia Sacra Urbis Romae. Dolichena et Heliopolitana*, L'Erma di Bretschneider, Rome, 369–456.

Speidel, M.

1994a *Riding for Caesar*, London.

1994b 'Germanen in der kaiserlichen Leibwache zu Rom', in B. and P. Scardigli (eds.) *Germani in Italia*, Rome, 151–7.

1994c *Die Denkmäler der Kaiserreiter*, Beihefte der Bonner Jahrbucher 50, Cologne.

Speidel, M. and Scardigli, B.

1990 'Neckarschwaben (Suebi Nicrenses)', *Arch.Korr.Mainz* 20, 201–7.

Stambaugh, J.E.

1988 *The Ancient Roman City*, Baltimore.

Stanley, F.H. jr

1990 'Geographical mobility in Roman Lusitania: an epigraphical perspective', *ZPE* 82, 249–69.

Stern, M.

1974–84 *Greek and Latin Authors on Jews and Judaism*, 3 vols., Jerusalem. [GLAJJ]

Stevens, G.

1994 'Immigration, emigration, language acquisition and the English language proficiency of immigrants in the U.S.', in B. Edmonston and J.S. Pastel (eds.) *Immigration and Ethnicity*, Washington D.C., 163–85.

Storey, G.R.

1997 'The population of Ancient Rome', *Antiquity* 71, 966–78.

Tabbernee, W.

1997 *Montanist Inscriptions and Testimonia: Epigraphic sources illustrating the history of Montanism*, Patristic Monograph Series 16, Macon, Ga.

Taglietti, F.

1994 'Un inedito bollo laterizio ostiense ed il commercio dell'olio betico', in *Epigrafia della produzione e della distribuzione*, CEFR 193, Rome, 156–93.

Talbert, R.J.A.

1984 *The Senate of Imperial Rome*, Princeton.

Tataki, A.B.

1998 *Macedonians Abroad*, MELETHMATA 28, Paris.

Teixidor, J.

1979 *The Pantheon of Palmyra*, EPRO 79, Leiden.

Thomasson, B.E.

1961 'Aus einer stadtrömischen Inschriftensammlung', *OpuscRom* 3, 179–90.

Thylander, H.

1951–2 *Inscriptions du port d'Ostie*, Lund.

Tilly, C.

1978 'The historical study of vital processes', in C. Tilly (ed.) *Historical Studies of Changing Fertility*, Princeton, 3–56.

Toynbee, J.M.C.

1971 *Death and Burial in the Roman World*, London.

1973 *Animals in Roman Life and Art*, London.

Toynbee, J.M.C. and Ward-Perkins, J.B.

1956 *The Shrine of St Peter and the Vatican Excavations*, London.

Turcan, R.

1958 'Origines et sens de l'inhumation a l'époque impériale', *REA* 60, 323–47.

1996 *The cults of the Roman Empire*, tr. A. Nevill, Oxford.

Urso, G.

1994 'Il concetto di "alienigena" nella guerra annibalica', in M. Sordi (ed.) *Emigrazione e immigrazione nel mondo antico*, Contributi dell' Istituto di Storia Antica 20, Milan, 223–36.

Väänänen, V. (ed.)

1973 *Le iscrizioni della necropoli dell'Autoparco vaticano*, Acta Instituti Romani Finlandiae 6, Rome

Vermaseren, M.J.

1977 *Corpus cultus Cybelae Attidisque*, EPRO 50, Leiden. [CCCA]

Vidman, L.

1969 *Sylloge inscriptionum religionis Isiacae et Sarapiacae*, Religionsgeschichtliche Versuche und Vorarbeiten 28, Berlin. [SIRIS]

1990 'Ägypter ausserhalb von Ägypten in der Kaiserzeit', in M. Ta'eva and D. Bojad'iev (eds.) *Studia in honorem Borisi Gerov*, Sofia, 259–66.

Vismara, C.

1986 'I cimiteri ebraici di Roma', in A. Giardina (ed.) *Società romana e impero tardantico*, vol. 2, Bari, 351–92.

Vulpe, R.

1925 'Gli Illiri nell'Italia imperiale romana', *EphDacor* 3, 129–259.

Walker, S.

1985 *Memorials to the Roman Dead*, London.

Walters, J.C.

1998 'Romans, Jews, and Christians: the impact of the Romans on Jewish/Christian relations in first-century Rome', in K.P. Donfried and P. Richardson (eds.) *Judaism and Christianity in First-century Rome*, Grand Rapids, 175–95.

Ward-Perkins, J.B.

1992 *Marble in Antiquity*, Archaeological Monographs of the British School at Rome 6, London.

Weaver, P.R.C.

Familia Caesaris, London.

Wells, C.M.

1997 ' "The daughters of the regiment": sisters and wives in the Roman army', in W. Groenman-van Waateringe et al. (eds.) *Roman Frontier Studies 1995*, Oxbow Monographs 91, Oxford, 571–4.

Wessel, C.

1989 *Inscriptiones Graecae Christianae veteres occidentis*, ed. A. Ferrua and C. Carletti, Bari. [IGCVO]

White, L.M.

1998 'Synagogue and society in imperial Ostia: archaeological and epigraphic evidence', in K.P. Donfried and P. Richardson (eds.) *Judaism and Christianity in First-century Rome*, Grand Rapids, 30–68.

Whittaker, M.

1982 *Tatian: Oratio ad Graecos and Fragments*, Oxford.

Wiedemann, T.E.J.

1992 *Emperors and Gladiators*, London.

Williams, M.H.

1989 'The expulsion of the Jews from Rome in AD 19', *Latomus* 48, 765–84.

1994a 'The organisation of Jewish burials in ancient Rome in the light of evidence from Palestine and the Diaspora', *ZPE* 101, 165–82.

1994b 'The structure of Roman Jewry re-considered – were the synagogues of ancient Rome entirely homogeneous?', *ZPE* 104, 129–41.

1997 'The meaning and function of *Ioudaios* in Graeco–Roman inscriptions', *ZPE* 116, 249–62.

1998 'The structure of the Jewish community in Rome', in M. Goodman (ed.) *Jews in a Graeco–Roman World*, Oxford, 215–28.

Williams, W.

1967 'Antoninus Pius and the control of provincial embassies', *Historia* 16, 470–83.

Winter, J.G.

1933 *Life and Letters in the Papyri*, Ann Arbor.

Wrigley, E.A.

1967 'A simple model of London's importance in changing English society and economy, 1650–1750', *P&P* 37, 44–70. Reprinted in *People, Cities and Wealth*, Oxford, 1987, 133–56.

Zappata, E.

1996 'Les divinités dolichéniennes et les sources épigraphiques latines', in G.M. Bellelli and U. Bianchi (eds.) *Orientalia Sacra Urbis Romae. Dolichena et Heliopolitana*, Rome, 87–256.

Zevi, F.

1973 'P. Lucilio Gamala senior e i "Quattro tempietti" di Ostia', *MEFRA* 85, 555–81.

Zgusta, L.

1984 *Kleinasiatische Ortsnamen*, Beiträge zur Namenforschung Beiheft 21, Heidelberg.

INDEX